# PREVENTION OF CHILD MALTREATMENT

Related Titles in the
**WILEY SERIES ON PERSONALITY PROCESSES**

IRVING B. WEINER, *Editor*
*University of South Florida*

# Prevention of Child Maltreatment: Developmental and Ecological Perspectives

*Edited by*
Diane J. Willis
E. Wayne Holden
Mindy Rosenberg

*University of Oklahoma Health Sciences Center*
*The University of Maryland School of Medicine*
*Sausalito, California*

A WILEY-INTERSCIENCE PUBLICATION
JOHN WILEY & SONS
New York • Chichester • Brisbane • Toronto • Singapore

**Library of Congress Cataloging-in-Publication Data**

Prevention of child maltreatment : developmental and ecological
  perspectives / edited by Diane J. Willis, E. Wayne Holden, Mindy
  Rosenberg.
       p.    cm. — (Wiley series on personality processes)
  Includes bibliographical references.
  ISBN 0-471-63419-0
  1.  Child abuse—Prevention.  I. Willis, Diane J.  II. Holden, E.
Wayne, 1956–    .  III. Rosenberg, Mindy Susan.  IV. Series.
  [DNLM: 1. Child Abuse—prevention & control.  WA 320 P944]
HV6626.5.P74  1992
362.7′67—dc20
DNLM/DLC
for Library of Congress                        91-15035

Printed in the United States of America

10 9 8 7 6 5 4 3 2 1

**Printed and bound by Malloy Lithographing, Inc..**

*In memory of my loving brother, Herb Bynum Willis.
(DJW)*

*To Jeanette and Dean Holden for their love, support and
encouragement along the way. (EWH)*

*In memory of my loving mother, Marilyn Rosenberg.
(MR)*

# Contributors

MARK ABER, Ph.D.
Assistant Professor of Psychology
University of Illinois
Champaign, Illinois

THOMAS S. ALTEPETER, Ph.D.
Assistant Professor
Department of Psychology
University of Wisconsin-Oshkosh
Oshkosh, Wisconsin

ANNE H. COHN, D.P.H.
Executive Director
National Committee for Prevention
  of Child Abuse
Chicago, Illinois

DEBRA COHN, Ph.D.
Children's Hospital
Child Abuse Program
Columbus, Ohio

MARY M. CORCORAN, M.A.
Doctoral Candidate
Department of Psychology
Auburn University
Auburn, Alabama

JAN L. CULBERTSON, Ph.D.
Associate Professor
Department of Pediatrics
University of Oklahoma Health
  Sciences Center
Director of Neuropsychological
  Services
Child Study Center
Oklahoma City, Oklahoma

DENNIS DROTAR, Ph.D.
Professor of Psychology
Case Western Reserve University
School of Medicine, and
Division of Child and Adolescent
  Psychiatry
Cleveland Metropolitan General
  Hospital
Cleveland, Ohio

DAVID FINKELHOR, Ph.D.
Co-Director
Family Research Laboratory
University of New Hampshire
Durham, New Hampshire

JAMES GARBARINO, Ph.D.
President, Erikson Institute for
  Advanced Study in Child
  Development
Chicago, Illinois

E. Wayne Holden, Ph.D.
Assistant Professor of Pediatrics
The University of Maryland School
  of Medicine
Baltimore, Maryland

Charles F. Johnson, M.D.
Professor of Pediatrics
The Ohio State University
Director, Child Abuse Program
Children's Hospital
Columbus, Ohio

Joan Kaufman, Ph.D.
Post Doctoral Fellow
Western Psychiatric Institute
University of Pittsburgh
Pittsburgh, Pennsylvania

Keith L. Kaufman, Ph.D.
Assistant Professor of Pediatrics
  and Psychology
The Ohio State University and
  Children's Hospital
Columbus, Ohio

Jan McCleery, R.N., B.A.
Director, Quality Improvement
Licking Memorial Hospital
Newark, Ohio

Gary B. Melton, Ph.D.
Carl Adolph Happold Professor of
  Psychology and Law
Director, Law/Psychology Program,
  and Center on Children,
  Families, and the Law
University of Nebraska-Lincoln
Lincoln, Nebraska

N. Dickon Reppucci, Ph.D.
Professor of Psychology
Director of Graduate Studies
University of Virginia
Charlottesville, Virginia

Mindy S. Rosenberg, Ph.D.
Private Practice
Sausalito, California

Cynthia J. Schellenbach, Ph.D.
Assistant Professor of Psychology
University of Notre Dame
Notre Dame, Indiana

Daniel J. Sonkin, Ph.D.
Private Practice
Sausalito, California

Nancy Strapko, Ph.D.
Post Doctoral Fellow
Plymouth State University
Plymouth, Massachusetts

C. Eugene Walker, Ph.D.
Professor and Director of Pediatric
  Psychology
Department of Psychiatry and
  Behavioral Sciences
University of Oklahoma Health
  Sciences Center
Oklahoma City, Oklahoma

Diane J. Willis, Ph.D.
Professor of Medical Psychology
Department of Pediatrics and
Director of Psychological Services
Child Study Center
University of Oklahoma Health
  Sciences Center
Oklahoma City, Oklahoma

Edward Zigler, Ph.D.
Sterling Professor of Psychology
Director, Bush Center in Child
  Development and Social Policy
Yale University
New Haven, Connecticut

# Acknowledgments

The expertise and knowledge of several individuals enriched us as we began this book. Division 37, Children, Youth and Families, of the American Psychological Association provided initial support and direction for this project. Division 37 is an effective and outstanding advocacy organization on behalf of children and out of the executive committee of this group the idea for the book was born. Numerous individuals provided input early on in the project and a debt of gratitude is extended to them. Michael Roberts, Ph.D., in Kansas reviewed the original outline for the book and provided constructive and helpful comments. Gary Melton, Ph.D., who wrote a chapter in the book is credited for his leadership in advocacy and for many years was the backbone of Division 37. Anne Cohn and Deborah Daro are both guiding lights in the prevention of child abuse and we thank them for their pioneering spirits.

It's been a privilege to work with the U.S. Advisory Board on Child Abuse and Neglect during the 1989–91 year, and the staff of the National Center on Child Abuse and Neglect. These dedicated, caring, and hard working individuals published a working document that Congress and the States can utilize as a blueprint for the care and protection of children. Diane Broadhurst, contracted to work with the Board, permitted the use of her research on the history of legislation in the area of child protection, and she contributed enormously to early drafts of the Advisory Boards publication.

Finally, we would like to thank Sheila Deaton in Oklahoma City and Kathy Kiel in Maryland for their patience in typing and retyping manuscripts and correspondence related to the project.

# Series Preface

This series of books is addressed to behavioral scientists interested in the nature of human personality. Its scope should prove pertinent to personality theorists and researchers as well as to clinicians concerned with applying an understanding of personality processes to the amelioration of emotional difficulties in living. To this end, the series provides a scholarly integration of theoretical formulations, empirical data, and practical recommendations.

Six major aspects of studying and learning about human personality can be designated: personality theory, personality structure and dynamics, personality development, personality assessment, personality change, and personality adjustment. In exploring these aspects of personality, the books in the series discuss a number of distinct but related subject areas: the nature and implications of various theories of personality; personality characteristics that account for consistencies and variations in human behavior; the emergence of personality processes in children and adolescents; the use of interviewing and testing procedures to evaluate individual differences in personality; efforts to modify personality styles through psychotherapy, counseling, behavior therapy, and other methods of influence; and patterns of abnormal personality functioning that impair individual competence.

IRVING B. WEINER

*University of South Florida*
*Tampa, Florida*

# Foreword: Child Abuse Prevention

A multidisciplinary team was sitting down by the river bank one afternoon. A pediatrician, a social worker, a policeman, an attorney, a psychologist and a parent aide. As they sat enjoying the afternoon sun, one of them noticed a strange object bobbing in the water. The object was carried by the current closer and closer to where they were seated. When it got quite close, it became clear that the object wasn't so strange after all—it was a small child.

An alert member of the team quickly dove into the water, swam to the child, gently grabbed him and pulled him ashore. The child was near drowned. The team went into action, working together, sharing their expertise; within moments they had helped the child regain consciousness. With a sense of success, they sat down on the river bank once again to relax in the afternoon sun.

Not much time had passed when, gazing up the river, a member of the team noticed another strange object in the water. As it got closer, it was obvious that this too was a small child. With the experience of the first rescue fresh in mind, the team went into action. One swam out and brought the child ashore. The others were ready and immediately began the procedures to save the child's life. Again the team was successful. And feeling great triumph, the team once more settled down on the river bank.

But their moment of relaxation was brief. For as they looked upstream, they could see one more now not-so-strange object floating in the water, and then another and then another. Indeed, as far as the eye could see the water was dotted with small children on the verge of drowning. Recognizing the futility of fishing the children out one after another and working to resuscitate them, one member of the team bolted up and declared to the others "We're wasting our time here saving these babies one by one. I'm going to work upstream and find out why the children are falling in the river in the first place."

And so it is that when we come to speak of child abuse we must concern ourselves with why the children are falling in the river and what it is we can do to stop them. We must talk of prevention, of doing things so abuse does not happen in the first place. It is simply not sufficient for us to respond to the problem after it has occurred after the damage has been done.

It is neither humane nor sensible to wait until a child is hurt. Not only do preventive approaches spare children the pain, which should be ample reason enough to pursue them, but they also can save dollars.

The numbers are staggering regardless of how broad or narrow the definition of child abuse one uses. Each year in the United States reports of suspected abuse and neglect run close to two million. About half of these reports demand further protective services. At least 1,200 children die as a result of maltreatment each year; the number could run as high as 5,000. At least as many others suffer permanent physically handicapping conditions. And all experience some kind of emotional or developmental trauma. This is a lot of broken bones and shattered spirits and lives prematurely and cruelly terminated.

Intervening early can keep children from suffering the emotional and developmental ravages of abuse which can lead to teenage runaways, school problems, juvenile delinquency, drug and alcohol abuse, teenage prostitution, suicide attempts, and later abusive behavior. The costs of these social problems are enormous. A preventive approach to child abuse can help avoid such costs.

There are those who do not believe prevention will work. They believe prevention is simply not possible because child abuse is caused in large part by values and conditions that we as a society tolerate: poverty, unemployment, sexism, media violence, drug abuse. There are beliefs that unless we can do away with all social ills, we will not be able to do away with child abuse. It is quite clear, for example, that in certain population groups inadequate income and no access to jobs do contribute to the possibility of child abuse. Yet, there is a lot we know about child abuse that has little to do with the conditions or values of our society. We know, for example, that even within the so-called "underclass," finances alone do not explain why child abuse occurs. There are other factors, related to awareness and education about child development, which can indeed be addressed without major social change.

Then there are other skeptics who believe that we cannot prevent child abuse because we do not know how. Certainly as we study the prevention literature, and look for research that will survive close scientific scrutiny, we find few studies which prove definitely that we can prevent child abuse. Some individuals say that with so little good research, we really do not know much at all. Indeed if we are looking for perfect programs or perfect solutions we won't find them—with a problem as complex as child abuse and so deeply imbedded in the unpredictable nature of human behavior there are no perfect approaches. However, when we step back and look broadly at the issues of child abuse, the factors which cause it, and the context in which it occurs, we see that we actually know a tremendous amount about the possibilities of prevention.

To be sure there remains a need to do more testing and more measuring to see if what our common sense, our intelligence and our experiences tell us are promising approaches, are in fact effective. Yet, we have expanded our knowledge about prevention in the past decade or so. For example, in 1974 when our federal government first became officially involved with child abuse we would have had a hard time mapping out possible prevention strategies for physical abuse. Today those strategies are well defined and widely know. And, in 1980, as national attention began to focus on the sexual victimization of children, we could not have identified a set of possible sexual abuse prevention strategies; our knowledge was undeveloped. We had begun to think only about prevention strategies aimed at children. Today it's possible to identify various ways of intervening with sexual abuse, including strategies directed at potential perpetrators.

Our challenge now is to be conscious of what we have learned, to monitor our expanding knowledge base, and to continually pull in new insights, new experiences which contribute to our ability to understand why abuse happens and how it can be stopped. And then, our commitment must be to base our policies and our program decisions and our budget allocations on that which we have learned.

The value of this book, truly the first primer on prevention issues and child abuse, is that it does pull together the extant knowledge base. It presents a comprehensive review of the literature from both developmental and ecological perspectives; it draws on both scientific insights and clinical experience. This book is important. Its contents are precious—for it contains the beginning answers of how to reduce the size of an egargiously large public health problem. It guides the reader upstream to understand why the babies are falling in the river in the first place and how to begin to stop them. The messages here are powerful if we do not pay attention to the ample recommendations provided we have only ourselves to blame as the child abuse problem grows in our country.

ANNE H. COHN, D.P.H.
Executive Director
National Committee for Prevention of Child Abuse

# Contents

# CHAPTER 1

# Child Maltreatment Prevention: Introduction and Historical Overview

DIANE J. WILLIS, E. WAYNE HOLDEN, AND MINDY ROSENBERG

A leading authority on prevention once stated that no mass disorder has ever been brought under control or eliminated by treating the disorder (Albee, 1990, personnel communication). To combat the serious problem of child abuse and neglect, we must begin to initiate prevention strategies. In June 1990, the U.S. Advisory Board on Child Abuse and Neglect issued its first report to Congress and the Secretary of the Department of Health and Human Services. The report stressed the need for a national strategy on child abuse and neglect and presented 31 recommendations, three of which dealt specifically with prevention. The report noted that there are often conflicting demands for monies between those wanting treatment services and those wanting prevention programs. An example of this conflict is demonstrated in the Adoption Assistance and Child Welfare Act of 1980 (P.L. 96-272).

> The law has two divergent components: (1) a Title IV-B child welfare services program focused in part on "preventative services" that can avoid the need for children to be removed from their families, and (2) a Title IV-E foster care maintenance program that is focused on support for substitute care and treatment providers. There is currently taking place an important re-assessment within the child welfare community of whether too much of a funding focus has been given to out-of-home care and treatment of children, at the expense of adequate prevention-oriented "family preservation services" designed to protect children within their own homes.
>
> *U.S. Advisory Board Report, 1990, pp. 82–83*

The need for a focus on prevention of child maltreatment is apparent to mental health service providers, professionals in the judicial and child welfare systems, and families whose lives have been affected by child abuse/neglect. There is no question that preventing maltreatment saves lives, prevents serious mental health sequelae, and preserves limited mental health resources in the United States. But how do we effectively prevent a problem with such complex etiology? There is confusion about the definition of child abuse and neglect,

1

controversy about the etiological factors which result in maltreatment, and a diversity of opinion regarding which prevention approaches are most effective. This book addresses these prevention issues from a developmental and ecological perspective. It is intended to review our current knowledge, examine the research on etiological factors, and critically evaluate the efficacy of prevention efforts to date. The text is divided into three sections, with the first section focusing on age-related prevention issues from the prenatal/perinatal period through adolescence. The second section focuses on child abuse prevention within the context of current treatment delivery systems such as the health care and social service systems, parent training, and the legal system. The third section focuses on future directions for research and clinical service in the prevention of child maltreatment.

In this introductory chapter, we review the definition, incidence and impact of child maltreatment, provide an overview of prevention issues, and review the history of child maltreatment including legislation enacted to combat the problem.


## DEFINING CHILD MALTREATMENT

In 1974, Congress enacted the Child Abuse Prevention and Treatment Act known as P.L. 93-247 which defines child abuse as the "physical or mental injury, sexual abuse, negligent treatment, or maltreatment of a child under the age of eighteen by a person who is responsible for the child's welfare under circumstances which indicate that the child's health and welfare is threatened thereby."

While the intent of the Act is to protect children, the law is vague and poses problems for mental health caregivers, professionals in the child welfare and judicial systems, and researchers. Other definitions of child abuse proposed by various states and organizations, including the Child Welfare League of America, range from very broad to very narrow. For example, one state law *lists* actions considered abusive, including "skin bruising, malnutrition, burns, etc." (Giovannoni and Becerra, 1979, p. 7), while the Child Welfare League defines abuse as denial of "normal experiences that produce feelings of being loved, wanted, secure, and worthy" (Giovannoni and Becerra, 1979, p. 88). Zigler and Hall (1989) stated the issues quite succinctly:

> A major dilemma facing modern workers is the lack of a widely accepted definition or set of definitions to describe child abuse. The seriousness of this void must not be underestimated, for the practical ramifications are many. The definition of child abuse will affect how cases are classified, how placement decisions are made, how eligibility for social and legal services is determined, and how the abusers and the abused child will be viewed by others and by themselves.

Although an in-depth discussion of the definitional issues of child abuse and neglect is beyond the scope of this book, a detailed review of definitional problems can be found in Giovannoni (1989) and Zigler and Hall (1989). Since prevention programs are based on some definition of risk criteria, however, it is important to arrive at a consensus regarding the definition of child abuse and neglect.

## INCIDENCE

There are two factors which seriously affect the accuracy of child abuse incidence data: the lack of consensus about the definition of child abuse, and the lack of a consistent, state-by-state data collection system. Because of these factors, the data available on incidence should be considered approximations. Reports indicate that the incidence of child abuse has increased dramatically since 1974 when 60,000 cases were reported. By 1980, 1.1 million children were reported for abuse, and in 1989 the figure had more than doubled to 2.4 million. In 1989, between 1,200 to 5,000 children *died* as a result of abuse. It is estimated that 2.5 percent of all children in the United States are abused and neglected each year (National Center on Child Abuse and Neglect [NCCAN], 1988).

The abuse of children has clearly reached epidemic proportions, causing the U.S. Advisory Board on Child Abuse and Neglect (1990) to call their first report, *Critical First Steps in Response to a National Emergency*. When 3,145 children died and 21,269 were left paralyzed as a result of polio, this disease was viewed as an epidemic and a national Mothers' March on Polio occurred (Public Health Service, 1964). And research by Jonas Salk led to development of the Salk vaccine. As a result of such nationwide prevention efforts, polio for all practical purposes has been eradicated. But efforts to prevent child maltreatment will not be as simple as administering a vaccine. The complexities of the problem in terms of dealing with human frailties, social ills, and economic factors are so great that prevention by a vaccine, as in the case of polio, seems quite appealing. Prevention of child maltreatment, however, will require a coordinated, nationwide effort and considerably more research into etiological factors.

## ETIOLOGY

Child maltreatment is not only an enormous and serious problem, it is a complex problem that occurs across all socioeconomic strata. Numerous factors likely interact for child abuse to occur. Certain factors contributing to abuse, while not meant to be inclusive, are worthy of mentioning because of their significance. Poverty and increased substance abuse are leading contributors to child maltreatment. Children born or reared in poverty are seven times more likely to be abused than children living in homes where the income is above $15,000 per year (NCCAN, 1988). Garbarino & Crouter (1978) reported that neighborhoods with a high poverty rate have higher rates of maltreatment. While child abuse and neglect occur in all socioeconomic levels, poverty increases the likelihood of their occurrence. Additionally, a dramatic increase in child maltreatment coincides with parental substance abuse (U.S. Department of Health and Human Services [DHHS], 1990; Finkelhor, 1986). Chasnoff (1989) estimated that as many as 375,000 drug-exposed children may be born annually, many of whom may end up in foster care. States are reporting an increase in child maltreatment by parents who are abusing crack or cocaine. Mitchel (1989) reported that "73% of New York's neglect related child fatalities in 1987 resulted from parental drug use; in 1985, this figure was 11%" (p. 3). Poor parenting skills, parents with mental health problems, dysfunctional neighborhoods in inner cities, and poverty-stricken rural communities coupled with the lack of community-based services add to the stress that contributes to child maltreatment. In this book, authors will discuss numerous prevention programs demonstrated to be effective in reducing stress on families and in reducing the incidence of maltreatment.

## IMPACT OF CHILD MALTREATMENT

What is the impact of child maltreatment and the impact of family/parental dysfunction? The psychological damage to children (and youth) as a result of abuse or neglect can have a lasting effect on self esteem and behavior. Children exposed to emotional abuse or chronic neglect grow up feeling unloved. Those subjected to physical and sexual abuse may become aggressive or depressed. Aber and Cicchetti (1984) examined socioemotional development in maltreated children and found poor peer relations, cognitive deficits, behavior problems, and psychopathology. Willis (1987) found that physically abused children placed in nurturing, stable foster homes made significant gains in cognitive and behavioral functioning over a six to nine month period.

Over the years, the need for mental health services has increased dramatically, and this need may be linked to the increased incidence of abuse and neglect. The number of children served in classrooms for the mentally handicapped or learning disabled has increased minimally compared to the number of children requiring placement in classrooms for the emotionally or behaviorally disordered. Tuma (1989) reported that 15 percent to 19 percent of the 63 million children and youth in the U.S. suffer from problems requiring mental health intervention, and Knitzer (1982) reported that 3 percent to 8 percent of the child population are seriously emotionally disturbed. According to Tuma (1989, p. 189), "Some of the most severe environmental risk factors associated with higher rates of mental health problems in children are poverty, minority ethnic status, parental psychopathology, physical or other maltreatment, a teenage parent, premature birth and low birth weight, parental divorce, and serious childhood illness." Given the significant impact of child maltreatment, it is clear that prevention programs must be initiated at every level of our society in order to combat the high incidence of mental health problems, the increased stress on families, and the high rate of child abuse and neglect.

## PERSPECTIVES ON PREVENTION

On a general level, prevention refers to intervention that occurs before the development of a disorder to either prevent the disorder itself or prevent some manifestation of the disorder. With respect to child maltreatment, this refers to efforts to reduce the actual occurrence or the negative sequelae of physical abuse, sexual abuse, psychological maltreatment, and neglect. *Primary prevention*, i.e., early intervention prior to maltreatment, when effective, changes the rate of occurrence of maltreatment. With the rise in child fatalities and child abuse statistics, efforts must be made to intervene at a primary level.

Effective prevention requires an accurate understanding of the etiological or risk factors associated with the development of the problem. The initial step in developing a preventive intervention program is establishing reliable criteria for determining the presence of a disorder or problem. After the problem is clearly defined, investigations are conducted to isolate risk factors. Preventive intervention trials designed to reduce risk prior to the development of a particular condition are then instituted. This may involve altering environment, host, or agent factors. Finally, wide-scale programs are implemented at the community level, based on the results of preventive intervention trials, to decrease the incidence and prevalence of the target condition. Over the course of the last several decades, the public health profession has enjoyed substantial success in reducing the incidence and prevalence of disease through the use of these methods.

With reference specifically to the prevention of child mental health problems, Lorion, Price, & Eaton (1989) have defined the prevention of psychopathology in children and families as altering the course of events from *pathological outcome* to *normative development*. In addition to an understanding of etiology and risk for a particular condition, this definition implies that knowledge of psychosocial competence, protective factors, and normative development are important in the prevention of mental health problems. Other authors also have noted the importance of focusing on normal development in the prevention of problems in youth and their families. For example, Rolf (1985) and Cowen & Work (1988) highlighted the importance of promoting competence during normative developmental transitions as a strategy for preventing negative mental health outcomes. Given the multiple causative factors implicated in child maltreatment (Belsky, 1980), altering the developmental course by bolstering protective factors to promote psychosocial competence may be as salient a prevention strategy as isolating the effects of and reducing risk factors.

George Albee, a leading proponent of primary prevention of child and adult disturbances, held a national conference on primary prevention at the University of Vermont in 1975. This conference has been so successful that it is now an annual event called the "Vermont Conference on the Primary Prevention of Psychopathology." In a brief historical perspective on the primary prevention of childhood mental disorders, Albee (1982) wrote about the major revolutions in the field of mental health:

> The first of these occurred when Pinel struck off the chains and brought the insane from the dungeons of Paris up into the light. The humanitarian movement followed. The second revolution was instituted by Freud and led to the gradual understanding of the dynamic causation of mental and emotional disturbances. The third revolution was the development of community based intervention, early help for persons in comprehensive community mental health centers with a variety of services reached through a single entry door.

> Now we are on the verge of a fourth mental health revolution. It is a revolution involving a shift towards efforts at prevention. It recognizes the impossibility of ever bringing the epidemic of emotional distress under control by attempts at helping single individuals. It accepts the doctrine that prevention is the only meaningful approach to widespread distress.

> The fourth revolution makes new demands on those of us already in the field. It means that we must think through our new responsibilities and our new areas of emphasis. We must find ways to untangle the complex web of causation.

> We must stop focusing our exclusive attention on the individual child, and lift our eyes, shift our focus to the family, the neighborhood, and the community. We must see individual pathology as a reflection of more general social pathology and we must become active in efforts at changing and improving living conditions in our society by reducing needless stress and improving competence and coping skills in children. (*p. 8*).

## CATEGORIES OF PREVENTION

In addition to understanding the basic prevention paradigm, it is important to differentiate preventive interventions into relevant categories. Caplan (1964) suggested the use of the terms primary, secondary, and tertiary prevention to refer to the goals, population focus, and the timing of delivery of preventive interventions. *Primary prevention* strategies are directed at the total population in an effort to reduce the incidence or rate of occurrence of new cases. These strategies do not focus on risk factors or risk groups and are implemented well before any early signs of disorder. An example of primary prevention is the addition of fluoride in water to prevent cavities. The fluoride reaches everyone, young and old, who drink water. Installing metal detectors in airports to screen all passengers is another primary prevention strategy.

Social primary prevention activities include prenatal programs, parent education programs, sex abuse education programs, and preschool programs such as Headstart.

*Secondary prevention* involves early identification of target individuals who are at risk; it is designed to reduce overall prevalence of a disorder. An example of a secondary preventive intervention would be providing support and counseling from paraprofessional volunteers to at-risk children in the school system (Weissberg & Allen, 1986). Crisis intervention for emotional distress, early intervention for abused children and their parents, and telephone crisis lines are other examples of secondary prevention.

*Tertiary prevention* is targeted at individuals with already diagnosed conditions. Although difficult to differentiate from treatment, tertiary prevention is designed to reduce the adverse consequences associated with a disease state or disorder, or to prevent the individual from being incapacitated.

Gordon (1983) proposed an alternative system for classifying preventive interventions that are designed to reduce psychopathology and behavioral problems. He argued that the differences between behavioral/mental health problems and infectious diseases warrants a greater focus on *who* receives the preventive intervention. He proposed using the terms "universal interventions," "selected interventions," and "indicated interventions" to describe prevention strategies for psychopathology and behavioral problems. Similar to primary prevention, universal interventions are targeted to all segments of the population and by necessity are mass distributed as well as inexpensive. Selected interventions are targeted at high-risk populations and are designed to reduce incidence of a disorder. Finally, indicated interventions are targeted to reduce sequelae of a disorder in individuals who are currently displaying a diagnosable condition.

This book reviews the literature on preventive interventions that are targeted at widely varying populations and that are instituted at different points in the continuum of pathology (that is, ranging from the absence of any disorder to diagnosable psychopathology). An appreciation of the differences between universal, selected, and indicated interventions is apparent in nearly every chapter. Uneven progress has been made in preventing child maltreatment depending upon the level of intervention and the population that has been targeted for change. For example, many secondary or selected intervention strategies have been evaluated with reasonable outcome data supporting their efficacy. Primary or universal interventions, however, have not received as much attention and it is unclear how effective these strategies actually may be in either the short or long term.

A cautionary note regarding the applicability of prevention efforts to child maltreatment is important. The public health paradigm has been most successful in the prevention of infectious diseases. Single pathogen disorders are directly amenable to epidemiological research and intervention strategies designed to promote risk factor reduction. The rapid progress that has been made in the area of human immunodeficiency virus (HIV) infection over the last decade attests to the power of public health methods in isolating patho-genic agents, defining risk factors, and developing preventive interventions (Glasner & Kaslow, 1990). However, the multiple, interacting etiological factors involved in the development of mental health problems such as child maltreatment render these phenomena less directly amenable to epidemio-logical and other public health methods. In addition, the situation is further complicated by the absence of reliable criteria for defining child maltreatment in general and in its various forms. The prevention of problems that are embedded in complex, social ecological causative frameworks, as noted by Gary Melton's chapter in this volume, may require reshaping the traditional public health paradigm so that interpersonal/family problems with complex etiologies can be successfully investigated and controlled. As Albee (1983) pointed out, effective prevention programs do *not* even have to untangle the complex question of etiology. If stress on families can be reduced, if we can enhance social coping skills, and if we provide supportive networks, many forms of child maltreatment may likely be prevented.

## HISTORICAL OVERVIEW OF CHILD MALTREATMENT

The U.S. government has been involved in the care and protection of children and families since the beginning of this century. Government concern for child welfare issues can be traced to 1909 and the first White House Confer-ence on Children. For instance, the U.S. Children's Bureau, founded in 1912, continues to promote the health, welfare, growth and development of chil-dren. The 1935 Social Security Act was a major thrust for the development of child welfare services for all children in need of care and protection, and the Fair Labor Standards Act of 1938 sought an end to the abuse and ex-ploitation of children in the work force.

Recent government response to child abuse and neglect dates from the early 1960s. Prompted by the work of Dr. C. Henry Kempe and his colleagues, (Kempe, Silverman, Steele, Droegemueller, & Silver, 1962), the Children's Bureau focused on the problem of abuse, beginning with model state reporting statutes designed to improve the reporting of suspected child abuse and ne-glect. By 1967, every state had enacted a child abuse and neglect reporting law. In 1974, Congress passed the Child Abuse Prevention and Treatment Act (P.L. 93-247), which established the National Center on Child Abuse and Neglect and underscored the government's commitment to provide fund-ing and technical assistance for child abuse and neglect services to state and local governments.

In 1978, this act was expanded to include child pornography and adoption law reform. That same year the Indian Child Welfare Act was passed, re-turning jurisdiction of Native American children to their tribes and outlining placement priorities for these children in out-of-home care. In 1980, the Adoption Assistance and Child Welfare Act provided for reasonable efforts to prevent out-of-home placements and to reunify families in which placement had occurred. And in 1984, Congress expanded the National Center's responsibilities further by adding the "Baby Doe" provisions, which required programs and procedures for responding to reports of medical neglect, including reports of withholding medically indicated treatment from disabled infants with life-threatening conditions.

In 1987, the House of Representatives Select Committee on Children, Youth, and Families issued *Abused Children in America: Victims of Official Neglect*, a report confirming, "the increasing tragedy of child abuse and child neglect in America, as well as the decline in resources available to serve these children."

The following years, Congress passed the Child Abuse Prevention, Adoption, and Family Services Act of 1988 (P.L. 100-294) which, among other provisions, extended the authority for the National Center on Child Abuse and Neglect and specified its duties and staff qualifications; provided for research, grants and program activities; established the U.S. Inter-Agency Task Force on Child Abuse and Neglect made up of representatives of Federal agencies with responsibility for programs and activities related to child abuse and neglect; and established the U.S. Advisory Board on Child Abuse and Neglect, a group of experts appointed by the Secretary of Health and Human Services to address related policy and legislative issues.

In enacting P.L. 100-294, Congress reaffirmed its interest in providing services to abused and neglected children and their families and signaled its intent to ensure that the National Center would benefit from the advice of experts in the field of child abuse and neglect. While the United States has made considerable progress in enacting laws to protect children, little has been done in the prevention area. The goal of the current U.S. Advisory Board on Child Abuse and Neglect, over the next few years, is to provide ideas for legislation which would improve prevention efforts and increase funding for research into the causes and effects of child maltreatment.

## DEVELOPMENTAL PERSPECTIVE ON PREVENTION

The integration of developmental perspectives into classification, treatment, and prevention of child psychopathology has become a priority over the last two decades. Kazdin (1989) recently noted that substantial progress has been made in this area and emphasized the need for construction of a true developmental psychopathology. As an example of the problems encountered in this area, Cicchetti, Toth & Bush (1988) reviewed the evidence for developmental changes across a number of disorders and provided a model to guide the direction of further research into developmental transitions. They noted the relative paucity of research in this area to date and hence the difficulty in constructing accurate conceptual and theoretical models. However, with rapid growth in the field of developmental psychopathology, the research base for our understanding of developmental effects on child disorders is beginning to emerge.

The increased interest in developmental models of childhood problems has been fueled by the rapid expansion of information on normative child development (Horowitz & O'Brien, 1989) and advances in the understanding of the functioning of families (Carter & McGoldrick, 1988). Basic theoretical and conceptual information is now available to plot the *normal* developmental course and to begin to understand deviations from this course. It is important, however, to focus more specifically on individual developmental stages in order to clearly understand the factors within each stage that promote competent development or result in psychopathology. A study of disturbed attachment relationships between maltreated infants and preschool children and their caregivers (Cicchetti, 1987) is one example of the type of work that needs to be conducted in order to develop more comprehensive transactional models of the etiology and sequelae of child maltreatment.

Recent authors have underscored the importance of integrating developmental perspectives into childhood prevention research and community prevention programs (Cowen & Work, 1988; Lorion et al., 1989; Rolf, 1985). Empirical research that examines the interactions between developmental trajectories and preventive interventions is clearly needed. This book attempts to conceptually integrate a developmental perspective into child maltreatment prevention by presenting chapters that review issues germane to the prenatal/ perinatal period, infancy and preschoolers, school-aged children, and adolescents. It is clear from the authors' presentations that less empirical study on developmental factors has been conducted than is currently needed to make informed public policy decisions. This book is intended to provide a foundation for those interested in developing a clearer understanding of the linkages between developmental stages and the interactions among risk factors, protective factors, and preventive interventions in child maltreatment, with the hope that such information will hasten the development of effective preventive interventions over the next decade.

## ECOLOGICAL PERSPECTIVE ON CHILD MALTREATMENT

In addition to focusing on developmental stages, this book emphasizes an ecological perspective on child maltreatment prevention. Broadly construed, social ecological models of child maltreatment suggest that etiological factors occur at multiple levels of the environmental context. These approaches consider causal factors at the level of the individual, as well as variables at the levels of family, community, and culture in explanatory models. Ecological models assume multivariate causality, and assume that interactional effects across different levels of the social ecological context influence the incidence and prevalence of child maltreatment.

Bronfenbrenner (1979) initially popularized the use of ecological constructs in the area of child development. His ecological model of human development has had a substantial influence on general child development research as well as more specific research and program development in child welfare. Belsky (1980) extended this perspective to the area of child maltreatment, and subsequent work (Rosenberg & Reppucci, 1985) has highlighted the importance of ecological perspectives in the prevention of child maltreatment.

The chapters in this volume devoted to the health care/social services system, the legal system, and parent training directly underscore important issues within specific ecological niches that impact on the prevention of child maltreatment. These chapters provide information for those working within these systems as well as those interested in understanding the impact of factors at different levels of the environmental context on child maltreatment. Furthermore, the remaining chapters on developmental periods, the prevention of specific forms of maltreatment, and research/policy issues also present various facets of ecological approaches that are directly applicable to the construction of comprehensive etiological models that include both risk and protective factors.

## OVERVIEW OF CHAPTERS

The book is divided into three sections. In the first section, the chapters outline the ecological-developmental perspective to child-abuse prevention as it applies to the different stages of child and family development and the various forms of child maltreatment. E. Wayne Holden, Diane J. Willis, and Mary M. Corcoran focus on the prenatal/perinatal period of infant and family development and review the research on child maltreatment prevention during this critical transition to parenting. Jan L. Culbertson and Cynthia Schellenbach examine preventive interventions for infants and preschool children and their parents in the context of an integrative model for prediction of effective parenting and positive attachment. Mindy S. Rosenberg and Daniel J. Sonkin discuss two high-risk family situations for school-aged children, substance-abusing caregivers and marital violence, and the implications for developing preventive interventions for these families. The dynamics of adolescent maltreatment are addressed by James Garbarino, who incorporates current research to generate hypotheses for further study and development of preventive strategies.

Whereas the above authors concentrate their discussion primarily on child physical abuse, the following three chapters expand to cover additional forms of child maltreatment. Dennis Drotar targets child neglect and provides a critical analysis of the empirical literature concerning prevention. The next two chapters focus on sexual abuse prevention. David Finkelhor and Nancy Strapko review the evaluation studies on educational programs for sexual abuse prevention while Gary Melton offers a provocative critique of the feasibility of preventing sexual abuse.

The theme of the second section is child abuse prevention and current service delivery systems. In the legal domain, N. Dickon Reppucci and Mark S. Aber examine the ethical dilemmas raised by using the legal system to combat the problem of child maltreatment. Child abuse prevention in the health care and social service systems is discussed by Keith L. Kaufman, Charles F. Johnson, Debra Cohn, and Janet McCleery. The rationale underlying parent education, the most commonly used preventive strategy in child maltreatment programs, and research supporting its effectiveness is addressed by Thomas S. Altepeter and C. Eugene Walker.

In the last section, Joan Kaufman and Edward Zigler address the theme of future directions by identifying the critical issues in child maltreatment prevention programming, research, and policy. *Prevention of Child Maltreatment* purports to summarize the prevention literature to date and stimulate ideas for future research and prevention programs.

## REFERENCES

Aber, J. L., & Cicchetti, D. (1984). Socioemotional development in maltreated children: An empirical and theoretical analysis. In H. Fitzgerald, B. Lester, and M. Yogman (Eds.), *Theory and research in behavioral pediatrics. Vol. II.* New York: Plenum Press.

Albee, G. (1982). A brief historical perspective on the primary prevention of childhood mental disorders. In Frank, M. (Ed.). *Primary prevention for children and families.* New York: Haworth Press.

Albee, G. (1983). *Prevention and promotion in mental health.* Testimony presented on behalf of American Psychological Association and Association for the Advancement of Psychology before the U.S. Senate Committee on Labor and Human Resources, April 26.

Albee, G. (1990). Personal communication.

Belsky, J. (1980). Child maltreatment: An ecological integration. *American Psychologist, 35,* 320–335.

Bronfenbrenner, U. (1979). *The ecology of human development: Experiments by nature and design.* Cambridge, MA: Harvard University Press.

Caplan, G. (1964). *Principles of preventive psychiatry.* New York: Basic Books.

Carter, B. & McGoldrick, M. (1988). *The changing family life cycle: A framework for family therapy.* New York: Gardner Press.

Chasnoff, I. (1989). Drug use and women: Establishing a standard of care. *Annals of the New York Academy of Sciences. 208.*

Cicchetti, D. (1987). Developmental psychopathology in infancy: Illustration from the study of maltreated youngsters. *Journal of Consulting and Clinical Psychology, 55,* 837–845.

Cicchetti, D., Toth, S. & Bush, M. (1988). Developmental psychopathology and incompetence in childhood: Suggestions for intervention. In B.B. Lahey & A.E. Kazdin (Eds.), *Advances in clinical child psychology Vol. 11* (pp. 1–71). New York: Plenum Press.

Cowen, E. L. & Work, W. C. (1988). Resilient children, psychological wellness, and primary prevention. *American Journal of Community Psychology*, *16*, 591–607.

Finkelhor, D. (1986). *A sourcebook in child sexual abuse*. Beverly Hills: Sage Publications.

Garbarino, J. and Crouter, K. (1978). Defining the community context of parent-child relations: The correlates of child maltreatment. *Child Development*, 49, 604–616.

Giovannoni, J. and Becerra, R. M. (1979). *Defining child abuse*. New York: The Free Press.

Giovannoni, J. (1989). Definitional issues in child maltreatment. In Cicchetti, D. and Carlson, V. (Eds.) *Child maltreatment: Theory and research on the causes and consequences of child abuse and neglect*. New York: Cambridge University Press. (pp. 3–37).

Glasner, P. D. & Kaslow, R. S. (1990). The epidemiology of human immunodeficiency virus infection. *Journal of Consulting and Clinical Psychology*, *58*, 13–21.

Gordon, R. (1983). An operational definition of prevention. *Public Health Reports*, *98*, 107–109.

Horowitz, F. D. & O'Brien, M. (Eds.), (1989). Special Issue: Children and their development: Knowledge base, research agenda, and social policy application. *American Psychologist*, *44*, 94–445.

Kazdin, A. E. (1989). Developmental psychopathology: Current research, issues, and directions. *American Psychologist*, *44*, 94–445.

Kempe, C. H., Silverman, F. N., Steele, B., Droegemueller, W. and Silver, H. R. (1962). The Battered Child Syndrome. *Journal of the American Medical Association*, *17*, 181.

Knitzer, J. (1982). *Unclaimed children*. Washington, DC: Children's Defense Fund.

Lorion, R. P., Price, R. H. & Eaton, W. W. (1989). The prevention of child and adolescent disorders: From theory to research. In D. Shaffer, I. Philips & N. B. Enzer (Eds.), *Prevention of mental disorders, alcohol, and other drug use in children and adolescents* (pp. 55–9). Rockville, MD: Office for Substance Abuse Prevention.

Mitchel, L. B. (1989). Report on fatalities from NCPCA. *Protecting Children: American Association for Protecting Children*, *6*, 3–5.

National Center on Child Abuse and Neglect, (1988). *Study of National Incidence and Prevalence of Child Abuse and Neglect: 1988*. Washington, DC, U.S. Department of Health and Human Services.

Public Health Service, (1964). *Morbidity and Mortality Weekly Report*, Washington, DC: U.S. Department of Health, Education and Welfare, 4–5.

Rolf, J. E. (1985). Evolving adaptive theories and methods for prevention research with children. *Journal of Consulting and Clinical Psychology*, *53*, 631–646.

Rosenberg, M. S. & Reppucci, N. D. (1985). Primary prevention of child abuse. *Journal of Consulting and Clinical Psychology*, *53*, 576–585.

Tuma, J. (1989). Mental health services for children: The state of the art. *American Psychologist*, *44*, 188–199.

U.S. Department of Health and Human Services (1990). *Child abuse and neglect:*

*Critical first steps in response to a national emergency.* Washington, DC: U.S. Government Printing Office: Stock No.: 017-092-00104-5.

U.S. Department of Health and Human Services. (1990). *Crack babies.* Washington, DC: Office of Evaluation and Inspections.

Weissberg, R. P. & Allen, J. P. (1986). Promoting children's social skills and adaptive interpersonal behavior. In B. S. Edelstein & L. Michelson (Eds.), *Handbook of prevention* (pp. 153–175). New York: Plenum Press.

Willis, D. J. (1987). Symposium: Critical issues in child abuse prevention. New York: American Psychological Association Annual Convention.

Zigler, E. & Hall, N. W. (1989). Physical child abuse in America: Past, present, and future. In Cicchetti, D. and Carlson, V. (Eds.) *Child maltreatment: Theory and research on the causes and consequences of child abuse and neglect* (pp. 3–37). New York: Cambridge University Press.

# A Developmental Perspective on Child Maltreatment Prevention

# CHAPTER 2

# *Preventing Child Maltreatment During the Prenatal/Perinatal Period*

E. WAYNE HOLDEN, DIANE J. WILLIS, AND MARY M. CORCORAN

Conception, pregnancy and subsequent childbirth encompass one of the most important transition periods in development. Changes occur simultaneously at multiple levels of influence from the biological to the psychological to the relational/social system level. In comparison to other developmental transitions, the changes occurring during the prenatal/perinatal period commence at a relatively rapid rate, influencing not only the mother and developing fetus, but also other family members and the social and professional helping networks who are connected with them. Relationships between individuals and between different components of the social ecological context can change substantially as a function of the transitions experienced during this developmental period. The resulting biopsychosocial framework that emerges postnatally serves as an important foundation for later individual and family development.

As a period of developmental transition, and perhaps even crisis, the prenatal/perinatal period provides opportunities for enhancing competencies and reducing risks that may have implications for lifelong developmental processes for both children and parents. For example, an expectant parent may be influenced by contacts with the health care community that provide information, coping assistance and social support. These contacts can be instrumental in enhancing expectant parents' sense of competence, developing parenting skills, strengthening family relationships, and identifying as well as modifying risk factors for subsequent child maltreatment.

Given the transitional nature of the prenatal/perinatal period and its importance as a foundation for later development, it comes as no surprise that this developmental period has received substantial attention within the child maltreatment area. Three major sets of literature specifically address the issue of child maltreatment during the prenatal/perinatal period. The first set of literature has focused on the identification of factors during this period that predict subsequent child maltreatment (Altemeier, O'Connor, Vietze, Sandler, & Sherrod, 1982). The second set of literature consists of reports of primary and secondary prevention programs that have been instituted during the prenatal/perinatal period (Cohen, Gray & Wald, 1984). The third set of literature, which has received far less attention, is the investigation of maltreatment directed toward the fetus or neonates. This latter area has consisted primarily of clinical descriptions and theoretical conceptualizations rather than empirical investigations (Condon, 1986). In combination with the growing literature on maternal health risk behaviors, however, the information available on fetal abuse and neglect is important to consider in the further refinement and extension of the role of the prenatal/perinatal period in the prevention of child maltreatment.

The primary purpose of this chapter is to review and integrate the literature that is currently available on the prenatal/perinatal period and the prevention of child maltreatment. Initial attention will be given to defining a normative ecological model for categorizing the variables of interest during this transitional period. Risk factors that have been identified in the literature will be integrated into the model to provide a foundation for the discussion of prevention programs. Research evaluating preventive interventions based in the prenatal/perinatal period will then be considered. The literature on fetal abuse/ neglect and maternal health risk behaviors will also be addressed. Finally, conclusions will be drawn and recommendations made for future research and program implementation.

## A NORMATIVE ECOLOGICAL MODEL
## OF THE PRENATAL/PERINATAL PERIOD

Since Belsky's (1980) initial proposal for an ecological model of child maltreatment, substantial progress has been made in refining and extending the ecological perspective. Ecological models are concerned with identifying, and specifying the effects of causal agents at multiple levels of the environmental context. Although individuals are considered to be important components, contextual influences at the levels of the family, community and culture are also emphasized. Ecological models assume multivariate causality and posit important interactional effects between components at different levels of the social ecological context.

One might argue that ecological models are currently in vogue in the child maltreatment area and that their relevance to both treatment (Garbarino, Guttmann & Seeley, 1986) and prevention (Rosenberg & Reppucci, 1985) have been established. The models that are available, however, are often static and disregard developmental changes. To promote further progress in both prevention and treatment, ecological conceptualizations that highlight factors specific to individual developmental periods and provide linkage be-

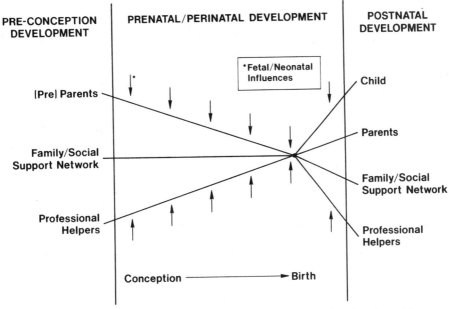

**Figure 2.1.** Developmental social ecological model of the prenatal/perinatal transition.

tween developmental periods are needed (Rolf, 1985). To have relevance for both primary and secondary prevention, these conceptualizations require a competence focus and a normative orientation.

One framework that can be used to conceptualize the ecological factors involved in the developmental transitions during the prenatal/perinatal period is illustrated in Figure 2.1. This figure depicts changes from prior to conception through postnatal development across four areas of the social ecological context that are present during the prenatal/perinatal period. These categories include 1) the fetus/neonate, 2) parents, 3) family/social support networks, and 4) the professional helpers.

Conception initiates a transitional period in which individual social ecological factors and the relationships between these factors are subject to change. The existing relationships between potential parents, their families/social support networks and professional helpers prior to conception are challenged by the presence of the fetus and the tasks of childbearing. Within this model, the fetus/neonate serves as a catalyst for promoting changes that by the end of the prenatal/perinatal period result in a modified social ecological matrix that includes the newborn child and that is the foundation for later development. In the ensuing discussion, each level of influence will be individually considered, while interactions and the potential for bidirectional causal combinations will also be addressed.

## The Fetus/Neonate

Conception, subsequent development of the fetus, and birth have important implications as biological events that can potentially prompt changes in the social environment. Normative development predicts a linear stage-like progression in growth and biological functioning such that potential for viability outside the womb increases as a function of time. In addition, although variability exists between mother-fetus pairs, indices of fetal existence and subsequent development based in biological changes (for example, morning sickness, quickening, expansion of the mother's abdomen) cue both the mother and other members of her social network to change. The resulting responses represent the beginnings of a reciprocal relationship between the fetus and its impending extrauterine environment that can become the basis for changes in the relationship between parents, extended family members, informal social supports and professional helpers. Birth and the subsequent physical condition of the neonate following birth also serve as important factors that further effect the interactional sequences among components of the social ecological context.

## The Parents

Both as individuals and as a relationship entity, parents exert substantial influence on and are substantially influenced by the developmental events of the prenatal/perinatal period. The relationship that develops between the parents and fetus assumes critical importance with respect to the provision of adequate prenatal care. This relationship is also an important precursor of later parent-child interactions.

More attention has been directed towards investigating the role of the mother than the father during the prenatal/perinatal period. Determination of the mother's adjustment to pregnancy is a well-researched topic with a number of variables specified as important to the adjustment process (Hees-Stauthamer, 1985). On a subjective level, the physical and emotional experiences of pregnancy appear to be important factors that determine the mother's attitudes towards the pregnancy, subsequent behavior and, in some cases, obstetrical outcome (Entwistle & Doering, 1981). For example, Fleming and associates (1988) reported that maternal pregnancy and postpartum mood were significant predictors of mother-infant interaction at one and three months following birth. Depressed mothers were more likely to display less affection and less responsiveness toward their infants. A recent investigation (Labs & Wurtele, 1986) has suggested that maternal health locus of control beliefs with respect to the developing fetus may be an additional cognitive factor to consider. Those expectant mothers who believed that they had control over fetal health outcomes (that is, were internally oriented) on a measure of fetal health locus of control were less likely to report engaging in behaviors such as drug use, smoking, caffeine intake, and poor nutrition that represented health risks for fetal development.

Maternal experience of and beliefs about pregnancy can also be influenced by the interpersonal context in which the fetus-mother axis exists. Marital adjustment during pregnancy has been reported to be a significant predictor of maternal pregnancy adjustment (Goldberg & Easterbrook, 1984). From a transitional perspective, maternal coping with the multiple internal and interpersonal changes experienced during pregnancy may result in a reduction or an increase in stress. The anxiety and stress associated with normative transitions during the prenatal/perinatal period can prompt the development of maternal coping strategies that may become a basis for later parental competencies. Some of these coping mechanisms represent healthy and effective methods for reducing stress, whereas others such as alcohol use may result in direct harm to the developing fetus.

The last two decades have witnessed an increasing emphasis on the role of the father in the prenatal/perinatal period of development (May & Perrin, 1985). The father has become an active participant in the birth process through the family centered childbirth movement, and the developmental transitions that the father experiences during the prenatal/perinatal period have been recognized as important research topics (Roopnarine & Miller, 1985). The role of the father during the prenatal/perinatal period is far from being completely understood. However, interventions conducted during the prenatal/perinatal period to enhance paternal-child interactions postnatally have been effective, at least in the short term (Parke & Beitel, 1986). This underscores the importance of continuing to investigate the role of the father in prenatal/perinatal development.

Although the marital relationship may undergo substantial change during the prenatal/perinatal period, the relationship itself is also an important source of stability and support. Marital satisfaction measured prenatally has been significantly associated with pregnancy adjustment and postnatal parenting attitudes (Belsky, Spanier & Rovine, 1983; Goldberg & Easterbrook, 1984; Oates & Heinicke, 1985). A bidirectional causal relationship may also exist between neonatal characteristics and the marital relationship. It has been reported that infant temperamental variations exert influence on marital adjustment during the transition to parenthood (Sirignano & Lachman, 1985). A circular relationship between these two sets of variables is consistent with a social ecological conceptualization of the prenatal/perinatal period. The interactions between variables at different levels of the social ecological context is an important factor that has been relatively neglected in prior research but should be included in the development of future explanatory models.

### Family/Social Support Network

Both the nuclear and extended family are important factors at the social systems level during the prenatal/perinatal period. The childbearing period has been recognized as a developmental stage in its own right within family life cycle theory (Carter & McGoldrick, 1980). Changes occurring during this stage of family development may have implications for multigenerational relationships within extended family systems. Within the nuclear family, re-lationships shift between expectant parents and, in multiparous couples, be-tween parents and existing children as childbirth approaches. Changes in the nuclear family do not occur in a systemic vacuum. Family of origin issues can exert substantial influence over the direction of nuclear family transitions during the prenatal/perinatal period. Belsky and Isabella (1985) recently stated that parents' self-report of how they were reared and their own parents' marital relationship were significantly related to changes in their ratings of marital adjustment across the transition to parenthood. Furthermore, multi-generational relationships involving grandparents and other extended family members can be either directly or indirectly renegotiated during the prenatal/perinatal period (Sherwen, 1987).

The beneficial value of social support on both physical and psychosocial functioning has been recognized with increasing frequency within the general psychological literature (Barrera, 1986; Cohen & Wills, 1985). With respect to pregnancy and subsequent childbirth, it has been reported that social sup-port at the time of birth mediates more positive outcomes for both neonate and mother (Klaus et al., 1986) and social support during pregnancy predicts better maternal adjustment to pregnancy even among teenage mothers (Unger & Wandersman, 1985). Support networks outside of the family may include informal relationships, work environments or formal groups such as childbirth education classes or La Leche League meetings. Support systems that are present prior to conception may function to buffer the additional stress of childbearing, or new support systems may be formed that meet the specific needs of the prenatal/perinatal transition.

As recently indicated by Seagull (1987), however, the preventive effects of social support are quite likely complex and determined by a number of other factors that are also present in the social ecological context during the prenatal/perinatal period. For example, at moderate levels of life stress, social support may have a buffering effect, but at high levels of life stress social support may be relatively ineffective in preventing maladaptive outcomes. The differential effects of social support at varying levels of stress, may be moderated by family factors and variations in the linkages between family systems and social support networks. Further research is required to specify accurately the relative influence of variables at different levels of the social ecological context on the effects of social support.

## Professional Helpers

The provision of prenatal care and medical assistance during the birth process provides a time-limited opportunity for the engagement of professional sup-port and for professional input into the emergent social ecological context. The role of professional helpers can be instrumental in assisting the renegotiation of relationships between family members (Sherwen, 1987) and in linking families with support systems that otherwise may not have been available (Crockenberg, 1985). For some families, this represents the only period in development that a systematic, stable relationship with the medical/health care context occurs over time. For the professional community, it represents an opportunity to support the development of a healthy, growth-enhancing foundation for later child and family development. Problematic relationships between professional helpers and potential parents or their families prior to conception may complicate development of an effective helping relationship during the prenatal/perinatal period. An inconsistent relationship characterized by random contacts with multiple health care professionals or hostility between the health care system and families can negatively impact on the support that can be potentially provided by health care professionals during the prenatal/perinatal period.

## Summary

The model proposed in this section offers a framework for categorizing the influence of pertinent social ecological variables during the prenatal/perinatal developmental period. In addition to the four levels discussed above, it should be emphasized that differences in cultural context, the interactions between social ecological levels, and historical factors such as changes in health care delivery are also involved in determining the outcome of the events of this developmental period. Although preconception relationships between social-ecological components were not specifically addressed, they provide a foundation for the promotion of positive or negative change across the prenatal/ perinatal transition. The rigidity of preconception relationships may be an important factor to consider when evaluating the likelihood of change during the prenatal/perinatal transition. The proposed model will be used as a basis for the review of literature on risk factors associated with the prenatal/perinatal period in the following section.

## RISK FACTORS

Substantial attention has been devoted to identifying factors during the prenatal/perinatal period that are predictive of subsequent child maltreatment. Some of these factors concern events that occurred prior to conception—for example, mother's childhood experiences—while others first manifested themselves during the prenatal/perinatal period: maternal attitudes toward pregnancy, birth complications, etc. Time of assessment of these factors has varied with some investigations assessing risk prenatally, others assessing risk perinatally, and still others evaluating the risk status of prenatal/perinatal factors retrospectively; that is, after the occurrence of child maltreatment.

Enhanced methodological rigor in recent research has yielded results that often contradict earlier findings which suggested a relatively strong, almost direct influence of single variables for risk of subsequent child maltreatment. Current researchers are emphasizing the importance of multivariate approaches that capitalize on the enhanced predictive power of sets of multiple risk factors. Although the assessment and determination of risk status is fraught with controversy and represents a deficit orientation to child maltreatment prevention, a substantial proportion of the literature has been directed towards this issue.

## Medical Care

Over the last two decades several researchers have investigated the risk status of variables at the level of the fetus/neonate. In early retrospective, less well controlled investigations (cf. Lynch & Roberts, 1977), medical problems occurring during pregnancy or complications at birth were associated with higher risk for subsequent child maltreatment. More recent research utilizing sophisticated retrospective designs or prospective methodologies (Benedict, White, & Cornely, 1985; Caplan, Watters, White, Parry, & Bates, 1984; Egeland & Vaughn, 1981; Leventhal, Egerter & Murphy, 1984), however, has failed to substantiate such an association. In addition to differences in methodological rigor, changes in medical care provided to families who have experienced substantial pregnancy and birth complications over the last decade may have influenced the outcome of the more recent investigations. Advances in neonatology and obstetrical care in combination with the recognition of the importance of the prenatal/perinatal period to subsequent development have generally resulted in enhanced professional contact and support when complications arise (Sherwen, 1987). The interactions between enhanced health care delivery and fetal/neonatal medical complications may be important to consider in the determination of risk status for later child maltreatment in subsequent research.

 ## Infant Temperament

Many of the models developed to help provide understanding of the etiology of child abuse include characteristics of the child as important variables (e.g., Snyder, Hampton & Newberger, 1983). Having a child with a difficult temperament is considered to be a child-produced stressor which may interact with other environmental stressors and parental factors to increase the potential for child maltreatment. Although many clinicians believe that difficult temperament is related to maltreatment (Carey, 1986), this viewpoint is supported by little empirical evidence. Sherrod, Altemeier, O'Connor and Vietze (1984) included infant temperament, measured at either one or three months, as one of many variables in a prospective investigation of child maltreatment.

They reported that difficult temperament, as perceived by mothers in the study, was significantly related to subsequent abuse. However, other researchers (Sroufe & Waters, 1982) have reported that within their research program there was no clear evidence that temperamental characteristics of the infant increased potential for subsequent child maltreatment. Valid and reliable estimates of temperamental variations are impossible to collect prenatally, and no investigators to date have researched the specific relationship between temperament measured just following birth and rates of subsequent child maltreatment. Infant temperament is yet another variable that has been emphasized clinically despite conflicting empirical evidence for its effects.

## Maternal Variables

At the level of the parents, primary attention has been directed toward maternal characteristics in the prediction of risk for subsequent child maltreatment. Demographic variables including maternal age, race, socioeconomic status, educational level and marital status have been investigated as well as historical and psychological factors. In the following paragraphs individual parental factors that have been investigated will be addressed.

Young maternal age as a predictor of subsequent child maltreatment was evaluated in 10 separate investigations with mixed results. Six of the studies which did not support age as a risk factor were generally well-controlled prospective investigations (Altemeier et al., 1982; Bolton & Laner, 1981; Earp & Ory, 1980; Hunter, Kilstrom, Kraybill, & Loda, 1978; Kinard & Klerman, 1980; Murphy, Orkow, & Nicola, 1985). Those four studies which found younger mothers to be at greater risk for subsequent child maltreatment utilized retrospective designs (Agathonos, Stathacopoulou, Adam, & Nakou, 1982; Benedict et al., 1985; Caplan et al., 1984; Leventhal et al., 1984). In addition, two of these four investigations (i.e., Agathonos et al., 1982; Caplan et al., 1984) did not control for socioeconomic status (SES). When researchers controlled for SES in the previously cited prospective investigations, age no longer surfaced as an important predictive variable. A similar pattern of results across investigations was obtained for single marital status during pregnancy.

Lack of financial resources (Bolton & Laner, 1981; Caplan et al., 1984; Hunter et al., 1978) and lower educational level (Agathonos et al., 1982; Caplan et al., 1984; Egeland & Brunnquell, 1979) have received somewhat more support as potential risk factors. Racial status, however, has not been found to be a significant predictor of subsequent child maltreatment (Altemeier et al., 1982). Histories that include a criminal record (Caplan et al., 1985) or loss of a previous child (Altemeier et al., 1982; Benedict et al., 1985), however, have also been reported to increase risk status.

Maternal history of childhood maltreatment and/or negative perceptions of childhood nurturance has received support in both prospective and retrospective investigations (Agathonos et al., 1982; Altemeier et al., 1982;

Hunter et al., 1978; Murphy et al., 1985). In a prospective investigation specifically designed to evaluate history of abuse in expectant mothers (Altemeier, O'Connor, Sherrod, Tucker, & Vietze, 1986), it was reported that those mothers who were maltreated as children differed from controls on a number of proximal variables (e.g., lower self image, greater social isolation, greater stress, and more aggression) potentially important in subsequent child maltreatment. However, incidence rates of child maltreatment did not differ significantly between the two groups when the infants ranged from 21 to 48 months of age. In a recent review of this literature, Kaufman and Zigler (1987) discussed the current status of the transgenerational transmission of child maltreatment. They concluded that this variable should be approached cautiously with an appropriate appreciation for the methodological problems in the research supporting the history of child maltreatment as a risk factor. The results of retrospective investigations have inflated the importance placed on this risk factor in clinical situations. Clearly, history of child maltreatment may enhance risk in some cases, but there are many cases where parents who were maltreated as children do not subsequently maltreat their own children. Once again, the complexity of factors that are involved in any act of child maltreatment must be underscored, with the use of multivariate approaches in risk factors research clearly indicated.

A wide range of maternal psychological variables during the prenatal/perinatal period have been evaluated as predictors of subsequent child maltreatment. Their value in the assessment of risk has been supported across individual investigations. Negative maternal attitude toward the pregnancy (either unwanted or unplanned) has been a significant predictor of increased risk in all six of the investigations that evaluated that variable (Agathonos et al., 1982; Altemeier et al., 1982; Brunnquell et al., 1981; Egeland & Brunnquell, 1979; Murphy et al., 1985; Zuravin, 1987). Zuravin (1987) additionally reported that negative maternal attitudes may be more predictive of subsequent neglect than physical abuse. Other maternal psychological characteristics that have received some support as predictors of increased risk include poor self image, aggression/anger, impulsivity, emotional difficulties, lack of knowledge of parenting and psychiatric difficulties.

## Paternal Characteristics

It is important to note that fathers have been relatively neglected in the assessment of risk status for later child maltreatment during the prenatal/perinatal period. Although marital status and spouse conflict (Agathanos et al., 1982; Caplan et al., 1984) have both been reported to be significant predictors of risk specific paternal characteristics remain an untapped, yet potentially important source of information. Further research with fathers may allow us to gain an increased understanding of paternal risk factors as well as protective factors that may lead to the enhancement of parenting competencies during this developmental period.

## Social Isolation

Several variables at the family/social support level have been investigated in addition to marital status and spouse conflict. It has been reported that the absence of social support and social isolation during the prenatal/perinatal period are significant predictors of increased risk for subsequent child maltreatment (Agathanos et al., 1982; Egeland & Brunquell, 1979; Hunter et al., 1978; Murphy et al., 1985). However, two investigations (Altemeier et al., 1982; Caplan et al., 1984) failed to find a significant relationship between social support indices and child maltreatment. There is stronger evidence for a relationship between social isolation and child neglect than between social isolation and child abuse (Seagull, 1987).

## Environmental Stressors

Levels of perceived environmental stress including health related stressors, financial stressors, and life events stressors have received consistent support as risk factors which predict higher subsequent incidence rates (Altemeier et al., 1982; Benedict et al., 1985; Caplan et al., 1984; Friedrich & Wheeler, 1982; Justice & Duncan, 1976; Murphy et al., 1985; Pelton, 1978). Large family size or inadequate child spacing may also be conceptualized as a stressor and has been cited in prospective investigations as an indicator of heightened risk (Altemeier et al., 1982; Hunter et al., 1978).

## Other Possible Risk Factors

Interactions may exist between social support and life stress that moderate any predictive relationships. This is particularly likely given the interactional nature of stress level and social support in the life stress-physical illness relationship (Barth & Schinke, 1983; Cohen & Wills, 1985). Very little attention, however, has been given to investigating the interactions between variables in the determination of risk status for subsequent child maltreatment.

Furthermore, minimal attention has been devoted to the level of professional helpers in the determination of risk. None of the previously cited studies addressed variables that were directly related to the involvement of professional helpers. The vast majority of the literature is deficit oriented and the protective influences of enhanced professional support and guidance during the prenatal/perinatal period have been relatively neglected in empirical investigations. This may reflect a bias that is, in part, determined by the process of health care delivery in the United States. Crockenberg (1985) reported that cross-national differences in the provision of prenatal care to expectant teenagers resulted in the experience of less social support for those receiving services in the United States as opposed to those receiving services in Great Britain. Nurse home visitation was a consistent part of the prenatal care that was delivered in Great Britain and was not a part of the services offered to the United States sample.

## Summary

The ability to identify risk factors that accurately predict subsequent child maltreatment during the prenatal/perinatal period has important implications. Several primary and secondary prevention programs have been based on the identification of high-risk groups, however, risk factors that were used to select target populations frequently have received contradictory support in the literature. For example, Olds (1982), focused their prevention program on primiparous women who were either teenagers, unmarried, or of low socioeconomic status (SES). These three factors were reviewed in this section and low SES was the only variable with data which consistently supported its predictive validity. It should be noted, however, that the three factors, in combination, may produce enhanced risk and that combining variables to identify risk groups is consistent with the multivariate causal modeling that is needed in this area. In our review, negative maternal attitudes towards pregnancy and high stress levels are two of the very few factors investigated that have shown consistent evidence that they do indeed place a woman at high risk for subsequent child maltreatment.

The literature on risk factors is just beginning to address, on a conceptual level, variables that promote healthy relationships or serve to reduce risk for child maltreatment (Cicchetti & Rizley, 1981; Rosenberg, 1987). The deficit orientation that has largely characterized previous research has ignored protective factors that may play important roles in determining outcome. As the issue of resiliency is addressed more frequently in empirical research in the general area of child psychopathology (Rutter, 1987), those working in the area of child maltreatment should begin to include more comprehensive sets of both protective and risk enhancing variables in research designs. As our proposed model suggests, it is likely that multiple factors will be identified at several different levels of the social ecological context that interact to determine risk status. Multivariate research designs should yield a clearer understanding of prenatal and perinatal risk for subsequent child maltreatment in future investigations.

## PREVENTION STRATEGIES

Preventive interventions that have been instituted during the prenatal/perinatal period are based on the results of research that has specifically investigated variables that are risk factors for subsequent child maltreatment. In addition, developmental research based on the prenatal/perinatal period has also been used as a basis for the development of specific prevention strategies. Evaluations of these interventions have reflected their underlying foundations, with outcome measures largely limited to the assessment of proximal variables within ecological models of child maltreatment. Subsequent child maltreatment incidence rates have not been universally included in outcome evaluations. In reviewing the outcome literature on the prevention of child maltreatment during the prenatal/perinatal period, some attention will be directed towards developmental research from which specific intervention strategies have emerged. First, comprehensive prenatal/perinatal interventions will be reviewed. Second, programs focusing on early/extended contact and perinatal information will be evaluated. Community-level interventions will then be addressed followed by a critique of the literature in this area.

### Comprehensive Prenatal/Perinatal Programs

Several comprehensive prevention programs that were implemented during the prenatal/perinatal period have been reported in the literature. These programs varied widely in both scope and content. In some, interventions were initiated prenatally and extended well into early infancy; whereas in others interventions were only conducted during the prenatal/perinatal period. Although preventive interventions were typically instituted within health care settings, the status of individuals who had direct contact with families varied substantially across investigations. More specificially, those individuals having direct contact with families ranged from paraprofessional volunteers to physicians. Evaluations of these programs has not been universally systematic and methodologically rigorous. Anecdotal outcome descriptions characterize much of the literature that is available and, in cases where data were collected, the approaches to data analysis and interpretation were often less than comprehensive. The accurate measurement of distal as well as proximal outcome variables with respect to child maltreatment has been neglected in a majority of these program evaluations.

A number of authors described programs that have been developed to prevent child maltreatment through enhanced involvement between professional helpers and parents or families beginning in the prenatal/perinatal period. Ayoub and Jacewitz (1982) presented an in-depth description of a secondary prevention program for at-risk parents that identified potential participants through both formal and informal prenatal screening methods. A major portion of the program was devoted to training professionals in the community to informally screen parents using criteria across four areas— biological, psychological, social, and interactional—and to make referrals for further evaluation and intervention to the program. Comprehensive hospital care at birth, outpatient clinic care for the child following birth, and in-home visits by public health nurses and volunteers were provided to families who participated in the program. Unfortunately, no outcome data were presented regarding the enhancement of parental competencies or the prevention of subsequent child maltreatment. Even if such data were available it would have been impossible to evaluate the specific effects of prenatal/perinatal interventions due to the presence of extensive contact during both the prenatal/perinatal and postnatal periods. The program, as designed, had several positive aspects with perhaps the most important being the active linking of existing community resources to create a professionally based screening and helping network to prevent child maltreatment.

Cooper, Dreznick & Rowe (1982) described a comprehensive prevention program for primiparous mothers with contact beginning at the seventh prenatal month and extending until the child was one year old. Their approach provided prenatal, perinatal and postnatal support and education to parents. The decriptive information that is presented may be useful to those individuals who are creating new programs as the authors detail some of the issues involved in establishing and maintaining prevention programs within health care contexts. Although the descriptive information that is presented may be useful to those individuals who are creating new programs, there was no attempt to systematically evaluate the outcome of their prevention efforts.

Grindley (1981) provided an excellent conceptual discussion of the role of the nurse in the prevention of child maltreatment during the prenatal/perinatal period. She underscored a number of informal avenues for providing support and potentially enhancing subsequent parenting competencies. However, similar to Cooper and associates (1982), no outcome data regarding the effectiveness of the suggested interventions were reported. Similarly, Helfer (1987) discussed the importance of prenatal/perinatal programs to prevent child maltreatment and qualitatively reviewed six existing programs. Although recommendations were made for systematic outcome research in the future, no quantitative outcome data for the existing programs were reported.

Gray and associates (1977) were the first authors to report the results of a well-designed evaluation of a prenatal/perinatal child maltreatment secondary prevention program. They identified 100 high-risk mothers prenatally utilizing a comprehensive screening battery. The mothers were randomly assigned to either an intervention or control group. Preventive interventions began at birth and included a higher frequency of contact with a pediatrician, weekly home health nurse visits, and greater linkage with other professional helpers in the community. At follow up, between 17 and 35 months postpartum, the preventive interventions had positive effects on child maltreatment. The control and treatment groups differed significantly in severity of child maltreatment with less severe episodes reported for the high-risk mothers who had received enhanced contact with professionals. Five of the children from the control group were hospitalized for injuries, while none of the children from the intervention group required hospitalization. A subsequent report (Gray, Cutler, Dean & Kempe (1979) supported the positive effects that regular visitation by home health nurses can have on severity of subsequent child maltreatment. No serious injuries were reported as a result of abuse or neglect for several hundred high-risk families who received home health nurse visitation for 18 months postpartum. Although the interventions used by these authors began at birth, they extended well into the period of postnatal development making it impossible to determine the specific effects of perinatal contact on severity of subsequent child maltreatment.

An intensive secondary prevention program encompassing the prenatal, perinatal, and postnatal periods of development was also included in the demonstration projects of the Collaborative Research of Community and Minority Group Action to Prevent Child Abuse and Neglect (Gray, 1983). Beginning in the last trimester of pregnancy, trained paraprofessionals (for example, experienced volunteer mothers and grandmothers) provided emotional support, information, and transportation assistance to primiparous mothers and their spouses from a low-income, high risk for child maltreatment urban area. An additional component of the program was the development of a support group for the parents that met on a regular basis. The program was intentionally designed to intensively impact on a limited number of parents. Just over 700 total contacts were made with 28 participating families during the first year with most contacts occurring prior to three months postpartum.

Evaluation of the project included comparisons between a control group and the participants. Families were assigned to the two groups on a random basis. Unfortunately, only proximal outcome variables were measured with the instruments employed consisting of self-report measures. Moreover, the pre/post evaluation data were collected for only approximately one-half of each group. On the Broussard Neonatal Perception Inventory, however, parents participating in the intervention group displayed a significant change in the positive direction from pre to post testing. It appeared that the prevention program provided sufficient support to high risk mothers to produce positive changes in their perceptions of their infants. The only significant difference on the Bavolek Adolescent/Adult Parenting Inventory was at pretest with the intervention group displaying more unrealistic expectations than the controls. No data on subsequent child maltreatment incidence rates were reported. It is important to note, however, that evaluation efforts were hampered by premature termination of funding for this demonstration project. The initial evaluation data are encouraging and suggest that intensive contacts by paraprofessionals may be an effective prevention strategy with high risk mothers.

Another comprehensive secondary prevention program for high-risk parents was conducted in Belgium (Soumenkoff, Marneffe, Gerard, Limet, Beeckmans & Hubinot, 1982). High-risk parents were identified prenatally and followed by a specialized prevention team including a gynecologist, nurse, child psychiatrists, and social workers. The team followed the identified cases through birth and into the postnatal period. Interventions included enhanced support by members of the high-risk team (for example, increased frequency of contact, extended contact during appointments, and easy access to appointments) and repeated psychosocial interventions devised by the team during weekly meetings to alter unfavorable socioeconomic factors or parental emotional maladjustment. Evaluation of the program consisted of intensive analysis of outcomes for the participants with some comparisons to outcomes for other mothers delivering in the same health care setting who did not participate in the program. High rates of personality problems and emotional disturbance were found among the high-risk parents. The preventive interventions appeared to be somewhat effective in lowering the prematurity rate for the sample. Intensive psychotherapeutic interventions conducted by the child psychiatrists in a minority of the cases were also reported to be effective in lowering the risk for subsequent child maltreatment. Anecdotal evidence indicated that the team concept had a positive effect on the relationships among health care personnel. These results, however, should be interpreted cautiously since they are based primarily on outcome analyses that only included the participants or comparisons of intervention and control groups that were not randomly assigned to receive preventive services. In addition, outcome assessments reflected clinical impressions rather than scores on well standardized tests.

The most well-designed comprehensive prevention program to date has been conducted by Olds and associates (1980, 1982, 1984, 1986a, 1986b) in upstate New York. Labeled the Prenatal/Early Infancy Project, this secondary prevention program has provided comprehensive nurse home visitation services to expectant mothers and their families in rural Appalachia. An important characteristic of this project has been a rigorous evaluation methodology that included the random assignment of subjects to four specific treatment groups and the evaluation of prenatal, birth and postnatal outcome variables. Both proximal and distal outcome variables with respect to child maltreatment were included in the evaluation component. The four treatment levels that were evaluated in the study included 1) a control group that participated in the pre-post collection of evaluation data, but did not receive services, 2) a minimal intervention group that received assistance in transportation for attending medical appointments, 3) a group that received extensive nurse home visitation prenatally and transportation assistance, and 4) a group that received extensive nurse home visitation postnatally in addition to the services provided to group 3. Nurse home visitation consisted of parent education, attempts to enhance family and other informal social supports, and linkage with professional helpers in the community.

The effects of the preventive interventions conducted within this program have been reported with respect to prenatal/perinatal outcomes (Olds, Henderson, Tatelbaum & Chamberlin, 1986a) and postnatal parent-child interactions as well as child maltreatment rates (Olds, Henderson, Chamberlin & Tatelbaum, 1986b). In comparisons of mothers who received nurse home visitation versus those not receiving this intervention prenatally, positive effects were noted for the former groups across a wide range of prenatal and perinatal variables including specific behaviors of the mother, amounts of social support within and outside the family, and utilization of professional helping services in the community. Positive effects of nurse home visitation on birth weight and length of gestation were particularly apparent for adolescents aged 18 and under and mothers who smoked during gestation.

Postnatal effects of this prevention program were also analyzed by comparing groups receiving nurse home visitation versus those who did not receive this intervention. Among the highest risk mothers (for example, age 18 or under, unmarried, and lower SES) and among teenage mothers generally, marginally significant differences were obtained between the intervention and nonintervention groups in the area of subsequent child maltreatment rates. Poor, unmarried teenagers who did not receive the prevention services displayed higher rates of referral for abuse or neglect by 2 years postpartum. In eight of the thirty-two cases (i.e., 25% of the control sample) either substantiated abuse or neglect had occurred. In contrast, child maltreatment was reported to local authorities for only one of the forty cases that received nurse home visitation services. Mothers in the nurse-visited group also perceived their children as less irritable, and the group at greatest risk who received intervention displayed less restrictive and more nurturing behavior in parent-child interactions when compared to the high-risk mothers who did not receive preventive intervention. Emergency room visits for the infants were less frequent for the families receiving nurse home visitation across both the first and second postnatal years. Furthermore, nurse home visitation appeared to moderate the potential deleterious effects of low perceived control. Lack of personal control was a significant predictor of child maltreatment incidence rates and emergency room visits in the comparison group, but not among the mothers receiving nurse home visitation.

The well-conceived experimental design and rigorous evaluation methodology used in the Prenatal/Early Infancy Project sets the results from this program apart from other available literature. Although the effects of prenatal/perinatal versus postnatal contact were not analyzed separately, the results suggest that comprehensive prevention services provided through nurse home visitation can have a significant positive effect on a number of proximal and distal variables important in the prevention of child maltreatment. More evaluative research of this type needs to be done to develop a clearer understanding of the preventive effects of comprehensive approaches during the prenatal/perinatal period.

## Early and Extended Perinatal Contact

One set of developmental research that has had substantial influence on the prevention of child maltreatment during the prenatal/perinatal period is conceptually and theoretically rooted in bonding and attachment theory. Beginning with the initial work of Klaus and Kennell (1972), the notion of a critical sensitive period for maternal-infant and paternal-infant bonding in the immediate postpartum has received significant attention. The increase in extended contact immediately following birth and rooming-in of neonates with mothers in obstetrical units across the country is a direct product of the belief that early and extended contact promotes healthy parental-infant bonding and attachment. Theoretically, early parent-neonate contact immediately following birth would enhance bonding by creating heightened parental emotional responses, and extended contact via rooming-in would increase parental sensitivity to neonatal behavioral cues (Wilson, 1984).

The research base supporting the notion that contact during this sensitive period is *necessary* for the development of effective parent-child relationships has been challenged in several critical reviews (Lamb & Hwang, 1982; Goldberg, 1983; Herbert, Sluckin & Sluckin, 1982). The period of time in which successful attachment and bonding can occur may be much less restricted than originally suggested. Reviewers of this literature, however, have indicated that early and extended perinatal contact appears to have some short-term positive effects and that it is relatively easy and cost effective to implement.

Proponents of early and extended contact have invesigated its effects on subsequent child maltreatment. O'Connor, Vietze, Sherrod, Sandler & Altemeier (1980) randomly assigned 301 primiparous mothers to rooming-in or no rooming conditions to evaluate the impact of extended maternal-neonate contact on subsequent rates of child maltreatment. At approximately 17 months after birth, 12 cases of abuse or neglect had been identified with only 2 of the 12 cases occurring in families that received rooming in. In a subsequent study, however, risk status for child maltreatment established prenatally interacted with rooming-in (O'Connor, Vietze, Sherrod, Sandler, Gerrity & Altemeier, 1982). High-risk mothers, in comparison to low-risk mothers, benefitted minimally when specific observational indices of postnatal mother-infant interaction were used as outcome measures. Anisfeld and Lipper (1983), however, reported that mothers who experienced lower levels of social support may benefit more from early contact than mothers who had higher levels of social support. The data presented in this latter study are limited to the first two days following birth limiting the generalization of the conclusions with respect to later child maltreatment.

A demonstration project evaluating the effects of early and extended contact was conducted as part of the Collaborative Research of Community and Minority Group Action to Prevent Child Abuse and Neglect (Gray, 1983). Mothers were assigned to four groups differing in the amounts and timing of contact between mother and neonate. Initial evaluation of the outcome of the program with self-report measures of maternal attitudes and maternal perceptions of the neonate revealed no significant differences across the four groups participating in the program. High rates of subject attrition across the four groups, however, may have biased the outcome evaluation.

One other study to date has systematically addressed the issue of the effects of extended and early contact on subsequent maltreatment (Siegel, Bauman,

Schaefer, Saunders & Ingram, 1980). Over 300 low-income women were randomly assigned to either an extended contact group, a postnatal home visit group, a group that combined both interventions, or a control group. Only those mothers who had uncomplicated deliveries participated in the follow up. Home visits were not significantly related to parent-child attachment or child maltreatment. Although early and extended contact was associated with better parent-child attachment, it did not have any significant effects on later child maltreatment. Interestingly, demographic variables were the best predictor of postnatal parenting. The authors conclude that more sweeping changes in social policy initiatives may be necessary to impact on the background variables that were more predictive of problematic postnatal parenting in their investigation.

There have been a number of investigations that have evaluated the impact of the father's early and extended contact at birth on subsequent paternal-infant interactions (see Parke & Beitel, 1986 for an excellent review). Unfortunately, subsequent child maltreatment incidence rates have not been included as outcome measures. Although the evidence of basic developmental research is mixed regarding positive effects, amount of paternal-neonatal contact at birth may be an important variable to investigate further in the prevention of child maltreatment.

## Perinatal Information

Other researchers have focused on providing information to parents during the initial pospartum period to enhance subsequent parent-child interactions and thereby prevent child maltreatment. These approaches have capitalized on the contact between health care personnel and parents that naturally occurs during hospitalization for birthing. These interventions have been directed towards facilitating the development of parent-infant synchrony or influencing parents' perceptions of the neonate and cognitions regarding the nature of parenting.

There have been a relatively large number of investigations which have evaluated the effects of demonstrating newborn capabilities to parents on subsequent parent-child interactions (Belsky, 1982; Belsky, 1985; Myers, 1982; Pannabecker, Emde & Austin, 1982; Szajnberg, Ward, Krauss & Kessler, 1987; Widmayer & Field, 1980; Worobey & Belsky, 1982). These interventions have had positive effects on parent-child interactions measured observationally several weeks to several months postnatally. In at least one investigation (Widmayer & Field, 1980), positive effects have also been noted in the area of infant development. The Brazelton Neonatal Behavioral Assessment Scale (Brazelton, 1984) has typically been employed in the demonstration of newborn capabilities to mothers, fathers, or both parents. The results of these investigations suggest that the positive effects of Brazelton demonstrations may be dependent on active exposure in which parents are encouraged to elicit responses and subsequently practice eliciting responses with their newborn child at home (Widmayer & Field, 1980; Worobey & Belsky, 1982; Myers, 1982). However, a recent well-controlled study by Belsky (1985) has indicated that motivational factors may be the most significant variables determining the effectiveness of this intervention in enhancing parent-child interactions. Although promising, this approach warrants further investigation especially considering the fact that no investigation conducted to date has evaluated the effects of these interventions on subsequent rates of child maltreatment.

Provision of information during the perinatal period has taken other forms besides displaying newborn capabilities to parents. One of the four perinatal demonstration projects in the Collaborative Research of Community and Minority Group Action to Prevent Child Abuse and Neglect (Gray, 1983) focused on evaluating the effects of providing information across a wide range of parenting topics to a predominantly Caucasian group of middle-class mothers. The preventive intervention also included a social support component. Trained volunteers visited mothers during their hospital stay to provide them with pamphlets and videotaped materials on parenting topics. They continued having contact with the parents until one month postnatally. Initial evaluation of the program indicated that there were no significant differences between control and treatment group mothers on the Broussard Neonatal Perception Inventory or the Bavolek Adult/Adolescent Parenting Inventory. However, follow-up data when the children were between 12 and 15 months old indicated that treatment mothers were more involved with their children and provided a more nurturing child-rearing environment than controls. In addition, younger mothers who participated in the treatment group displayed more functional parenting attitudes at follow up. The results of this program highlight the need for long term follow-up in the absence of short term change. The positive effects of a preventive intervention may take some time to evolve in participating parents.

Videotape technology has also been utilized to impact on fathers during the initial postpartum period. Parke and associates (1980) reported that a videotape presentation of three fathers feeding, diapering, and playing with their children during the mother's post-birth hospitalization affected several aspects of father's attitudes and behavior during the first three postnatal months. Fathers who viewed the videotape were more knowledgeable about infant capabilities and displayed increased caretaking activities for infant sons. Interactions with their infants became more affectionate and more contingent on infant behavior from postpartum assessment to the three-month follow up. This research indicates that targeting the father as a focus of preventive intervention may be effective in enhancing competent paternal-infant interactions.

## Community-Level Interventions

One of the four perinatal intervention programs that was funded as part of the Collaborative Research of Community and Minority Group Action to

Prevent Child Abuse and Neglect (Gray, 1983) targeted its prevention efforts at the community-wide systems level in a five-county rural region of Indiana. Community organization strategies and consultation to community agencies were used to enhance the emphasis placed on prenatal/perinatal support for families and in-hospital bonding procedures at the time of birth. Evaluation of the effects of the program was conducted at several levels, but a comparison community matched on relevant variables was not included as a control group and baseline data were not collected prior to the intervention. Although it did appear that substantially more prenatal and perinatal services were provided across the five participating counties during the intervention period, and that more effective linkages between helpers in the community were created, this did not appear to have a significant effect on individual maternal perceptions of closeness to infants. No data were presented on the subsequent incidence of child maltreatment. This innovative program illustrates the potential promise of targeting interventions at the community level and the methodological difficulties associated with evaluating community wide prevention strategies to reduce child maltreatment.

Direct links between individual perceptions and systems change are consistent with a social ecological conceptualization of child maltreatment. The absence of a relationship in this program may have been mediated by the cross sectional nature of data collection. Extended periods of time may be an important factor to include when attempting to assess the effects of systems wide change on the individual level. Clearly, this innovative program illustrates the potential promise of targeting interventions at the community level, but also the methodological difficulties associated with evaluating community wide prevention strategies to reduce child maltreatment.

## Summary

It is apparent from our review of the literature that a number of prevention strategies are available for implementation during the prenatal/perinatal period. The empirical support for the effectiveness of these strategies, however, varies widely and several questions persist regarding their applicability and ultimate utility in large-scale program development and planning. Further progress on both methodological and conceptual levels is necessary for the continued refinement of information on the effectiveness of specific prevention programs in this area.

The literature, as it now stands, is in its beginning stages. A number of important issues germane to the process of child maltreatment prevention during the prenatal/perinatal period are yet to be investigated. For example, the interactions between level of risk for subsequent child maltreatment and the effectiveness of specific prevention strategies has not been addressed, although it is a critical question with respect to prevention programming.

Comparison of the effects of comprehensive versus circumscribed prevention approaches on both proximal and distal variables in child maltreatment is an important issue that also needs to be addressed by future investigators. An additional area requiring investigation is the effectiveness of paraprofessionals versus professionals in the implementation of specific prevention strategies. Utilization of a social ecological/developmental perspective on the prenatal/ perinatal transition, as outlined previously, may help both researchers and program developers to efficiently sort and classify the multiple variables impacting on the outcome of preventive interventions. Expansion of prevention programs to include consideration of variables at all levels of the social ecological context may enhance the ultimate effectiveness of specific prevention strategies by specifying the conditions under which they will produce an optimal effect.


## FETAL/NEONATAL MALTREATMENT
## AND MATERNAL HEALTH RISK BEHAVIORS

The phenomenon of violence directed towards the fetus or neonate has existed for quite some time. For example, neonaticide can be traced back to the Roman empire by citing the practice of throwing defective infants into the Tiber river. These ancient pratices were supported by legal mandates that guaranteed the right of parents to murder their children (Resnick, 1980). Fetal/neonatal maltreatment, however, is a topic of interest beyond its historical significance. Several recently published case studies (Chasnoff, Burns, Schnoll, Burns, Chisum & Kyle-Spore, 1986; Condon, 1986; MacKenzie, Collins & Popkin, 1982; Morey, Begleiter & Harris, 1981; Slayton & Soloff, 1981) have documented the continuing occurrence of fetal/neonatal maltreatment and underscored the need for preventive interventions. Scientific interest in this area has emerged against a background of general concern for the effects of maternal behaviors on fetal development, as well as efforts to more clearly delineate the various forms of child maltreatment.

Broadly construed, fetal/neonatal maltreatment includes nearly any behavior resulting in harm to the fetus or neonate. Due to space considerations, only selected portions of the relevant literature will be reviewed with no emphasis placed on parent-mediated behaviors. Although abortion has been considered by some to fit within this area, it will not be included in this discussion. Data on maternal health risk behaviors, however, will be included in this section. Research on maternal health risk behaviors provides an empirical foundation that complements and extends the primarily clinical case descriptions that have been published on fetal/neontal maltreatment.

A recent review of the fetal abuse/neglect literature by Condon (1986) highlighted several important issues that have relevance for prevention programming in this area. First, and perhaps most important, is the recognition that fetal abuse and neglect may take many forms and that intent to harm the fetus does not necessarily have to be present on a conscious level. For example, blatant drug abuse during pregnancy may be conceptualized as a form of fetal abuse because of the well documented teratogenic effects. Second, from an etiological standpoint, fetal abuse/neglect is likely a complex, multidetermined act. Condon (1986) speculates about causative factors that extend across the four levels of the previously presented social ecological model. Fathers as well as mothers may be involved in the perpetration of abusive or neglectful acts directed towards the fetus. Third, the concept of fetal neglect is presented and related to maternal nutritional inadequacy during pregnancy. Finally, it is suggested that a relationship may exist between fetal abuse/neglect and the following problems: 1) subsequent child maltreatment, 2) neonaticide, and 3) maternal health risk behaviors. Although a discussion of the issue of prevention per se is not included, the article emphasizes early assessment and intervention as important steps in minimizing the effects of such behaviors on the fetus.

Large-scale investigations evaluating the hypotheses generated from clinical case descriptions have not been undertaken to date. On theoretical and conceptual levels, however, it appears that factors related to the occurrence of fetal/neonatal maltreatment may increase risk for subsequent child maltreatment. Furthermore, fetal/neonatal maltreatment, as conceptualized by Condon (1986), appears to be amenable to preventive intervention at multiple levels of the social ecological context during pregnancy. It may be important to begin these interventions prior to conception or as early as possible in pregnancy, once valid and reliable risk factors are identified. Preliminary research investigating the process of fetal attachment for both mothers and fathers (Condon, 1985) irritation toward or the urge to harm the fetus (Condon, 1987), and maternal beliefs regarding fetal health locus of control (Labs & Wurtele, 1986) may prove useful in the development of prediction models and prevention strategies.

Closely related to the phenomenon of fetal/neonatal maltreatment is the growing body of literature on maternal health risk behaviors during pregnancy. Primary attention has been directed toward drug and alcohol use (Abel, 1981; Chasnoff et al., 1986), smoking patterns (Hoff, Wertelecki, Blackburn, Mendenhall, Wiseman & Stampe, 1986; Kleinman & Kopstein, 1987), and nutritional status (Stockbauer, 1987). In general, maternal health risk behaviors during pregnancy have decreased across the last two decades primarily due to increased information provided to the general public regarding negative birth outcomes. However, research examining behavioral and psychological effects of drug use, alcohol use, and smoking on later child development has suggested that increasingly subtle long-term effects are associated with lower doses of drugs, alcohol and nicotine than was previously suspected (Abel, 1985; Fried, 1983).

These data highlight the need for placing further emphases on decreasing the frequencies of maternal health-risk behaviors and promoting competent coping with the stresses of pregnancy. This conclusion can be made irrespective of the outcome of risk factors research which continues to debate the relationship between drug use during pregnancy and subsequent child maltreatment. An example of preventive intervention targeting maternal health risk behaviors was reported by Larsson and Bohlin (1987). Professional support and guidance during prenatal health care contacts was effective in reducing significantly rates of alcohol consumption for high-risk mothers and subsequent rates of fetal alcohol syndrome in neonates.

This brief overview of fetal/neonatal maltreatment and maternal health risk behaviors was not intended to be comprehensive. It was included to emphasize the growing importance of these areas and to indicate that greater integration of these topics into risk factors research and prenatal/perinatal prevention programming directed towards postnatal child maltreatment is needed. Utilization of social ecological models that emphasize multiple causation and developmental change across the prenatal/perinatal transition may facilitate this task in both future research and clinical applications.

## CONCLUSIONS AND RECOMMENDATIONS

The intent of this chapter was to provide a comprehensive review of child maltreatment prevention during the prenatal/perinatal period and to conceptualize this area within a model encompassing both social ecological and developmental perspectives. The model that was presented at the beginning of this chapter was used as a guide for examining the literature that has been published in this area. In general, researchers have focused on the relationship between specific variables within the broader ecological context of the prenatal/perinatal period. It is clear that we have developed some understanding of (1) the factors operating to enhance risk for subsequent child maltreatment, (2) the process of conducting, as well as the effects of, preventive interventions, and (3) the phenomenon of fetal maltreatment and its potential relationship to maternal health risk behaviors. There is a need for greater integration of these three areas to more clearly understand the effects of the multiple causative factors operating within the context of the prenatal/perinatal period. Adequate tests of ecological and developmental models in this area will only be possible as integration across research areas and settings occurs, and more complex methodologies that increasingly include developmental and ecological factors are employed in research designs.

Despite the numerous research problems noted throughout this review, it is important to realize that this is a relatively young area of investigation and that the process of conducting research is quite complex and time consuming. A large body of literature has amassed that in general supports continued investigation. Moreover, second-generation research is beginning to overcome the methodological problems that plagued earlier investigators (cf. Altemeier et al., 1986; Olds et al., 1986b). Continued financial support at the local, state, and Federal levels is needed to complete the prospective, longitudinal research that is fundamentally important to further advancement in this area. Even with adequate funding, it will likely take quite some time before comprehensive, empirically based answers are available to address the critical questions confronting the prenatal/perinatal prevention area.

In the meantime, however, high incidence rates of child maltreatment and resulting physical or psychological trauma argue for the establishment of service-based prevention programs. The prenatal/perinatal period provides multiple opportunities for accessing families to conduct preventive intervention through health care system contacts. Based on the current literature, it is recommended that service programs adopt comprehensive prevention programs that have solid conceptual foundations and follow populations from the prenatal period to birth and into the postnatal period of development. It also appears important to focus on the notion of risk by targeting high-risk groups for secondary prevention. Furthermore, service-based prevention programs should place an emphasis on systematic evaluation of outcome and utilize the results of progam evaluations to refine the delivery of services. Greater accountability at the level of clinical application may generate information that provides answers to those conducting more controlled investigations.

# REFERENCES

Abel, E. L. (1981). Behavioral teratology of alcohol. *Psychological Bulletin: 90*, 564–581.

Abel, E. L. (1985). Fetal alcohol effects: Advice to the advisors. *Alcohol & Alcoholism: 20*, 189–193.

Agathonos, H., Stathacopoulou, N., Adam, H., & Nakou, S. (1982). Child abuse and neglect in Greece: Sociomedical aspects. *Child Abuse & Neglect: 6*, 307–311.

Altemeier, W. A., O'Conner, S., Sherrod, K. B., Tucker, D., & Vietze, P. M., (1986). Outcome of abuse during childhood among pregnant low income women. *Child Abuse & Neglect: 10*, 319–330.

Altemeier, W. A., O'Connor, S., Vietze, P. M., Sandler, H. M., & Sherrod, K. B. (1982). Antecedents of child abuse. *The Journal of Pediatrics: 100*, 823–829.

Anisfeld, E., & Lipper, E. (1983). Early contact, social support, and mother-infant bonding. *Pediatrics: 72*, 79–83.

Ayoub, C. & Jacewitz, M. M. (1982). Families at risk of poor parenting: A model for service delivery, assessment, and intervention. *Child Abuse & Neglect, 6*, 351–358.

Barrera, M. (1986). Distinctions between social support concepts, measures, and models. *American Journal of Community Psychology, 14*, 413–445.

Barth, R. P., & Schinke, S. P. (1983). Coping with daily strain among pregnant and parenting adolescents. *Journal of Social Service Research, 7*, 51–63.

Belsky, J. (1980). Child maltreatment: An ecological integration. *American Psychologist, 35*, 320–335.

Belsky, J. (1982). A principled approach to intervention with families in the newborn period. *Journal of Community Psychology, 10*, 66–73.

Belsky, J. (1985). Experimenting with the family in the newborn period. *Child Development, 56*, 407–414.

Belsky, J., & Isabella, R. A. (1985). Marital and parent-child relationships in family of origin and marital change following the birth of a baby: A retrospective analysis. *Child Development, 56*, 342–349.

Belsky, J., Spanier, G. B., & Rovine, M. (1983). Stability and change across the transition to parenthood. *Journal of Marriage and the Family, 45*, 567–577.

Benedict, M. I., White, R. B., & Cornely, D. A. (1985). Maternal perinatal risk factors and child abuse. *Child Abuse & Neglect, 9*, 217–224.

Bolton, F. G., & Laner, R. H. (1982). Maternal maturity and maltreatment. *Journal of Family Issues, 2*, 485–508.

Brazelton, T. B. (1984). *Neonatal Behavioral Assessment Scale* (2nd ed.). Philadelphia: J. B. Lippincott.

Brunnquell, D., Crichton, L., & Egeland, B. (1981). Maternal personality and attitude in disturbances of child rearing. *American Journal of Orthopsychiatry, 51*, 680–691.

Caplan, P. J., Watters, J., White, G., Parry, R., & Bates, R. (1984). Toronto multi-agency child abuse research project: The abused and the abuser. *Child Abuse & Neglect, 8*, 343–351.

Carey, W. B. (1986). Further thoughts on temperament. *Journal of Developmental & Behavioral Pediatrics, 7*, 120–121.

Carter, E. A., & McGoldrick, M. (1980). The family life cycle and family therapy: An overview. In E. A. Carter & M. McGoldrick (Eds.), *The Family Life Cycle: A framework for family therapy*. New York: Gardner Press.

Chasnoff, I. J., Burns, W. J., Schnoll, S. H., Burns, K., Chisum, G., & Kyle-Spore, L. (1986). Maternal-neonatal incest. *American Journal of Orthopsychiatry, 56*, 577–580.

Cicchetti, D., & Rizley, R. (1981). Developmental perspectives on the etiology, intergenerational transmission, and sequelae of child maltreatment. *New Directions for Child Development, 11*, 31–55.

Cohen, S., Gray, E., & Wald, M. (1984). *Preventing child maltreatment: A review of what we know*. Chicago: National Committee for the Prevention of Child Abuse.

Cohen, S., & Wills, T. A. (1985). Stress, social support, and the buffering hypothesis. *Psychological Bulletin, 98*, 310–357.

Condon, J. T. (1985). The parental-foetal relationship—A comparison of male and female expectant parents. *Journal of Psychosomatic Obstetrics and Gynecology, 4*, 271–284.

Condon, J. T. (1986). The spectrum of fetal abuse in pregnant women. *The Journal of Nervous and Mental Disease, 174*, 509–516.

Condon, J. T. (1987). "The battered fetus syndrome", preliminary data on the incidence of the urge to physically abuse the unborn child. *The Journal of Nervous and Mental Disease, 175*, 722–725.

Cooper, H., Dreznick, J. & Rowe, B. (1982). Perinatal coaching—A new beginning. *Social Casework, 63*, 35–40.

Crockenberg, S. (1985). Professional support and care of infants by adolescent mothers in England and the United States. *Journal of Pediatric Psychology*, *10*, 413–428.

Earp, J. A., & Ory, M. G. (1980). The influence of early parenting on child maltreatment. *Child Abuse & Neglect*, *4*, 237–245.

Egeland, B., & Brunnquell, D. (1979). An at-risk approach to the study of child abuse: Some preliminary findings. *Journal of the American Academy of Child Psychiatry*, *18*, 219–235.

Egeland, B., & Vaughn, B. (1981). Failure of "bond formation" as a cause of abuse, neglect, and maltreatment. *American Journal of Orthopsychiatry*, *51*, 78–84.

Entwisle, D. R., & Doering, S. G. (1981). *The First Birth*. Baltimore, MD: Johns Hopkins Press.

Fleming, A. S., Ruble, D. N., Flett, G. L., & Shaul, D. L. (1988). Postpartum adjustment in first-time mothers: Relations between mood, maternal attitudes, and mother-infant interactions. *Developmental Psychology*, *24*, 71–81.

Fried, P. A. (1983). Soft drug use during pregnancy: The Ottawa prospective study. In P. Firestone, P. McGrath, & Feldman (Eds.), *Advances in Behavioral medicine in Children and Adolescents*. Hillsdale, NJ: LEA.

Friedrich, W. N., & Wheeler, K. K. (1982). The abusing parent revisited: A decade of psychological research. *The Journal of Nervous and Mental Disease*, *170*, 577–587.

Garbarino, J., Guttmann, E., & Seeley, J. (1986). *The Psychologically Battered Child*. San Francisco: Jossey Bass.

Goldberg, S. (1983). Parent-infant bonding: Another look. *Child Development*, *54*, 1355–1382.

Goldberg, W. A., & Easterbrook, M. A. (1984). Role of marital quality in toddler development. *Developmental Psychology*, *20*, 505–514.

Gray, E. B. (1983). *Final report: Collaborative research of community and minority group action to prevent child abuse and neglect. Vol. I: Perinatal interventions*. Chicago: National Committee for Prevention of Child Abuse.

Gray, J. D., Cutler, C. A., Dean, J. G., & Kempe, C. H. (1977). Prediction and prevention of child abuse and neglect. *Child Abuse & Neglect 1*, 45–58.

Gray, J. D., Cutler, C. A., Dean, J. G., & Kempe, C. H. (1979). Prediction and prevention of child abuse and neglect. *Journal of Social Issues*, *35*, 127–139.

Grindley, J. F. (1981). Child abuse: The nurse and prevention. *Nursing Clinics of North America*, *16*, 167–177.

Helfer, R. E. (1987). The perinatal period, a window of opportunity for enhancing parent-infant communication: An approach to prevention. *Child Abuse & Neglect*, *11*, 565–579.

Herbert, M., Sluckin, W. & Sluckin, A. (1982). Mother-to-infant 'bonding'. *Journal of Child Psychology and Psychiatry*, *23*, 205–221.

Hees-Stauthamer, J. C. (1985). *The first prenancy: An integrating principle in female psychology*. Ann Arbor, Michigan: UMI Rersearch Press.

Hoff, C., Wertelecki,W., Blackburn, W. R., Mendenhall, H., Wiseman, H., & Stampe, A. (1986). Trend associations of smoking with maternal, fetal, and neonatal morbidity. *Obstetrics & Gynecology*, *68*, 317–321.

Hunter, R., Kilstrom, N., Kraybill, E., & Loda, F. (1978). Antecedents of child abuse and neglect in premature infants: A prospective study in a newborn intensive care unit. *Pediatrics, 61,* 629–635.

Justice, B., & Duncan, D. F. (1976). Life crisis as a precursor to child abuse. *Public Health Reports, 91,* 110–115.

Kaufman, J., & Zigler, E. (1987). Do abused children become abusive parents? *American Journal of Orthopsychiatry, 57,* 186–192.

Kinard, E. M., & Klerman, L. V. (1980). Teenage parenting and child abuse: Are they related? *American Journal of Orthopsychiatry, 50,* 481–488.

Klaus, M. H., & Kennell, J. H. (1976). *Maternal Infant Bonding.* St. Louis: Mosby.

Klaus, M. H., Kennell, J. H., Robertson, S. S., & Sosa, R. (1986). Effects of social support during parturition on maternal and infant morbidity. *British Medical Journal, 293,* 585–587.

Kleinman, J. C., & Kopstein, A. (1987). Smoking during pregnancy, 1967–80. *American Journal of Public Health, 77,* 823–825.

Labs, S. M., & Wurtele, S. K. (1986). Fetal Health Locus of Control Scale: development and validation. *Journal of Consulting and Clinical Psychology, 54,* 814–819.

Lamb, M. E., & Hwang, C.-P. (1982). Maternal attachment and mother-infant bonding: A critical review. In M. E. Lamb & A. L. Brown (Eds.), *Advances in Developmental Psychology* (Vol. 2). Hillsdale, NJ: Erlbaum.

Larsson, G., & Bohlin, A.-B. (1987). Fetal alcohol syndrome and preventive strategies. *Pediatrician, 14,* 51–56.

Leventhal, J. M., Egerter, S. A., & Murphy, J. M. (1984). Reassessment of the relationship of perinatal risk factors and child abuse. *American Journal of Diseases in Children, 138,* 1034–1039.

Lynch, M. A., & Roberts, J. (1977). Predicting child abuse: signs of bonding failure in the maternity hospital. *British Medical Journal, 1,* 624–626.

Mackenzie, T. B., Collins, N. M., & Popkin, M. E. (1982). A case of fetal abuse? *American Journal of Orthopsychiatry, 52,* 699–703.

May, K. A., & Perrin, S. P. (1985). Prelude: Pregnancy and birth. In S. M. H. Hanson & F. W. Bozett (Eds.), *Dimensions of Fatherhood.* New York: Sage.

Morey, M. A., Begleiter, M. L., & Harris, D. J. (1981). Profile of a battered fetus. *Lancet, 8258(2),* 1294–1295.

Murphy, S., Orkow, B., & Nicola, R. M. (1985). Prenatal prediction of child abuse and neglect: A prospective study. *Child Abuse & Neglect, 9,* 225–235.

Myers, B. J. (1982). Early intervention using Brazelton training with middle-class mothers and fathers of newborns. *Child Development, 53,* 462–471.

Oates, D. S., & Heinicke, C. M. (1985). Prebirth prediction of the quality of the mother-infant interaction: The first year of life. *Journal of Family Issues, 6,* 523–542.

O'Connor, S., Vietze, P. M., Sherrod, K. B., Sandler, H. M., Gerrity, S., & Altemeier, W. A. (1982). Mother-infant interaction and child development after rooming-in: Comparison of high-risk and low-risk mothers. *Prevention in Human Services, 1,* 25–43.

O'Connor, S., Vietze, P. M., Sherrod, K. B., Sandler, H. M., & Altemeier, W. A.

(1980). Reduced incidence of parenting inadequacy following rooming-in. *Pediatrics*, *66*, 176–182.

Olds, D. L. (1980). Improving formal services for mothers and children. In J. Garbarino & S. H. Stocking (Eds.), *Protecting Children from Abuse and Neglect: Developing and maintaining effective support systems for families*. San Francisco: Jossey-Bass.

Olds, D. L. (1982). The prenatal/early infancy project: an ecological approach to prevention of developmental disabilities. In J. Belsky (Ed.), *In The Beginning*. New York: Columbia University Press.

Olds, D. L. (1984). Case studies of factors interfering with nurse home visitors' promotion of positive care-giving methods in high risk families. *Early Childhood Development and Care*, *16*, 149–166.

Olds, D. L., Henderson, C. R., Chamberlin, R., & Tatelbaum, R. (1986a). Preventing child abuse and neglect: a randomized trial of nurse home visitation. *Pediatrics*, *78*, 65–78.

Olds, D. L., Henderson, C. R., Tatelbaum, R., & Chamberlin, R. (1986b). Improving the delivery of prenatal care and outcomes of pregnancy: a randomized trial of nurse home visitation. *Pediatrics*, *77*, 16–28.

Pannabecker, B. J., Emde, R. N., & Austin, B. C. (1982). The effects of early extended contact on father-newborn interaction. *Journal of Genetic Psychology*, *141*, 7–17.

Parke, R. D., & Beitel, A. (1986). Hospital-based intervention for fathers. In M. E. Lamb (Ed.), *The Father's Role: Applied Perspectives*. New York: Wiley and Sons.

Parke, R. D., Hymel, S., Power, T. G., & Tinsley, B. R. (1980). Fathers and risk: A hospital based model of intervention. In D. B. Sawin, R. C. Hawkins, L. O. Walker, & J. H. Penticuff (Eds.), *Psychosocial Risks in Infant-environment Interactions*. New York: Bruner/Mazel.

Pelton, L. H. (1978). Child abuse and neglect: The myth of classlessness. *American Journal of Orthopsychiatry*, *48*, 608–617.

Resnick, P. J. (1980). Murder of the newborn: A psychiatric review of neonaticide. In G. J. Williams & J. Money (Eds.), *Traumatic Abuse and Neglect of Children at Home*. Baltimore, MD: Johns Hopkins University Press.

Rolf, J. E. (1985). Evolving adaptive theories and methods for prevention research with children. *Journal of Consulting and Clinical Psychology*, *53*, 631–646.

Roopnarine, J. L., & Miller, B. C. (1985). Transitions to fatherhood. In S. M. H. Hanson & F. W. Bozett (Eds.), *Dimensions of Fatherhood*. New York: Sage.

Rosenberg, M. S. (1987). New directions for research on the psychological maltreatment of children. *American Psychologist*, *42*, 166–171.

Rosenberg, M. S., & Reppucci, N. D. (1985). Primary prevention of child abuse. *Journal of Consulting and Clinical Psychology*, *53*, 576–585.

Rutter, M. (1987). Psychosocial resilience and protective mechanisms. *American Journal of Orthopsychiatry*, *57*, 316–331.

Seagull, E. A. W. (1987). Social support and child maltreatment: A review of the evidence. *Child Abuse & Neglect*, *11*, 41–52.

Sherrod, K. B., Altemeier, W. A., O'Connor, S., & Vietze, P. M. (1984). Early prediction of child maltreatment. *Early Child Development and Care, 13,* 335–350.

Sherwen, L. N. (1987). *Psychosocial Dimensions of the Pregnant Family.* New York: Springer.

Siegel, E., Bauman, K. E., Schaefer, E. S., Saunders, M. M., & Ingram, D. D. (1980). Hospital and home support during infancy: impact on maternal attachment, child abuse and neglect, and health care utilization. *Pediatrics, 66,* 183–190.

Sirignano, S. W., & Lachman, M. E. (1985). Personality changes during the transition to parenthood: the role of perceived infant temperament. *Developmental Psychology, 21,* 558–567.

Slayton, R. I., & Soloff, P. A., (1981). Psychotic denial of third trimester pregnancy. *Journal of Clinical Psychiatry, 42,* 471–473.

Snyder, J. C., Hampton, R., & Newberger, E. H. (1983). Family dysfunction: Violence, neglect, and sexual misuse. In. M. D. Levine, W. B. Carey, A. C. Crocker, & R. T. Gross (Eds.), *Developmental-behavioral Pediatrics.* Philadelphia: W. B. Saunders.

Soumenkoff, G., Marneffe, C., Gerard, M., Limet, R., Beeckmans, M., & Hubinont, P. O. (1982). A coordinated attempt for prevention of child abuse at the antenatal care level. *Child Abuse & Neglect, 6,* 87–94.

Sroufe, L. A., & Waters, E. (1982). Issues of temperament and attachment. *American Journal of Orthopsychiatry, 52,* 743–747.

Stockbauer, T. W. (1987). WIC prenatal participation and its relation to pregnancy outcomes in Missouri: A second look. *American Journal of Public Health, 77,* 813–818.

Szajnberg, N., Ward, M. J., Krauss, A., & Kessler, D. B. (1987). Low birth-weight prematures: preventive intervention and maternal attitude. *Child Psychiatry and Human Development, 17,* 152–165.

Unger, D. G., & Wandersman, L. P. (1985). Social support and adolescent mothers: Action research contributions to theory and application. *Journal of Social Issues, 41,* 29–45.

Widmayer, S. M., & Field, T. M. (1980). Effects of Brazelton demonstration on early interactions of preterm infants and their teenage mothers. *Infant Behavior and Development, 3,* 79–89.

Wilson, A. L. (1984). Promoting a positive parent-baby relationship. In C. H. Kempe & R. E. Helfer (Eds.), *The Battered Child* (4th ed.). Chicago, IL: University of Chicago Press.

Worobey, J., & Belsky, J. (1982). Employing the Brazelton scale to influence mothering: an experimental comparison of three strategies. *Developmental Psychology, 18,* 736–743.

Zuravin, S. J. (1987). Unplanned pregnancies, family planning problems, and child maltreatment. *Family Relations, 36,* 135–139.

# CHAPTER 3

# Prevention of Maltreatment in Infants and Young Children

JAN L. CULBERTSON AND CYNTHIA J. SCHELLENBACH

Child maltreatment is a growing national concern, despite the major efforts directed toward understanding its etiology and prevention. The number of child abuse reports has increased in recent years, and reports of fatalities resulting from child abuse have increased dramatically (Daro, 1989). Nearly one and a half million cases of child abuse occur in the United States each year (Daro & Mitchell, 1987). This means that an estimated 16.13 children per 1,000 experienced abuse or neglect serious enough to suffer demonstrable injuries. The problem is even more serious when we consider the number of children who experience abuse or endangerment of health and safety through abuse and neglectful treatment (25.2 children per 1,000). Infants and toddlers appear to be more vulnerable to serious physical injury and neglect, as suggested by the greater incidence of deaths in children under the age of three.

Since infants and young children are disproportionately represented among the cases of severe and fatal abuse, prevention efforts directed toward families of young children are needed. Yet, according to Daro (1989), prevention efforts have been extremely difficult to establish for several reasons:

1. Child abuse has many causes, and prevention efforts typically have been unidimensional rather than multidimensional.
2. There is a low base rate for child abuse in the United States, and primary prevention efforts directed populationwide are expensive and will go to persons who do not need to hear it.
3. There is no prediction formula which accurately distinguishes the abuser from the nonabuser.
4. Finally, raising children in America is considered to be primarily a private or family issue, and many parents do not welcome societal intervention (Daro, 1989). As Belsky (1980) pointed out, parenthood

often is construed in terms of ownership, and there is widespread societal belief that children are property to be handled as parents choose.

Effective prevention programs, by definition, must be based on some concept of the etiology of maltreatment, and must make attempts to intervene around those specific variables known to be related to maltreatment (Cohen, Gray & Wald, 1984). To address this issue, researchers have been active in studying the etiology of child maltreatment. Yet, much of the early research has relied on retrospective research designs, conceptual models that postulated isolated or single causes for child maltreatment, and there has been a lack of theoretical foundation from previous empirical findings (Belsky, 1980; Cicchetti & Aber, 1980; Cicchetti & Rizley, 1981; Egeland & Brunnquell, 1979; Pianta, Egeland, & Erickson, 1989). Despite the advances made in theory and research in child maltreatment over the past 30 years, only recently have there been attempts to develop integrated theoretical models (Pianta et al., 1989). Both Garbarino (1977) and Belsky (1980) proposed ecological models to integrate divergent etiological viewpoints regarding child maltreatment. Within the past 10 years, these ecological models have provided a foundation for the design of other integrative research models on child maltreatment (Pianta et al., 1989).

The purpose of this chapter is to review the literature on etiology of infant-toddler maltreatment within the context of a proposed ecological model for prediction of the quality of parenting. Specifically, the research on such factors as psychosocial adjustment or parental personality characteristics, knowledge of child development and parenting skills, maternal health, child characteristics, and social support is discussed. Discussion of these risk factors in the context of an ecological model is designed to facilitate understanding of the complex interrelationships among child abuse risk factors, and to provide an integrative model for future research. Specifically, the model is designed to predict the quality of parenting and subsequent attachment during the infancy and toddler years. By considering research relevant to each of the constructs, support for the following conclusions will be provided: 1) The quality of parenting and subsequent attachment is determined by constructs depicting individual differences among parents, the unique characteristics of their children, as well as the social context in which the parent-child relationship is embedded; 2) the sources of influence operate in unique ways to predict different types of parenting dysfunction and attachment disorders. Finally, examples of prevention programs derived from aspects of the proposed ecological model are presented, along with suggestions for future research.

Before describing the proposed model for prediction of quality of parenting, Belsky's ecological conceptualization of child maltreatment is discussed as a foundation for the model to be presented in the remainder of this chapter.

## AN ECOLOGICAL FRAMEWORK FOR CHILD MALTREATMENT

Belsky (1980) suggested a conceptual framework for integrating diverse theories of etiology of child maltreatment. These theories include psychological disturbance in parents, abuse-eliciting characteristics of children, dysfunctional patterns of family interaction, stress-inducing social forces, and abuse-promoting cultural values. Belsky's conceptual framework drew heavily on the work of Bronfenbrenner (1977, 1979) related to the ecology of human development. It conceptualized child maltreatment as a "social-psychological phenomenon" that is determined by multiple forces at work across four different levels: in the individual (*ontogenetic* development), the family (the *microsystem*), the community (the *exosystem*), and the culture (the *macrosystem*) in which both the individual and family are embedded (Belsky, 1980). Belsky also incorporated Tinbergen's (1951) methods of analysis, with particular emphasis on the need to consider ontogenic development by examining from a developmental perspective why a parent grows up to behave in an abusive or neglectful way. Tinbergen's methods of analysis included examining the immediate antecedents of abuse, which could help explain why child abuse or neglect occurs at a particular point in time, and the consequences of abuse which help one understand the possible functions of abusive or neglectful behavior. Belsky combined Tinbergen's concern for ontogenic development with Bronfenbrenner's concern for the ecology (or the context) in which development takes place to develop a conceptual framework for interpreting the data available on etiology of child maltreatment. Belsky assumed that child maltreatment is multiply determined by forces within the individual, the family, the community and the culture, and he assumed that these multiple determinants are nested ecologically with one another (Belsky, 1980).

At the level of the individual, the focus is on the attributes that the abusive parent brings with him/her into the family setting and the parenting role. These variables may include the parents' personality traits, their socialization experiences (e.g., exposure to violence, parental rejection, and inappropriate developmental expectations for children). At the family or microsystem level of analysis, there is examination of the family setting, or the immediate context in which child maltreatment takes place. These variables may include dysfunctional interactions among family members, conflictual spousal relationships, or potential abuse-eliciting child characteristics. At the exosystem, or community level, the influence of such social contexts as work, the neighborhood, informal social networks, socioeconomic factors, unmanageable stress, and degree of social isolation are considered. Finally, at the macrosystem, or cultural, level of analysis, one considers the cultural belief systems and values that may foster the abusive and neglectful behavior by the influence they exert on ontogenic development and the micro- and exosystems (Belsky, 1980). These variables may include the sanctioning of corporal punishment to control child behavior, attitudes toward violence as a legitimate means of settling disputes, and parenthood construed as ownership of the child (Belsky, 1980).

The ecological model proposed by Belsky allows one to examine the existing literature on etiology of child maltreatment within the four levels of analysis, and with the assumption that there are multiple and interactive determinants of maltreatment. As recent reviews have suggested (Pianta et al., 1989; Wolfe, 1985), there has been a shift from a psychiatric model of maltreatment which emphasized static traits of individuals as causes of maltreatment to process-oriented conceptual models in which multiple influences of a variety of risk and protective factors are considered simultaneously. Using an ecological approach allows one to consider these potential multiple determinants of maltreatment in developing research or prevention programs.

The ecological approach is now applied specifically through discussion of a multidimensional model for depicting the parental, social and child characteristics that interact to predict quality of parenting and subsequent attachment.

## MODEL FOR PREDICTION OF PARENTING RISK

Research has provided a clear knowledge base on factors that are related to risk for abuse. According to the ecological framework delineated by Belsky, evidence indicates that risk for abuse is linked to risk factors in the parent, the child, the parent-child relationship, and the quality of the social support system provided to the parent and child. As Belsky (1984) suggested, the quality of parenting is multiply determined by characteristics of the parent, the child, and the social context. In this section, the characteristics of these three constructs are further specified in a model designed to predict parenting and attachment among high-risk parents (See Figure 3.1). The framework specifies the constructs required to depict the correlates of risk in the parent-child relationship. As in the Belsky (1984) model, it is assumed that parenting is multiply determined by the characteristics of the parent (specified as psychosocial adjustment, maternal health, knowledge of child development and parenting skill), by the characteristics of the child (developmental status, health, temperament), as well as the quality of the social context in which the parent-child relationship is embedded.

Although the model depicted in Figure 3.1 postulates both direct and indirect influences on parenting behavior, these relationships may be summarized as follows: To parent the infant and young child effectively, individuals must display capabilities that are sensitively attuned to the infant's developmental capabilities and to the developmental task; and the ability to nurture a variety of outcomes including emotional security, sense of autonomy, and socialization in the limits for appropriate behavior. Indeed, the literature suggests that the nature of parenting changes with the age of the child. A developmental approach to child abuse prevention focuses on the

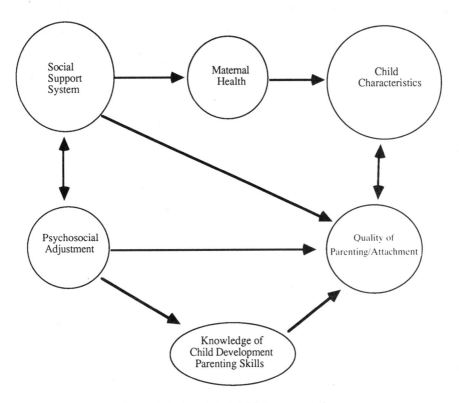

**Figure 3.1.** A model of child abuse prevention.

causes and correlates of abuse as a function of child characteristics (Cicchetti & Rizley, 1981). For example, the task of parenting an infant is very different from parenting a school-age child or adolescent. The infant thrives with a parent who is able to provide a predictable and stable environment, who is attentive, emotionally responsive, and nurturant.

The child-rearing issues differ for parents of the school-age child, however. Trickett and Susman (1988) indicated that abusive parents are less satisfied with the performance of their children, particularly with respect to social and school competence issues. Furthermore, research on the correlates of adolescent abuse indicated that parental issues of control and limit-setting in response to the growing independence of the adolescent were the central problems leading to abuse. Given the utility of the developmental approach to parenting, it follows that a model for predicting parenting should be based on a developmental approach. Thus the risk factors for parents of infants are likely to be unique in comparison with the risk factors for parents of adolescents.

Effective parenting during the early years is based on knowledge of the developmental capabilities of the infant and the skills to respond appropriately to the infant's needs. The model depicted in Figure 3.1 suggests the following direct and indirect influences on quality of parenting: To respond sensitively to the infant or young child, the parent must be cognitively and behaviorally prepared with knowledge of child development and parenting skills. This knowledge base depends on direct support and information from the parents' social support network and on the direct effects of the parents' own experience of child rearing as an influence on individual psychosocial adjustment. The social support system also has a direct relationship to maternal health, and maternal health is related to child characteristics such as prematurity, low birth weight, or handicapping conditions. The unique characteristics of the child (e.g., sensitivity to maternal cues, responsivity, temperament) are reciprocally related to the quality of parenting and subsequent attachment.

The utility of the model is measured by the extent to which it serves as an organizer for research on risk factors that are linked to abuse. Moreover, the model is useful in evaluating the impact of specific preventive efforts aimed at enhancing or changing variables depicted in the constructs in the model. Finally, the model provides guidelines for the development of future empirical and applied efforts systematically aimed at the prevention of abuse toward infants and toddlers.

In the next section, the literature on attachment and its relation to child maltreatment is examined. Crittenden and Ainsworth (1989) argued that researchers in the field of maltreatment needed a workable model that could both explain the pattern of occurrence and nonoccurrence of child maltreatment and describe the process by which maltreatment is transmitted from one person to another. They proposed that attachment theory can be helpful in integrating much of the existing knowledge about maltreatment in a manner compatible with ecological theory. Within the context of the previously described model, positive attachment and effective parenting are viewed as optimal outcomes. Attachment theory provides one theoretical framework within which the relationships among constructs in the model may be interpreted. The growing literature on the relationship between attachment and maltreatment will be reviewed in the following section.


## ATTACHMENT AND ITS RELATION TO MALTREATMENT

Attachment is defined by Ainsworth (1973) as "a hypothetical construct indicating an affectional tie that one person forms to another specific person, binding them together in space and enduring over time" (p. 1). It is important to note that attachment relationships may be different between a given infant and different caregivers. An infant's primary attachment(s) develop over the course of the first year. Bowlby has distinguished four main phases of attachment. The first involves a relatively undistinguishable phase of social responsiveness in which signaling behaviors are emitted during times of stress. Ainsworth (1989) refers to these behaviors as "attachment behaviors." As the infant begins to discriminate one person from another, attachment behaviors begin to be directed differentially toward certain caregivers. By about the middle of the infant's first year, a number of developments occur which herald a more sophisticated level of attachment between infant and caregiver. The infant by this age has developed better locomotion, directed reaching and grasping, and "proximity-keeping" behaviors which enable the more effective maintainance of proximity with the caregiver. In addition, the infant has developed the ability for internal representation of the caregiver, even when the caregiver is not present. According to Ainsworth (1989), the infant at this time is capable of attachment and is most likely attached to a primary caregiver as well as one or a few other familiar persons. The infant gradually builds up expectations of the caregiver's responses to attachment behaviors over the first year and begins to organize these expectations into what Bowlby (1982) has termed "working models" or "representational models" of the physical environment, attachment figures, and the self (Ainsworth, 1989). In other words, infants who experience their caregiver as being consistently accessible and responsive to their signals will develop the expectation that this is how their caregiver will behave in the future, and will internalize an image of themselves as competent in eliciting the caregiver's response and worthy of support and protection. The working model of the self that develops from the early attachment relationship(s) is felt to significantly affect the behavior in subsequent relationships (Bretherton, 1985).

Between three or four years of age, the child becomes capable of what Bowlby (1982) termed a "goal-directed partnership" with the caregiver, made possible by the increased effectiveness of communication between the partners as the child's language abilities increase, and also made possible by the child's more sophisticated ability to understand the perspective of another person. As the child's cognitive perspective-taking develops, it becomes possible for the child to understand the caregiver's motivations and plans, and to negotiate mutually acceptable plans. With the child's increased competence and confidence in the attachment figure comes the ability to sustain separation from the attachment figure for increasingly longer periods of time. Thus, the child's sense of security depends not so much on the actual presence of the attachment figure, but on the mutual trust and understanding that has been built up in the partnership (Crittenden & Ainsworth, 1989).

In an attempt to study the strength and quality of the attachment relationship, Ainsworth & Wittig (1969) developed an experimental laboratory procedure called the *Strange Situation*, which led to development of a classification system for parent-infant attachment relationships. The *Strange Situation* paradigm involves a sequence of separation and reunion episodes between an infant, his/her caregiver and a stranger; the paradigm is designed to study the responses of the infant to the separation, and thus assess the strength and quality of attachment. The major classifications of secure, anxious/avoidant, and anxious/ambivalent attachment have stood the test of time through many replications in studies (e.g., Belsky, Rovine, & Taylor, 1984; Egeland & Farber, 1984; Grossmann, Grossmann, Spangler, Suess, and Unzer, 1985). The long-term stability of earlier reported patterns of attachment is currently under investigation, and there is growing evidence for both cross-generational and within-subject longitudinal stability of the patterns (Crittenden & Ainsworth, 1989; Main, Kaplan & Cassidy, 1985).

Adjustments to the classificatory system have been made to account for the behavior of disturbed children, including maltreated children (Carlson, Cicchetti, Barnett & Braunwald, 1989). These adjustments to the three major patterns of attachment came about as researchers began to work with high-risk infants who were maltreated or from low socioeconomic environments and found to be unclassifiable according to the original system. Several groups of investigators (Crittenden, 1985a; Lyons-Ruth, Connell, Zoll, & Stahl, 1987; & Main & Hesse, 1990) have described classification systems in which these children are observed to display components of the three major attachment patterns, combined in unusual ways. These children also exhibited bizarre behaviors such as stilling, slow movements, freezing and depressed affect; incomplete, undirected, and interrupted movements and expressions; asymmetrical and mistimed movements, stereotypies and postures; and apprehension toward the caregiver (Main & Solomon, 1990). The most common characteristic is that these children seem to have no workable strategy for dealing with the stresses of separation from their primary caregiver, thus leading to their characterization as "disorganized."

Crittenden & Ainsworth (1989) have argued that anxious (or insecure) attachment is a critical concept in the etiology of family maltreatment. From the perspective of attachment theory, they have proposed several hypotheses which may explain the behavior of maltreated children and maltreating parents. They assumed that the behavior of individuals in maltreating families can provide a basis for inferring the nature of the "representational models" developed by these individuals, and that these representational models can serve as the basis for predicting the nature of other relationships. Crittenden (1985a, 1985b, 1988) has compared the mother-infant interaction in maltreating and nonmaltreating families to infer the nature of the underlying representational models and to predict both the nature of the child's attachment to his/her mother and the mother's relationships with professionals and others in her social network. Based on this research, *abusing* mothers have been shown to have representational models tied to issues of conflict, control, and rejection. They expect that others will try to dominate them and will reject them when they press to have their needs met. Their representational model assumes that others have physical and psychological resources, but that these resources will not be made available to them. This situation often may result in the affect of anger. In contrast, *neglecting* mothers have been shown to have representational models centered around the concept of helplessness. They do not see others as being able or willing to give them what they need;

they likewise do not consider themselves effective at eliciting the support and help of others. Their affect often consists of emptiness and depression. Mothers who are *adequate* have representational models centered around competence and reciprocity. They often perceive others as helpful and responsive and perceive themselves as capable of eliciting help or support from others when it is needed. They also are capable of providing support to others and often have the affect of satisfaction.

Given the wide range of behaviors exhibited by caregivers in the attachment relationship, the question arises as to whether infants can form secure attachment relationships with these caregivers. Bowlby (1973) addressed this issue by stressing the importance of the attachment relationship to the infant's survival and therefore the ability of the infant to form attachments to caregivers who vary across a wide continuum of sensitivity or nurturance. He noted:

> A special but not unusual situation in which there is conflict between attachment behavior and withdrawal is when the attachment figure is also the one who elicits fear perhaps by threats or violence. In such conditions young creatures, whether human or nonhuman, are likely to cling to the threatening or hostile figure rather than run away from him or her.
>
> *Bowlby.*

Bowlby clearly thought that maltreatment did not prevent the formation of an attachment relationship; however, he questioned the *quality* of that relationship and the nature of the representational models of the self and the larger social environment that are established under conditions of maltreatment. Assuming that individuals in maltreating families would form anxious attachments with family members, the underlying internal representational models of the self and others would be expected to be distorted. The working models for describing abusing/neglecting families in terms of attachment theory have been tested empirically, and a review of a few seminal studies follows.

A number of investigators have found that both abused and neglected children in the preschool age range (1 to 4 years) are anxiously attached to their mothers (Crittenden, 1985a, 1985b; Egeland & Sroufe, 1981a; Gaensbauer & Harmon, 1982; Schneider-Rosen, Braunwald, Carlson, & Cicchetti, 1985) and particularly display the anxious/avoidant pattern of attachment. Several studies have demonstrated, through the Strange Situation methodology, that maltreated children do form attachment relationships with their parents, and that these attachments are likely to be more insecure than those of nonmaltreated children (Crittenden, 1985a, 1988; Egeland & Sroufe, 1981a, 1981b; Lamb, Gaensbauer, Malkin & Schultz, 1985; Schneider-Rosen et al., 1985; Schneider-Rosen & Cicchetti, 1984).

Studies of parent-child interaction also have allowed investigators to infer the quality of the attachment relationship. Maternal insensitivity (i.e., interference and/or unresponsiveness) in interaction with her child has been associated with child anxiety in the Strange Situation (Ainsworth, Blehar, Waters, & Wall, 1978; Belsky, Rovine, & Taylor, 1984; Crittenden, 1985a; Sroufe, 1985). Abusing mothers were consistently observed to be more harsh, controlling, interfering, and negative when interacting with their children (Burgess & Conger, 1978; Crittenden, 1981, 1985a; Crittenden & Bonvillian, 1984; Dietrich, Starr, and Weisfeld, 1983; Mash, Johnson & Kovich, 1983; Robinson & Solomon, 1979; Wasserman, Green & Rhianon, 1983). In contrast, neglecting mothers were found to be insensitively understimulating (Crittenden, 1985a). Belsky et al. (1984) and Lyons-Ruth et al. (1987) have shown that mothers whose interaction style was primarily intrusive and characterized by covert hostility were more likely to have infants who demonstrated an avoidant style in the Strange Situation. Mothers whose interaction style was passive, withdrawn, and lacking initiative were more likely to have infants who were insecure/resistant-ambivalent in the Strange Situation. Thus, distinct patterns of maternal interactional style have been linked reliably to particular insecure patterns of attachment in the Strange Situation (Carlson et al., 1989).

Crittenden & Ainsworth (1989) argued that patterns of attachment behavior, as described in the previous paragraph, affect the direction of children's future developmental courses, rather than interrupting or arresting development at a certain stage. Insecure attachment relationships are presumed to leave family members more vulnerable to stresses inherent in the environment (i.e., employment, financial stresses) and less able to maintain stable relationships with other adults. Both individual differences and environmental experiences can affect the developmental outcome for a given person.

Effective parenting and attachment are desirable outcomes as depicted in the model in Figure 3.1. However, multiple constructs in the model are thought to relate to effective parenting and attachment, and they work together to predict the quality of these outcomes. Each of these constructs, and the research evidence to support them as potential etiological factors in maltreatment, is examined in turn.

## PARENTAL CHARACTERISTICS

### Psychosocial Adjustment

Research indicates that there is a direct relationship between maltreatment and the enduring characteristics of the parents; namely, the psychosocial adjustment and personality of the parents have a direct influence on quality of parenting. Early literature on the personality characteristics and social adjustment of abusive parents indicated that these parents tended to experience problems in social relationships that were related to atypical personality characteristics. For example, early studies suggested that parental characteristics such as role reversal (Steele & Pollack, 1974), lack of empathy for children (Bavolek, 1979), and excessive rigidity were characteristic of abusive parents. In a study designed to differentiate parents on level of child abuse potential, Milner and Wimberly (1980) reported that loneliness, rigidity, interpersonal problems, and lack of self-control were most strongly predictive of high child abuse potential. Of these factors, rigidity and problems with family and friends showed the strongest relationship to child abuse potential. Other studies have suggested that low self-esteem, impulsivity, or an internalized feeling of lack of control may be related to parental functioning.

However, these and other studies have been unable to determine a replicable, specific pattern of personality characteristics or traits among abusing parents (Parke & Collmer, 1975; Wolfe, 1985). Rather than continuing to examine static personality characteristics as potential risk factors for maltreatment, recent research has focused more on process-oriented variables, such as the way in which the caretaker *feels* about the role of parenting and other affective and cognitive aspects of the caretaker-child relationship (Brunnquell, Crichton & Egeland, 1981; Newberger, 1980; Newberger & Cook, 1983; Sameroff & Feil, 1984). According to Pianta et al., (1989), these studies demonstrate rather consistently that among maltreating parents, there is a ". . . lack of understanding of the complexity of social relationships, especially caretaking, and their feelings about meeting the needs of another person" (p. 205). These researchers suggest that ". . . the parent that provides good quality care is able to take the child's perspective and understand the child's behavior in terms of the context or situation and the developmental level of the child" (p. 206). These studies reaffirm the importance of a developmental approach to studying parental determinants of maltreatment.

Recent studies (Main & Hesse, 1990) suggest that parents' unresolved personal conflicts related to traumatic events or developmental issues of nurturance in their own experience of parenting may place them at greater risk for problems in the ability to parent effectively and may lead to a dysfunctional parent-child attachment relationship. Aber & Zigler (1981) argue strongly for consideration of the developmental level of maltreating parents in research, prevention and clinical intervention. The considerations would include the parents' cognitive stage, resolution or lack of resolution of dependency and autonomy issues, their internal (or representational) models of relationships, and their own history of parenting. An example of the process by which developmental experiences may influence parenting behaviors can be seen in parents who experience early deprivation of nurturance. These parents, as adults, may be likely to suffer from feelings of inadequacy and low self-esteem that may affect their interpersonal relationships and lead to social isolation or other more serious psychological disorders that affect the quality of parenting.

The developmental origins of interpersonal problems among abusive parents have been studied extensively, but some of this research led to conclusions which are no longer accepted. For instance, early research suggested a strong association between experience of abuse as a child and mistreatment of one's own children (Kempe & Kempe, 1978; Spinetta & Rigler, 1972). The limitations of this body of research are both methodological and conceptual. First, this assertion has been based largely on clinical case evidence, and as such, has been challenged in more recent research (Kaufman & Zigler, 1987). Second, the design of the studies is retrospective and lacking in comparison groups of parents who experienced maltreatment and did not subsequently abuse their own children. More recent prospective studies indicate that factors such as early and continued family instability, isolation, and problems in the mother-child relationship were effective predictors of abuse when compared to nonabusive, matched control groups (Newberger, Newberger & Hampton, 1977). Hunter and Kilstrom (1979) based their work on a study of parents with abusive histories who did not mistreat their own children compared to those who did abuse their children. Findings indicated that nonrepeaters showed a strong awareness of the psychological impact of their childhood and a conscious determination to rear their own children in a different way. In addition, the nonrepeaters utilized support from a broad network of social support systems. In another prospective study, Egeland and Brunnquell (1979) reported that factors that differentiated abusive from nonabusive mothers were an understanding of the psychological complexity of her infant, the quality of the mother's caregiving skills, and the infant's social responsiveness.

More recent research (Egeland, Jacobvitz, and Papatola, 1987) reported that 70 percent of parents who had experienced abuse as children were observed to maltreat or provide borderline care for their own children. A striking contrast was reported for the sample of mothers who had positive experiences with their own parents, all of whom (with a single exception) provided adequate care for their own children. Further, 26 percent of the parents who had been abused also provided adequate care for their children. The parents who provided adequate care were likely to have received emotional support during their own childhoods, had been involved in psychotherapy, and were currently involved in marriage with a stable partner. It is important to note that this study utilized a sample of lower socioeconomic status mothers who were likely to experience multiple-risk factors.

The data summarized thus far illuminate the relationship between psychosocial adjustment and potential for abuse among parents. The data indicate that parents' developmental experiences in the family of origin affect directly the quality of parenting offered to their own infant children. Rather than focusing on a psychopathological method of parental personality dysfunction, integrative research in recent years has been more process oriented and has pointed to the relationship between parental affective and cognitive factors and maltreatment. In addition to the research on psychosocial adjustment of parents, the quality of parenting also is influenced by the parent's knowledge of child development and parenting skill.

## Knowledge of Child Development and Parenting Skills

Research has indicated a strong relationship between knowledge of child development and potential for abuse (Larrance & Twentyman, 1983). Milner and Wimberly (1980) underscored the excessive rigidity in expectations of parents who are high in child abuse potential. Other researchers agree that abusive parents are less able to assess the developmental needs of their children (Newberger & Cook, 1983). Larrance and Twentyman (1983) reported that abusing mothers were less knowledgeable than a matched comparison group regarding the developmental capabilities of their children. In this research, the pattern of inaccuracies was not clear. In some situations, parents had higher than average expectations, and in other situations they had lower than average expectations. Further, abusing mothers tended to judge their children to be significantly more aversive than the children of other parents (Larrance & Twentyman, 1983). These mothers also judged their children to be significantly more likely to engage in annoying behaviors. In addition, abusive mothers tended to attribute their children's failures to internal causes and their children's successes to external causes. The opposite and more positive pattern was true for the nonabusive comparison group of mothers. In general, empirical research suggests that abusive parents tend to have a limited repertoire of parenting skills (Burgess & Conger, 1978) as well as inappropriate expectations for child behavior.

More recent research has focused on the dimensions of parental nurturance and control examined in theoretical work on child-rearing and parenting skill (Maccoby & Martin, 1983). In an examination of child-rearing attitudes of abusive parents, Trickett and Susman (1988) reported that abusive parents are less satisfied with their children and perceive child-rearing to be more difficult than the control parents. Abusive parents also tended to report less enjoyment of the parental role and a stronger desire to express negative affect. In the same study, researchers reported that while both control and abusive parents valued physical punishment, there were clear differences in the types of parental control utilized by the parents. Abusive parents tended to be more punitive than the nonabusive parents. In addition, the abusive parents were more likely than control parents to use severe physical punishment and less likely to use reasoning as a form of discipline. The abusive parents in this sample also were unable to encourage autonomy and independence, age-appropriate tasks for their school-age children, as much as the comparison group of nonabusive parents.

The data reviewed thus far substantiates a strong link between parenting skill and knowledge of child development and potential for maltreatment. Some authors have suggested that other parental characteristics, such as health status and health practices of the parent, also may influence risk in the parent-child relationship. For example, poor prenatal care or poor maternal health may lead to infant prematurity, low birth weight, or other child characteristics that increase stress for the parent.

## Maternal Health

Poor physical health and poor health practices of the mother appear to increase the risk for infant problems such as prematurity, low birth weight, and congenital handicaps. The model presented earlier in the chapter (Figure 1) suggests that maternal health influences child characteristics, and that these child characteristics may in turn create risk in the parent-child relationship. For example, maternal practices such as drug or alcohol abuse may have a deleterious effect on maternal health and also may affect the developing fetus in a way to impair the child's subsequent health, behavior, and development. Children exposed to drugs and alcohol *in utero* may be born prematurely or experience serious withdrawal symptoms. Their health is fragile, and they may require specialized medical care following birth (Daro & Mitchell, 1990). These children also are prone to learning difficulties, attentional deficits and hyperactivity, and severe behavioral and psychosocial adjustment problems (Willis & Holden, 1990). Parenting such children is a challenge in any case, but especially for parents whose own health and social needs are a factor. It is a growing national concern that offspring of substance-abusing mothers are disproportionately represented among the children entering the foster care system, presumably because of maternal abuse and/or neglect. According to the U.S. Advisory Board on Child Abuse and Neglect Report (1990), the association between child abuse/neglect and substance abuse is apparent in a number of public statistics. In 1989, Los Angeles County Department of Children's Services received referrals on over 2,400 newborn infants affected by prenatal exposure to drugs and alcohol. In New York City, 7.6 per 1000 newborns are found to be addicted (U.S. Advisory Board on Child Abuse & Neglect, 1990). Daro & Mitchell (1990), in reporting the results of the National Committee for Prevention of Child Abuse 1989 Annual 50 State Survey, reported that as many as 375,000 drug-exposed children may be born nationwide each year. Clearly, the importance of considering maternal health practices as a risk factor in child maltreatment is established.

The literature relating other aspects of maternal health to child maltreatment is more confounded than that related to substance abuse. Social factors such as poverty, ethnic status, neighborhood dysfunction, mental health problems of the parent, and special needs of the child have been strongly associated with higher rates of child maltreatment (U.S. Advisory Board on Child Abuse and Neglect, 1990). Many of the same factors also are associated with poor maternal health and subsequent infant health problems or handicapping conditions. Common sense would suggest that the relationship between maternal health, child characteristics, and parenting is strong, but empirical demonstration of this correspondence is lacking. The literature to date fails to disentangle the effects of social and health risks in the parent-child relationship.

Clearly there is a need for empirical studies to examine the effects of maternal health as a risk factor in child maltreatment and to examine factors which may serve to buffer the parent-child system to prevent maltreatment. For instance, empirical studies already demonstrate the positive effects of social support on maternal health status and psychiatric symptoms (Carveth & Gottlieb, 1979). Further delineating the types of social support that are helpful for which families under what circumstances is needed.

The model of parenting risk has emphasized that developmental transitions and child characteristics influence the nature of the parenting task. Some authors also suggest that characteristics of the child may contribute to the child's own maltreatment. The next section first describes the developmental transitions and characteristics of infants and preschool children that may influence risk in the parent-child relationship, and then reviews the literature on child characteristics as a potential influence on risk for maltreatment.

## CHILD CHARACTERISTICS

### Developmental Transitions

The characteristics of the young child may contribute to the challenge of the parenting task. The developmental approach implies that the nature of the parenting task is shaped by the unique characteristics of the child. Thus, it has been suggested earlier in the chapter that the risk factors for parents of infants and toddlers are likely to operate in unique ways compared to ways in which risk factors operate for parents of adolescents. For the infant, effective parenting appears to be based upon the ability to understand the developmental needs of the infant and to respond empathically to the infant. Providing a stable and predictable environment of attentive care-taking also is essential to promote the infant's development of trust in the environment (Erikson, 1968). As the infant begins to take a more active role in initiating and controlling interactions, the coordination and reciprocity of the relationship is a critical correlate of positive parenting. The degree to which the infant and parent are able to coordinate their behavior is known to be critical for the establishment of a successful and trusting relationship (Tronick & Cohn, 1989). These researchers suggest that coordination may be measured behaviorally in terms of synchronicity that is expressed in the coordination of movements, gaze patterns, and affective interactions.

The developmental challenges during the toddler years include a movement from dependence to greater self-reliance, the beginning of compliance to social rules and values, and the psychological process of individuation and separation. All of these developmental tasks focus on a striving for individual autonomy or independence characteristic of the toddler years. Thus, the increasing psychological independence and physical mobility of the toddler, together with the negativism typical of toddlers, shift the parenting issues to highlight a balance of control and appropriate limits for the toddler. Many parents find this task more challenging than providing care for the infant.

In addition to the normative characteristics of early childhood, research suggests that special characteristics of the child such as temperament or physical handicaps may influence the nature of the parenting task.

## Child Characteristics as Etiological Risk Factors

The critical question to be raised is: Are some child characteristics difficult to manage or nonrewarding enough to elicit maltreatment in parents who would not otherwise maltreat a normal child? The literature on this issue has been mixed over the past few years. Early literature suggested that the child's behavior exerts a powerful enough influence on the parent-child relationship to change parent behavior (Bell, 1968). Other researchers reported that child characteristics such as prematurity, handicapping conditions, or facial features influenced parents to maltreat because the children were difficult to manage or nonrewarding (Belsky, 1980; McCabe, 1984). However, more recent literature concludes that there is little evidence that child characteristics alone are powerful enough to cause a parent to maltreat (Pianta et al., 1989). Maccoby & Martin (1983) presented an extensive review of the socialization process, examining the bidirectionality of effects in the parent-child relationship. They concluded that, although child effects on parent behavior are important in isolated parent-child interaction episodes, the effects are short-term and do not appear to account for the variability in care-taking outcomes over time.

Thomas and Chess (1977) first described the wide range of temperamental differences related to sleep and feeding states, arousal level, activity, and social behavior in infants and toddlers. These temperamental traits fall on a continuum from "easy" to "difficult" and are thought to be present from the time of early infancy. Some authors have demonstrated an association between physical abuse and difficult temperamental traits such as increased irritability, fussiness, and dependency (Gil, 1970). Other child behavioral traits have been associated with maltreatment. Terr (1970) noted an increased incidence of hyperactivity or mental retardation in a sample of physically abused children, although these results must be viewed cautiously due to the difficulty in measuring intelligence and behavioral symptoms accurately in abused children. Patterson (1983) reported an association between aggressive boys' behavior and the quality of parenting responses, and Kempe (1971) noted an increased risk for physical abuse in children who were premature or adopted. Despite these reports, reviews by Brachfield, Goldberg, & Sloman, (1980), Crnic, Greenberg, Ragozin, Robinson, & Basham (1983), and Sameroff & Chandler (1975) concluded that it is not possible to predict that certain children will be maltreated based on their characteristics alone. Pianta et al. (1989) underscored the "power of parental responsiveness and the caretaking milieu in overcoming early developmental difficulties" (p. 209). Many of the studies claiming a causal relationship between child characteristics and maltreatment are hampered by methodological problems such as retrospective designs, measures of infant temperament that are not predictive of later behavior, and the general inability to separate the effects of the child's behavior from the possibility that poor parenting resulted in a child with these characteristics (Pianta et al., 1989).

A major theme of this chapter is that the antecedents of child maltreatment are multifactorial, involving factors at the individual, family, community, and cultural levels. The importance of child characteristics as etiological risk factors in maltreatment must be viewed in this same ecological context. That is, the child becomes an active part of the socialization process by placing demands on parental time and resources and having an idiosyncratic set of cues for responsiveness and sensitivity (Pianta et al., 1989). However, the parents' own resources and readiness to parent, or the support system available to the parents in the larger social environment may make a difference in whether or not these child characteristics create insurmountable stress and result in maltreatment.

Now that parent psychosocial characteristics, knowledge of child development and parenting skills, maternal health and child characteristics have been examined as possible etiological factors in maltreatment, the ecological model suggests the importance of moving beyond the individual and family levels to the broader context in which abuse may occur. Garbarino (1977) suggested that the social context of child rearing is a critical factor in determining the quality of parenting. The next section explores the effects of social support on parenting.

## SOCIAL SUPPORT AND ITS EFFECTS ON PARENTING

The ecological framework highlights the need to assess the social context as a component in preventing dysfunction in the parenting relationship. The beneficial impact of social support on general health and psychological health is well-documented (Gottlieb, 1981; Mitchell & Trickett, 1980; Turner, 1983). The direct positive relationship of social support has also been established in empirical work (Colletta, 1981; Colletta & Lee, 1983; Crockenburg, 1981; Pascoe, Loda, Jeffries, & Earp, 1981). In addition, research supports the relationship between social support, parenting, and child development (Crockenburg, 1981), particularly with respect to quality of attachment. Thus, the presence of social support is related to positive child-rearing and subsequent child development. In examining the specific case of child maltreatment, the research has established a link between the absence of social support (or social isolation) and maltreatment. For example, Crittendon (1985b) reported that among qualitatively different groups of maltreating parents, maltreatment status accounted for 35 percent of the variance in quality of attachment, and parental satisfaction with social network accounted for 20 percent of the variance over and above the effects of maltreatment status. Specifically, Crittendon (1985b) found three patterns of social support that were related to styles of child-rearing, ranging from stable, open, and cooperative to unstable, closed, and hostile. The study indicated that the optimal social support system was associated with most positive styles of parenting.

The positive effects of social support on parental functioning may be examined by analyzing the types and sources of social support, and the mechanisms through which social support functions to enhance parenting. Understanding the functions of social support will provide a framework for suggesting the most effective child abuse prevention programs.

Recent research has stressed the need to view social support as a multi-dimensional construct (Dean & Lin, 1977; Kaplan, Cassel, & Gore, 1977; Thoits, 1982). On the basis of these empirical efforts, the critical dimensions for defining social support appear to be the sources of social support, the types and functions of support, and the effects of the support on specific outcomes (i.e., the quality of parenting and child outcome). The importance of these dimensions will be stressed in the review of the effects of social support from an ecological framework (Belsky, 1980; Garbarino, 1977).

## Types of Social Support

The types of social support have been conceptualized in both theoretically-derived systems and empirically-derived systems. Belsky (1984) suggested that social support functions in three general ways to affect parenting: 1) by providing emotional support; 2) by providing instrumental assistance; and 3) by providing social expectations and sanctions for appropriate parenting behavior. Emotional support is defined as the acceptance directed toward an individual, through verbal support or a caring, affectionate atmosphere. Instrumental assistance refers to the provision of practical help with tasks (such as child care and transportation) and the provision of advice directed toward problem-solving. Social expectations are sanctions or guidelines which function to provide boundaries for appropriate behavior.

Similar categories of social support were described in an empirically-derived typology developed by Gottlieb (1978). Four categories of behavior were suggested: 1) emotionally sustaining behaviors (talking or encouraging); 2) problem-solving (advising, directing, referring); 3) indirect personal influence and availability; 4) environmental action—action taken to alleviate stressors in the environment. Recent research underscores the importance of measuring specific types of support, since the use of a composite measure weakened the ability to detect relationships between social support and outcome (Feiring, Fox, Jaskir, & Lewis, 1987). A review of the types of social support according to the sources of support within the ecological framework follows. This section continues with a review of the relationship of types and sources of support to outcomes (e.g., parenting and attachment).

An examination of the links between social support and quality of parenting highlight three distinct sources of support that affect quality of parenting: immediate family support, a social network of friends and extended family, and formal systems of support present in the social context including professional and community support.

### The Immediate Family

Evidence indicates that support from the spouse and kin is related to the quality of parenting among samples of both normal and premature infants. In general, research indicates that a tightly knit support network was positively associated with parental sense of competence (Abernethy, 1973). Pascoe et al. (1981) reported that contact with social network and supportiveness was correlated positively with mothers' avoidance of punishment of her offspring.

Spousal support plays an especially significant role in promoting the quality of mothers' relationships with infants and preschool children. Early research documented the positive impact of husbands' supportiveness on mothering during infancy (Pederson, 1982). In a classic study by Sears, Maccoby, and Levin (1957), these researchers indicated that mothers' positive regard for their husbands was systematically related to the praise directed toward their children. More recent research indicates that spousal support can facilitate optimal maternal behavior with premature infants (Crnic et al., 1983). Indeed, research indicates that availability of support enhances maternal sensitivity, nurturance, and positive attitudes toward parenting in mothers of at-risk infants (Crockenburg, 1981). Pascoe and Earp (1984) further documented the relationship by reporting that mothers of at-risk infants who were given more social support also provided more stimulating environments for their children regardless of the number of life changes they experienced. Social support from fathers also had a strong positive relationship to interaction despite the risk status of the infant (Feiring et al., 1987).

While some researchers (Belsky, 1984) have asserted that the impact of the marital relationship is mediated by psychological adjustment; other more recent research suggests that when differences in psychological adjustment are accounted for, mothers are warmer and more sensitive when they are involved in close, confiding marriages (Cox, Owen, Lewis, & Henderson, 1989).

Turning to the literature on another high-risk group of parents, researchers have underscored the importance of social support as a major factor in promoting adolescent adjustment to pregnancy. Social support from partner and family of origin appeared to be critical factors directly relating to adolescent feelings of adjustment, life satisfaction, and positive parenting. Unger and Wandersman (1985) reported that support from family of origin was associated with feelings of adjustment at a prenatal assessment, but this association was not evident at a postnatal assessment. In a more recent study on the effects of specific sources of social support, Unger and Wandersman (1988) reported that both family and partner support were important in determining life satisfaction among adolescent parents.

The literature also suggests a relationship between social support and increased responsivity and affection of adolescent mothers toward their children (Colletta, 1981; Crockenburg, 1981). When the father of the child and the grandmother provided child care, adolescent mothers' perceptions of support were associated with more positive parenting skills. On the basis of evidence from these studies, it appears that partners and the family of origin are salient sources of support for high-risk adolescent mothers. Indeed, studies indicate that relatives (especially grandmothers) are the most frequent providers of childcare assistance to adolescent mothers (Furstenburg & Crawford, 1978). Moreover, teens who received support from the family of origin experienced easier transitions to parenthood (Panzarine, 1986). Thus, it would appear that family members and partners are critical sources of support, particularly for high-risk mothers during the prenatal and postnatal periods.

### Community and Professional Support

Consideration of parent-child relationships within a social context necessarily highlights the factors in the community that support or strain family relationships. Literature on the relationship of community factors to child maltreatment indicates that the larger community may affect parent-child relationships by providing:

1. Guidelines and feedback on standards for appropriate behavior toward children (Caplan, 1974; Caplan & Killilea, 1976)
2. An index of the level of social risk inherent in the neighborhood (Garbarino & Sherman, 1980)
3. Direct support to family by members of the social network (friends, professionals).

Any comprehensive review of the literature leads to the conclusion that child maltreatment is concentrated among high-risk families who are socially and economically disadvantaged. High-risk families tend to be socially isolated from support systems that provide the necessary functions mentioned earlier (Garbarino & Crouter, 1978). Particularly important is the feedback and monitoring function of community support systems. As Caplan (1974) suggested, "They tell him (the individual) what is expected of him and guide him in what to do. They watch what he does and they judge his performance" (pp. 5–6). Abusive families tend to be isolated from external monitoring and guidelines for appropriate parenting behavior.

The second way in which the social context affects maltreatment is through the influence of an impoverished social context (Garbarino & Crouter, 1978; Garbarino, 1989). In explaining his concept of the impact of social impoverishment on child maltreatment, Garbarino differentiated two concepts of risk. The first concept refers to the absolute rate of maltreatment that is concentrated in lower socioeconomic neighborhoods. As Garbarino and his colleagues have suggested, socioeconomic status accounts for 40 percent of the variation across neighborhoods. The second meaning of risk involves the quality of the neighborhood in providing family support through services, standards to ensure safety for children, and a community commitment to enhance life, children, and families.

The final arena in which the community affects maltreatment is through the direct support of friends and professionals in the community. For example, Powell (1980) reported that the quality of mothering as defined by verbal and emotional responsivity was more likely to occur for mothers who had regular and weekly contact with friends than with those who did not have contact with friends.

The literature suggests that professional support consistently has positive effects on high-risk single and young parents. Crockenburg (1986) compared two groups of mothers ages 17 to 19. One group received regular, professional support from home visitors in England. The comparison group of similar socioeconomic status resided in the United States and received no professional support. Crockenburg (1986) reported that the English mothers engaged in smiling toward their infants more frequently than the American mothers and that professional support predicted positive maternal behaviors. In another study, Olds and his colleagues (Olds, Henderson, Tatelbaum, & Chamberlin, 1986) reported that a group of young, single mothers in rural New York state who received professional support in the form of information and instrumental assistance were observed to restrict and punish their children less frequently in comparison to a group who received no professional support. More recently, Culbertson, Willis and Buck (1989) reported that a group of lower socioeconomic status teen mothers who received regular professional home visiting had higher total scores on the Home Observation for Measurement of the Environment Scale (HOME) compared to teen mothers who received only short-term hospital based intervention or no intervention. Interestingly, however, there were no significant differences between the improvement of the mothers who received the home intervention for six months in comparison to those who received intervention for 12 months during the postnatal period.

Comprehensive programs also have been successful in producing gains regarding specific risk factors among abusive parents. Specific gains have included ability to understand and respond to the child's developmental needs (Field, Widmayer, Stringer, Ignatoff, 1980), and improved mother-child interaction as demonstrated by use of less punitive discipline (Olds et al., 1986).

On the basis of this review of social support, it is apparent that the evidence supports a direct relationship between social support and quality of parenting. The effects of social support may be observed in both direct and indirect relationship to quality of parenting. The direct effects of social support may be observed in the positive impact of spousal support on quality of parenting (Crnic et al., 1983), on the benefit derived from support of family (Unger & Wanderman, 1985), friends (Powell, 1980), and professionals (Olds et al.,

1986). Social support also has a direct relationship to the parents' knowledge of child development (Field et al., 1980) which, in turn, influences quality of parenting. Social support is effective in reducing perinatal risk through general impact on maternal health (Olds et al., 1986). Social support may be mediated through psychosocial adjustment. Adjustment has a direct influence on quality of parenting (Egeland et al., 1987).

The model of parenting risk can be used to integrate available data on the effectiveness of prevention programs to reduce the risk for abuse. Child abuse prevention programs have focused on the following constructs derived from the model:

1. Knowledge of child development and parenting skill—increasing the parents' knowledge of child development and parenting skill
2. Psychosocial adjustment—providing a therapeutic group experience to nurture self-esteem
3. Maternal health—providing adequate transportation and outreach to high-risk parents in order to reduce perinatal and postnatal risk
4. Social support or providing professional formal support and facilitating informal support among parents.

Comprehensive programs have implemented these objectives through intensive, multipurpose intervention programs with high-risk parents and their children. Descriptions of a few model programs follow.

## MODEL PROGRAMS FOR PREVENTION OF MALTREATMENT

### Outreach Program Model

*Nurse home-visiting of young, single, poor mothers during prenatal and postnatal period.* The program designed by Olds incorporated three major goals: 1) parent education regarding fetal and infant development; 2) the involvement of family members and friends in child care and support of the mother; and 3) the linkage of family members with other health and human services. Of the 400 women who participated in the program, 47 percent were younger than 19 years of age; 62 percent were unmarried; and 61 percent were low socioeconomic status. Despite the similarities in demographic characteristics at intake, those who received the most intensive intervention had significantly lower incidence of reported child abuse over the two-year post-birth study period. While 19 percent of the comparison group at greatest risk for maltreatment (i.e., poor, unmarried teens) were reported for abuse or neglect, only 4 percent of their nurse-visited counterparts were reported. Although these results were not true for older program participants, the dramatic gains realized with the first-time, teen mothers suggest that this intervention may be particularly effective with young first-time mothers. In addition to having a lower reported rate of child abuse, those infants whose mothers received ongoing nurse home visits had fewer accidents and were less likely to require emergency room care. The mothers also reported less frequent need to punish or restrict their children (Olds et al., 1986).

## Center-Based Program Model

*Minnesota Early Learning Design (MELD).* One of the most widely disseminated models is the Minnesota Early Learning Demonstration (MELD), an intensive two-year parenting education and support program (Staff, 1985). MELD's mission is to get families off to a good start and to eliminate the potential for maltreatment by never allowing abusive or neglectful patterns to begin. MELD believes that there is no one right way to parent, and participants are encouraged to make the child-rearing choices that are appropriate for them. The program demonstrates that if participants are supported in their efforts to be good parents, if they are exposed to good information and alternative ways of addressing child-rearing issues, they will be able to make the choices that enhance their children's well-being as well as their own. A typical MELD group includes 10–20 mothers who meet for two or three hours weekly. While the group lasts for two years, the meetings are scheduled in four, six-month phases that include 20 meetings each and are led by extensively trained parent volunteers. The topics discussed during these meetings include health issues, child development, child guidance, family management and personal growth. Although the program has never been evaluated in terms of child abuse prevention, the immediate outcomes demonstrated by program participants are encouraging. A recent evaluation of the MELD Young Mom's program conducted by the Child Welfare League of America noted that 80 percent of the participants had finished or were completing high school compared to an overall school completion rate of only 20 percent for the general adolescent parent population. Also, while 25 percent of teenage mothers experience a repeat pregnancy within a year of their first birth, MELD for Young Mom participants had a repeat pregnancy rate of only 10–15 percent. Changes also were noted in the parents' use of physical discipline: The percentage of parents who spanked their children decreased from 56 percent at the start of the program to only 12 percent at the conclusion of services.

## Hospital-Based Programs

*The First Steps Program.* This is a primary prevention program which provides education, emotional support, and referrals to adolescent mothers at three sites in Georgia (Staff, 1984). The First Steps Programs has the following goals: 1) emotional support for adolescent parents; 2) planning for the arrival of the baby, particularly regarding availability of support and material needs for the infant; 3) preparation of the adolescent mother for parenthood including the easing of changes in relationships with spouse or partners, siblings, or friends; 4) increasing awareness of community resources to serve the family; 5) reducing social isolation; and 6) identifying families with special problems.

The services are initiated during the last trimester of pregnancy and continue on a weekly basis through the use of volunteers to the mothers and infants during the first three months of life.

## CHOOSING A PREVENTION MODEL

Reaching the full spectrum of parents of infants and toddlers will require some combination of program components and methods. Outreach programs may be more beneficial for parents who are isolated or parents with multiple risk factors such as single parenthood, infant prematurity, or adolescent parenthood. Center-based models may be more appropriate for the motivated parents who are likely to benefit from a social support network in the community focused on parenting.

Few researchers have systematically examined the constructs and outcomes that influence and predict quality of parenting and attachment. A close examination of the model presented earlier in this chapter suggests that multiple constructs must be considered in designing child abuse prevention programs.

A comprehensive program would improve the psychosocial adjustment of the parent, knowledge of child development and parenting skill, health status, social support, and parenting as affected by the unique characteristics of the child. Several points should be stressed regarding the interpretation of the model. First, parents will differ in the profile of factors that influence quality of parenting and subsequent attachment. One parent may require preventive efforts directed at one or two construct domains, while another may have multiple risk factors. These factors often are correlated, and the effects of each on poor parenting outcomes increase multiplicatively rather than additively (Rutter, 1979). Accordingly, prevention programs directed at infants and toddlers and their parents must be consistent with the parent-child needs. Additional evaluative research that focuses on the relationships between constructs and quality of parenting would provide a theoretical foundation for the design of prevention programs.

## CONCLUSIONS

In this chapter, we have explored a variety of potential etiological factors related to maltreatment within the context of an ecological model for prediction of the quality of parenting and attachment. Rather than focusing on static personality or behavioral traits of the parent and child, we have reviewed research that has emphasized the complex intercorrelations among risk factors at the level of the individual, the family, the community, and the culture. We also have pointed out the many areas in which further research is needed. The ecological model is intended to serve as an organizer for research on risk factors linked to abuse and to assist in evaluating the impact of preventive efforts aimed at enhancing or changing various constructs depicted in the model. Finally, the model provides guidelines for the development of future empirical and applied efforts systematically aimed at the prevention of abuse toward infants and young children.

## REFERENCES

Aber, J. L. & Zigler, D. (1981). Developmental considerations in the definition of child maltreatment. In R. Rizley & D. Cicchetti (Eds.), *New directions in child development: Developmental perspectives in child maltreatment.* San Francisco: Jossey-Bass.

Abernethy, V. D. (1973). Social network and response to the maternal role. *International Journal of Sociology of the Family, 3,* 86–92.

Ainsworth, M. D. S. (1973). The development of infant-mother attachment. In B. Caldwell & H. Ricciutti (Eds.), *Review of Child Development Research: Vol. 3.* Chicago: University of Chicago Press.

Ainsworth, M. D. S. (1989). Attachments beyond infancy. *American Psychologist,* 44(4), 709–716.

Ainsworth, M. D. S., Blehar, M. C., Waters, E., & Wall, S. (1978). *Patterns of attachment: A psychological study of the strange situation.* Hillsdale, NJ: Erlbaum.

Ainsworth, M. D. S. & Wittig, B. A. (1969). Attachment and exploratory behavior of one-year-olds in a strange situation. In B. M. Foss (Ed.), *Determinants of infant behavior—IV.* London: Methuen.

Bavolek, S. J. (1979, October). *Educational settings for the primary prevention of child abuse and neglect birth adolescents.* Paper presented at the Fourth National Conference on Child Abuse and Neglect, Los Angeles.

Bell, R. (1968). A reinterpretation of the direction of effects in studies of socialization. *Psychological Review, 75,* 81–95.

Belsky, J. (1980). Child maltreatment: An ecological integration. *American Psychologist, 35,* 320–335.

Belsky, J. (1984). The determinants of parenting: A processes model. *Child Development, 55,* 83–96.

Belsky, J., Rovine, M., & Taylor, D. G. (1984). The Pennsylvania Infant and Family Development Project, III: The origins of individual differences in infant-mother attachment: Maternal and infant contributions. *Child Development, 55,* 718–728.

Bowlby, J. (1969/1982). *Attachment and loss, Vol. I: Attachment* (2nd Ed.). New York: Basic Books.

Bowlby, J. (1973). *Attachment and loss, Vol. II: Separation.* New York: Basic Books.

Brachfield, S., Goldberg, S. & Sloman, J. (1980). Parent-infant interaction in free play at 8 and 12 months: Effects of prematurity and immaturity. *Infant Behavior and Development, 3,* 289–305.

Bretherton, I. (1985). Attachment theory: Retrospect and prospect. In I. Bretherton & E. Waters (Eds.), Growing points of attachment: Theory and research. *Monographs of the Society for Research in Child Development, 50,* 3–36.

Bronfenbrenner, U. (1977). Toward an experimental ecology of human development. *American Psychologist, 32,* 513–531.

Bronfenbrenner, U. (1979). *The ecology of human development.* Cambridge, MA: Harvard University Press.

Brunnquell, D., Crichton, L., & Egeland, B. (1981). Maternal personality and attitude in disturbances of child rearing. *American Journal of Orthopsychiatry, 51,* 680–691.

Burgess, R. L. & Conger, R. D. (1978). Family interaction in abusive, neglectful, and normal families. *Child Development, 49,* 1163–1173.

Caplan, G. (1974). *Support systems and community mental health.* New York: Behavioral Publications.

Caplan, G., & Killilea, M. (1976). *Support systems and mutual help.* New York: Grune & Stratton, 1976.

Carlson, V., Cicchetti, D., Barnett, D. & Braunwald, K. (1989). Finding order in disorganization: Lessons from research on maltreated infants' attachments to their caregivers. In D. Cicchetti & V. Carlson (Eds.), *Child Maltreatment.* New York: Cambridge University Press.

Carveth, W. & Gottlieb, B. (1979). The measurement of social support and its relation to stress. *Canadian Journal of Behavioral Science, 11,* 179–186.

Cicchetti, D. & Aber, L. (1980). Abused children-abusive parents: An overstated case? *Harvard Educational Review, 50,* 244–255.

Cicchetti, D. & Rizley, R. (1981). Developmental perspectives on the etiology, intergenerational transmission, and sequelae of child maltreatment. *New Directions for Child Development, 11,* 31–55.

Cohen, S., Gray, E. & Wald, M. (1984). *Preventing child maltreatment: A review of what we know.* Working Paper #024. National Committee for Prevention of Child Abuse.

Colletta, N. D. (1981). Social support and the risk of maternal rejection by adolescent mothers. *Journal of Psychology, 109,* 191–197.

Colletta, N. D., & Lee, D. (1983). The impact of support for Black adolescent mothers. *Journal of Family Issues, 4,* 127–143.

Cox, M. J., Owen, M. T., Lewis, J. M., & Henderson, V. K. (1989). Marriage, adult adjustment, and early parenting. *Child Development, 60,* 1015–1024.

Crittenden, P. M. (1981). Abusing, neglecting, problematic and adequate dyads: Differentiating by patterns of interaction. *Merrill-Palmer Quarterly, 27,* 1–18.

Crittenden, P. M. (1985a). Maltreated infants: Vulnerability and resilience, *Journal of Child Psychology and Psychiatry and Allied Disciplines, 26*(1), 85–96.

Crittenden, P. M. (1985b). Social networks, quality of childrearing, and child development. *Child Development, 56,* 1299–1313.

Crittenden, P. M. (1988). Relationships at risk. In J. Belsky & T. Nezworski, (Eds.), *Clinical implications of attachment theory* (pp. 136–174). Hillsdale, NJ: Erlbaum.

Crittenden, P. M. & Ainsworth, M. D. S. (1989). Child maltreatment and attachment theory. In D. Cicchetti and V. Carlson, (Eds.), *Child Maltreatment*. New York: Cambridge University Press.

Crittenden, P. M. & Bonvillian, J. (1984). The effect of maternal risk status on maternal sensitivity to infant cues. *American Journal of Orthopsychiatry, 54*, 250–262.

Crnic, K. A., Greenberg, M. T., Ragozin, A. S., Robinson, N. M., & Basham, R. (1983). Effects of stress and social support on mothers and premature and full-term infants. *Child Development, 54*, 209–217.

Crockenberg, S. B. (1981). Infant irritability, mother responsiveness, and social support influences on the security of infant-mother attachment. *Child Development, 52*, 857–865.

Crockenburg, S. (1986). Professional support for adolescent mothers. Who gives it, how adolescent mothers evaluate it, and what they prefer: *Infant Mental Health Journal, 7*, 49–58.

Culbertson, J., Willis, D., & Buck, P. (1989). *Effects of home intervention in reducing risk for maltreatment in teen mothers.* Unpublished manuscript.

Daro, D. (1989, October). *Child abuse prevention: Major gains and continued limitations.* Paper presented at The Eighth National Conference on Child Abuse and Neglect, Salt Lake City, UT.

Daro, D. & Mitchell, L. (1987). Deaths due to maltreatment soar: The results of the 1986 annual 50 state survey. Chicago: National Committee for Prevention of Child Abuse.

Daro, D. & Mitchell, L. (1990). Current trends in child abuse reporting and fatalities: The results of the 1989 annual 50 state survey. Chicago: National Committee for Prevention of Child Abuse.

Dean, A., & Lin, N. (1977). The stress-buffering role of social support: Problems and prospects for systematic investigation. *Journal of Nervous and Mental Disease, 165*, 403–417.

Dietrich, K. N., Starr, R. & Weisfeld, G. E. (1983). Infant maltreatment: Caretaker-infant interaction and developmental consequences at different levels of parenting failure. *Pediatrics, 72*, 532–540.

Egeland, B. & Brunnquell, D. (1979). An at-risk approach to the study of child abuse: Some preliminary findings. *Journal of the American Academy of Child Psychiatry, 18*, 219–235.

Egeland, B. & Farber, E. A. (1984). Infant-mother attachment: Factors related to its development and changes over time. *Child Development, 55*, 753–771.

Egeland, B., Jacobvitz, D., & Papatola, K. (1987). Intergenerational continuity of abuse. In R. Gelles & J. Lancaster (Eds.) *Child abuse and neglect: Biosocial dimensions.* New York: Aldine.

Egeland, B. & Sroufe, A. (1981a). Attachment and early maltreatment. *Child Development, 52*, 44–52.

Egeland, B. & Sroufe, A. (1981b). Developmental sequelae of maltreatment in infancy. *New directions for child development: Developmental perspectives on child maltreatment, 11*, 77–92.

Erikson, E. H. (1968). *Identity: Youth and crisis.* New York: Norton.

Feiring, C., Fox, N. A., Jaskir, J., & Lewis, M. (1987). The relation between social support, infant risk status, and mother-infant interaction. *Developmental Psychology, 23,* 400–405.

Field, T. M., Widmayer, S. M., Stringer, S., & Ignatoff, E. (1980). Teenage, lower-class, black mothers and their pre-term infants: An intervention and follow-up. *Child Development, 51,* 426–436.

Furstenberg, F. F., & Crawford, A. G. (1978). Family support: Helping teenage mothers to cope. *Family Planning Perspectives, 10,* 322–333.

Gaensbauer, T. J. & Harmon, R. J. (1982). Attachment behavior in abused/neglected and premature infants: Implications for the concept of attachment. In R. N. Emde & R. J. Harmon (Eds.), *The development of attachment and affiliative systems.* New York: Plenum.

Garbarino, J. (1977). The human ecology of child maltreatment: A conceptual model for research. *Journal of Marriage and the Family, 39,* 721–727.

Garbarino, J., & Crouter, A. (1978). Defining the community context for parent-child relations: The correlates of child maltreatment. *Child Development, 49,* 604–616.

Garbarino, J., & Sherman, D. (1980). High-risk families and high-risk neighborhoods. *Child Development, 51,* 188–198.

Garbarino, J. (1989). The human ecology of early risk. In S. Meisels and J. Shonkoff (Eds.) *Handbook of early intervention.* Boston: Cambridge University Press.

Gil, D. G. (1970). *Violence against children: Physical abuse in the United States.* Cambridge, MA: Harvard University Press.

Gottlieb, B. H. (1978). The development and application of a classification scheme of informal helping behaviors. *Canadian Journal of Behavioral Science, 10,* 105–115.

Gottlieb, B. H. (1981). *Social networks and social support.* Beverly Hills: Sage.

Grossmann, K. E., Grossmann, K., Spangler, G., Suess, G., & Unzer, L. (1985). Maternal sensitivity and newborns' orientation responses as related to quality of attachment in Northern Germany. In I. Bretherton & E. Waters (Eds.), Growing points of attachment theory and research. *Monographs of the Society for Research in Child Development, 50,* 233–256.

Hunter, R. S., & Kilstrom, N. (1979). Breaking the cycle in abusive families. *American Journal of Psychiatry, 136,* 1320–1322.

Kaplan, B. H., Cassel, J. C., & Gore, S. (1977). Social support and health. *Medical Care, 15,* 47–58.

Kaufman, J., & Zigler, E. (1987). Do abused children become abusive parents? *American Journal of Orthopsychiatry, 57,* 186–192.

Kempe, C. H. (1971). Pediatric implications of the battered baby syndrome. *Archives of Disease in Childhood, 46,* 28–37.

Larrance, D. T., & Twentyman, C. T. (1983). Maternal attribution and child abuse. *Journal of Abnormal Psychology, 92,* 449–457.

Lyons-Ruth, K., Connell, D., Zoll, D. & Stahl, J. (1987). Infants at social risk: Relationships among infant maltreatment, maternal behavior, and infant attachment behavior. *Developmental Psychology, 23*(2), 223–232.

Maccoby, E. E., & Martin, J. A. (1983). Socialization in the context of the family: Parent-child interaction. In P. H. Mussen (Series Ed.) and E. M. Hetherington

(Vol. Ed.), *Handbook of Child Psychology, Vol. 4: Socialization, Personality, and Social Development.* New York: Wiley.

Main, M., Kaplan, N. & Cassidy, J. (1985). Security in infancy, childhood and adulthood: A move to the level of representation. In I. Bretherton & E. Waters (Eds.), Growing points in attachment theory and research. *Monographs of the Society for Research in Child Development, Vol. 50*(1 & 2), 66–104 (Serial No. 209).

Main, M. & Hesse, E. (1990). Parents' unresolved traumatic experiences are related to infant disorganized attachment status. In M. Greenberg, D. Cicchetti, & M. Cummings (Eds.), *Attachment in the preschool years.* Chicago: University of Chicago Press.

Main, M. & Solomon, J. (1990). Procedures for identifying infants as disorganized/disoriented during the Ainsworth Strange Situation. In M. Greenberg, D. Cicchetti, and M. Cummings (Eds.), *Attachment during the preschool years.* Chicago: University of Chicago Press.

Mash, E. J., Johnston, C. & Kovitz, K. (1983). A comparison of the mother-child interactions of physically abused and non-abused children during play and task situations. *Journal of Clinical Child Psychology, 12,* 337–346.

McCabe, V. (1984). Abstract perceptual information for age level: A risk factor for maltreatment? *Child Development, 55,* 267–276.

Milner, J. S., & Wimberley, R. C. (1980). Prediction and explanation of child abuse. *Journal of Clinical Psychology, 36,* 875–884.

Mitchell, R. E., & Trickett, E. J. (1980). Task force report: Social networks as mediators of social support. *Community Mental Health Journal, 16,* 27–43.

Newberger, E., Newberger, C., & Hampton, R. (1977). Pediatric social illness: Toward an etiologic classification. *Pediatrics, 60,* 178–185.

Newberger, C. M. (1980). The cognitive structure of parenthood: Design a descriptive measure. *New directions in child development, 7,* 45–67.

Newberger, C. M., & Cook, S. J. (1983). Parental awareness and child abuse: A cognitive-developmental analysis of urban and rural samples. *American Journal of Orthopsychiatry, 53,* 512–524.

Olds, D. L., Henderson, C. R., Tatelbaum, R., & Chamberlin, M. (1986). Improving the delivery of prenatal care and outcomes of pregnancy: A randomized trial of nurse home visitation. *Pediatrics, 77,* 16–28.

Panzarene, S. (1986). Stressors, coping, and social supports of adolescent mothers. *Journal of Adolescent Health Care, 7,* 153–161.

Parke, R. D. & Collmer, C. W. (1975). Child abuse: An interdisciplinary analysis. In F. D. Horowitz (Ed.), *Review of child development research.* Chicago: University of Chicago Press.

Pascoe, J. M., Loda, F. A., Jeffries, V., & Earp, J. A. (1981). The association between mother's social support and provision of stimulation to their children. *Developmental and Behavioral Pediatrics, 2,* 15–19.

Pascoe, J. M., & Earp, J. A. (1984). The effect of mothers' social support and life changes on the stimulation of their children in the home. *American Journal of Public Health, F4,* pp. 358–360.

Patterson, G. (1983). Stress: A change agent for family process. In M. Rutter and N.

Garmezy (Eds.), *Stress coping and development in children* (pp. 235–264). New York: McGraw-Hill.

Pedersen, F. (1982). Mother, father, and infant as an interactive system. In J. Belsky (Ed.), *In the beginning: Readings on infancy.* New York: Columbia University Press.

Pianta, R. Egeland, B. & Erickson, M. F. (1989). The antecedents of maltreatment: Results of the Mother-Child Interaction Research Project. In D. Cicchetti & V. Carlson, (Eds.). *Child Maltreatment.* New York: Cambridge University Press.

Powell, D. R. (1980). Personal social networks as a focus for primary prevention of child maltreatment. *Infant Mental Health Journal, 1,* 232–239.

Robinson, E. & Solomon, F. (1979). Some further findings on the treatment of the mother-child dyad in child abuse. *Child Abuse and Neglect, 3,* 247–251.

Rutter, M. (1979). Protective factors in children's responses to stress and disadvantage. In M. W. Kent & T. W. Rolf (Eds.), *Social competence in children* (pp. 49–74). Hanover, NH: University Press of New England.

Sameroff, A. J. & Chandler, M. J. (1975). Reproductive risk and the continuum of caretaking casualty. In F. D. Horowitz (Ed.), *Review of child development research.* Chicago: University of Chicago Press.

Sameroff, A. J. & Feil, L. A. (1984). Parental concepts of development. In I. Sigel (Ed.), *Parental belief systems: The psychological consequences for children.* Hillsdale, NJ: Erlbaum.

Schneider-Rosen, K., Braunwald, K. G., Carlson, V., & Cicchetti, D. (1985). Current perspectives in attachment theory: Illustration from the study of maltreated infants. *Monographs of the Society for Research in Child Development, 50,* 194–210.

Schneider-Rosen, K. & Cicchetti, D. (1984). The relationship between affect and cognition in maltreated infants: Quality of attachment and the development of visual self-recognition. *Child Development, 55,* 648–658.

Sears, R. R., Maccoby, E. E., & Levin, H. (1957). *Patterns of child rearing.* White Plains: Row, Peterson, and Co.

Spinetta, J. J., & Rigler, D. (1972). The child abusing parent: A psychological review. *Psychological Bulletin, 77,* 296–304.

Sroufe, L. A. (1985). Attachment classification from the perspective of infant-caregiver relationships and infant temperament. *Child Development, 56,* 1–14.

Staff, (1984). First steps: A program for new families. *First Steps Newsletter.* Atlanta: Georgia Council on Child Abuse.

Staff, (1985). Minnesota Early Training Design (M.E.L.D.) Minnesota: Minneapolis.

Steele, B. F., & Pollack, C. B. (1974). A psychiatric study of parents who abuse infants and young children. In R. E. Helfer and C. H. Kempe (Eds.), *The battered child* (2nd edition). Chicago: University of Chicago Press.

Terr, L. (1970). A family study of child abuse. *American Journal of Psychiatry, 127,* 665–671.

Thoits, P. A. (1982). Conceptual, methodological, and theoretical problems in studying social support as a buffer against life stress. *Journal of Health and Social Behavior, 23,* 145–159.

Thomas, A. & Chess, S. (1977). *Temperament and development*. New York: Bruner-Mazel.

Tinbergen, N. (1951). *The study of instinct*. London: Oxford University Press.

Trickett, P. K., & Susman, E. J. (1988). Parental perceptions of child-raising practices in physically abusive and non-abusive families. *Developmental Psychology, 24,* 270–276.

Tronick, E. Z., & Cohn, J. F. (1989). Infant-mother face-to-face interaction: Age and gender differences in coordination and the occurrence of miscoordination. *Child Development, 60,* 85–92.

Turner, R. J. (1983). Direct, indirect, and moderating effects of social support on psychological distress and associated conditions. In H. B. Kaplan (Ed.). *Psychosocial stress: Trends in theory and research* (pp. 105–155). New York: Academic Press.

Unger, D. G., & Wandersman, L. P. (1985). Social support and adolescent mothers: Action research contributions to theory and practice. *Journal of Social Issues, 41,* 29–45.

Unger, D. G., & Wandersman, L. P. (1988). The relation of family and partner support to the adjustment of adolescent mothers. *Child Development, 59,* 1056–1060.

United States Advisory Board on Child Abuse and Neglect. (1990). *Child abuse and neglect: Critical first steps in response to a national emergency*. US DHHS Publication No. 017-092-00104-5. Washington, DC: U.S. Government Printing Office.

Wasserman, G. A., Green, A. & Rhianon, A. (1983). Going beyond abuse: Maladaptive patterns of interaction in abusing mother-infant pairs. *Journal of the American Academy of Child Psychiatry, 22,* 245–252.

Willis, D. J. & Holden, E. W. (1990). Etiological factors contributing to deviant development. In J.H. Johnson & J. Goldman, (Eds.), *Developmental assessment in clinical child psychology: A handbook*. New York: Pergamon Press.

Wolfe, D. A. (1985). Child-abusive parents: An empirical review and analysis. *Psychological Bulletin, 97,* 462–482.

# CHAPTER 4

# The Prevention of Child Maltreatment in School-Age Children

MINDY S. ROSENBERG AND DANIEL J. SONKIN

The school-age period has not received its share of attention in the empirical evaluation of prevention programs for child *physical* abuse, in contrast to the extensive literature on maltreatment prevention in the prenatal/perinatal and preschool periods (see Holden, Willis, & Corcoran, p. 17; and Culbertson & Schellenbach, p. 47). Efforts to prevent *sexual* abuse per se have been the main focus of maltreatment prevention programs during the school-age period (see Finkelhor and Strapko, p. 150; and Melton, p. 168; Haugaard & Reppucci, 1988). There has been no shortage of other types of prevention programs that intervene directly with school-age children, such as competency enhancement and social skill-building programs (Durlak & Jason, 1984), or those that prevent a particular behavioral problem including substance abuse (Albino, 1984), school maladjustment (Cowen, Trost, Dorr, Lorion, Izzo, & Isaacson, 1975), or social isolation (e.g., Conger & Keane, 1981). By drawing attention to the gap in maltreatment preventive programs for school-age children and their families, this chapter will hope to restimulate interest in thinking about the needs of this population.

This chapter begins by providing the rationale for intervening to prevent child maltreatment during the school-age period, followed by a discussion of parenting tasks encountered during the elementary school years. Examples of two problematic family situations in which children are at risk for maltreatment will be analyzed: substance-abusing caregivers and marital violence. Within each family situation, attention is given to the nature of the problem as it affects school-age children and their parents, and specific issues to consider in developing preventive interventions for that population.

## RATIONALE FOR MALTREATMENT PREVENTION DURING THE SCHOOL-AGE PERIOD

There are several reasons to target school-age children and their families for child maltreatment prevention efforts. First, statistics on age of onset for various types of maltreatment suggest that the developmental period spanning the ages of six through 12 years represents the highest risk period for at least one type of maltreatment; namely, sexual abuse (Finkelhor & Baron, 1986). Second, by reviewing the statistics on the various ages at which maltreated children come to the attention of authorities (as opposed to the age at which maltreatment actually begins), it is apparent that elementary school-age children are identified in substantial numbers as experiencing all types of maltreatment. Some of these children may have been abused or neglected since infancy or early childhood but the maltreatment was detected once the child entered school. For others, the maltreatment may have begun sometime after the child entered school. However, the fact that so many children are identified as potentially maltreated during this developmental period suggests a third reason for planning preventive interventions at this time, and that is to take advantage of the child's (and thereby the family's) expanding connection with the community once the child enters school. Even the most isolated families will need to contend with the myriad changes brought on by their child's increased involvement with school and other community settings. A more detailed discussion of each of these reasons for targeting this population of children and their families follows.

## ONSET OF MALTREATMENT DURING THE SCHOOL-AGE YEARS

Are elementary school-age children at greater risk than children of other ages for experiencing certain forms of maltreatment? The answer to this question appears to be *yes* for the onset of sexual abuse. As Finkelhor and Baron (1986) note in their review of studies on children's age at onset of sexual abuse, vulnerability to this form of maltreatment increases between the ages of six to seven years and then again at 10 years. However, during the ages of 10 to 12 years, children are sexually victimized at more than twice the average rate. The National Incidence Study (1982) reports that half the female victims of sexual abuse are 11 years old or younger, yet the incidence rate for sexual abuse is highest among adolescent females aged 12 to 17 years. One should note that the sampling strategy may have skewed the age distribution of reported cases because those agencies included in the study (e.g., public schools) tend to have more contact with older children; while agencies who typically see younger children (e.g., day care centers, medical clinics) were not sampled. With this caveat in mind, the findings indicate that although children between the ages of six and 11 years are 33 percent of the general child population, they represent 36 percent of substantiated maltreatment cases in the sample. Both the 1982 and the more recent 1988 study report that the incidence of child physical abuse increased with age (U.S. Department of Health and Human Services, 1988). In contrast to preschool children (i.e., ages 0–5 years) whose percentage of fatalities are disproportionately high (74%), elementary school-age children sustain 2 percent of the fatalities, and approximately equal percentages of injuries and/or impairments that can be classified as "serious" or "moderate."

Similarly, the American Humane Association's (1987) study of child maltreatment cases reported to child protective service agencies indicated that six to 11 year-old children represent approximately 31 percent of all children in the United States and 33 percent of reported maltreatment cases. Regardless of which study's results are cited, it is clear that a substantial percentage of school-age children are reported as experiencing all forms of maltreatment, although information is not available on the children's age at which maltreatment began. The identification of substantiated cases during the school-age period does not tell us how many of those children experienced the cumulative effects of maltreatment that began earlier in their lives and how many children were reported maltreated shortly after the fact. Additionally, the data does not provide information about how many children are living in family circumstances that place them at risk for maltreatment.

## CHILD AND FAMILY TRANSITION TO SCHOOL

A major developmental task facing families with children aged five to six years is the child's transition from primarily family-dominated involvement to school and community activities. For some children, this transition occurs much earlier if the child is in family day care or attends a day care center or preschool. Although the transition to school for these families continues to represent an important developmental milestone for the child and initiates a series of life cycle changes within the family, the transition is probably not as dramatic as the one faced by families who have remained fairly isolated from social contact. Insular mothers (Wahler, 1980) and those parents who are isolated from formal and informal support networks during stressful periods tend to be at greater risk for child abuse and neglect than parents who are better-connected to their community and can rely on others outside the immediate family for support (Garbarino & Crouter, 1978). For the latter group of families, the child's transition to school is a step toward connecting the family to the outer community and an opportunity to reduce isolation. The relevance for prevention programming is not only that schools have recently become a central conduit for the delivery of many types of prevention services, but more importantly, that all children who reach school-age are mandated to attend elementary school, and therefore, become a part (to a greater or lesser extent) of an institution outside of their family and are exposed to a wider range of people, activities, and opportunities than they had been before.

## NORMATIVE TASKS FOR PARENTS DURING THE SCHOOL-AGE PERIOD

Throughout the family life cycle, parents and children are confronted with the challenge of mastering developmental tasks related to the corresponding life cycle stages. Much has been written about the *normal* family life cycle, deviations in that cycle that include divorce and remarriage, and family life cycle variations of specific populations such as the poor and different cultural groups (e.g., Carter & McGoldrick, 1980). Researchers interested in the enhancement of healthy parent-child relationships and the prevention of dysfunctional ones, including maltreatment, have focused their attention on the early stages of the family life cycle such as the transition to parenthood, and the determinants of healthy and high-risk parenting throughout the child's development (Belsky & Vondra, 1989; Pianta, Egeland, & Erickson, 1989; Wolfe, 1987).

Current thinking in the field of parenting and child maltreatment per se uses an ecological model to conceptualize factors that contribute to healthy and abusive parent-child relationships (Belsky, 1980; Garbarino, 1977). In brief, the model suggests that parental functioning is multiply determined, and is influenced by factors that relate to the personality or psychological health of the parent (e.g., parents' experience with or exposure to violence as a child), child characteristics (e.g., temperament) and contextual sources of stress and support (e.g., quality of the marital relationship, access to formal and informal support systems) (Belsky & Vondra, 1989; Wolfe, 1987). Acknowledgement is also given to macrosystem factors such as the child-rearing values and practices characteristic of the society or subculture in which the individuals, families, and communities are embedded. In addition, distinctions are made between chronic risk characteristics or conditions (i.e., vulnerability factors), short-term stresses (i.e., challengers), and factors that can offset stress and vulnerability (i.e., protective factors) in understanding the determinants of parental functioning (Belsky & Vondra, 1989; Cicchetti & Rizley, 1981).

It should be noted that the nature of family relationships evolves over time, so that what we actually observe during the school-age period is a product of how the family resolved previous transitions (e.g., transition to parenthood, to a family with young children) and coped with acute and/or chronic stressors encountered over the family life cycle. However, specific qualities of parental behavior developed as children grow older may lessen the likelihood of problematic parent-child relationships and child maltreatment. These include: 1) co-parenting; 2) authoritative parenting; 3) positive modeling of negotiation and communication skills; and 4) permeable family boundaries. Throughout childhood there is a continuing need for parents to approach children as a unified couple (or as co-parents if divorced), giving the child relatively consistent messages about discipline, school, peers, and other important aspects of the child's life. Likewise, parents must maintain their authority but at the same time be flexible enough to respond to the child's needs for autonomy and independence. Another way in which parents help their children develop in healthy ways is by modeling positive negotiation and communication skills which the child in turn will demonstrate with peers and adults outside of the family. Lastly, when the child enters school, the parents are faced with the task of creating a permeable boundary between the family, school, and the community across which information can easily flow and families can take advantage of and participate in community activities.

## FAMILY SITUATIONS PLACING CHILDREN AT RISK FOR MALTREATMENT

Two family situations are discussed that place school-aged children at risk for experiencing physical and psychological maltreatment: caregiver substance abuse, and marital violence. Within each situation, attention is given to the nature of the problem, the potential developmental obstacles posed by the family situation and the issues involved in designing preventive interventions.

### Caregiver Substance Abuse

Within the last three years, attention has been rivited to the problem of drug abuse in our society. Politicians, the media, mental health professionals, and local community leaders are in the midst of what appears to be an overwhelming battle against substance abuse. We are only beginning to document the social repercussions of substance abuse, i.e., the links between abuse of drugs to other social problems including homicide, suicide, AIDS, marital violence, the birth of crack-addicted infants and their sequelae of developmental problems, and child maltreatment. For purposes of definition, substance abuse refers to a "maladaptive pattern of psychoactive substance use indicated by either continued use despite knowledge of having a persistent or recurrent social, occupational, psychological or physical problem that is caused or exacerbated by use of the substance, or recurrent use in situations in which use is physically hazardous (e.g., driving while intoxicated)" (American Psychiatric Association, 1987, p. 169). Psychoactive substances include alcohol, amphetamines, cannabis, cocaine, hallucinogens, inhalants, opioids, PCP, and sedatives, hypnotics, or anxiolytics.

### *Overview of the Problem*

The emerging statistics on the relationship between caregiver substance abuse and child maltreatment indicate that drugs figure prominently in families where maltreatment occurs. In a national interview study of 1,681 families with children from birth to 17 years with documented child maltreatment, 10.88 percent of respondents reported on first interview that alcohol or drug dependence was a significant stressor in their family (American Association for Protecting Children, 1988). The National Committee for the Prevention of Child Abuse (Daro & Mitchell, 1989) surveyed their state liaison offices to gather information on the relationship between substance abuse and child maltreatment and found a number of dramatic results. Sixty-eight percent of those surveyed across the country reported substance abuse to be the dominant characteristic of their caseload, but specific states reported even greater problems. The Washington, DC office alone found that almost 90 percent of caretakers on child abuse caseloads were active substance abusers. Illinois statistics on the number of infants reported to protective services as a result of parental substance abuse reflected a 132 percent increase from 1987 to 1988, while New York's child neglect-related fatalities in substance-abusing homes rose from 11 percent in 1985 to 73 percent in 1987. Overall, the National Committee estimates that 675,000 children annually are seriously maltreated by drug-abusive caretakers, which translates into one out of 13.3 children with a substance-abusive parent experiences serious abuse (Daro & Mitchell, 1989).

Children who grow up in families with substance-abusing parents or caregivers are at risk for experiencing physical abuse and neglect directly, or psychological maltreatment indirectly. As Garbarino and Vondra (1987) indicate, whether caregivers physically harm children while under the influence of drugs or make substances easily available for children's use, they serve as inappropriate models and may even encourage behavior that is clearly damaging to children's psychological and physical health. In the case where children's parents are alcoholic, physical child abuse may occur when inhibitions are diminished as a result of alcohol intake, and parents are less likely to suppress aggressive or impulsive behavior (Martin & Walters, 1982). When substance abuse contributes to parental noninvolvement and emotional unavailability, then questions of physical and psychological neglect become paramount. Howard, Beckwith, Rodning, & Kropenske (1989) sum up the relationship between parental substance abuse and psychological maltreatment this way: "Parents who are addicted to drugs have a primary commitment to chemicals, not to their children" (p. 8).

An example of pervasive caregiver neglect is illustrated by the behavior of crack-addicted mothers. One of the tragic realities of crack addiction is that women, typically single mothers, comprise a substantial number of the population affected, and that they have abdicated their parental role for the pursuit of crack. Children are left alone for long periods of time without the basic necessities of food and clothing, and while high on crack, mental health professionals find these mothers oblivious to their children's needs and unreachable psychologically. The example of crack-addicted mothers represents the extreme end of the neglect continuum, but there are less blatant illustrations of noninvolvement in substance-abusing caretakers that also qualify as psychological neglect. Parents whose substance preoccupation takes precedence in their lives are unable to attend consistently to their children's emotional needs or provide the psychological guidance so crucial to the nurture of school-age children, such as encouraging the development of competencies, fostering a positive self-concept, supporting academic learning, monitoring peer relationships, and helping develop self-discipline and self-control. Moreover, children who observe caregiver substance abuse may be learning powerful messages about the strategies that adults use to handle emotion (e.g., anger, anxiety, pain), interpersonal conflict, and that obtaining and using substances take priority over children's socioemotional and physical well-being.

## Issues in Prevention

For the most part, preventive interventions with substance-abusing caretakers who are also at risk for maltreating children have focused on mothers of infants and very young children, usually no older than preschoolers. Project Futures in Illinois is a good example of such a program, serving cocaine-dependent women and their children from birth to 2 years in a multiagency cooperative where services are designed with the dual purpose of preventing drug abuse and child maltreatment. Since researchers and mental health professionals are only beginning to document the psychological and developmental sequelae of children born to substance-abusing parents, there is comparatively less information available about the cumulative psychological effects for school-aged children. Preventive programs for parents of school-age children with a dual substance and child abuse emphasis are rare at the present time. A crucial first step before designing empirically based interventions for prevention of substance and child abuse is to generate basic research data on the risk factors that predispose parents to both situations. Moreover, the ecological context that places caregivers at risk for abusing alcohol and maltreating their children may differ from one that promotes abuse of harder substances, such as cocaine. For purposes of this chapter, it would also be helpful to investigate the ways in which these risk factors may interact with the demands of raising school-age children.

Efforts to prevent the onset of substance abuse apart from child maltreatment and vice versa have been launched through media campaigns. At present, however, there has been no attempt to inform the public of the potential relationship between the two social problems. Media campaigns rest on the assumption that increased understanding of the issue and where and how to reach for help are the basis for any preventive effort (Rosenberg & Reppucci, 1985). Increasing public awareness about caregiver substance abuse and the heightened risk of child maltreatment cannot proceed without the concomitant focus on training professionals to identify and respond in a coordinated manner to both problems. Mental health professionals, physicians, nurses, and social service staff are beginning to join forces across disciplines to meet the challenge of working with this difficult population.

One example of an innovative approach to the joint problems of substance and child abuse is illustrated by a program at San Francisco General Hospital to support grandmothers caring for grandchildren as a result of their daughters' drug and alcohol abuse, mental illness, or incarceration (D. Miller & S. Trupin, personal communication, February, 1990). The program began in response to observations noted by physicians and nurses in outpatient public health clinics that the medical problems of a sizable number of poor, black, middle-age to elderly female patients began to worsen, and the women missed appointments and showed indications of despair and depression. When questioned further, it became apparent that the women were under significant stress from trying to assume child-rearing responsibilities as a result of their daughters' abdication of their parenting role, leaving children unsupervised and in potentially dangerous situations. Although it is not uncommon in the African-American community for grandmothers to help care for their grandchildren, this particular situation is complicated by the duress of having a drug-addicted daughter and the unique psychological problems that these children demonstrate, either as a result of being drug-exposed *in utero* and/or as a consequence of their home environment. Thus, these grandmothers and great-grandmothers who thought they were finished with parenting duties and were looking forward to their golden years were now forced into caring for children ranging in age from infancy to adolescence.

Initially, Doriane Miller, an internist, and Sue Trupin, a nurse, began a weekly social support and mutual self-help group for grand- and great-grandmothers to share their anger, rage, and frustration at being forced into the primary caretaker role, to educate themselves about the present difficulties of raising young children in contrast to 20 years ago, and to develop strategies for coping with their drug-addicted or mentally ill adult children. Over time, the group also took on an advocacy role, as for example, in trying to change the local department of social services' policy that made it difficult for relatives to qualify for child-related financial support without first adopting the children. Grandparents attend and are vocal participants at public hearings related to families and drug abuse, they have testified at city agencies, a department of public health, and at Assemblyman Thomas Bates' committee on drug abuse. Miller and Trupin have also testified to the House Select Committee of Children, Youth, and Families on the effects of crack cocaine on the extended family.

Over 30 grandmothers have participated in the support groups since their inception in approximately 1990, and several of these women have now begun additional support groups in other communities. Although empirical information is not yet available, the group leaders plan to track the effects of group participation on self-esteem, self-efficacy, coping strategies, and medical status. Anecdotal reports from physicians suggest that group participation is associated with improved medical prognosis and a decrease in depressive symptoms. With regard to the children, group leaders observed that because of their myriad behavioral and emotional problems, it is not uncommon for the leaders to make treatment referrals to psychologists. Consideration is also being given to the possibility of forming children's support groups.

At this point, there is no empirical data on whether this type of intervention actually prevents child abuse and neglect, but there are several reasons why it merits consideration as a preventive strategy and further investigation with child maltreatment prevention as a distal programmatic goal. First, in many cases, the grandmothers assumed childcare responsibilities as a direct result of court action in which the child was found abused, neglected, abandoned, or in danger of maltreatment during a dependency hearing. In other cases, children were observed to be neglected, and grandmothers informally took over childcare duties. In either situation, the children were at risk, or had already experienced some form of maltreatment. Then, intervention by the grandmothers could be considered secondary prevention in some cases and tertiary prevention in others, however, because the children themselves often present the grandmothers with overwhelming behavioral and emotional demands, the stress of raising these children contribute to the women's medical problems, depression, anger and resentment. Support groups could function to reduce the risk of child abuse and neglect while in the grandmothers' care. By providing enough support and access to essential resources, such intervention could also help the grandmothers continue to care for their grandchildren and prevent unnecessary out-of-home placements.

The Marin Institute for the Prevention of Alcohol and Other Drug Problems in California is an example of an organization that works with grassroots community groups to facilitate the development of solutions to the prevention of substance abuse in participating communities (Wechsler, 1988). Although the Institute is not currently involved in programs that focus on the dual problem of substance abuse and child maltreatment, their work can serve as an example of how to use community organizing principles to generate support for the development of preventive programs for this challenging problem.

One of the strategies used to garner community support for the prevention of substance abuse is the following. Typically, a community organizer is invited in by a grass-roots group to help form a council composed of lay people representing a cross-section of the community. The councils' goal is to develop a prevention plan to answer the specific needs of that community. At this writing, three communities are in the process of writing their plans, each approaching substance abuse prevention from a different angle. One community is particularly concerned with the problem of crack cocaine and its relationship to child maltreatment and other social issues. This council has discussed the need for more research on the relationship between substance abuse, marital violence, and child maltreatment and recognizes the need for professional and public education and training. Hopefully, the development of preventive interventions that address both substance abuse and child maltreatment will be the next step in this exciting process. By empowering lay people to identify and respond to the unique needs of their community, we may find that the development of preventive interventions more closely matches the needs of the targeted population.

## Marital Violence

Although increasing attention in this country has been focused on battered women since the mid-1970s, in the years since 1985 substantial research and mental health efforts have been concentrated on marital violence including battered women, men who batter, and the children who may be the sole witnesses to the violence between their parents. Until recently, however, researchers tended to isolate marital violence from other forms of violence toward family members (Rosenberg, 1987a), so that early studies in this area did not articulate the potential linkages between wife battering and child physical or sexual abuse. The tragic case of Lisa Steinberg in New York City, the six-year-old girl who was beaten by her "adoptive" father and left dying while his battered partner Hedda Nussbaum, looked on helplessly, is a clear illustration of the potential relationship between wife battering and child maltreatment (*Newsweek December 12, 1988, pp. 56–61*).

### Overview of the Problem

In their initial national survey data of spouse and child abuse in 2,143 families, Straus, Gelles, and Steinmetz (1980) found that 12 percent of spouses reported an incident of marital violence in the previous year; 28 percent said there had been a violent incident in the course of their marriage; and 3.6 percent of parents acknowledged using severe violence against their child in the previous year. Based on these estimates, the authors extrapolated that there were approximately 1.8 million women victimized annually by their husbands and 1.7 million abused children in the United States in 1975. The 1985 survey replication with 3,520 families indicated that the overall couple violence rate declined from 160 per thousand families in 1975 to 158 per thousand families a decade later (Straus & Gelles, 1986). Similarly, the replication data indicated that rates of severe violence toward children had decreased as well. In 1975, 36 parents per 1,000 of children aged three to seventeen reported using severe violence toward their children; while in 1985, that figure dropped to 19 parents per 1,000 (Gelles & Straus, 1988). Although the validity of the second survey's results has been subjected to much methodological criticism, the authors (Gelles & Straus, 1988; Straus & Gelles, 1986) believe that there has been a decrease in the rate of violence toward children and, to a lesser extent, toward women. Included among their explanations in support of their data are increased alternatives for battered women, the availability of prevention and treatment programs, and legal deterrence.

What is the relationship between marital violence and physical child abuse? Based on the initial national survey data, Straus (1983) found that seven to 10 percent of parents who reported no instances of marital violence abused their children frequently during the previous year. In contrast, fathers who abused their wives frequently during the previous year had dramatically elevated rates of abuse toward their children. For mothers, the rate of child abuse for those who experienced their husband's violence was almost double to those who had never been beaten.

Similarly, in their sample of violent, discordant, and satisfactorily-married couples, Rosenberg and Rossman (1989) identified two family environments where school-aged children were at risk for abuse as measured by the Child Abuse Potential Inventory (Milner, 1980). In the first case, families were of low socioeconomic status and defined by the presence of couple physical and verbal aggression and high dissatisfaction with the marital relationship. The second case was a magnification of the first, in that these families were also of low socioeconomic status, had the highest level of couple physical violence, were the least satisfied maritally, and represented the most dangerous environment for children (i.e., the greatest potential for abuse).

Children who witness their parents' violence but are not themselves abused physically are also at risk for experiencing a range of behavioral and socio-emotional problems (Rosenberg, 1987b; Rosenberg & Rossman, 1990). Many in the field of family violence research and service consider witnessing marital violence one form of psychological maltreatment (e.g., Rosenberg, 1987a; Walker & Edwall, 1987). In fact, the greatest risk factor for abusing one's spouse as an adult male is to have witnessed marital violence as a child (Hotaling & Sugarman, 1986). Unfortunately, there are no epidemiological studies on the incidence or prevalence of children who witness marital violence, although Carlson (1984), projecting from the Straus et al. (1980) national survey data estimates that at minimum, 3.3 million children between the ages of three and 17 are at risk for exposure to marital violence. Therefore, children who grow up in families witnessing their parents' violence are also at risk for experiencing physical and/or psychological abuse, and constitute an important group to consider when designing prevention programs.

### Issues in Prevention

In general, programs to prevent child maltreatment in the context of marital violence have been relatively rare, and in the cases where such programs exist, they have not been subjected to longitudinal, carefully controlled evaluation that we are just beginning to see in child maltreatment prevention programs (cf. Daro, 1988; Olds & Henderson, 1989). For the most part, programs have either focused on preventing child maltreatment or preventing marital violence (Straus & Smith, 1990; Swift, 1988). It remains an empirical question as to which combination of prevention strategies are appropriate to address the dual problems of child abuse and marital violence.

Swift (1988) adapted a systems-oriented prevention formula from George Albee (1981) to organize the major factors associated with behavioral and social problems such as family violence:

$$\text{Incidence of Dysfunction} = \frac{\text{Stress} + \text{Risk Factors}}{\text{Social Supports} \times \text{Coping Skills} \times \text{Self-Esteem}}$$

As Swift explains, prevention strategies aimed at changing the equation's numerator have focused on reducing environmental or intrapersonal sources of stress while those aimed at the denominator have focused on ways of increasing environmental or interpersonal social supports or improving intrapersonal skills and abilities. Since risk factors tend to be personal characteristics or situations that are out of people's control (e.g., gender), they are often difficult to modify. In the case of marital violence and child abuse, stressors may be chronic or temporary, and may include such factors as unemployment, pregnancy, and poverty. Examples of risk factors in child physical abuse and marital violence are children with handicaps, gender, and parents' experience with or exposure to severe violence in their childhoods. Social supports refer to informal (i.e., relatives, friends) and formal resources (i.e., mental health and medical personnel, religious leaders) that offer help with childrearing and support through listening to problems, providing feedback or advice, and decreasing isolation. Coping skills include broad areas of competence and those behavioral and emotional skills specific to the target problem(s). For instance, parenting and marital communication and problem-solving skills are relevant to outcomes of family violence. Self-esteem refers to individuals' perceptions of their personal resources and abilities. The factors in this equation can be applied to such prevention goals as preventing the development of abusive behavior or preventing victimization (e.g., strengthening coping skills, ensuring children's safety).

Researchers and clinicians have proposed a variety of family violence prevention ideas that speak to each of the components of the above equation. For example, Swift (1988) describes programs to reduce stress (e.g., providing specific job skills to the unemployed), to reduce risk status (e.g., support, education, and respite care for parents with children who have handicapping conditions), and to increase social support, coping skills and self-esteem. In the domain of coping skills, Straus and Smith (1990) suggest that family problem-solving courses and workshops be offered through high schools, religious organizations, or other community groups, to provide skills for resolving interpersonal conflicts through negotiation, compromise, and reciprocity. Whereas these ideas have been offered as strategies to prevent family violence, it still remains an empirical question as to whether they actually do reach their distal prevention goal of reducing the incidence of marital violence and child maltreatment.

Parent education and related support services have traditionally been included as core components of a multifaceted network of services to prevent child maltreatment and enhance healthy child development (Cohn, 1983; Daro, 1988; Rosenberg & Reppucci, 1985; Zigler & Hall, 1989). Similarly, shelters for victims of domestic violence have typically made available parent education and support services to women with children who participate in their residential and out-client programs. Parenting information has been delivered in the form of group meetings, individual sessions, and/or during naturally occurring problem situations between mothers and children while at the shelter. Women are also taught to identify and attend to their partners' signals of impending violence and to develop strategies to ensure their children's safety, should they decide to return to their partner. Shelters routinely have a house policy of nonviolence that frequently challenges the women's use of physical disciplinary strategies towards their children and presents multiple opportunities to discuss alternative, nonviolent childrearing techniques. However, in addition to handling generic parenting difficulties, it is not uncommon for shelter staff to identify family situations where children are at risk for maltreatment, to observe extremes in parenting behavior that qualify as physical abuse and neglect, or to learn that a child has been sexually abused. Thus, the shelters are in a unique position to provide preventive services to this high-risk population and to intervene and stop maltreatment that has already occurred (i.e., tertiary prevention). In addition, both shelters and researchers are in a position to work collaboratively and collect data about the effectiveness of such programs to prevent child maltreatment.

## CONCLUSION

It is now well known that child maltreatment is multiply determined, and therefore prevention programs need to take a multifaceted approach to developing effective interventions. The most successful programs integrate a number of components that address the various factors implicated in the etiology of child maltreatment (e.g., stressors, risk factors, support systems, development of coping skills). Many programs, however, sacrifice the distal goal of preventing child maltreatment for immediate proximal goals and as a result seldom know the ultimate long-term effectiveness of their interventions.

More recently, both researchers and clinicians have realized that there is considerable overlap in the various types of child maltreatment. In addition, we now understand that child maltreatment does not occur in isolation from other significant social problems. Therefore, continued cross-fertilization between the various interest groups within the child maltreatment field will help promote more comprehensive prevention programs. Likewise, creating links between the child maltreatment field and other areas of social concern will help expand our understanding of these problems by focusing on situations of particular risk for child maltreatment, such as drug addiction, marital violence, poverty, and homelessness.

Although hundreds of child maltreatment prevention programs currently exist across the country, few programs make themselves known through publications and those that do are often anecdotal descriptions rather than methodologically sound evaluation. It is important that links are created between community based organizations and researchers. The agency has the advantage of having its finger on the pulse of the community. The academic has the understanding of theory, assessment and evaluation strategies. Therefore, a combined effort can make a greater difference than either one could do alone. Innovative ideas can be the seeds and the fruits of such cooperative commitment time, resources, research and evaluation efforts.

## REFERENCES

Albee, G. W. (1981). Preventing psychopathology in the community mental health centers. In *The health care system and drug abuse prevention: Toward cooperation and health promotion.* (DHHS Publication No. ADM 81-1105) Washington, DC: U.S. Government Printing office.

Albino, J. E. (1984). Prevention by acquiring health-enhancing habits. In M.C. Roberts & L. Peterson (Eds.), *Prevention of problems in childhood* (pp. 200–231). New York: John Wiley & Sons.

American Association for Protecting Children (1987). *Highlights of official child neglect and abuse reporting 1985.* Denver, CO: American Humane Association.

American Association for Protecting Children (1988). *Highlights of official child neglect and abuse reporting, 1986.* Denver, CO: American Humane Association.

American Psychiatric Association (1987). *Diagnostic and statistical manual of mental disorders* (3rd ed. rev.). Washington, DC: Author.

Belsky, J. (1980). Child maltreatment: An ecological integration. *American Psychologist, 35,* 320–335.

Belsky, J., & Vondra, J. (1989). Lessons from child abuse: The determinants of parenting. In D. Cicchetti & V. Carlson (Eds.), *Child maltreatment: Theory and research on the causes and consequences of child abuse and neglect* (pp. 153–202). Cambridge, MA: Cambridge University Press.

Carlson, B. E. (1984). Children's observations of interparental violence. In A. R. Roberts (Ed.), *Battered women and their families: Intervention strategies and treatment programs* (pp. 147–167). New York: Springer.

Carter, E. A., & McGoldrick, M. (Eds.). (1980). *The family life cycle: A framework for family therapy.* New York: Gardner Press.

Cicchetti, D., & Rizley, R. (1981). Developmental perspectives on the etiology, intergenerational transmission and sequelae of child maltreatment. *New Directions for Child Development, 11,* 31–56.

Cohn, A. (1983). *An approach to preventing child abuse.* Chicago: National Committee for Prevention of Child Abuse.

Conger, J. C., & Keane, S. P. (1981). Social skills intervention in the treatment of isolated or withdrawn children. *Psychological Bulletin, 90,* 478–495.

Cowen, E. L., Trost, M. A., Dorr, D. A., Lorion, R. P., Izzo, L. D., & Isaacson, R. V. (1975). *New ways in school mental health: Early detection and prevention of school maladaptation.* New York: Human Sciences Press.

Daro, D. (1988). *Confronting child abuse: Research for effective program design.* New York: The Free Press.

Daro, D. & Mitchell, L. (1989). *Child abuse fatalities continue to rise: Results of the 1988 annual fifty state survey.* Chicago: National Committee for the Prevention of Child Abuse, Fact Sheet No. 14.

Durlak, J. A., & Jason, L. A. (1984). Preventive programs for school-aged children and adolescents. In M.C. Roberts & L. Peterson (Eds.), *Prevention of problems in childhood* (pp. 103–132). New York: John Wiley & Sons.

Finkelhor, D., & Baron, L. (1986). High-risk children. In D. Finkelhor (Ed.), *A sourcebook on child sexual abuse* (pp. 60–88). Beverly Hills: Sage.

Garbarino, J. (1977). The human ecology of child maltreatment: A conceptual model for research. *Journal of Marriage and the Family, 39,* 721–726.

Garbarino, J., & Crouter, A. (1978). Defining the community context for parent-child relations: The correlates of child maltreatment. *Child Development, 49*, 604–616.

Garbarino, J., & Vondra, J. (1987). Psychological maltreatment: Issues and perspectives. In M. R. Brassard, R. Germain, & S. N. Hart (Eds.), *Psychological maltreatment of children and youth* (pp. 25–44). New York: Pergamon Press.

Gelles, R. J., & Straus, M. A. (1988). *Intimate violence: The definitive study of the causes and consequences of abuse in the American family*. New York: Simon & Schuster.

Haugaard, J., & Reppucci, N. D. (1988). *Child sexual abuse*. San Francisco: Jossey-Bass.

Hotaling, G. T., & Sugarman, D. B. (1986). An analysis of risk markers in husband to wife violence: The current state of knowledge. *Violence and Victims, 1*, 101–124.

Howard, J., Beckwith, L., Rodning, C., & Kropenske, V. (1989). The development of young children of substance-abusing parents: Insights from seven years of intervention and research. *Zero to Three, 9*, 8–12.

Martin, M. J., & Walters, J. (1982). Familial correlates of selected types of child abuse and neglect. *Journal of Marriage and the Family, 44*(2), 267–276.

Milner, J. S. (1980). *The child abuse potential inventory: Manual*. Webster, NC: Psytec Corporation.

Olds, D. L., & Henderson, Jr., C. R. (1989). The prevention of maltreatment. In D. Cicchetti & V. Carlson (Eds.), *Child maltreatment: Theory and research on the causes and consequences of child abuse and neglect* (pp. 722–763). Cambridge, MA: Cambridge University Press.

Pianta, R., Egeland, B., & Erickson, M. F. (1989). The antecedents of maltreatment: Results of the Mother-Child Interaction Research Project. In D. Cicchetti & V. Carlson (Eds.), *Child maltreatment: Theory and research on the causes and consequences of child abuse and neglect* (pp. 203–253). Cambridge, MA: Cambridge University Press.

Rosenberg, M. S. (1987a). New directions for research on the psychological maltreatment of children. *American Psychologist, 42*, 166–171.

Rosenberg, M. S. (1987b). Children of battered women: The effects of witnessing violence on their social problem-solving abilities. *Behavior Therapist, 10*(4), 85–89.

Rosenberg, M. S., & Reppucci, N. D. (1985). Primary prevention of child abuse. *Journal of Consulting and Clinical Psychology, 53*, 576–585.

Rosenberg, M. S., & Rossman, B. B. R. (1989, August). *Children of violent parents: Child coping and control*. Paper presented at the annual convention of the American Psychological Association, New Orleans, LA.

Rosenberg, M. S., & Rossman, B. B. R. (1990). The child witness to marital violence. In R. T. Ammerman & M. Hersen (Eds.), *Treatment of family violence: A sourcebook* (pp. 183–210). New York: Wiley & Sons.

Straus, M. A. (1983). Ordinary violence, child abuse, and wife beating: What do they have in common? In D. Finkelhor, R. J. Gelles, G. T. Hotaling, & M. A. Straus (Eds.), *The dark side of families: Current family violence research* (pp. 213–234). Beverly Hills: Sage.

Straus, M. A., & Gelles, R. J. (1986). Societal change and change in family violence from 1975 to 1985 as revealed by two national surveys. *Journal of Marriage and the Family, 41*, 75–88.

Straus, M. A., Gelles, R. J., & Steinmetz, S. K. (1980). *Behind closed doors: Violence in the American family.* New York: Doubleday/Anchor.

Straus, M. A., & Smith, C. (1990). Family patterns and primary prevention of family violence. In M. A. Straus & R. J. Gelles (Eds.), *Physical violence in American families: Risk factors and adaptation to violence in 8,145 families* (pp. 507–528). New Brunswick, NJ: Transaction Publishers.

Swift, C. F. (1988). Stopping the violence: Prevention strategies for families. In L. A. Bond & B. M. Wagner (Eds.), *Families in transition: Primary prevention programs that work* (pp. 252–285). Beverly Hills: Sage.

United States Department of Health and Human Services (1982). *National study of the incidence and severity of child abuse and neglect* (DHHS Publication No. OHDS 81-30329). Washington, DC: U.S. Government Printing Office.

United States Department of Health and Human Services (1988). *National study of the incidence and prevalence of child abuse and neglect.* Washington, DC: U.S. Government Printing Office.

Wahler, R. G. (1980). The insular mother: Her problems in parent-child treatment. *Journal of Applied Behavior Analysis, 13*, 207–219.

Walker, L. E. A., & Edwall, G. E. (1987). Domestic violence and the determination of visitation and custody in divorce. In D. J. Sonkin (Ed.), *Domestic violence on trial: Psychological and legal dimensions of family violence.* New York: Springer.

Wechsler, R. (1988). Community organizing principles for local prevention of alcohol and drug abuse. In A. Mecca (Ed.), *Prevention 2000: A public/private partnership.* Berkeley, California: The California Health Research Foundation.

Wolfe, D. A. (1987). *Child abuse: Implications for child development and psychopathology.* Beverly Hills, CA: Sage.

Zigler, E. & Hall, N. W. (1989). Child abuse in America. In D. Cicchetti & V. Carlson (Eds.), *Child maltreatment: Theory and research on the causes and consequences of child abuse and neglect* (pp. 38–75). Cambridge, MA: Cambridge University Press.

# CHAPTER 5

# *Preventing Adolescent Maltreatment*

JAMES GARBARINO

Abuse and neglect are embedded in a wide range of adolescent problems—delinquency, parricide, running away, and prostitution—to name but four that are mentioned frequently in research and clinical reports, with the degree of coincidence being in excess of 65 percent in some samples. These problems provide an important link in the contextual understanding of efforts to prevent adolescent maltreatment. A second aspect of that context is public and professional stereotypes about adolescents.

Some of the most prominent observers of adolescence in the 1950s and 1960s saw negative stereotypes of youth as both the cause and effect of adolescent alienation from the adult world. Classics such as Paul Goodman's *Growing Up Absurd* (1956), Edgar Friedenberg's *The Vanishing Adolescent* (1959) and *The Dignity of Youth and Other Atavisms* (1965) explored this theme. Goodman's title is self-explanatory. Friedenberg emphasized the way adults often regard adolescents, generally with fear and contempt. High schools are the principal arena in which adult society plays out this theme:

> They are problem-oriented and the feelings and needs for growth of their captives and unenfranchised clientele are the least of their problems; for the status of the teenager in the community is so low that even if he rebels, the school is not blamed for the conditions against which he is rebelling. What high school personnel become specialists in, ultimately, is the *control* of large groups of students. (Friedenberg, 1965, pp. 92–93)

Twenty years later, as controlling school crime and meeting basic scholastic requirements have become dominant issues, Friedenberg's analysis remains appropriate. What is more, as public sympathy for troubled adolescents turns

The author acknowledges the assistance of Andrew Kelley, Wendy Gamble, Janet Sebes, and Cynthia Schellenbach in the research and literature review upon which the chapter is based. [Based in part upon an invited address to Division 37 (Children, Youth, and Families) of the American Psychological Association's Annual Convention, August 25, 1984, Toronto, Canada.]

to public support for *get tough* (e.g., through *tough love* programs), Frieden-berg's words may come to be applied with equal validity to families and the models for parents.

In her book *Children Without Childhood* (1983), Marie Winn speaks of the "myth of the teenage werewolf":

> A pervasive myth has taken hold of parents' imagination these days, contributing to their feeling of being powerless to control the fates of their children: the myth of the teenage werewolf. Its message is that no matter how pleasant and sweet and innocent their child might be at the moment, how amiable and docile and friendly, come the first hormonal surge of puberty and the child will turn into an uncontrollable monster. (p. 14)

These images of adolescence contribute to the context in which the dynamics of adolescent maltreatment take place, *and in which those who would prevent it must operate.* These images find their professional parallel in the widely held images of adolescence as necessarily stormy and stressful (*Sturm und Drang*) (Garbarino, Kelley, & Schulenberg, 1985; Kelley & Garbarino, 1985). In this view, adolescents experience conflict and turmoil as a *normal* part of their development. Many who hold this view most strongly have studied or worked professionally with disturbed adolescents engaged in deviant behavior.

Along these lines, Anna Freud (1958) wrote of the difficulty of distinguishing normality from psychopathology in adolescence:

> . . .adolescence constitutes by definition an interruption of peaceful growth which resembles in appearance a variety of other emotional upsets and structural upheavals. The adolescent manifestations come close to symptom formation of the neurotic, psychotic or dissocial order and merge almost imperceptibly into borderline states, initial, frustrated or fully fledged forms of almost all the mental illnesses. Consequently, the differential diagnosis between the adolescent upsets and true pathology becomes a difficult task." (p. 267)

Anna Freud viewed adolescence as a developmental disturbance derived from the reawakening of libidinal impulses that marks the movement from the latency period into the pubertal period. Teenagers experience psychic conflict as they try to balance their Oedipal impulses with what society dictates as correct behavior. Childhood defenses (repression, rationalization, and projection) keep these Oedipal desires from awareness, and thereby permit escape from uncomfortable and threatening turmoil.

As the individual matures, this defensive balance (preliminary and precarious as it is) becomes more and more inappropriate. It can't accommodate the powerful sexual drives that are resurgent in adolescence. Adolescents must overthrow their old systems and build new ones. This process results in the rebellion, the ups and downs, and the dramatic changes that Anna Freud saw as being typical of adolescence.

Although this "period of upheaval" is a healthy, normal expression of development, adolescents will reject their parents in response to the unacceptable desire to possess the opposite sex parent, and enter into a series of intense but brief romantic involvements with their peers as they learn to accept and adapt to their new-found sexuality.

This behavior will be perceived as rebellion. It provides a theoretical explanation for the stereotyped view of adolescents as being necessarily rebellious. It is interesting to recall what Anna Freud (1958) wrote concerning what is occurring when such "structural upheavals" and "rebellious" activities do *not* occur.

> . . .we all know individual children who as late as the ages of 14, 15, or 16 show no such outer evidence of inner unrest. They remain, as they have been in dealing with the latency period, 'good' children, wrapped up in their family relationships, considerate sons of their mothers, submissive to their fathers, in accord with the atmosphere, ideas, and ideals of the childhood background. Convenient as this may be, it signifies a delay of normal development and is, as such, a sign to be taken seriously. . . . These are children who have built up excessive defenses against their drive activities and are now crippled by the results, which act as barriers against the normal maturational processes of phase development. They are perhaps more than any others, in need of therapeutic help to remove the inner restrictions and clear the path for normal development, however 'upsetting' the latter may prove to be. (p. 265)

From A. Freud's psychoanalytic perspective, the exhibition of "storm and stress" in the form of conflict with parents is not only a *natural* experience but it is also a *necessary* occurrence for normal adolescent development to occur. The "upholding of a steady equilibrium during the adolescent process is in itself abnormal" (A. Freud, 1958, p. 275). This undermines the validity of adolescent acting out behaviors as indicators of disrupted development, family conflict, or psychopathology. As such it may undermine our ability to deal with adolescent maltreatment by casting its results as "just a phase," when in fact it is a genuine crisis. Preventing adolescent maltreatment may depend upon our ability to take seriously its consequences and origins.

But is the storm and stress view valid? Anthropologists such as Margaret Mead and Ruth Benedict challenged it on the basis of their observations in other cultures. Survey research in the United States indicates that while adolescence is usually a time of family challenge *adolescents are not normally either crazy or highly rebellious.*

The first systematic research evidence that teenagers in modern Westernized societies do not necessarily experience major problems of adjustment was presented by two sociologists, Westley and Elkin (1956). Their small sample of middle-class adolescents in Montreal, Canada, reported little turmoil. Instead, they presented a picture of relative calm and stability. Douvan and Adelson (1966) conducted a study in which they extensively interviewed over 3,000 adolescents. The sample was constructed in such a way as to be representative of the entire United States population of boys and girls facing adolescence, although it was restricted to teenagers in school and somewhat underrepresented low income and racial minority youth. In this broad, more representative sample, there also was little evidence of *major* turmoil and conflict.

In fact, their data presented a picture of the *typical* adolescent as a somewhat conservative and conforming individual, to which Anna Freud might respond that this only shows how widespread is the problem of abnormal placidity.

> The adolescent at the extremes responds to the instinctual and psychosocial upheaval of puberty by disorder, by failures of egosynthesis, and by a tendency to abandon earlier values and object attachments. In the normative response to adolescence, however, we more commonly find an avoidance of inner and outer conflict, premature identity consolidation, ego and ideological constriction, and a general unwillingness to take psychic risks. The great advantage of the survey technique is that it allows us to study these adolescents who make up the middle majority, who evoke neither grief nor wonder, and who all too often escape our notice. (Douvan & Adelson, 1966, p. 351)

Douvan and Adelson's study has been criticized for the fact that their interviewers were not mental health professionals (and thus presumably were more likely to miss signs of distress), but subsequent studies that *have* employed mental health professionals interviewing nonpatient populations have confirmed the finding that the majority of adolescents do *not* show overt signs of disorder. Of course, the psychoanalytically-oriented professional could respond that this shows that most adolescents suffer from the problem of no problems.

One of the most extensive early studies of adolescent normality was the Normal Adolescent Project carried out by Daniel Offer and his colleagues (Offer, 1969; Offer & Offer, 1973, 1974, 1975). Offer directed an eight-year project using a sample of 73 typical middle-class, male teenagers in the Midwest United States. The boys were assessed at various times from their freshman to senior years of high school. The assessment procedure consisted of parent interviews, psychological tests, and psychiatric interviews. In addition, 61 of the original 73 subjects were assessed in the same manner during their four years of college (and this reference to college attendance indicates the relative affluence of the sample).

Offer and his colleagues identified three major patterns of growth for these adolescents. *Continuous growth* refers to a gradual, smooth transition from adolescence to young adulthood, free from the turbulence and turmoil predicted by the storm-and-stress theorists. *Surgent growth* refers to a less gradual developmental pattern, where growth occurs in spurts, between which development appears arrested. Most of the teenagers in this study developed in one of these two models—experiencing little or no stress and discomfort on their way to normal, adaptive adjustment to adulthood. A third pattern of growth was termed *tumultuous growth*, and corresponds to the kind of inner turmoil and crisis pattern the storm and stress hypothesis predict for all adolescents. Twenty-one percent of the sample evidenced this kind of developmental process, a large enough minority to show that there are sufficient troubled adolescents to sustain the professional stereotype of storm and stress, but too few to validate the claim that it is the typical adolescent pattern.

In another study, Rutter, Graham, Chadwick, and Yule (1976) studied a large representative sample of all of the 14-to-15 year olds on the Isle of Wight in Great Britain. They found only a very slight increase in psychopathology from middle childhood to adolescence and a very low incidence of rejection or relationship difficulties between adolescents and parents. Interestingly, however, they found that about 22 percent of their sample reported that they *often* felt miserable or depressed, and were having trouble sleeping. This is almost the exact percentage that reported this pattern in the studies by the Offers (1973, 1974, 1975). About 44% reported feeling miserable and depressed *at times*. We should note that in Michael Rutter's study (1976) the incidence of psychopathology (as assessed by a formal psychiatric interview) was 16.3 percent among their sample, so that there is a difference between reporting depression and being considered clinically depressed.

Therefore, we have evidence from two fairly large-scale studies that about 20 percent of nonpatient adolescents report experiencing serious turmoil as they grow up. This is far short of the majority predicted by storm and stress theorists, and it tells us that we should be alert to families that are experiencing a high level of conflict, for it is not typical or normal to do so. In a survey of college students, Balswick and Macrides (1975) found that only 22 percent reported that they had been rebellious as teenagers.

In their study of middle-class families of adolescent boys, Bandura and Walters (1959) also found little evidence of storm and stress. When teenagers did exhibit aggressive behavior, such as fighting physically with their parents, it was found that these youth presented the same problems as when they were children. It was only when they became bigger and stronger that they could overpower their parents, a finding to which we will return. Bandura and Walters concluded: "Our findings suggest . . . that the behavioral characteristics exhibited by children during the so-called adolescent stage are lawfully related to, and consistent with, pre-adolescent behavior" (Bandura and Walters, 1963, p. 196). Subsequent research tends to confirm this conclusion (Ebata, 1986).

The general conclusion that profound conflict and turmoil across all life's domains is not the typical pattern of development for adolescents receives support from other studies of nonclinical populations (Grinker, Grinker & Timberlake, 1962; Hamburg, Coelho & Adams, 1974; Oldham, 1978; Weiner, 1970). It seems fairly well established then that when one looks at the data, the typical adolescent is *not* one who is experiencing far-reaching psychic disturbance as a matter of predetermined developmental course. Keep in mind also, that no period in the human life course is totally free from stress and conflict. Adolescents certainly have no monopoly on storm and stress, no more so than toddlers or middle-agers. All this reveals that seriously troubled youth should be taken seriously, and that the behaviors often identified as symptoms of adolescent maltreatment are usually indicators of genuinely serious problems, often problems of family breakdown associated with the special challenges of adolescence.

But why do negative stereotypes of adolescence continue? Why is the myth of the teenage werewolf so durable? Several hypotheses are plausible. From a psychoanalytic perspective, the negative stereotype may serve an important function for adults. It may act as a kind of defense mechanism by transferring onto adolescents responsibility for the envy that the no-longer-young feel for the sexuality and freedom of the young. It may also serve to justify the structures of social control that adults impose in schools and in families.

From a more ecological perspective, these negative stereotypes are part of the larger macrosystems that rationalize and organize social relations (Bronfenbrenner, 1979; Garbarino & Associates, 1985). In this view negative stereotypes of adolescence reflect a combination of factors: Resistance to change in power dynamics, naïve overgeneralization from the behavior of the *tumultuous* minority to the *continuous* majority of teenagers, and a lack of empathy and absence of self-understanding on the part of adults who do not see the parallels between adolescent and adult behavior.

Whatever the source of these negative stereotypes, they are real and they contribute to the problems of troubled youth in troubled families. They justify unresponsive parenting and exacerbate family conflict of the serious variety. They color and interpret the normal challenges to the family system that *do* inhere in adolescence in modern societies. All told, they seriously complicate the task of preventing adolescent maltreatment. To overcome this obstacle, it is essential to see clearly the challenges faced by parents dealing with adolescents.

## THE CHALLENGE OF BEING PARENT TO AN ADOLESCENT

What does adolescence mean for the family as a whole? For one thing, it means adjusting patterns of authority and interaction to incorporate a *new person.* Developmental psychologist John Hill (1980) has looked at the research on this matter, and he concludes that:

> Studies where family interaction is directly observed suggest that there may be a period of temporary disequilibrium in early adolescence while the family adjusts to having a new person in the household—"new" in stature, "new" in approaching reproductive capability, new in cognitive competence—but this disequilibrium in no way approaches the shoot-out that many parents are led

to expect from media reports. Instead, in most families, there appears to be a period of adaptation to the primary changes, a period when both parents and their newly adolescent children work out—often not consciously—what these changes mean for their relationships. (p. 33)

At its heart, the task of being parent to an adolescent (and adolescent to a parent) substantially differs from the parent-child relationship in ways which have implications for preventing adolescent maltreatment (Garbarino & Gilliam, 1980; Garbarino, Schellenbach, Sebes, & Associates, 1986).

The adolescent's power is much greater than the child's. This includes physical power, of course, including the capability for physical retaliation if assaulted by a parent. The adolescent requires a reorganization of family roles. The enhanced power that comes with adolescence accompanies the need to redefine family roles, and is often a destabilizing force, particularly when parents and/or adolescents have little motive or facility for flexible negotiation and compromise. These changes in power and role set in motion challenges to the family. A family's success or failure in meeting these challenges depends in large measure upon the character of the human ecology within which that family is embedded.

## A DEVELOPMENTAL APPROACH TO THE ECOLOGY OF MALTREATMENT

Researchers have come to recognize that adolescence provides an important illumination of basic developmental processes. Models of adolescence reveal heightened attention to the role of culture and society in development, as observers seek to relate individual identity formation to social change and ideological transformation. These issues are ripe for an ecological perspective, with its insistence upon attention to interactive effects, to the relations of individuals and social systems, to the interaction of biology and society, of personality and culture, of organismic systems and social systems, and to the interplay of science and policy (Bronfenbrenner, 1979; Garbarino & Associates, 1982). These issues emerge in a review of the challenges to family systems inherent in Western-style adolescence, as has been indicated earlier. But this same ecological perspective sheds light on the very concept of maltreatment as it applies to adolescents.

### Maltreatment as a Social Judgment

To label a pattern of behavior as *maltreatment* is to make a social judgment (Garbarino & Gilliam, 1980; Garbarino, Guttmann, & Seeley, 1986). It is to assert that a particular pattern of behavior is inappropriate and puts the "victim" at risk for impaired development. There is no objective reality to the concept of maltreatment apart from the historical process in which negotiated settlements between science and culture, professional expertise and community standards, arise, are affirmed, revised, reconsidered, and reaffirmed. The concept of maltreatment is thus intrinsically social and historical in nature. What *then* was acceptable may *now* become redefined or "discovered to be" inappropriate and damaging.

Whereas once it was entirely appropriate to transport a young child on the front seat of an automobile, it is now an act of neglect to do so. A generation of improved scientific knowledge and professional expertise have provided the basis for child advocacy aimed at altering community standards of care. The result is a redefinition of *neglect*. It is within this fundamental process (i.e. that defining maltreatment is an act of science-based advocacy) that we must understand adolescent maltreatment. We start from the proposition that adolescent maltreatment only exists insofar as advocates define a standard of care that receives community endorsement.

Practitioners have long recognized that the service needs of children and adults differ markedly, with respect to issues of informed consent, placement, verbally mediated therapy, and other aspects of intervention. Placing adolescents on this continuum of maturity has proven even more difficult. This is particularly evident in our efforts to understand and deal with abuse and neglect. Most approaches differentiate between child abuse and spouse abuse, but only recently have a few researchers, practitioners, or policy makers differentiated *child* abuse and neglect from *adolescent* maltreatment. However, both policy and services should reflect changes in the meaning, causes, correlates, and effects of maltreatment as a function of development and maturation (Cicchetti & Rizley, 1981; Garbarino, Schellenbach & Sebes, 1986).

The issues for school-age children differ from those for infants, or even for three-year olds, for that matter. The infant is a perfect victim in two senses. First, the infant can do virtually nothing to protect itself from abuse and is totally defenseless against neglect. The battered baby is victimized in direct proportion to the parent's impulses and the presence of internal and external constraints, which are often few. The infant experiences neglect in exact proportion to the parent's failure to provide care, thus being liable to nonorganic failure to thrive. What is more, the infant's capacity to signal its plight to others is limited and largely unconscious. On the other hand, the infant is perfectly blameless when victimized. There is no issue of culpability raised, as there often is when the victim of assault is a spouse or an adolescent.

In contrast to infants, school-age children have better resources. They can adapt to the parent to minimize abuse by assuming whatever role will appease the parent, e.g, by being extremely compliant, innocuous, or responsible. They can counteract neglect by fending for themselves to some degree. Their ability to communicate their plight is greater because of language skills and attending school offers many opportunities to do so. Finally, they are likely to have larger independent social networks from which to draw nurturance, support, and protection. However, what they gain in power they lose in credibility as a victim. This sort of developmental contrast is essential when we consider adolescent maltreatment.

When a child reaches adolescence, developmental shifts and changes in social expectations for caregiving and socialization come together to shift the standards which guide appropriate behavior in family relationships. Some forms of behavior by parents toward their offspring which were appropriate (if not particularly wise) in childhood may become abusive in adolescence. For example, the psychological connotations and behavioral response to spanking a three or four year old (*control through force*) are usually different from those of spanking a 15 year old. Likewise, a permissive policy of *control through indulgence* that is possible in response to the child's relatively benign impulses may become untenable in adolescence, for even the most permissive parent cannot fully indulge the more powerful impulses of the adolescent. Also, managing every detail of a four year old's daily existence (*control through intrusion*) may be acceptable, while the same intrusiveness with a teenager would be entirely inappropriate and is likely to produce a strong adverse reaction leading to family conflict.

This is crucial because observational research (Reid, 1986) shows that abusive families are behaviorally differentiated from nonabusive families in their handling of the 5-10 percent of parent-child interactions that are negative. Nonabusive families are able to conclude, or at least terminate, these negative interactions quickly. Abusive families are ineffective and become enmeshed in escalating conflict. It is possible that some of the families using the strategies enumerated earlier (control through force, indulgence, or intrusion) become abusive in adolescence because these approaches are no longer adequate to prevent or put the lid on negative exchanges and prevent the escalation of conflict.

Adolescents typically demand a more nearly equal role in family decision-making. Observational research presents a picture of the youth challenging the parents (particularly the father) for a more active role in leading family discussions and decision-making (Steinberg & Hill, 1980).

These factors, combined with differences in our culture's view of adolescents (with suspicion) and in our institutional treatment of them (with little compassion), suggest that the phenomenon of adolescent maltreatment will differ from child abuse. In fact, as we shall see, in their interpersonal dynamics and cultural interpretation, such destructive relations may more closely resemble spouse abuse than the maltreatment of children. Efforts to understand adolescent maltreatment may serve as a bridge to constructing a much needed, general life-course theory of domestic violence, one that can integrate policy and services in this area.

### A Life-Course Perspective

Figure 5.1 places abused adolescents on a circular continuum relating abused wives, maltreated children, and abused elders. The central issue is power,

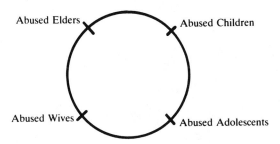

**Figure 5.1.** Continuum of abuse victims.

the ability to determine one's own behavior, and influence the actions of others. Children and the frail elderly are nearly powerless, though their behavior can have a significant effect on what happens to them. Teenagers gain power because of increases in the ability to think, argue, and act that adolescence brings. Just as wives in a patriarchal and sexist society are powerful enough to threaten the authority of husbands, teenagers can challenge parental authority. Paradoxically, because children and the elderly are powerless they are perfect victims for two reasons. First, they are easily victimized. Second, they elicit sympathy once they are abused. Teenagers are closer to wives in being imperfect victims, in both respects.

One piece of evidence of the greater power of abused teens and wives is the fact that they sometimes are involved in reciprocal assault (cf. Browne, 1987; Post, 1982). Obviously, children and elderly cannot match the strength of the parent generation, but abuse has been identified as a contributing factor in many assaults by adolescents, from relatively minor incidents to parricide (Garbarino & Gilliam, 1980). Wives who kill their husbands often do so in retaliation for abuse, usually at the culmination of a long period of mutual assault in which wives are the chronic losers. Straus, Gelles, & Steinmetz (1980) reported assault by youth against their parents in some 10 percent of American families. The likeness between adolescent and wife abuse extends beyond these power dynamics, of course. The two groups are likely to face similar psychodynamic issues, including ambivalence about dependency and separation in their relationships with family authority figures. For example, both may engage in repeated attempts to flee the home, only to return when the challenges of independent living and/or the pain of separation is too great.

This analysis of the conceptual issues involved in understanding the developmental context of adolescent development sets the stage for examining the research on adolescent maltreatment with an eye to implications for prevention as a matter of policy and practice. We can begin with a catalog of the studies.

## RESEARCH FINDINGS ABOUT ADOLESCENT MALTREATMENT

Research on adolescent maltreatment is limited to a handful of small-scale studies and several major surveys. Before examining the substance of this small body of research it is worth cataloging the available data sources.

The surveys are the National Incidence Study (1988), the American Humane Association's annual tabulation (1982), and the national probability sample assessed for domestic violence by Straus, Gelles, & Steinmetz (1980). The small-scale studies include clinical and questionnaire studies of identified or suspected cases of adolescent maltreatment (see Garbarino, Schellenbach & Sebes, 1986, for a complete review).

In the mid 1970s, the National Incidence Study collected data on suspected abuse and neglect which occurred in a sample of 26 U.S. counties located in 10 states. In addition to child protective service agencies, other local agencies were surveyed, including schools, hospitals, police, and courts. This resulted in the identification of what would be projected nationally to be approximately 650,000 distinct cases. This study is being replicated, with results expected in 1988.

The American Humane Association's National Study of Child Abuse and Neglect Reporting tabulates and analyzes cases reported to and accepted by official child protective service agencies. The reports are compiled on a state by state basis and approximately 80 percent of the states participate in the program. The study reports "occasion analyses" that shed light on child-adolescent contrasts.

Straus, Gelles, & Steinmetz (1980) assessed the level of violence in a national sample of more than 1000 U.S. families that contained two parents and at least one child three years of age or older in the mid 1970s. This survey was replicated (with some differences in sampling approach and survey methodology) in the mid 1980s (Straus & Gelles, 1986).

In addition to these large-scale national surveys, some 7 small scale studies serve to illuminate adolescent maltreatment. Berdie and colleagues (1983) studied 163 families from two separate samples. The subjects were being served by specialized adolescent maltreatment programs. Farber and his colleagues (1984; 1986) studied 77 families in which an adolescent was being served by an adolescent maltreatment demonstration treatment project. These adolescents had been identified by a local protective service agency (40 percent of the sample), a runaway youth center (31 percent), a hospital abuse team (20 percent), or some other agency (9 percent).

Garbarino and his colleagues (1980; 1984) studied two samples: 209 cases of maltreatment (100 of which involved adolescents) reported to a local child protective service agency and 61 families representing a spectrum of adolescent adjustment problems (22 of whom were later judged to have experienced maltreatment). Libby & Bybee (1979) studied all 25 cases of adolescent abuse reported to a local child protection agency over a ten-month period. They excluded all sexual abuse cases from the analysis.

Lourie (1977) surveyed 258 cases and conducted an in-depth clinical assessment of 70 of the cases of confirmed adolescent abuse reported to a local child protection agency. Pelcovitz and his colleagues (1984) studied 33 adolescents (from 22 families) reported to a local child protective service agency and referred to a hospital-based treatment program.

The large-scale surveys and the smaller studies began to map the social terrain of adolescent maltreatment. The National Incidence Study indicated that despite public and professional emphasis on *child* abuse and neglect, *adolescent* maltreatment accounts for some 47 percent of the known cases of maltreatment (42 percent of the cases according to Holmes & Olsen's (1986) analysis of these same data which eliminated all unsubstantiated cases). This finding is especially dramatic since teenagers account for only 38 percent of the population under the age of 18. As noted earlier, adolescent cases are less likely to be reported to protective service agencies, and this is the presumable source of the discrepancy.

Studies confined to specific localities report findings somewhere between the National Incidence Study and the American Humane Association figures (Morgan, 1977). This seems to derive from differences in local reporting and definitional practices, as well as from differences in the composition of the populations included.

Much of the existing body of research on abuse and neglect is based on hospital and protective service samples. This has biased designs and findings against adolescent victims who are less likely to be identified and served by these agencies. The National Incidence Study found that adolescent abuse cases were less likely to be reported to the protective services system than were cases involving abuse of other age groups (24 percent for children vs. 61 percent for adolescents). An analysis conducted by the American Humane Association (Trainor, 1984), indicated, however, that the likelihood that adolescents will receive services once reported to protective services has risen as professional awareness of the problem has grown (e.g., from 33 percent receiving services in 1976 to 55 percent in 1982). Adolescent maltreatment tends to be associated with problematic acting-out behavior of the teenager or dysfunction within the family, and tends to be dealt with as such by agencies other than protective services. These cases may often be buried under the labels of *dysfunctional families*, *school adjustment problems*, *running away*, *acting out*, or *marital problems*, even when there is no apparent difference in the level of abuse experienced (Farber et al., 1984). This has implications for sampling in studying adolescent maltreatment as well as for policies and practices designed to prevent it.

## RESEARCH-BASED HYPOTHESES AND IMPLICATIONS FOR POLICY AND PRACTICE IN PREVENTING ADOLESCENT MALTREATMENT

Drawing upon the available research, we now are in a position to put forth seven hypotheses concerning the prevention of adolescent maltreatment. Each is based upon an attempt to synthesize existing findings.

HYPOTHESIS NO. 1. *Prevention programs should target adolescent maltreatment, because the incidence of adolescent maltreatment equals or exceeds the incidence of child maltreatment.* We cannot justify the current disregard for adolescent victims that is evident in service delivery systems. Adolescent victims are numerous and exhibit many signs of harm (Burgdorff, 1980). The National Incidence Study reports that adolescents receive less severe physical injuries and experience more psychological maltreatment, and more sexual abuse than do youngsters (Olson & Holmes, 1983). The National Incidence Study reported that physical assault constitutes a smaller proportion of cases (42 percent vs. 52 percent) while psychological abuse accounts for a larger proportion (32 percent for adolescents vs. 25 percent for children.)

HYPOTHESIS NO. 2. *Females appear more likely to be abused as they pass through adolescence than in childhood, while risk for males peaks early and generally declines through adolescence. Therefore, prevention programs should give special attention to the issues faced by families with female adolescents.* The National Incidence Study reported females outnumbering males two to one (Olsen & Holmes, 1983). Small studies tend to confirm this, with the reported figures ranging from 55% female (Garbarino, Schellenbach & Sebes, 1984) to 77% (Lourie, 1977). There are few exceptions, such as the 45% female figure in the Pelcovitz (1984) study. This suggests that services that are attuned to adolescent females must be especially vigilant for evidence of maltreatment. This evidence is to be found in direct and indirect reports by young people. For example, Farber and his colleagues (1984) used the Conflict Tactics Scale (c.f. Straus, Gelles, & Steinmetz, 1980) as an instrument to detect maltreatment of adolescents. Many clinicians rely upon open-ended intake interviews for all adolescents receiving social, educational, or health services, including physical and mental health services.

HYPOTHESIS NO. 3. *Some cases of adolescent maltreatment are simply a continuation of abuse and neglect begun in childhood; others represent the deterioration of unwise childhood patterns or the inability of a family that functioned well in childhood to meet new challenges in adolescence. Child abuse prevention programming is insufficient to deal with the problem of adolescent maltreatment, because it does not deal with adolescent onset situations but is essential to reduce the overall problem of maltreated teenagers.* The relative proportion of adolescent maltreatment cases in the two categories (child vs. adolescent onset) varies from study to study based in part, it seems, on differences in definition and/or sampling. Lourie (1977) concluded that 90 percent of adolescent abuse cases begin in adolescence. In Libby and Bybee's study (1979) 80 percent were so described. Garbarino and Gilliam (1980) reported a 50-50 split. Pelcovitz (1984) observed a 57 percent adolescent onset. Farber and Joseph (1986) reported that 29 percent displayed adolescent onset, while 51 percent began in childhood but became qualitatively more severe in adolescence, and 21 percent were severe through childhood into adolescence. Berdie and her colleagues (1983) concluded that 24 percent of their adolescent cases began in adolescence.

Taken together, the existing studies tell us that there is a distinctly adolescent genesis in a significant number of adolescent maltreatment cases. This means that our preventive efforts must not be limited to programs and policies aimed exclusively at infancy and early childhood. They should address the special issues involved in the transition from childhood to adolescence (e.g. negotiated role transitions in families). Thus, for example, the late elementary and early junior high school period is a high priority period for interventions that teach nonviolent conflict resolution skills to both parents and youth.

HYPOTHESIS NO. 4. *Unlike families at high-risk for child maltreatment, families at high-risk for destructive parent-adolescent relations are socioeconomically equivalent to low-risk families. Therefore, prevention programs should reach across the board, regardless of socioeconomic resources.* Despite the finding that family income is not a powerful predictor of risk for adolescent maltreatment, some research does suggest that a *feeling* of deprivation and strained resources associated with larger family size may play a role (Vondra, 1986). The big social class differences that characterize *child* maltreatment cases are largely absent (or at least are attenuated) in the case of adolescent maltreatment. This is evident in the National Incidence Study. Adolescent abuse families were half as likely as child maltreatment cases to be earning less than $7,000 per year, and three times as likely to be earning $15,000 per year or more. Nonetheless, 66 percent of the adolescent maltreatment cases had family incomes below $15,000— with 25 percent below $7,000 and 33 percent above $15,000 (Burgdorff, 1980). Berdie and colleagues (1983) reported that about 51 percent of the families in her study had incomes less than $15,000. Garbarino and Gilliam (1980) had reported findings consistent with the National Incidence Study. What is more, when they compared adolescent onset cases with childhood onset-adolescent maltreatment cases, they found even more striking differences. The adolescent onset cases were about half as likely to be in the poverty group as the child onset (and child maltreatment) cases. In the protective service-based sample, adolescent onset families were four times as likely to have incomes in excess of $11,000 (in 1978 dollars): 42 percent versus 11 percent. Garbarino and colleagues (1984) report no difference in family income between families judged to be abusive and families judged nonabusive; about half of each group of families have incomes of nearly $20,000 (in 1982 dollars).

Several studies have used measures of social class that are not based on income. The National Incidence Study reports higher educational levels for parents of maltreated adolescents than maltreated children. Farber and Joseph (1986) report that their families were predominantly lower class with an average Hollingshead Index of 53. Pelcovitz and his colleagues (1984) report that 59 percent of their families were classified in the two top socioeconomic groups, with a five-point Hollingshead Index. Libby and Bybee (1979) indicate that only 12 percent of their families were located in the lowest (of eight) socioeconomic status categories. Garbarino and his colleagues (1984) report no difference between families judged to be abusive and comparable nonabusive families on a Hollingshead Index.

These findings, too, tell us that conventional public welfare approaches aimed exclusively at *child* abuse are insufficient to deal with *adolescent* maltreatment. A more broadly-based and community-oriented mental health approach is in order. Service institutions that are regularly in contact with middle-class families must be drawn into efforts to deal with adolescent maltreatment. These include private clinics, schools, churches, and civic groups. Of course the good news here is that these families may have a good prognosis for responding to preventive programming.

HYPOTHESIS NO. 5. *Families at high-risk for maltreatment in adolescence are more likely to contain stepparents. Therefore, stepfamilies should be a special target for preventive programming aimed at adolescent maltreatment.* A variety of analyses point to the stepparent-adolescent relationship as a very risky one, particularly among families in which adolescents exhibit developmental pathology (e.g., Kalter, 1977; Daly & Wilson, 1981). Studies of maltreatment tend to confirm this. Libby & Bybee (1979) reported that 28 percent of their families were stepfamilies; an additional 8 percent were adoptive. Berdie and colleagues (1983) reported that 25 percent of their families were step, and 31 percent had no father figure in the home. Olson and Holmes' (1983) analysis of data from the National Incidence Study revealed that 40 percent of the adolescent maltreatment cases contained a stepparent. Garbarino and colleagues (1984) found that 41 percent of the families judged to be abusive were stepfamilies, versus none judged nonabusive. Farber & Joseph (1986) reported that only 30 percent of their adolescents were living with both biological parents.

These data suggest that special programming for persons involved in stepfamily relationships is imperative. This is a high priority target, particularly in cases where youths evidence disrupted psychosocial development before entering a step-arrangement. Indeed, where research has addressed this matter at all (e.g., Garbarino, Schellenbach, Sebes, & Associates, 1986) it has suggested that it is the challenge of coping with a teen who is already at risk because of prior disruption (e.g., divorce) that tends to precipitate maltreatment crises in stepfamilies.

HYPOTHESIS NO. 6. *Adolescents at high risk for maltreatment are less socially competent and exhibit more developmental problems than their peers. Therefore, prevention programs must respond to the additive and interactive nature of adolescent maltreatment (i.e., that adolescence may be precipitating and/or exacerbating patterns of difficulty rooted in childhood).* Most studies have commented upon the aversive and/or dysfunctional character of the adolescent victim of maltreatment. Libby & Bybee (1979) reported that in more than 90 percent of the cases they studied, specific abusive incidents were *preceded* by negative adolescent behavior, such as disobeying or arguing. Was this negative behavior the result of earlier maltreatment? The studies do not provide clear evidence on this score. None offers the kind of prospective, longitudinal design that would be necessary. Certainly in a general way parents are responsible for the outcomes evidenced by their children. However, it is undeniable that maltreatment is not the sole source of problematic development in children. Temperamental problems, parent-child mismatches, negative extrafamilial influences, and genetic predisposition to pathology all play a role. Although we cannot be confident about the pattern of causation, the pattern of association is evident: preventing adolescent maltreatment involves helping parents (and other adults) work effectively and nonabusively with troubled and troublesome teenagers.

Berdie and her colleagues (1983) report that 49 percent of their adolescent maltreatment victims exhibited significant clinical indicators of depression. Problems such as nervous habits, isolation, poor social skills with peers, lethargy, low self-esteem; low frustration tolerance, temper outbursts, and stubbornness characterized from 45–70 percent of the adolescents, depending upon which problem is being considered in the analysis.

Garbarino and his colleagues (1986) used the Achenbach Child Behavior Checklist to assess the presence of problems in abused adolescents. Having selected a sample to maximize the presence of such problems (i.e., the overall group's score is at the 85th percentile on such problems), the important finding was in the contrast between maltreated and nonmaltreated youth. The abused group was significantly more problem-ridden (the 90th versus the 80th percentiles): evidencing between 50 percent and 100 percent more problems, depending upon the type of problems being considered and the source of the report. The difference was greater for externalizing problems (e.g., aggression, delinquency) than for internalizing problems (e.g., somatic complaints, obsessive-compulsive behavior, withdrawal). Programming and policy that is aimed at adolescent maltreatment should be a high priority for institutions serving adolescents who evidence developmental problems. These youth are the principal high-risk group to be targeted for preventive and protective intervention.

HYPOTHESIS NO. 7. *Families characterized as high risk for adolescent maltreatment are also at high risk on the dimensions of adaptability, cohesion, support, discipline, and interparental conflict. Therefore, prevention programs aimed at adolescent maltreatment should adopt a broadly based approach to supporting and redirecting family systems. However, these programs should recognize that in some cases servicing the family may be untenable, and direct services to support the adolescent as an independent individual may be the most practical approach.* Lourie's (1977) model of family functioning offered three categories of adolescent abuse: 1) families that continued a childhood pattern; 2) families that escalated from harsh (though nonabusive by community standards) punishment in childhood to abuse in adolescence; and 3) families that functioned normally in childhood but in which the transition to adolescence precipitated abuse. This early formulation figures prominently in many subsequent analyses of family functioning in adolescent maltreatment.

Libby and Bybee (1979) reported that 13 of their 25 cases could be characterized as "reasonably well-functioning families who had recently been under stress." The other 12 cases were characterized by "psychopathology or disturbed behavior by either the adolescent or parents." Few cases seemed to be attributable to the high stress/social isolation syndrome that is characteristic of many child maltreatment families. In contrast, Berdie and her colleagues (1983) concluded that "adolescent maltreatment families, like many child maltreatment families, are multiproblem families with high rates of divorce and separation, financial stresses and family conflict." Farber and Joseph (1986) omit comment directly on family functioning, but do report that an analysis of adolescent problems did not find differences based upon Lourie's classification of maltreatment types, with its implicit classification of families.

Pelcovitz and colleagues (1984) conducted a clinical analysis of their 22 adolescent maltreatment families. They classified cases into childhood and adolescent onset. The eight childhood onset families (14 adolescents) were characterized in the multiproblem child abuse mode; that is, they manifested intergenerational abuse, spouse abuse, and developmentally inappropriate demands, all the elements of what Helfer and Kempe (1976) term "the world of abnormal rearing." The 14 adolescent-onset families (19 adolescents) fell into two categories on the basis of multiple, independent clinical assessments: seven "authoritarian" and seven "overindulgent."

The authoritarian families were characterized by paternalistic, harsh, rigid, domineering styles of childrearing. This was coupled with denial of parental feelings toward each other and about the family system. Abuse typically arose from adolescent challenge (e.g. acting out and testing behavior) that was met with overwhelming parental force. The high priority placed upon control provided the foundation for high levels of force.

In contrast, the overindulgent families were characterized by parental efforts to compensate for the emotional deprivation that they had experienced in their own childhood (e.g., 12 of the 14 parents had lost one or both of their parents during childhood). These families made few demands upon their children, set few limits, and desired a high level of emotional gratification from them. When the children reached adolescence and sought to form primary attachments outside the home or began to act impulsively in important social settings, the overindulgent parents reacted with excessive force.

Garbarino and his colleagues (1986) have contrasted the family system of families judged to be abusive with that of families judged to be nonabusive. They used an assessment of family adaptability and cohesion (FACES, c.f. Olson, 1985) to assess the overall interaction. Abusive families tended to score in the "chaotic" and "enmeshed" categories, on adaptability and cohesion, respectively. Nonabusive families scored lower on these scales, putting them in the more normal "flexible" and "connected" range. On a measure of interparental conflict, adolescents in the abusive families tended to rate their parents as evidencing more conflict. However, the average difference masks the fact that some abusive families evidenced extremely high conflict while others evidenced extremely low conflict. This pattern was evident in a two-year follow-up in which it appeared that some families dealt with conflict by expelling the adolescent, while others simply suppressed all manifestations of conflict through a conspiracy of silence.

Adolescents in the abusive families tend to describe their parents as being much more punishing. This is also found in an assessment of attitudes and values concerning punishment which measures risk for abuse (Sebes, 1983). The Adolescent Abuse Inventory (AAI) taps parental commitment to abusive versus nonabusive responses toward adolescent behavior. An analysis that defined any family with at least one parent in the top quartile of risk (based upon the AAI score) correctly classified as abusive or non-abusive 100% of the families that had been so described on the basis of the adolescent's comparable description of self (Sebes, 1983). This measure correctly identified 85 percent of abusive families using the descriptions of outside observers. An assessment of stressful life changes (A-FILE) (Olson, 1985) indicated 50% more recent changes in the lives of adolescents in abusive families than in nonabusive families.

Adolescent maltreatment is most likely to arise when troubled youth live within a high-risk family. In part, we should direct our efforts towards identifying family patterns in *childhood* that bode ill for effective adjustment in adolescence. Overindulgence and authoritarianism are the two parenting patterns that appear most frequently in the existing research. Parent education programs should seek to identify these high-risk patterns in childhood and redirect them toward more adaptive patterns that cast neither the child nor the parent in a dictatorial role but rather establish norms and practices of reciprocal negotiation that evolve from appropriate use of parental authority. This will help to pave the way for an effective transition to adolescence. In part, also, intervention programs should focus upon the adolescent period itself. They should stress the normal demands for adaptation that adolescence brings for youth and adult alike. Effective conflict resolution and communication skills will provide the foundation for accomplishing this important process of adaptation and preventing the deterioration of parent-child relations that may result in adolescent maltreatment.

These then are the keys to preventing adolescent maltreatment: effective intervention in child abuse to stop the child's developmental deterioration into adolescence, effective intervention with troubled adolescents to prevent them from exceeding parental coping capacity, and the promulgation of non-violent conflict resolution skills for parents and youth as part of a broad campaign to improve family functioning in adolescence.

## REFERENCES

American Humane Association. (1982). *Annual Report of the National Study of Child Abuse and Neglect Reporting.* Denver, CO: American Humane Association.

Balswick, J. O., & Macrides, C. (1975). Parental stimulus for adolescent rebellion. *Adolescence, 10,* 253–266.

Bandura, A., & Walters, R. H. (1963). *Social learning and personality development.* New York: Holt, Rinehart & Winston.

Berdie, J., Berdie, M., Wexler, S., & Fisher, B. (1983). *An empirical study of families involved in adolescent maltreatment.* San Francisco, CA: URSA Institute.

Browne, A. (1987). *When battered women kill.* New York: Free Press.

Burgdorff, K. (1980, December). *Recognition and reporting of child maltreatment: Findings from the National Incidence and Severity of Child Abuse and Neglect.* Prepared for the National Center on Child Abuse and Neglect, Washington, D.C.

Burgess, B., & Garbarino, J. (1983). Doing what comes naturally? An evolutionary perspective on child abuse. In D. Finkelhor, R. Gelles, G. Hataling, & M. Straus (Eds.), *The dark side of families* (pp. 88–101). Beverly Hills, CA: Sage.

Cicchetti, D., & Rizley, R. (1981). Developmental perspectives on the etiology, intergenerational transmission, and sequelae of child maltreatment. *New Directions for Child Development,* No. 11, 31–52.

Daly, M., & Wilson, M. (1981). Child maltreatment in sociobiological perspective. *New Directions for Child Development,* No. 11, 93–112.

Douvan, E., & Adelson, J. (1966). *The adolescent experience.* New York: John Wiley & Sons.

Ebata, A. Stability of depression in early adolescence. Unpublished dissertation, Pennsylvania State University, University Park, PA, 1986.

Farber, E., & Joseph, J. (1986). The maltreated adolescent: Patterns of physical abuse. *Child Abuse and Neglect.*

Farber, E., McCoard, W. D., Kinast, C., & Falkner, D. (1984). Violence in the families of adolescent runaways. *Child Abuse and Neglect, 8,* 295–300.

Friedenberg, E. Z. (1959). *The vanishing adolescent.* Boston: Beacon Press.

Friedenberg, E. Z. (1965). *The dignity of youth and other atavisms.* Boston: Beacon Press.

Freud, A. (1958). Adolescence. *Psychoanalytic Study of the Child, 13,* 255–278.

Garbarino, J. & Associates (1982). Children and families in the social environment. New York: Aldine DeGruyter.

Garbarino, J., & Gilliam, G. (1980). *Understanding abusive families.* Lexington, MA: Lexington Books.

Garbarino, J., Kelley, A., & Schulenberg, J. (1985). Adolescence: An introduction. In J. Garbarino & Associates (Eds.), *Adolescent development: An ecological perspective.* Columbus, Ohio: Charles E. Merrill.

Garbarino, J., Schellenbach, C., Sebes, J., & Associates. (1986). *Troubled youth, troubled families.* New York: Aldine Publishing Co.

Garbarino, J., Sebes, J., & Schellenbach, C. (1984). Families at-risk for destructive parent-child relations in adolescence. *Child Development, 55,* 174–183.

Garbarino, J., Guttmann, E. and Seeley, J. (1986). *The Psychologically Battered Child.* San Francisco: Jossey-Bass Publishers.

Goodman, P. (1956). *Growing up absurd.* New York: Vintage.

Grinker, R. R., Sr., Grinker, R. R., Jr., & Timberlake, J. (1962). A study of mentally healthy young males (homoclites). *Archives of General Psychiatry, 6,* 405–453.

Hamburg, D. A., Coehlo, G. V., & Adams, J. E. (1974). Coping and adaptation: Steps toward a synthesis of biological and social adaptation. In G. V. Coelho, D. A. Hamburg, & J. E. Adams (Eds.), *Coping and adaptation.* New York: Basic Books.

Helfer, R., & Kempe, C. H. (1976). *Child abuse and neglect: The family and the community.* Cambridge, Mass: Ballinger.

Hill, J. P. (1980). The family. In M. Johnson (Ed.), *Seventy-ninth yearbook of the national society for the study of education.* Chicago: University of Chicago Press.

Kalter, N. (1977). Children of divorce in an outpatient psychiatric population. *American Journal of Orthopsychiatry, 47,* 40–51.

Libby, P., & Bybee, R. (1979). The physical abuse of adolescents. *Journal of Social Issues, 35,* 101–126.

Lourie, I. (1977). The phenomenon of the abused adolescent: A clinical study. *Victimology, 2,* 268–276.

Morgan, R. (1977). The battered adolescent: A developmental approach to identification and intervention. *Child Abuse and Neglect, 1,* 343–348.

National Center on Child Abuse and Neglect, Study Findings (1988). *Study of The national incidence and prevalence of child abuse and neglect.* (DHHS Publication). Washington, DC: U.S. Government Printing Office.

Offer, D. (1969). *The psychological world of the teenager: A study of normal adolescent boys.* New York: Basic Books.

Offer, D., & Offer, J. (1973). Normal adolescence in perspective. In J. C. Schoolar (Ed.), *Current issues in adolescent psychiatry.* New York: Brunner/Mazel.

Offer, D., & Offer, J. D. (1974). Normal adolescent males: The high school and college years. *Journal of the American College Health Association, 22,* 209–215.

Offer, D., & Offer, J. D. (1975). *From teenager to young manhood: A psychological study.* New York: Basic Books.

Oldham, D. G. (1978). Adolescent turmoil: A myth revisited. In S. C. Feinstein & P. L. Gioracchini (Eds.), *Adolescent psychiatry, Vol. VI.*

Olsen, L., & Holmes, W. (1983). Youth at risk: Adolescents and maltreatment. Boston, MA: Center for Applied Social Research.

Olson, D. H. (1985). *FACES.* St. Paul, MN: Family Social Service, University of Minnesota.

Pelcovitz, D., Kaplan, S., Samit, C., Krieger, R., & Cornelius, P. (1984). Adolescent abuse: Family structure and implications for treatment. *Journal of Child Psychiatry, 23,* 85–90.

Post, S. (1982). Adolescent parricide in abusive families. *Child Welfare. 61,* 445–455.

Reid, J. (1986). Social interactional patterns in families of abused and non-abused children. In C. Waxler & M. Radke-Yarrow (Eds.), *Social and biological origins of altruism and aggression.* Cambridge: Cambridge University Press.

Rutter, M., Graham, P., Chadwick, O. F. D., & Yule, W. (1976). Adolescent turmoil: Fact or fiction? *Journal of Child Psychology and Psychiatry, 17,* 35–36.

Sebes, J. M. (1983). *Determining risk for abuse in families with adolescents: The development of a criterion measure.* Unpublished doctoral dissertation, The Pennsylvania State University.

Steinberg, L., & Hill, J. (1980). Family interaction patterns during early adolescence. In R. Muuss (Ed.), *Adolescent behavior and society: A book of readings* (3rd ed.). New York: Random House.

Straus, M., Gelles, R., & Steinmetz, S. (1980). *Behind closed doors.* New York: Doubleday.

Straus, M. & Gelles, R. (1986). Societal change and change in family violence from 1975–1985 as revealed in two national surveys. *Journal of Marriage and the Family, 48,* 465–479.

Trainor, C. (1984). *A description of officially reported adolescent maltreatment and its implications for policy and practice.* Denver, CO: American Humane Association.

Vondra, J. (1986). Socioeconomic stress and family functioning in adolescence. In J. Garbarino, C. Schellenbach, J. Sebes and Associates, *Troubled Youth, Troubled Families* (pp. 191–234). New York: Aldine.

Weiner, I. B. (1970). *Psychological disturbance in adolescence.* New York: John Wiley & Sons.

Westley, W. A., & Elkin, F. (1956). The protective environment and adolescent socialization. *Social Forces, 35,* 243–249.

Winn, M. (1983). *Children without childhood.* New York: Penguin Books.

CHAPTER 6

# Prevention of Neglect and Nonorganic Failure to Thrive

DENNIS DROTAR

Practitioners who are called upon to intervene in a preventive fashion with neglected and nonorganic failure to thrive (NOFT) children face formidable challenges. Current patterns of health and mental health practice and reimbursability are usually directed toward manifest clinical problems rather than prevention (Iscoe, 1981). Moreover, the families whose children are most vulnerable to neglect and NOFT often must deal with emergent stresses which limit their potential to respond to preventive efforts. Meaningful progress in prevention has also been limited by a lack of a concerted national policy to sustain and enhance families' capacities to nurture children's developmental, health and nutritional needs (Frank, Allen, & Brown, 1985; Kammerman, 1980; *National Academy of Sciences*, 1976; Zigler, Kagan & Klugman, 1983). Finally, prevention efforts are limited by an inadequate scientific knowledge base concerning the practice of preventive care for psychosocial problems. Empirical demonstrations of prevention of neglect and NOFT are rare. Descriptions of clinical intervention with these conditions have generally not focused explicitly on prevention issues (Helfer, 1982). However, by being alert to the prospects for preventive intervention suggested by empirical studies practitioners can be effective advocates who encourage families to utilize primary and secondary prevention services. Based on research and clinical experiences, this chapter describes approaches to preventive clinical management of NOFT and child neglect and the implications for research and practice.

**DEFINITION OF NEGLECT**

Objective definition of neglect and NOFT is needed to identify target populations, develop specific intervention goals, and compare findings from stud-

The following work was supported in part by National Institute of Mental Health Prevention Research Center No. 30274.

TABLE 6.1.   Expressions of Child Neglect

| Parameter | Specific Deficit | Potential Outcome |
| --- | --- | --- |
| Parental attention and availability | Stimulation Responsiveness to child | Cognitive deficit Insecure attachment |
| Food/Nutrition | Limited or inappropriate food/ nutrition | Undernutrition Failure to thrive |
| Supervision | Supervision | Accidents |
| Medical care | Well child care Noncompliance | Illness Prolonged recovery |
| Environmental safety/cleanliness | Exposure to dangerous conditions | Illness/accidents |

ies in different communities (Besharov, 1982; Garrison, 1987; Hart & Haggard, 1987). However, omissions of parental caretaking behaviors characteristic of neglect are more difficult to describe and detect than acts of commission. Definitions of neglectful behavior also depend upon community standards for adequate parenting (Korbin, 1980). The definition of ideal parental behavior, threshold for inadequate parental behavior, and standards for child neglect vary considerably from community to community (Garbarino & Crouter, 1978a; Giovannoni & Becerra, 1979). Finally, the lack of adequate norms for different aspects of adaptive parental behavior limits our ability to objectively define child neglect. Zigler (1983) suggests that different working definitions of child maltreatment are needed for different purposes. For example, narrower definitions are required for legal action to protect family rights. On the other hand, broader definitions are required for provision of services and to focus attention on at-risk families. However, all definitions must have an appropriate range and clarify objectives and intended uses (Aber & Zigler, 1981).

Neglect can be defined as a continuum of acts of omission in parental caretaking which are deficient based on community standards and which have negative consequences on the child's psychological and/or physical health (Aber & Zigler, 1981; Garbarino, Guttman & Seeley, 1986; Hart & Haggard, 1987). As shown in Table 6.1, child neglect can be expressed by lack of parental attention, stimulation, and emotional availability, inadequate provision of food and nutrition to the child, problematic supervision, lack of medical care, inconsistent medical compliance, and lack of environmental safety and cleanliness.

The acute and long term consequences of deficient parental behavior on the child's health and psychological development vary with the child's age and the severity and chronicity of neglect. For purposes of research and practice, independent assessments of parenting behaviors are highly desirable. Useful measures of parental behaviors related to neglect include the Childhood Level of Living Scale (Polansky, Chalmers, Buttenwieser and Williams, 1982), the Home Scale measure of environmental stimulation (Caldwell & Bradley, 1980), behavioral assessment of parenting behaviors related to safety, basic parenting skills, including cleanliness and meal planning (Lutzker, 1984) and pediatric standards for frequency of well child care visits and immunizations for children (Chamberlin, 1976).

## DEFINITION OF NOFT

Nonorganic failure to thrive (NOFT) is defined as a severe deficit in the child's rate of weight gain (to below the 5th percentile) based on objective norms (Hammill et al., 1979) in the absence of major organic contributions to the growth deficit (Bithoney & Rathbun, 1983). It should be noted that NOFT is one of a spectrum of problems in which environmental and organic factors interact to produce growth deficits. For example, children with primary organic disorders whose growth and development are also affected by environmental influences have special intervention needs, too (Handen, Mandell & Russo, 1986).

Because identification of NOFT is based upon objective norms for physical growth and physical diagnostic tests, objective early recognition of NOFT is certainly feasible. However, in practice it is often very difficult to differentiate environmental from organic influences on physical growth (Bithoney & Dubowitz, 1985; Casey, 1985; Gordon & Vazquez, 1985a). To identify NOFT, one must determine whether there has been significant deceleration in child's rate of weight gain (Altemeier et al., 1985a), and conduct a thorough physical exam which includes such diagnostic tests as a complete blood count and urinalysis and a careful pediatric and family history (Bithoney & Rathbun, 1983), assessment of the child's current family situation, psychological development, behavior and documentation of weight gain when given an adequate caloric intake, sometimes during a hospitalization (Schmitt, 1978) are also required.

The labels of NOFT and neglect subsume a wide range of environmental and interactional problems (Drotar, in press). While there can be overlap between neglect and NOFT, these two problems are not synonymous (Ayoub and Milner, 1985; Kotelchuck, 1980). Some NOFT children are also severely neglected, while others may be adequately cared for except for their under nutrition. In addition, children may be neglected in several ways but adequately nourished.

## INCIDENCE AND PREVALENCE OF NEGLECT AND NOFT

In light of definitional problems and the lack of uniform record keeping, the incidence and prevalence of neglect and NOFT are very difficult to establish. One might expect variations in the incidence and prevalence of neglect and NOFT depending on neighborhood and community characteristics (Garbarino & Sherman, 1980). However, available surveys report that neglect is much more common than child abuse and that neglected children number in the hundreds of thousands (American Humane Association 1986; Nagi, 1977; National Center on Child Abuse and Neglect, 1981; Wolock & Horowitz, 1984). Nonorganic failure to thrive occurs frequently (10–20 percent prevalence) in certain rural and urban ambulatory care settings (Frank et al., 1985; Mitchell, Gorell & Greenberg, 1982) and accounts for between 1–5 percent of pediatric hospital admissions of young children (Berwick, 1980; Hannaway, 1970). The Massachusetts Department of Public Health (1983) reported that more than one third of children seen in the emergency room at Boston City Hospital had severe deficits for weight and height and a cited 10 percent statewide incidence of chronic malnourishment as defined by low height for age (Massachusetts Nutrition Survey, 1983).

## EFFECTS ON PHYSICAL HEALTH AND PSYCHOLOGICAL DEVELOPMENT

Cross-sectional retrospective and prospective studies consistently indicate that neglected and NOFT children have a wide range of acute and chronic health and developmental problems which are shown in Table 6.2.

### Physical Health

Neglected children may not be seen as frequently as necessary for well child care visits and immunizations. For this reason, the health problems of neglected children may be recognized later, and necessary medical treatment may be postponed (Nakou, Adam, Strathacopoulou & Agathonos, 1982). Children with NOFT have increased frequencies of health problems relative to controls both prior and subsequent to their diagnosis (Sherrod, O'Connor, Vietze, & Altemeier, 1984). By definition, all NOFT children suffer from malnutrition serious enough to effect physical health and psychological development (Barrett, Radke-Yarrow, & Klein, 1982; Bithoney & Dubowitz, 1985; Frank, 1985). In some cases problems which accompany NOFT such

TABLE 6.2.    Physical and Psychological Sequelae of Neglect and Failure to Thrive

| Physical Health Problems | | | Psychological Problems | | |
|---|---|---|---|---|---|
| Accident | Physical illness | Malnutrition | General/specific cognitive deficits | Insecure attachment | Affective disturbance |
| | Chronic nutritional deficits/illness | | Relationship difficulties Faulty problem solving & coping Low self-esteem | | |
| | | | Lowered academic achievement | Psychological symptoms | |

as severe malnutrition, and dehydration can be life threatening (Lozoff & Fanaroff, 1975). The costs of medical services for neglected and NOFT children incurred by hospitalization in pediatric acute care and psychosomatic units and rehabilitation hospitals are considerable (Sills, 1978; Singer, 1985). Finally, it is not uncommon for neglected and NOFT children to be placed in foster care at considerable cost to society (Hopwood & Becker, 1976; Shyme & Schroeder, 1978).

## Effects on Psychological Development

Although studies of the psychological consequences of neglect and NOFT are limited by methodological problems (Lamphear, 1986; Plotkin, Azar, Twentyman & Perri, 1981) taken together, available studies underscore the vulnerability for risk experienced by neglected and NOFT children and the need for prevention.

An extraordinary range of psychological functions can be disrupted by child neglect and NOFT. Neglected children have lower intellectual abilities compared to control groups (Ammerman, Cassisi, Hersen, & Van Hasselt, 1986; Polansky et al., 1981). Children with NOFT also show greater intellectual and motor deficits than control groups (Field, 1984; Singer & Fagan, 1984).

Neglect and NOFT can also be very disruptive to socioemotional development (Egeland, Sroufe & Erickson, 1983). For example, social withdrawal, depression and behavioral problems have been documented in deprived and NOFT children (Berkowitz, 1985; Leonard, Rhymes & Solnit, 1966; Skuse, 1984). Feeding problems and disturbances in attachment are frequently encountered in NOFT children (Chatoor, Dickson, Schaefer, & Egan, 1985; Gordon & Jameson, 1979). Relative to controls, neglected children may have more aggression, conduct disorders, problems in social development and attachment (Ammerman et al., 1986). Preschoolers and school-aged children with histories of NOFT have higher frequencies of behavioral problems than controls (Hufton & Oates, 1977; Oates, 1987; Oates, Peacock, & Forest, 1985; Pollitt & Eichler, 1976). Children who experience multiple problems of NOFT, neglect, and abuse are at special risk and demonstrate serious problems such as self harming behaviors, severe social withdrawal, and temper tantrums (Money, Wolff, & Annecillo, 1972). The costs to society in terms of lost human potential and treatment of emotional disorders of neglected and NOFT children are considerable.

Preventive interventions for neglected and NOFT children should be based on scientific understanding of the factors which give rise to NOFT, neglect, and psychological sequelae. Unfortunately, scientific knowledge of the etiology of neglect and NOFT is far from being definitive (Plotkin et al., 1981). However, a conceptual framework for preventive intervention in NOFT and neglect can be developed from multiple data sources.

1. Research concerning influences on parental competence.
2. Studies of early identification and prediction of neglect and NOFT.
3. Studies of the psychological development of NOFT and neglected children.
4. The results of outcome and intervention studies with disadvantaged and malnourished children.
5. Case descriptions and interventions with neglected and NOFT children.

## ETIOLOGY OF CHILD NEGLECT AND NONORGANIC FAILURE TO THRIVE

Modern theories of the etiology of child neglect and NOFT emphasize the mutual interaction of child and environment and the role of multiple interacting systems (neighborhood, family, parent-child relationship) as causal agents (Casey, 1982; Garbarino, 1977). Belsky and his colleagues' (Belsky, 1984; Belsky, Robins, & Gamble, 1984) process-oriented contextual theory of parental competence is a useful conceptualization of the factors which contribute to neglect and NOFT. For Belsky (1984), parental competence includes sensitivity to the child's developing abilities and communications and involvement with the child and is influenced by three sets of factors: 1) parental resources such as education, attitudes toward child rearing, and parents' experience of being nurtured as a child (Frommer & Shea, 1973); 2) child's characteristics, including temperament, physical health, age; and 3) family context, including marital relationship, the quality of family social networks and resources, employment, financial resources, and community resources. Belsky et al. (1984) suggest that parental competence is multiply determined but is most vulnerable when each of the three domains (parental resources, child care characteristics, family resources) are compromised. Available empirical evidence suggests that the competence of parents of NOFT and neglected infants is limited by multiple factors. For example, parents of NOFT and neglected infants may have lower intellectual ability, educational deficits, and personality deficits which restrict their competence and self-esteem (Bruenlin et al., 1983, Polansky et al., 1981). Child characteristics such as temperament, illness, and handicap may also contribute to child maltreatment (White, Benedict, Wolff, & Kelley, 1987). In some cases, NOFT infants' physical problems may intensify parents' childrearing burdens and contribute to parental perceptions of the child as sickly (Sherrod et al., 1984, Kotelchuck, 1980).

Finally, problems in the family context may deplete maternal resources and limit access to support. Families of neglected and NOFT infants have lower economic levels (Kanawati & McClaren, 1973; Pelton, 1978; Wolock & Horowitz, 1979), higher family stress (Altemeier et al., 1979), less available extended family for help with childrearing and greater social isolation than comparison groups (Bithoney & Newberger, 1987; Garbarino & Sherman,

1980; Kotelchuck & Newberger, 1983; Seagull, 1987). Family stress and crisis emerges as a general characteristic of children who present with various forms of maltreatment (Newberger, Hampton, Marx, & White, 1986).

Altemeier and his colleagues' prospective study of a high-risk sample of mothers followed from pregnancy provides empirical support for a multifactorial etiological model (Altemeier et al., 1979). Mothers who eventually maltreated their children were more likely to identify problems in their childhood, including feelings that they were not loved. In addition, frequent life stresses such as arguments with the father, especially intermittent contacts with the child's father differentiated high-risk mothers of maltreated children from those who did not maltreat their children (Altemeier, O'Connor, Sherrod, & Vietze, 1985). Such data are consistent with the notion that neglect and NOFT reflect an overload of parental and family stresses relative to parental resources for caretaking (McCubbin & Patterson, 1983; Sherrod, O'Connor, Altemeier, & Vietze, 1985). The quality of a mother's attention to the child may be particularly sensitive to problems in her social network (Wahler, 1980; Wahler & Dumas, 1984).

The factors which trigger NOFT and neglect should be differentiated from those that maintain these problems. For example, once neglect and NOFT develop, parents' caretaking burdens may be increased by the child's deficits in social responsiveness, feeding problems, or irritability (Pollitt, 1968; Powell & Low, 1983; Powell, Low & Spears, 1987). In some cases, progressive emotional disengagement between mother and child combine with nutritional deprivation to maintain a vicious cycle of cumulative psychological risk. Evidence from controlled studies suggests that NOFT and neglect may be mediated by deficiencies in maternal behavior (Bradley, Casey, & Wortham, 1984, Linscheid & Rasnake, 1985; Polansky et al., 1981; Pollitt, Eichler & Chan, 1975; Ramey, Haeger & Klisz, 1972; Ramey et al., 1975). Once patterns of deficient maternal-child interaction have been well established, parents may come to perceive the child as quiet, sickly, or not very competent (Ayoub & Milner, 1985; Kotelchuck, 1981). Such maladaptive interactional patterns may eventually effect the quality of the child's attachment to the mother (Drotar, Malone, & Nowak, 1985; Egeland, Sroufe, & Ericksen, 1983; Gordon & Jameson, 1979; Schneider-Rosen, Braunwald, Carlson, & Cicchetti, 1985). Once established, maternal lack of availability and a child insecurity to parent attachment may have powerful effects on such developmental parameters as the child's expectations of adult availability, affect, problem solving, social relationships, and ability to cope with the demands of new and stressful situations (Aber & Allen, 1987; Main, Kaplan, & Cassidy, 1985). Chronic patterns of diminished social exchange between mother and child may eventually limit the child's sense of efficacy and disrupt affective development (Trad, 1987). Rohner (1986) has amassed an impressive array of cross-cultural evidence for the negative effects of parental neglect and rejection on children's self-esteem and emotional stability.

TABLE 6.3.  Types of Prevention

| Families at Risk (Adolescent mothers economic disadvantage) | | ↓ | ↓ | ↓ |
|---|---|---|---|---|
| Pregnancy | Newborn | Onset FTT neglect | Recognition | Chronic health/ psychological problems |
| Primary | | Secondary | | Tertiary |

## TYPES OF PREVENTIVE INTERVENTION

This preliminary framework for the etiology of neglect and NOFT and associated risk suggests possible points for preventive intervention (Table 6.3).

For example, primary prevention with high-risk populations prior to the development of NOFT or neglect is directed toward deficits in parental competence and/or family support which may trigger neglect or NOFT. In contrast, secondary prevention begins after NOFT and neglect are identified and is directed toward the prevention of medical, developmental, and emotional sequalae.

### Early Identification of NOFT and Neglect

Studies of early identification of families at risk for neglect or NOFT can identify potential targets of preventive intervention. Because it is not feasible to provide preventive intervention to large numbers of families, clinicians need an objective way to identify families at special risk for child neglect and NOFT. However, it is very difficult to predict problems such as neglect and NOFT which occur relatively infrequently in the general population without identifying a prohibitively high number of families (Butler, Starfield, & Stenmark, 1984; Kotelchuck, 1979; Light, 1973). Predictive studies have yielded mixed results. Gray, Cutler, Dean, & Kempe (1972) identified a group of families at high vs. low risk for maltreatment based on interview, questionnaire and observations of parental behavior during labor, delivery, and the post-partum period. A relatively high percentage (10%) of the high-risk group eventually were diagnosed with serious abuse. Five children in this group compared to none in the low-risk group developed NOFT.

Altemeier et al. (1979, 1985), utilized a comprehensive data set including prenatal interview, chart reviews, neonatal factors including temperament and demographic factors to predict child maltreatment within a high-risk sample. A mothers' perception of her own nurturance as a child and current family stresses predicted NOFT and neglect.

Hunter et al.'s (1978) prospective follow up of premature and newborns, correctly identified 10 of the 255 (3.9%) as being reported for abuse or neglect.

Significant differences were found between abusive and nonabusive parents on social isolation, serious marital problems, closely spaced children, and a family history of child abuse and neglect.

With respect to specific measures, promising findings concerning the predictive efficacy of family stress checklist (Murphy, Orkow, & Nicola, 1985) and a parent attitude measure (Avison, Turner, & Noh, 1986) concerning child maltreatment have been reported. On the other hand, predictions of child maltreatment based on parent-child interactions (Starr, 1987) or self report data (Bolton et al., 1985) (see Holden, Willis, & Corcoran, Chapter 2.) have not been significant.

Taken together, these findings suggest that family demographics, stress, and maternal history may be useful predictors. However, predictions have not usually focused specifically on neglect or NOFT and have not been especially powerful. Predictions have generally demonstrated adequate sensitivity (the ability to correctly identify neglected or NOFT children) but low specificity (the ability to correctly identify children who will not be victims) (Brams & Coury, 1985). Consequently, widespread clinical application of screening instruments and labeling families at risk is not warranted (Duquette, 1982). However, practitioners may wish to utilize promising objective instruments (Avison et al., 1986; Murphy et al., 1985) to identify families with special needs for preventive services.

## STUDIES OF PRIMARY PREVENTION OF NOFT AND NEGLECT

Because of their continuous access to large numbers of parents and children at important times in family development such as during pregnancy, the newborn period, and during infancy, health practitioners (physicians and nurses) are in a unique position to identify children at risk for NOFT and neglect and institute primary prevention. Promising demonstrations of primary prevention of child maltreatment have been initiated in health care settings.

### Prenatal Home Visitation

Gray et al., (1977) assigned a high-risk group to an intervention vs. control condition. Intervention included pediatric visits and phone calls and weekly home visits by lay health persons who provided support, assessed problems, and coordinated services. No group differences in abuse reports, abnormal parenting, number of accidents, child immunizations or the child's scores on the Denver Developmental Screening Test were reported. However, the severity of children's injuries from accidents was less in the intervention group.

Larson (1980) found a reduction in the rate of accidents, a trend for higher scores on the HOME scale, a lower prevalence of interactional and feeding disorders, and greater level of paternal participation in families where the health visitor made a prenatal visit compared to families who received a visit six weeks post partum or a control group. On the other hand, no group differences were found in well child care visits, immunizations, and emergency room visits.

More recently, an interesting series of preventive intervention studies have been conducted by Olds and his colleagues (Olds, Henderson, Tatelbaum, & Chamberlin, 1986a; Olds, Henderson, Tatelbaum, & Chamberlin, 1986b). In the initial study, high-risk unmarried adolescent mothers from low-income families who were visited by nurses during their pregnancy became more aware of community services, attended child-birth classes, made more extensive use of the nutritional supplement program, and reported talking more frequently to family social service providers than mothers in the control group (Olds et al., 1986a). In a subsequent study, Olds et al., (1986b), assessed the efficacy of home visits including parent education concerning infant development, involvement of family members and friends in child care and support, and linkage of family with other health and human services. Low-income adolescent mothers who had a home visit during pregnancy, transportation to well child visits, and home visits during the first two years of life were compared with groups who received components of intervention (e.g., transportation) but not extensive home visitation. There was a trend for the home-visited groups to have fewer incidents of abuse and neglect (4%) than the comparison group (19%). The nurse visited mothers had infants with happier moods, demonstrated greater concern about the child's problems, punished their children less frequently, and provided the children with a greater number of play materials. In addition, the nurse-visited group was seen for fewer emergency room visits for upper respiratory infections in the first year and were seen fewer times and had fewer accidents in the second year. On the other hand, no differences were found in developmental quotient and on several interactional measures.

## Enhancing Maternal Child Contact During the Neonatal Period

Separation of mother and child during the neonatal period can disrupt the mother-child relationship and contribute to neglect and NOFT (Klaus & Kennell, 1982), especially in highly stressed families. Although the empirical evidence that child neglect and NOFT are failures of bond formation is tenuous (Egeland & Vaughn, 1981), several investigators have found positive effects of early and extended contact on the occurrence of child maltreatment. For example, Siegel et al., 1980 randomly assigned low-income pregnant women receiving care at a public prenatal clinic to one of four groups: 1) early and extended hospital contact with their newborn and home visits by a paraprofessional infant care worker; 2) early and extended contact only; 3) home visits only; and 4) routine hospital and follow-up care. Early and extended contact explained significant amounts of variance in several measures of maternal attachment as assessed by home observations. However, background variables (marital status, race, education, maternal intelligence) accounted for more variance in maternal-child interaction than the intervention. In addition, neither the home visit or extended contact intervention affected reports of child abuse and neglect or health care utilization.

In contrast, O'Connor et al., 1980 found that maternal rooming-in and early post-partum contact was associated with fewer (10 vs. 2) cases of parenting inadequacy, as measured by physical or sexual abuse, failure-to-thrive (FTT), relinquishment of caretaking responsibilities, abandonment, neglect, or admission for a mother/infant problem. However, the overwhelming majority of the women who did not experience extended contact with their infants did not demonstrate problems in parenting. The authors suggested that extended contact may be especially beneficial to mothers who are predisposed to parenting problems related to life stresses.

The above studies indicate that although preventive interventions designed to reduce early separation and/or enhance the degree of early contact between mother and child do not have powerful effects, the effects are generally positive. Although early contact between mother and child may not necessarily prevent the occurence of neglect and NOFT, it may provide a useful support.

## Preventive Pediatric Care

Anticipatory guidance and support for parents are useful preventive measures which can be provided in pediatric care. In addition, by monitoring of the child's health status and physical growth, practitioners can identify early signs of neglect and NOFT and initiate additional support (Schmitt, 1980). Although pediatric interventions have not been shown specifically to prevent neglect or NOFT, pediatric health supervision and anticipatory guidance may enhance competent parenting. For example, Gutelious et al. (1977) reported that health supervision emphasizing counseling and anticipatory guidance given during the first three years of life to firstborn infants from low-income families had positive effects on diet, eating habits, and toilet training. Casey & Whitt (1980) found that discussions of infant social development in the context of well-child supervision were associated with improved mother-infant interaction including maternal sensitivity and cooperativeness.

Group well child care may be a cost-effective model of preventive intervention (Christophersen, 1986). Thomas, Hassanein & Christophersen (1984) demonstrated that parent educational sessions using a group format were successful in helping the majority of parents (75%) to set their water heaters correctly as a burn prevention method. The group well child format may be an effective way of enhancing nutrition and feeding, supervision, and accident prevention and should be applied to populations at risk for NOFT and neglect.

## Nutritional Supplementation

Economic disadvantage may contribute to the development of neglect and NOFT by limiting the available resources for maternal and child nutrition (Frank et al., 1985; Wolock & Horowitz, 1979). Nutritional supplementation during pregnancy and lactation has been shown to enhance infant development (Birch & Gussow, 1970; Klein et al., 1976; Joos, Pollitt, Mueller, & Albright, 1983; Rush, Stein, & Susser, 1980). The combination of educational intervention and nutritional supplementation have shown positive effects on the cognitive development of Columbian children (Grantham-McGregor, Schofield, & Harris, 1983; McKay et al., 1978). Edozien, Switzer & Bryan (1979) found that beneficial effects on infant birth weight, weight gain, and reduction in anemia were associated with participation in the Women's Infant and Children (WIC) supplementary feeding plan. Hicks, Langham, & Takenaka (1982) reported that children in rural Louisiana whose mothers received nutritional supplementation early during their third trimester of pregnancy and throughout the child's first year had higher WISC scores and less frequent behavioral problems than siblings who began the supplemental feeding programs after one year of age.

The evidence concerning the positive effects of nutritional supplementation on child development suggests that practitioners should be alert to the presence of nutritional deficits in neglected and NOFT children and help families secure necessary resources to ensure adequate nutrition for themselves and their children.

## Enhancement of Parental
## Competence and Stimulation

Deficiencies in parental stimulation are a hallmark of NOFT and neglect (Bradley, Casey & Wortham, 1984; Polansky et al., 1981). Although evidence for the primary prevention of severe parenting deficiencies is limited, preventive interventions have been shown to result in positive immediate effects for many different types of children and programs (Casto & White, 1984; Frank, 1984; Greenspan & White, 1985). For example, Ramey and his colleagues have amassed impressive evidence that the cognitive development of fetally malnourished infants from high-risk, disadvantaged families can be enhanced by intensive (daily) center-based stimulation and parent intervention (Ramey, McPhee, & Yeates, 1982; Ramey, Yeates, & Short, 1984; Zeskind & Ramey, 1978). In addition, Field, Widmayer, Stringer, & Ignatoff (1980) found that a home-based parent-training intervention improved optimal face-to-face interaction, mental development, maternal attitudes, and physical growth (weight and length) in four-month-old infants. Provence's (1985) review of the efficacy of early intervention programs for high-risk disadvantaged children cites evidence for long-term effects for the Perry Preschool Project on children's school achievement (Schweinhart & Weikart,

1980) and for the Yale Child Welfare Program (Provence & Naylor, 1982) on children's school achievement, school attendance, and family functioning (Seitz, Rosenbaum, & Apfel, 1985).

Early intervention appears to have utility in preventing developmental deficits often associated with NOFT and neglect and should be utilized for high-risk families. However, variations in availability of early intervention programs may limit their utility in some communities.

## ADVOCACY FOR PRIMARY PREVENTION

Parents at risk for neglect and NOFT often have difficulty following through with recommendations for early preventive intervention unless considerable efforts are directed toward enhancing their accessibility to and motivation for such programs. The prevention-minded practitioner can function effectively as an advocate by encouraging parents' utilization of primary prevention services (Morse et al., 1977), especially those with the following characteristics:

1. Intervention prior to the development of neglect or NOFT.
2. Parent education concerning nutrition and child development.
3. Involvement of multiple family members in addition to the child's mother.
4. Advocacy and support.
5. Provision of concrete resources, especially nutritional supplementation.
6. Linkage between health care and community agencies.
7. Outreach to promote parents' engagement with programs.
8. Emphasis on enhancing parental competencies.

Preventive support services include the maternal and infant health programs for pregnant women, which provide comprehensive nutritional, educational, health, family planning services, and home visitation. During the neonatal period, liberal rooming-in, support services, nutrition education, support for breast feeding, home visitation during the neonatal period, and nutritional supplementation may be very beneficial. During early childhood, parents and children at risk for neglect and NOFT benefit from additional anticipatory guidance in feeding, discipline and child development, well child care visits, monitoring of the child's health and development, nutritional supplement (Schmitt, 1980) and compensatory education and stimulation.

### Special Issues in Primary Prevention Advocacy

Practitioners face several obstacles in helping families to utilize primary prevention services. Clinicians in health care settings have access to relatively large numbers of high-risk families, such as adolescent mothers from low-income families. On the other hand, practitioners who practice in mental health clinics may not have consistent access to children until after they have developed the chronic sequelae of NOFT or neglect. Clinicians' job responsibilities also vary in their focus on prevention. For example, a social worker or psychologist who works in a neonatal intensive care nursery may direct considerable energies toward direct preventive work (anticipatory guidance, advocacy, support) with parents of premature infants.

Prevention-minded practitioners can often create their own opportunities for preventive intervention. For example, a therapist evaluated 17-year-old Alice who was referred for acting out behavior and conduct disorder. In the course of the evaluation, Alice reveals that she is pregnant. After several heated discussions, Alice and her parents decide that it would be best if they raise the infant together. However, family conflicts escalate, and Alice's prenatal care suffers. With continued family counseling, the family conflicts are contained, and Alice eventually accepts referrals for prenatal care through the local maternal and child health agency and support through a program of home visitation administered by a community agency. Alice develops a good rapport with the home visitor who continues to provide support after the infant is delivered. With the comprehensive support of family counseling, prenatal care, and home visitation, Alice and her infant daughter got off to a good start, and the entire family participated supportively in her care.

Unfortunately, not all families respond positively to preventive services. One of the main frustrations of prevention-related advocacy is that families who are most in need of primary prevention services also are burdened by multiple stresses which may interfere with their ability to recognize the need for prevention or follow through with recommended services. In many cases, practitioners need to be extremely persistent to ensure that their referrals for preventive services are successful. In presenting recommendations for preventive services, it is very helpful to emphasize the concrete advantages of services to parent and child which may not be immediately apparent and to underscore the fact that the service has helped other parents. Many socially isolated parents do not wish to open themselves up to potential scrutiny or be singled out as a problem family. In some cases, families who are satisfied consumers of preventive services can be helpful in convincing skeptical parents. For example, a pediatric nurse practitioner tried in vain to convince a young mother to take advantage of a support program for adolescent parents offered by the university. She remained steadfast in her refusal to participate in the program. However, during one visit, she agreed to talk with another mother who had enjoyed her participation in the support program. The two mothers got along very well. The formerly recalcitrant mother agreed to visit the program, liked what she saw, and eventually participated.

The ability to be an effective advocate requires a thorough knowledge of community resources and the ability to work closely with professionals from many disciplines (Barth, Ash, & Hacking, 1986). Prevention-related services sometimes have very specific eligibility criteria (e.g., young pregnant mothers from certain communities, mothers with intellectual impairments). Other programs may have long waiting lists which render them ineffective for some families. The effective advocate needs to help families negotiate what is sometimes a difficult maze of services to ensure that the family takes advantage of services. The advocacy role also may involve direct intervention on behalf of a family. For example, a family lost their much-needed supplemental nutritional (WIC) benefits because they did not show up to have the child recertified. The parents did not understand the importance of the recertification process and neglected to continue the service. At one point, the parents came to the WIC office and became angry at the clerk who refused to recertify them. The advocate helped parents to calm down and negotiate with the WIC office to have the parents' benefits reinstated. Advocacy requires the ability and the time to go that extra distance with families in order to help them receive services.

## SECONDARY PREVENTION

The large number of cases of child neglect and NOFT attests to the difficulties of preventing such problems in current patterns of care delivery. Most practicing clinicians work with NOFT and neglected children who are already showing signs of these problems. In such cases, intervention can be effectively directed toward the prevention of physical and psychological problems associated with NOFT, child neglect, and concomitant risk factors.

### Intervention with Neglected Children

In most communities, the legally mandated agency for initial recognition and intervention with neglected children is county welfare protective services who evaluates reports of child neglect, assess the risk to the child, provide support and advocacy to parents. However, county welfare protective services workers are generally overburdened by large case loads and usually cannot provide comprehensive preventive services. As a consequence, workers must rely on community treatment resources. The availability of services designed specifically for prevention of chronic psychological and health disturbances in neglected or NOFT children is quite variable.

Recent studies provide data and ideas for innovative prevention programs. For example, Wolfe (1986) evaluated a preventive intervention program with abused and neglected children which focused on parents' problems in child management and development. One component involved training in child management skills, instruction, modeling, and rehearsal procedures. A second component involved activities designed to promote the child's adaptive abilities, especially in language and social interaction. Mothers critiqued their own behavior via videotape and had an opportunity to practice relaxation and positive coping responses with their child present. Mothers who received parent training also attended support group meetings and received periodic visits in their homes by caseworkers. The comparative treatment condition was a support group, operated by the agency. The parent training group showed a significant reduction in maternal depression and also had fewer problems associated with parenting risk. However, no treatment effects were found for child-rearing methods.

Brunk, Henggeler, & Whelen (1987) evaluated the relative efficacy of two alternative treatments of child abuse and neglect: 1) parent training modeled after Wolfe (1986); and 2) multisystemic family intervention based on Minuchin (1974). Families who received either treatment showed decreased parental psychiatric symptoms, reduced overall stress, and a reduction in the severity of identified problems. Multisystemic therapy was more effective in restructuring parent-child relations than parent training. On the other hand, parent training was more effective in reducing social problems. This study provides evidence for differential sensitivity of outcome variables to different types of intervention.

Lutzker (1984) has described a promising ecobehavioral intervention (Project 12 Ways) which focuses on the specific antecedents and consequences of abuse and neglect in the home setting. Project 12 Ways utilizes a comprehensive range of modalities including parent-child training (Peed, Roberts & Forehand, 1977), stress reduction, self control, and assertiveness training for parents, marital counseling, and specific training for parents in money management, health maintenance, nutrition, and home safety. Thus far, program efficacy has been demonstrated in well-documented case studies using empirical measures, follow up of subsequent instances of child abuse and neglect and lower rates of recidivism (10%) compared to a group that did not receive Project 12 Ways services. Such promising results suggest that interventions with neglected children should be tailored to specific deficits in parenting.

## Intervention with Nonorganic Failure to Thrive

Although most children with NOFT receive some form of nutritional and psychosocial treatment in modern pediatric practice, intervention programs vary considerably with the problems that accompany NOFT, local treatment practices, community resources, and family level of acceptance (Drotar, 1988). In some settings, treatment focuses almost exclusively on the medical management of acute physical (nutritional) problems. In other settings, intervention focuses on helping parents and family members provide more effective nurturing and stimulation for the child. Case reports have documented successful utilization of several intervention modalities such as parent-infant psychotherapy (Fraiberg, 1980, Lieberman & Birch, 1983), support and advocacy (Ayoub, Pfeifer, & Leichtman, 1979), behavioral interventions for feeding disorders (Linscheid & Rasnake, 1985), comprehensive behavioral and psychiatric intervention (Chatoor et al., 1985), and family-centered intervention (Drotar & Malone, 1982). Interventions such as hospitalization, nutrition, and stimulation (Whitten, Pettit, & Fischoff, 1969; Ramey et al., 1975) or outpatient counseling (Fitch et al., 1976) have not prevented cognitive deficits. However, few controlled studies of preventive intervention in NOFT have been reported, especially concerning socioemotional outcomes (Drotar, Malone, & Negray, 1979, 1980).

Drotar et al., (1985a, b) studied the efficacy of three alternative forms of outreach intervention for young NOFT infants. Family-centered intervention involved members of the family group (mother, father, or grandparents) in weekly home visits directed toward enhancement of family coping skills, support of the child's mother, and lessening the impact of dysfunctional family influences such as marital conflict (Drotar & Malone, 1982; Drotar et al., 1985a). Parent-centered intervention included supportive education focused directly on improving the quality of mother's interactions, nutritional management, and relationship with the child. In the third intervention plan, advocacy, the child's mother was seen for an average of six home visits focused on providing emotional support to help the mother stabilize the child's weight gain following hospitalization and to obtain available economic and community resources. In each group, intervention was terminated after 12 months at an average age of 18 months. Type of intervention did not have differential effects on physical growth, cognitive development, attachment, and ratings of behavior at 12–48 months (Drotar, 1985a, b). Although the majority of children showed good recovery of physical growth, cognitive development declined over time. However, this sample of NOFT children showed lower rates of chronic physical growth deficits, and less severe intellectual deficits than other NOFT populations (Singer & Fagan, 1984; Singer, 1985). The nonspecific effects of intervention including support for the mother, continuity of intervention from hospital to home, and outreach may have been more influential than specific intervention. In addition, individual differences in patterns (onset and duration) of NOFT, and demographic characteristics (income) were associated with differences in psychological outcomes and may have limited detectability of intervention effects (Drotar et al., 1985a).

## CLINICAL APPROACH TO SECONDARY PREVENTION

The general goals of secondary prevention with NOFT and neglect include correction of the acute physical and psychological consequences of these problems and interruption of patterns that are maintaining these problems. In order to reduce the likelihood of chronic health and psychological problems, secondary prevention must accomplish: 1) early recognition of neglect or NOFT; 2) reversal or stabilization of the child's symptoms and acute problems; 3) attention to factors (parental appraisal, problematic parent-child relationships, maladaptive parental behavior, and family interferences) that are contributing to psychological risk.

Family stresses which claim parental attention and parents' lack of access to health care interfere with early recognition of NOFT and neglect. For example, it is not uncommon for NOFT children to have severe growth and nutritional deficits for months prior to diagnosis (Drotar, 1985). Early identification of NOFT is important for several reasons. Reversal of serious growth deficits and prevention of chronic FTT and insecure attachments may be easier to accomplish with younger infants who have generally not developed significant feeding and behavior disorders (Drotar, 1985). Early recognition and intervention can lessen the time neglected or NOFT children experience the effects of undernutrition or limited stimulation.

Close monitoring of the child's general health, physical growth patterns, and parental adjustment can aid early detection of NOFT and neglect as in the following case: At the second well child visit, the pediatrician noted that Eddie, a five month old, had shown poor weight gain after doing relatively well right after birth. Eddie was also noted to be unkempt and had missed immunization and well child care visits. Inquiry concerning recent events suggested contributing factors to his NOFT and neglect. Eddie's father had been recently laid off which precipitated a financial crisis. The entire family had to go without food to save money. Eddie's mother diluted his formula, precipitating his poor weight gain. The family missed medical visits, because they did not have the money to pay for them. Once these problems were discovered, the family was helped to obtain emergency food and Eddie's mother was educated concerning his nutritional needs. His rate of weight gain was monitored weekly, and he eventually recovered from his NOFT.

Once NOFT or neglect are suspected, a thorough assessment of the family situation, the child's psychological status and physical health is needed to identify areas of competence and special risk (Drotar, Malone, & Negray, 1980). Information from several professional disciplines may be needed to develop a comprehensive plan for intervention (Berkowitz, 1985; Peterson, Washington, & Rathbun, 1984). One primary goal of intervention is to identify and correct physical and nutritional deficits. However, medical and nutritional intervention does not address the underlying factors which are perpetuating NOFT or neglect and is generally not sufficient to prevent chronic psychological and physical deficits (Drotar, Malone, & Negray, 1979; Drotar & Sturm, 1988; Kristiansson & Fallstrom, 1987). The author's experience and that of others (Ayoub & Jacewitz, 1982; Lutzker, 1984) suggests that secondary prevention requires a concerted effort to engage the parents, intervene to address the specific problems that are maintaining NOFT and neglect, and close and continuous follow up.

Engaging parents of NOFT and neglected children is a critical but difficult prerequisite for intervention. Parents are generally threatened by the prospect of intervention. To enhance parental participation in intervention, we have found it useful to actively initiate contact with parents, emphasize parents' unique role in helping their child, understand parents' concepts of their child's condition, emphasize parental strengths, and create a sense of optimism con-

TABLE 6.4.    Preventive Intervention with Nonorganic Failure to Thrive

| Etiology | Major Presenting Problem | Goals of Intervention |
|---|---|---|
| Underfeeding owing to lack of knowledge of child nutrition | Undernutrition | Nutritional education advocacy |
| Financial problems Dysfunctional parent-child relationship | Understimulation Feeding disorder | Reinforce maternal involvement Modify feeding patterns |
| Severe family dysfunction | Understimulation Disorganized feeding | Enhance family support Reduce level of family conflict Promote family cooperation concerning child's feeding |

cerning the child's future potential. Parents of NOFT and neglected infants can be effectively approached through a process of open negotiation (Katon & Kleinman, 1982) which emphasizes their sense of control and participation in the following ways: 1. Eliciting parents ideas of the causes and consequences of the child's neglect and NOFT. 2. Involving parents in the treatment planning process. 3. Presenting information and treatment recommendations to parents and other family members, especially fathers and grandparents. 4. Openly acknowledging differences in opinions. 5. Developing a working compromise with parents when conflict arises. 6. Monitoring progress of communication and providing corrective feedback when conflict arises.

## Clinical Intervention in NOFT

Recent research has suggested that NOFT is a heterogenous condition which subsumes several subtypes which differ in etiology, age of onset, and risk to the child (Chatoor et al., 1985; Drotar, 1985, a,b; Drotar, 1987; Linscheid & Rasnake, 1985; Woolston, 1983, 1985). For example, NOFT is a continuum of problems ranging from relatively discrete and time-limited influences on growth and development to more pervasive and chronic problems. Strategies of preventive intervention are based upon the hypothesized etiology or breakdown in the maternal-child relationship and anticipated effects on the child.

One type of NOFT reflects underfeeding that minimizes the child's nutritional needs or relates to depletion of family resources. Families who run out of food at the end of the month may limit food intake for everyone in the family. In such cases, parents may respond effectively to education concerning children's nutritional needs and/or advocacy to help obtain much needed resources. For example, Johnny presented with NOFT at three months of age. Although the factors which influenced his growth deficit were not initially apparent, a careful review of his history indicated that he had had an earlier infectious illness. At this time, his mother was advised to feed him clear liquids. However, she kept him on clear liquids for longer than necessary because she felt this would help him. She was reluctant to feed him too much following his illness, because she viewed him as physically vulnerable. When his growth deficit was identified, she attributed it to a physical illness. When the cause of his problem was pointed out to her, she felt badly, agreed to feed him more, and his weight gain improved.

In another case, the child's NOFT reflected an acute nutritional crisis secondary to family financial difficulty. For example, Alice's father was laid off unexpectedly which depleted the family's financial reserves. To save money, the parents reduced their own food intake and did not see the harm in diluting Alice's formula. Alice's NOFT improved when the family was referred to the emergency food center and Alice received WIC benefits which paid for her formula.

In other situations, NOFT reflects a maladaptive maternal-child relationship which disrupts the child's nurturing. In some cases, the interactional deficit is characterized by a lack of responsiveness, especially contingent responses to the child (Linscheid & Rasnake, 1985; Ramey et al., 1975). In other cases, the problem involves a conflictual relationship and high levels of aversive stimulation (Chatoor et al., 1985). The varied developmental origins of these problems including focalization of attachment (3–7 months) or separation and individuation (8–24 months) (Chatoor et al., 1985; Lieberman & Birch, 1985) may respond to different intervention approaches. For example, Fraiberg (1980) and colleagues have advocated a program of developmentally oriented guidance which combines education, support, and therapy to help mothers address the impact of conflicts experienced as a child on their capacity to respond to specific signals or demands from their child. Others have advocated parent training to help mothers modify specific maladaptive behaviors (Linscheid & Rasnake, 1985). For example, mothers with low rates of contingent interactions might be encouraged to increase their rate of responding. On the other hand, mothers who engage in conflictual interactions with their child may be encouraged to decrease the frequency of aversive interactions (Chatoor et al., 1985). Parent training approaches are highly individualized and may require a highly structured treatment environment (Chatoor et al., 1985; Linscheid & Rasnake, 1985).

Although some cases of NOFT respond favorably to intervention at the level of the mother-child dyad, in other instances disturbed parent-child relationships reflect broader family problems (Drotar & Malone, 1982; Drotar et al., 1985) such as conflicts between the child's mother and her parenting partner (spouse, boyfriend, or mother). Family problems may affect the child directly by increasing the conflict and disorganization around mealtimes or indirectly by depleting the mother's energy for child rearing or attention to the child's caretaking (Wahler, 1980; Wahler & Dumas, 1984). In such cases, focusing intervention on maternal-child relationship difficulties without attending to the broader family problems may not be sufficient to maintain long-term intervention gains. Family problems can interfere with the mother's capacity to follow through with interventions directed at improving her relationship with her child (Drotar et al., 1985). In such cases, family centered intervention involving multiple family members can enhance the child's nurturing by: 1) improving the overall organization and planning concerning the allocation of family resources; 2) reducing family conflicts and thus improving the quality of exchanges within the family; and 3) helping family members to protect the child from dysfunctional family influences.

In some cases, the child's NOFT reflects a family crisis which needs to be addressed. For example, it came to light that Bobby's NOFT related to his parents marital problems. Bobby's mother was involved in a conflictual marital relationship with her husband who abused her. Although she had wanted to separate from her husband, she needed support to accomplish this. The major focus of intervention was to help her obtain legal and emotional support to initiate and follow through with this separation.

Family-centered intervention can also help mothers to make positive changes in their relationships with family members and thereby free up her energies for her child as in the following case: Rashita, the mother of a young failure-to-thrive infant, was engaged in a highly conflicted relationship with two men which affected her ability to nurture her infant and her access to resources. When things were going well in her relationships with men, she was able to provide relatively well for her children's needs. However, when things became more difficult between her and her boyfriends, she would miss her well-child appointments and her relationship with the child suffered. Intervention provided support for Rashita to mobilize a more adaptive social network. Eventually, she moved in with her sister who helped care for the infant. At the same time she began to distance herself from her boyfriends and developed positive sources of social support within her family.

Families in which the child's caretaking is dispersed among many caretakers and disorganized family members may need help to focus their caretaking more effectively as in the case of Randy, who first presented with NOFT at two months of age. Randy's complex assortment of caregivers included his mother who lived alone with her four children, and four other adults, a great grandmother, two uncles and an aunt. Randy's mother was stressed by the burden of his care and often asked the other adults to help feed him. However, this pattern of group child rearing reduced her overall level of involvement with Randy and resulted in highly inconsistent care which culminated in decreased caloric intake and two hospitalizations. Following Randy's second hospitalization, the family was encouraged to change their pattern of care by increasing Randy's mother's involvement in his care, decreasing the overall number of caretakers, and enhancing the overall organization of his care. One effective approach to restructuring Randy's care was to encourage his great grandmother to support his mother's primary involvement in his care by helping to feed Randy's very active siblings (Drotar & Malone, 1982).

TABLE 6.5.   Preventive Intervention with Neglected Children

| Domain of Parental Caretaking | Method of Assessment | Intervention Goal |
|---|---|---|
| Limited attention/stimulation | Home Scale<br>Behavioral observation | Reinforce parental stimulation, day care or Head Start programs |
| Limited food/nutrition | Observation of feeding<br>Assessment of physical growth | Nutritional supplementation<br>Reinforce meal planning |
| Inadequate cleanliness | Health assessment<br>Observation | Training to enhance parental caretaking |
| Hazards in home | Observation<br>Home safety checklist | Behavioral training to improve safety |
| Inconsistent health care | Medical records<br>Health assessment | Direct advocacy<br>Reinforcement of compliance with health care |
| Family disorganization affecting the child's care | Observation<br>Family assessment | Marital counseling<br>Family crisis intervention |

## Clinical Intervention in Child Neglect

Child neglect subsumes a heterogenous group of problems which includes deficient attention or stimulation; responsiveness or availability; deficits in basic nutrition, supervision, and child care skills; and medical neglect (see Table 6.2). As with NOFT, a detailed assessment is needed to define specific areas of parental neglect, to develop intervention plans, and set priorities for intervention. Table 6.5 shows domains of parental caretaking that characterize neglect, potential ways of assessing these problems, and goals for intervention. Wherever possible, objective methods of assessment can be used to determine specific deficits in caretaking, to provide a baseline assessment, and to assess progress (Lutzker, 1984). Because neglect often involves multiple areas of parental caretaking, it is useful to implement intervention in stages to avoid overburdening parents. In setting priorities for intervention, it may be necessary to focus on problems that pose immediate threats to the child. For example, the combination of an unsafe home and active toddler and inconsistent parental supervision is potentially dangerous and necessitates primary consideration. Similarly, neglect of a child's health care can also result in serious health consequences and deserves attention. In situations where parents' resistance to intervention is formidable, it may be productive to initiate intervention with problems that parents consider difficult. For example, a mother who considers her child's behavior as problematic may wish to obtain help even though she does not regard her own parenting as a problem.

Effective preventive intervention with neglected children is often focused on helping parents change their interactions with their children. Because neglect is characterized by specific and generalized deficits in parenting, helping parents extend their repertoire of adaptive parenting skills is often a primary intervention goal (Lutzker, 1984). Parent training may involve general goals such as increasing the use of clear, understandable directions and generalized praise (Peed et al., 1981). Alternatively, effective parent training may also be directed toward specific neglectful behavior. For example in Project 12 Ways, Lutzker (1984) cited an interesting application of parent training to a mildly retarded, illiterate mother who had neglected the child's nutrition. Parent training resulted in significant changes in the mother's ability to plan nutritious meals. Project 12 Ways staff have also developed a home safety checklist to assess and modify unsafe homes. Lutzker and his colleagues' (1984) approach to enhance home safety included: education, modeling, practice, and feedback. Based on an assessment of home safety, parents were educated concerning dangers in the home and were instructed to make their homes safer by specific training concerning the number and location of hazards found in the home and to initiate safety changes. The process of child-proofing was modeled to the parents, and practice sessions were included in which parents demonstrated their competence. Case studies using a multiple baseline design indicated a reduction in the kinds and numbers of hazardous items found to be accessible to children.

### Support and Advocacy for Neglectful Parents

For optimal results, behavioral training for neglectful parents is accomplished within the context of a supportive relationship between parent and professional (Wahler & Dumas, 1984). The relationship with the parent trainer is especially important, because many mothers of neglected children are socially isolated and do not have positive contacts with other adults (Polansky et al., 1981). Parents of neglected children also require substantial support to enable them to initiate more adaptive behaviors on their children's behalf and to appreciate that they can make a positive difference in their children's lives. Some parents of neglected children have a generalized sense of helplessness learned in the course of interactions with their own parents (Polansky et al., 1981). As a consequence, parents may tend to underemphasize or deny their influence on their children. Parents' attitudinal bias that they cannot affect their children may need to be addressed by direct training and practice. Many parents of neglected children do not recognize their need for intervention partly because of family problems that they experience. For this reason, practitioners may need to actively initiate and negotiate intervention in accord with the patient step-by-step approach described earlier for families of NOFT infants. Finally, many of the parents of neglected infants are beset by financial difficulties and need direct help and advocacy to obtain resources for their families as well as training to make more effective use of available financial resources (Lutzker, 1984).

### The Impact of Family Dysfunction on Neglect

In some instances, the resources of parents of neglected children may be drained by serious family conflicts. Such families may not be able to effectively implement behavioral training because the level of family conflict or disorganization is too great. In other cases, the gains that are made by parent training may be limited by problematic relationships between the mother and other family members. At times, child neglect is a consequence of patterns of family life characterized by low energy, lack of planning, or chaotic mealtimes or sleep patterns. In such cases, marital counseling or family-centered crisis intervention may be helpful in mobilizing the family members to help the child as the following case illustrates: Johnny was a two-year-old child who showed signs of significant neglect. Because his parents missed a number of well-child appointments, the visiting nurse was assigned to visit the family in their home. This home visit provided revealing information concerning the factors that were influencing the child's neglect. Johnny's mother was significantly depressed. Owing to a recent breakup with Johnny's father, she had moved in with her mother and sisters. However, her sisters resented her presence which precipitated conflict. Johnny's mother lacked the energy and transportation to take him for his well-child visits. However, the family members listened intently to the nurse's discussion of Johnny's need for health care and eventually agreed to help his mother with his care.

### Coordinating Services for Neglected and NOFT Children

The parents of neglected and NOFT children often have a great many needs which may require the services of multiple community agencies. For example, parents may need financial and emotional support and nutritional resources. The child may need a high quality Head Start program or a pediatrician. In some cases of neglect and NOFT, the family's ability to care for this child may need to be monitored by county welfare protective services. In most communities, it is rare that comprehensive services for neglected or NOFT children are provided in a single agency. As a consequence, close coordination of services is needed to ensure that parents follow through with necessary interventions and to avoid counter-productive overlap of services or overburdening the family. Close coordination of services and monitoring of the child and family's progress is also necessary because of the risk experienced by the neglected or NOFT child. Although preventive intervention is generally directed toward preserving and supporting parents' relationship with the child, families with very serious problems may not be able to make use of intervention. When the child's health and psychological development continues to suffer, the NOFT or neglected child may benefit by removal from the parents.

### FUTURE DIRECTIONS

This chapter has focused on preventive clinical interventions provided to families. Interventions for neglect and NOFT may also be directed toward the parents' social network. For example, Garbarino and his colleagues have suggested that the concept of high-risk families can be extended to include high-risk neighborhoods (Garbarino & Crouter, 1978b; Garbarino, Crouter, & Sherman, 1977; Garbarino & Sherman, 1980). The capacity of the neighborhood to provide social and material support for parents may be a salient factor in the development of NOFT and neglect. Some parents of neglected and NOFT children compete for scarce social and financial support, are isolated from potential sources of support within family networks (Bithoney & Newberger, 1986), and engage in high rates of aversive interactions with family members (Wahler, 1980). Consequently, evaluation of interventions focused on promotion of the social engagement of high-risk parents may be a useful future direction. Enhancing the social competence of families of NOFT and neglected children may be another promising area of intervention.

Additional research is needed to articulate how family influences contribute to neglect and NOFT and to develop intervention approaches which address these problems. Research is also needed to describe individual differences in neglectful parenting behavior and the impact on the child. Intervention research needs to be expanded in several directions. For example, detailed case reports of behavioral analyses of neglect and NOFT with adequate base line and follow-up data are needed to document the effects of individualized interventions (Lutzker, 1984). In addition, practitioners who are providing services to neglected and NOFT children need to collect data concerning the characteristics of children, outcomes, and prognosis. Such information can help define the needs of neglected and NOFT children, population characteristics, and promising approaches to intervention. Randomized controlled studies which compare alternative approaches to preventive intervention are very much needed (Fantuzzo & Twentyman, 1986; Frank, 1984). Finally, prospective studies of factors which potentiate psychological risk or protect neglected or NOFT children from psychological or health disturbances (Rosenberg, 1987; Rutter, 1984, 1987; Schneider-Rosen et al., 1985) are needed to develop the knowledge base for preventive intervention.

## REFERENCES

Aber, J. L., & Allen, J. P. (1987). Effects of maltreatment in young children's socioemotional development: An attachment theory perspective. *Developmental Psychology*, *23*, 406–414.

Aber, J. L., & Zigler, E. (1981). Developmental perspectives on child maltreatment. In R. Rizley & D. Cicchetti (Eds.), *New directions for child development: Vol. 2* (pp. 1–29). San Francisco; Jossey-Bass.

Altemeier, W. A., Vietze, P., Sherrod, K. B., Sandler, H. M., Falsey, S., & O'Connor, S. (1979). Prediction of child maltreatment during pregnancy. *Journal of the American Academy of Child Psychiatry*, *18*, 205–219.

Altemeier, W. A., O'Connor, S., Sherrod, R. B., Yeager, T. D. & Vietze, P. M. (1985a). A strategy for managing nonorganic failure to thrive based on a prospective study of antecedents. In D. Drotar (Ed.), *New directions in failure to thrive: Implications for research and practice* (pp. 211–222) New York: Plenum.

Altemeier, W., O'Connor, Sherrod, K. & Vietze, P. (1985). Prospective study of antecedents for non-organic failure to thrive. *Journal of Pediatrics, 106,* 360–365.

American Humane Association (1986) *Highlights of the official child neglect and abuse reporting,* 1982. Denver, CO: D. Drotar.

Ammerman, R. J., Cassisi, J. E., Hersen, M., & Van Hasselt, V. R. (1986). Consequences of physical abuse and neglect in children. *Clinical Psychology Review, 6,* 291–310.

Ayoub, C., & Jacewitz, M. D. (1982). Families at risk of poor parenting: A model for service delivery, assessment, and intervention. *Child Abuse and Neglect, 6,* 351–358.

Ayoub, C. C., & Milner, S. S. (1985). Failure to thrive parental indicators, types and outcome. *Child Abuse & Neglect, 9,* 491–499.

Ayoub, C., Pfeifer, D., & Leichtman, L. (1979). Treatment of infants with non-organic failure to thrive. *Child Abuse & Neglect, 3,* 937–941.

Avison, W. R., Turner, R. J., & Noh, S. (1986). Screening evidence for problem parenting: Preliminary evidence on a promising instrument. *Child Abuse & Neglect, 10,* 157–170.

Barth, R. D., Ash, J. R., & Hacking, S. (1986). Identifying screening and engaging high risk clients in private non-profit child abuse prevention programs. *Child Abuse and Neglect, 1,* 99–109.

Barrett, D. E., Radke-Yarrow, M., & Klein, P. C. (1982). Chronic malnutrition and child behavior: Effects of early caloric supplementation on social and emotional functioning at school age. *Developmental Psychology, 18,* 541–566.

Belsky, J. (1984). The determinants of parenting: A process model. *Child Development, 55,* 83–96.

Belsky, J., Robins, E., & Gamble, W. (1984). The determinants of parental competence: Toward a contextual theory. In M. Lewis (Ed.), *Beyond the Dyad* (p. 251–279). New York: Plenum.

Berkowitz, C. (1985). Comprehensive pediatric management of failure to thrive: An interdisciplinary approach. In D. Drotar (Ed.), *New directions in failure to thrive: Implications for research and practice* (pp. 193–211). New York: Plenum.

Berwick, D. M. (1980). Nonorganic failure to thrive. *Pediatrics in review, 1,* 265–270.

Besharov, D. J. (1981). Toward better research on child abuse and neglect, *Child Abuse and Neglect, 5,* 383–390.

Birch, H. G., & Gussow, J. D. (1970). *Disadvantaged children: Health, nutrition and school failure.* New York: Grune & Stratton.

Bithoney, W. G., & Dubowitz, H. (1985). Organic concomitants of nonorganic failure to thrive. In D. Drotar (Ed.), *New directions in failure to thrive: Implications for research and practice* (pp. 47–68). New York: Plenum.

Bithoney W. G., & Newberger, E. H. (1987). Child and family attributes of failure to thrive. *Journal of Developmental & Behavioral Pediatrics, 8,* 32–36.

Bithoney, W. G., & Rathbun, J. M. (1983). Failure to thrive. In W. B. Levine, A. C. Carey, A. D. Crocker, & R. J. Gross (Eds.), *Developmental Behavioral Pediatrics* (pp. 557–572). Philadelphia: Saunders.

Bolton, F. G., Charlton, J. K., Gal, D. S., Laner, R. H., & Shumway, S. M. (1985). Preventive screening of adolescent mothers and infants: Critical variables in assessing risk for child maltreatment. *Journal of Primary Prevention, 5,* 169–185.

Bradley, R. H., & Casey, P. M. (1985). A transactional model of failure to thrive: A look at misclassified cases. In D. Drotar (Ed.), *New directions in failure to thrive: Implications for research and practice* (pp. 107–118). New York: Plenum.

Bradley, R. H., Casey, P. M., & Wortham, B. (1984). Home environments of low SES non-organic failure to thrive infants. *Merrill Palmer Quarterly, 30,* 393–402.

Brams, J. S., & Coury, D. L. (1985). Primary prevention of failure to thrive. In D. Drotar (Ed.), *New directions for failure to thrive: Implications for research and practice* (pp. 312–336). New York: Plenum.

Bruenlin, D. C., Desai, V. J., Stone, M. E., & Swilley, J. (1983). Failure to thrive with no organic etiology: A critical review. *International Journal of Eating Disorders, 2,* 25–49.

Brunk, M., Henggeler, S. W., & Whelan, J. P. (1987). Comparison of multisystemic therapy and parent training in the brief treatment of child abuse and neglect. *Journal of Consulting and Clinical Psychology, 55,* 171–178.

Butler, J. A., Starfield, B., & Stenmark, S. (1984). Child Health Policy. In H. W. Stevenson & A. E. Siegel (Eds.), *Child Development Research and Social Policy* (pp. 116–118). Chicago: University of Chicago Press.

Caldwell, B. M., & Bradley, R. H. (1980). *Home observation for the measurement of the environment.* Little Rock: University of Arkansas. *Center for Child Development and Education.*

Casey, P. H. (1982). Failure to thrive: A reconceptualization. *Journal of Developmental and Behavioral Pediatrics, 4,* 65–66.

Casey, P. H., & Whitt, J. K. (1980). Effect of the pediatrician on the mother-infant relationship. *Pediatrics, 65,* 815–820.

Casto, G., & White, K. (1984). The efficacy of early intervention programs with environmentally at-risk infants. In M. Frank (Ed.), *Infant Intervention Programs: Truths and Untruths* (pp. 37–50). New York: Haworth Press.

Chamberlin, R. W. (1976). What is "adequate well baby care." *Pediatrics, 58,* 772–755.

Chatoor, I., Dickson, L., Schaefer, S., & Egan, J. (1985). A developmental classification of feeding disorders associated with failure to thrive: Diagnosis and treatment. In D. Drotar (Ed.), *New directions in failure to thrive: Implications for research and practice* (pp. 235–259). New York: Plenum.

Christophersen, E. R. (1986). Accident prevention in primary care. *Pediatric Clinics in North America, 33,* 925–933.

Drotar, D. (1985). Environmentally based failure to thrive: Diagnostic subtypes and early prognosis. In B. Stabler & L. Underwood (Eds.), *Slow grows the child: Psychosocial aspects of growth delay.* Hillsdale, NJ: Erlbaum.

Drotar, D. (1988). Failure to thrive. In D. K. Routh (Ed.), *Handbook of Pediatric Psychology,* (pp. 71–107). New York: Guilford.

Drotar, D., & Malone, C. A. (1982). Family-oriented intervention in failure to thrive. In M. Klaus & M. O. Robertson (Eds.), *Birth interaction and attachment. Johnson and Johnson Pediatric Round Table, Vol. 6*, (pp. 104–112). NJ: Skillman.

Drotar, D., Malone, C. A., & Negray, J. (1979). Psychosocial intervention with the families of failure to thrive infants. *Child Abuse and Neglect, 3*, 927–935.

Drotar, D., Malone, C. A., & Negray, J. (1980). Environmentally based failure to thrive and childrens intellectual development. *Journal of Clinical Child Psychology, 9*, 236–240.

Drotar, D., Malone, C. A., Devost, L., Brickell, C., Mantz-Clumpner, C., Negray, J., Wallace, M., Woychik, J., Wyatt, B., Eckerle, D., Bush, M., Finlon, M. A., El-Amin, D., Nowak, M., Satola, J., & Pallotta, J. (1985a). Early preventive intervention in failure to thrive: Methods and early outcome. In D. Drotar (Ed.) *New directions in failure to thrive: Implications for research and practice*, New York: Plenum.

Drotar, D., Malone, C. A., & Nowak, M. (1985, April). Early outcomes in failure to thrive. Correlates of security of attachment. Paper presented at Biennial meeting of Society for Research in Child Development. Toronto.

Drotar, D., Nowak, M., Malone, C. A., Eckerle, D., & Negray, J. (1985b). Early psychological outcome in failure to thrive: Predictions from an interactional model. *Journal of Clinical Child Psychology, 14*, 105–111.

Drotar, D., & Sturm, L. (1988). Prediction of intellectual development in children with early histories of non-organic failure to thrive. *Journal of Pediatric Psychology, 13*, 281–295.

Drotar, D., Woychik, J., Mantz-Clumpner, C., Brickell, C., Negray, J., Wallace, M., & Malone, C. A. (1985c). The family context of failure to thrive. In D. Drotar (Ed.), *New directions in failure to thrive: Implications for research and practice.* (pp. 295–310.) New York: Plenum.

Duquette, D. N. (1982). Protecting individual liberties in the context of screening for child abuse. In R. H. Starr (Ed.), *Child abuse prediction: Policy implications* (191–204). Cambridge, MA: Ballinger.

Edozien, J. C., Switzer, B. R., & Bryan, R. B. (1979). Medical evaluation of the special supplemental food program for women, infants, and children. *American Journal of Clinical Nutrition, 32*, 677–692.

Egeland, B., Sroufe, L. A., & Erickson, M. H. (1983). Developmental consequences of difficult patterns of maltreatment. *Child Abuse and Neglect, 7*, 459–469.

Egeland, B., & Vaughn, B. (1981). Failure of bond formation as a cause of abuse, neglect, and maltreatment. *American Journal of Orthopsychiatry, 51*, 78–79.

Fantuzzo, J. W., & Twentyman, C. T. (1986). Child abuse and psychotherapy, research, emerging social concerns, and empirical investigation. *Professional Psychology Research and Practice, 17*, 375–380.

Field, T. M., Widmayer, S. M., Stringer, S., & Ignatoffi, E. (1980). Teenage lower class black mothers and their preterm infants: An intervention and developmental follow-up. *Child Development, 51*, 426–436.

Field, M. (1984). Follow-up developmental status of infants hospitalized for non-organic failure to thrive. *Journal of Pediatric Psychology, 9*, 241–256.

Fitch, M. J., Cadol, R. V., Goldson, E. J., Wendel, T. P., Swartz, D. F., & Jackson, E. K. (1976). Cognitive development of abused and failure to thrive children. *Journal of Pediatric Psychology, 1*, 32–37.

Fraiberg, S. (1980). Ed. *Clinical studies in infant mental health.* New York: Basic Books.

Frank, D. A. (1985). Biologic risks in "nonorganic" failure to thrive: Diagnostic and therapeutic implications. In D. Drotar (Ed.), *New directions in failure to thrive: Implications for research and practice* (pp. 17–20). New York: Plenum.

Frank, D. A., Allen, D., & Broun, J. L. (1985). In D. Drotar (Ed.), *New directions in failure to thrive: Implications for research and practice* (pp. 337–358). New York: Plenum.

Frank, M. (Ed.). (1984). *Infant intervention programs: Truths and untruths,* New York: Haworth Press.

Frommer, E., & Shea, G. (1973). Antenatal identification of women liable to have problems in managing their infants. *British Journal of Psychiatry, 123,* 149–156.

Garbarino, J. (1977). The human ecology of child maltreatment: A conceptual model for research. *Journal of Marriage and the Family. 39,* 721–735.

Garbarino, J., & Crouter, A. (1978a). A note on the problem of construct validity in assessing the usefulness of child maltreatment report data. *American Journal of Public Health, 61,* 598–600.

Garbarino, J., & Crouter, A. (1978b). Defining the community context of parent child relationships: The correlates of child maltreatment. *Child Development, 49,* 604–616.

Garbarino, J., Crouter, A., & Sherman, D. (1977). Screening neighborhoods for intervention: A research model for child protection services. *Journal of Social Service Research, 1,* 133–145.

Garbarino, J., Guttman, E., & Seeley, J. W. (1986). *The psychologically battered child: Strategies for identification, assessment and intervention.* San Francisco: Jossey-Bass.

Garbarino, J., & Sherman, D. (1980). High risk neighborhoods and high risk families: The human ecology of child maltreatment. *Child Development, 51,* 158–198.

Garbarino, J., & Stocking, S. H. (1980). *Protecting children from abuse and neglect: Developing and maintaining effective support systems.* San Francisco: Jossey-Bass.

Garrison, E. G. (1987). Psychological maltreatment of children: An emerging focus for inquiry and concern. *American Psychologist, 42,* 157–159.

Giovannoni, J. M., & Becerra, R. M. (1979). *Defining child abuse.* New York: Free Press.

Gordon, A. H., & Jameson, J. C. (1979). Infant-mother attachment in parents with non-organic failure to thrive syndrome. *Journal of the American Academy of Child Psychiatry, 18,* 96–99.

Gordon, E. F., & Vazquez, D. M. (1985a). Failure to thrive: An expanded conceptual model. In D. Drotar (Ed.), *New directions in failure to thrive: Implications for research and practice.* New York: Plenum.

Gordon, E. F., & Vazquez, D. M. (1985). Failure to thrive in an economically depressed community. In D. Drotar (Ed.), *New directions in failure to thrive: Implications for research and practice* (pp. 359–366). New York: Plenum.

Grantham-McGregor, S., Schofield, W., & Harris, L. (1983). Effect of psychosocial stimulation on mental development of severely malnourished children: An interim report. *Pediatrics, 72,* 239–243.

Gray, J. D., Cutler, C. A., Dean, J. G., & Kempe, C. N. (1977). Prediction and prevention of child abuse and neglect. *Child Abuse & Neglect, 1,* 45–50.

Greenspan, S. I., & White, G. R. (1985). The efficacy of preventive intervention: A glass half full? *Bulletin of the National Center for Clinical Programs, 5,* 1–5.

Gutelius, M. F., Kirsch, A. D., McDonald, S., Brooke, M. R., & McErlean, T. (1977). Controlled study of child health supervision. *Pediatrics, 60,* 294–304.

Hammill, P. V. V., Drizd, T. A., Johnson, C. L., Reed, R. B., Roche, A. F., & Moore, W. M. (1979). Physical growth: National Center for Health Statistics percentages. *American Journal of Clinical Nutrition, 32,* 607–629.

Hannaway, P. J. (1970). Failure to thrive—A study of 100 infants and children. *Clinical Pediatrics, 9,* 96–99.

Handen, B. C., Mandell, F., & Russo, D. C. (1986). Feeding induction in children who refuse to eat. *American Journal of Diseases of Children, 140,* 52–54.

Hart, S. N., & Haggard, M. R. (1987). A major threat to children's mental health— Psychological maltreatment. *American Psychologist, 42,* 160–165.

Helfer, R. S. (1982). A review of the literature on the prevention of child abuse and neglect. *Child Abuse & Neglect, 6,* 251–261.

Hicks, L. E., Langham, R. A., & Takenaka, J. (1982). Cognitive and health measures following early nutritional supplementation: A sibling study. *American Journal of Public Health, 12,* 1110–1118.

Hoffman-Plotkin, D., & Twentyman, C. T. (1984). A multimodal assessment of behavioral and cognitive deficits in abused and neglected preschoolers. *Child Development, 55,* 794–802.

Hopwood, N., & Becker, D. J. (1979). Psychosocial dwarfism: Detection, Evaluation and management. *Child Abuse and Neglect, 3,* 439–447.

Hufton, I. V., & Oates, R. K. (1977). Nonorganic failure to thrive: A long-term follow-up. *Pediatrics, 59,* 73–79.

Hunter, R. S., Kilstrom, N., Kraybill, E. N., & Loda, F. (1978). Antecedents of child abuse and neglect in premature infants: A prospective study in a newborn intensive care unit. *Pediatrics, 61,* 629–635.

Iscoe, I. (1981). Conceptual barriers to training of psychopathology. In J. M. Joffe & G. W. Albee (Eds.), *Prevention through polital action and social change* (pp. 110–134). Hanover, NH: University Press of New England.

Joos, S. K., Pollitt, E., Mueller, W. H., & Albright, D. L. (1983). The bacon chow study: Maternal nutritional supplementation and infant behavioral development. *Child Development, 54,* 669–676.

Kammerman, S. R. (1980). *Parenting in an unresponsive society.* New York: Free Press.

Kanawati, A. A., & McClaren, D. S. (1973). Failure to thrive in Lebanon II: An investigation of the causes. *Acta Paedeatrica Scandinavia, 62,* 571–576.

Katon, W., & Kleinman, A. (1981). Doctor-patient negotiation and other social science strategies in patient care. In L. Eisenberg & A. Kleinman (Eds.), *The relevance of social science for medicine* (pp. 153–282). Dordrecht, Holland: Reidel.

Klaus, M., & Kennell, J. (1982). *Parent- infant bonding.* St. Louis: C. V. Mosby.

Klein, R. E., Arrenabes, P., Delgado, H., Engle, P., Guzman, G., Irwin, M., Lasky, R., Lechtig, A., Martorell, R., Pivaral, V., Russell, P., & Yarbrough, C. (1976).

Effects of maternal nutrition on fetal growth and infant development, *Bulletin of the Pan American Health Organization*, *10*, 301–316.

Korbin, J. E. (1980). Cultural context of child abuse and neglect. *Child Abuse & Neglect*, *4*, 3–13.

Kotelchuck, M. (1979). Child abuse and neglect: Prediction and misclassification. In R. H. Starr (Ed.). *Child abuse prediction: Policy implications* (pp. 67–104). Cambridge, MA: Ballinger.

Kotelchuck, M. (1980). Nonorganic failure to thrive: The status of interactional and environmental theories. In B. W. Camp (Ed.), *Advances in Behavioral Pediatrics: Vol. 1* (pp. 29–51). Greenwich, CT: Jai Press.

Kotelchuck, M., & Newberger, E. H. (1983). Failure to thrive: A controlled study of family characteristics. *Journal of the American Academy of Child Psychiatry*, *22*, 322–328.

Kristiansson, B., & Fallstrom, S. P. (1987). Growth at the age of 4 years subsequent to early failure to thrive. *Child Abuse & Neglect*, *11*, 35–40.

Lamphear, V. S. (1986). Psychosocial adjustment of maltreated children: Methodological limitations and guidelines for future research. *Child Abuse & Neglect*, *10*, 63–69.

Larson, C. P. (1980). Efficacy of prenatal and postpartum home visits on child health and development. *Pediatrics*, *66*, 191–197.

Leonard, M. F., Rhymes, J. P., & Solnit, A. J. (1969). Failure to thrive in infants: A family problem. *American Journal of Diseases of Children*, *111*, 600–612.

Lieberman, A. F., & Birch, M. (1985). The etiology of failure to thrive: An interactional developmental approach. In D. Drotar (Ed.), *New directions in failure to thrive: Implications for research and practice* (pp. 259–278). New York: Plenum.

Light, R. J. (1973). Abused and neglected children in America: A study of alternative policies. *Harvard Educational Review*, *43*, 556–598.

Linscheid, T. R., & Rasnake, L. K. (1985). Behavioral approaches to the treatment of failure to thrive. In D. Drotar (Ed.), *New directions in failure to thrive: Implications for research and practice* (pp. 279–294). New York: Plenum.

Lozoff, E., & Fanaroff, A. (1975). Kwashiorkor in Cleveland. *American Journal of Diseases of Children*, *129*, 710–711.

Lutzker, J. R. (1984). Project 12 ways: Treating child abuse and neglect from an ecobehavioral perspective. In R. F. Dangel & R. A. Polster (Eds.), *Parent Training* (pp. 260–297). New York: Guilford.

Main M., Kaplan, N., & Cassidy, J. (1985). Security in infancy, childhood and adulthood: A move to the level of representation. In I. Bretherton & E. Waters (Eds.), *Growing points in attachment theory and research. Monographs for Society of Research in Child Development* (pp. 66–104). Chicago: University of Chicago Press.

Massachusetts Department of Public Health (1983). *Massachusetts Nutrition Survey*. Boston, MA.

McCubbin, H. I., & Patterson, J. M. (1983). Family transitions: Adaptation to stress. In H. I. McCubbin & C. R. Figley (Eds.), *Stress and the Family, Vol. 1, Coping with Normative Transitions* (pp. 5–25). New York: Brunner-Mazel.

McKay, H., Sinisterro, L., McKay, A., Gomez, H., & Lloaeda, P. (1978). Improving cognitive ability in chronically deprived children. *Science, 200*, 270–278.

Mitchell, W. G., Gorell, R. W., & Greenberg, R. A. (1980). Failure to thrive: A study in a primary care setting: Epidemiology and follow-up. *Pediatrics, 65*, 971–977.

Minuchin, S. (1974). *Families and family therapy.* Cambridge Mass: Harvard University Press.

Money, J., Wolff, G., & Annecillo, C. (1972). Pain agnosia and self injury in the syndrome of reversible somatotropin deficiency (psychological dwarfism). *Journal of Autism and Childhood Schizophrenia, 2*, 19–27.

Morse, A. E., Hyde, J. N., Newberger, E. H., & Reed, A. B. (1977). Correlates of pediatric social illness: Preventive implications of an advocacy approach. *American Journal of Public Health, 67*, 612–615.

Murphy S., Orkow, B., & Nicola, R. M. (1985). Prenatal prediction of child abuse and neglect: A prospective study. *Child Abuse & Neglect, 9*, 225–235.

Nagi, S. (1977). *Child Maltreatment in the United States*, New York: Columbia University.

Nakov, S., Adam, H., Strathacapoulou, N., & Agathonos, H. (1982). Health status of abused and neglected children and siblings. *Child Abuse & Neglect, 6*, 279–284.

National Academy of Sciences (1976). *Toward a National Policy for Children and Families*, Report of the Advisory Committee on Child Development, Washington, DC.

Newberger, E. H., Hampton, R. L., Marx, T. J., & White, K. M. (1986). Child abuse and pediatric illness: An epidemiological analysis and ecological reformulation. *American Journal of Orthopsychiatry, 56*, 589–600.

Oates, R. (1987). *Child abuse and neglect: What happens eventually.* New York: Brunner Mazel.

Oates, R. K., Peacock, A., & Forest, D. (1985). Long-term effects of non-organic failure to thrive. *Pediatrics, 75*, 36–40.

O'Connor, S., Vietze, P. M., Sherrod, K. B., Sandler, H. M., & Altemeier, W. K. (1980). Reduced incidence of parenting inadequacy following rooming in. *Pediatrics, 66*, 176–182.

Olds, D. L., Henderson, C. R., Chamberlin, R., & Tatelbaum, R. (1986a). Preventing child abuse and neglect: A randomized trial of nurse intervention. *Pediatrics, 78*, 65–78.

Olds, D. L., Henderson, C. R., Tatelbaum, R., & Chamberlin, R. (1986b). Improving the delivery of prenatal care and outcomes of pregnancy: A randomized trial of nurse home visitation. *Pediatrics, 77*, 16–28.

Peed, S., Roberts, M., & Forehand, R. (1977). Evaluation of the effectiveness of a standardized parent training program in altering the interaction of mothers and their noncompliant children. *Behavioral Modification, 1*, 323–350.

Pelton, L. H. (1978). Child abuse and neglect: Myth of classlessness. *American Journal of Orthopsychiatry, 48*, 608–617.

Peterson, K. E., Washington, J. S., & Rathbun, J. M. (1984). Team management of failure to thrive. *Journal of the American Dietetic Association, 84*, 810–814.

Plotkin, R. C., Azar, S., Twentyman, C. T., & Perri, M. G. (1981). A critical evaluation of the research methodology employed in the investigation of child abuse and neglect. *Child Abuse & Neglect*, *5*, 449–455.

Polansky, N. A., Chalmers, M. A., Buttenwieser, E., & Williams, D. P. (1981). *Damaged parents: Anatomy of child neglect* Chicago: University of Chicago Press.

Pollitt, E. (1973). The role of the behavior of the infant in Marasmus. *American Journal of Clinical Nutrition*, *26*, 264–270.

Pollitt, E., & Eichler, A. (1976). Behavioral disturbances among failure to thrive children. *American Journal of Diseases of Children*, *130*, 24–29.

Pollitt, E., Eichler, A., & Cham, C. K. (1975). Psychosocial development and behavior of mothers of failure to thrive children. *American Journal of Orthopsychiatry*, *45*, 525–537.

Powell, G. F., & Low, J. L. (1983). Behavior in non-organic failure to thrive. *Journal of Developmental & Behavioral Pediatrics*, *4*, 26–33.

Powell, G. F., Low, J., & Spears, M. A. (1987). Behavior as a diagnostic aid in failure to thrive. *Journal of Developmental and Behavioral Pediatrics*, *8*, 18–24.

Provence, S. (1985). On the efficacy of early intervention programs. *Journal of Developmental Pediatrics*, *6*, 363–366.

Provence, S., & Naylor, A. K. (1982). *Working with disadvantaged parents and their children, Scientific and practice issues*. New Haven: Yale University Press.

Ramey, C. J., Haeger, L., & Klisz, D. (1972). Synchronous reinforcement of vocal responses in failure to thrive infants. *Child Development*, *43*, 1449–1455.

Ramey, C. T., Starr, R. H., Pallas, J., Whitten, C. F., & Reed, V. (1975). Nutrition, response contingent stimulation and the maternal deprivation syndrome: Results of an early intervention program. *Merrill Palmer Quarterly*, *21*, 45–55.

Ramey, C. T., MacPhee, D., & Yeates, K. O. (1982). Preventing developmental retardation: A general systems model. In L. A. Bond & J. M. Joffe (Eds.), *Facilitating Infant and Early Childhood Development* (pp. 343–407). Hanover, NH: University Press of New England.

Ramey, C. T., Yeates, K. O., & Short, E. J. (1984). The plasticity of intellectual development: Insights from preventive intervention. *Child Development*, *55*, 1913–1925.

Rohner, R. P. (1986). *The warmth dimension: Foundations of parental-acceptance rejection theory*, Sage: Beverly Hills.

Rosenberg, M. S. (1987). New directions for research on the psychological maltreatment of children. *American Psychologist*, *42*, 166–171.

Rush, D., Stein, Z., & Susser, M. (1980). *Diet in pregnancy: A randomized controlled trial of nutritional supplements*. New York: Liss.

Rutter, M. (1984). Protective factors in children's responses to stress and disadvantage. In J. M. Jaffe, G. W. Albee, L. D. Kelly (Eds.), *Readings in the Primary Prevention of Psychopathology* (pp. 157–177). Hanover, NH: University Press of New England.

Rutter, M. (1987). Psychosocial resilience and protective mechanisms. *American Journal of Orthopsychiatry*, *57*, 316–331.

Schmitt, B. D., (Ed.). (1978). *The child protection team handbook*. New York: Garland STPM Press.

Schmitt, B. D. (1980). The prevention of child abuse and neglect: A review of the literature with recommendations for application. *Child Abuse & Neglect, 4,* 171–177.

Schneider-Rosen, K., Braunwald, V. G., Carlson, V., & Cicchetti, O. (1985). In I. Bretherton & E. Waters (Eds.), *Growing points of attachment therapy and research. Monograph Society for Research in Child Development, 50,* (194–210). Chicago: University of Chicago Press.

Schweinhart, L. J., & Weikart, D. P. (1980). *Young children grow up: The effects of the Perry Preschool Program on youths through age 15,* Ypsilanti, MI: High Scope Press.

Seagull, E. A. W. (1987). Social support and child maltreatment. *Child Abuse & Neglect, 11,* 41–52.

Seitz, V., Rosenbaum, L. K., & Apfel, N. V. (1985). Effects of family support intervention: A ten-year follow-up. *Child Development, 56,* 376–391.

Shapiro, V., Fraiberg, S., & Adelson, E. (1976). Infant-parent psychotherapy on behalf of a child in a critical nutritional state. *Psychoanalytic Study of the Child, 31,* 461–491.

Sherrod, K. B., O'Connor, S., Altemeier, W. A., & Vietze, P. (1985). Toward a semispecific multidimensional threshold model of maltreatment. In D. Drotar (Ed.), *New directions in failure to thrive: Implications for research and practice* (pp. 89–106). New York: Plenum.

Sherrod, K. B., O'Connor, S., Vietze, P. M., & Altemeier, W. A. (1984). Child health and maltreatment. *Child Development, 55,* 1174–1182.

Shyme, A. W., & Schroeder, A. G. (1978). *National study of social services to children and families.* Washington, DC. National Center for Child Advocacy: U.S. Children's Bureau.

Siegel, E., Bauman, K. E., Schaefer, E. S., Saunders, M. M., & Ingram, B. D. (1980). Hospital and home support during infancy: Impact on maternal attachment, child abuse and neglect and health care utilization. *Pediatrics, 66,* 183–190.

Sills, R. H. (1978). Failure to thrive: The role of clinical and laboratory evaluation. *American Journal of Diseases of Children, 132,* 967–969.

Singer, L. (1985). Extended hospitalization of failure to thrive infants: Patterns of care and developmental outcome. In D. Drotar (Ed.), *New directions in failure to thrive: Implications for research and practice* (p. 139–154). New York: Plenum.

Singer, L. T., & Fagan, J. F. (1984). The cognitive development of the failure to thrive infant. A three-year longitudinal study. *Journal of Pediatric Psychology, 9,* 363–383.

Skuse, D. (1984). Extreme deprivation in early childhood: II theoretical issues and a comparative review. *Journal of Child Psychology and Psychiatry, 25,* 543–572.

Starr, R. H. (1987). Clinical judgement of abuse proneness based on parent-child interactions. *Child Abuse & Neglect, 11,* 87–92.

Thomas, K. A., Hassanein, R. S., & Christophersen, E. R. (1984). Evaluation of group well child care for improving burn prevention practices in the home. *Pediatrics, 74,* 879–882.

Trad, P. V. (1987). Infant & childhood depression. *Developmental factors.* New York: Wiley.

Wahler, R. G. (1980). The insular mother: Her problems in parent-child treatment. *Journal of Applied Behavior Analysis, 13*, 207–219.

Wahler, R. G., & Dumas, J. E. (1984). Changing the observational coding styles of insular and noninsular mothers: A step toward maintenance of parent training effects. In R. F. Dangel & R. A. Polster (Eds.), *Parent Training* (pp. 379–416). New York: Guilford.

White, R., Benedict, M. I., Wolff, L., & Kelley, M. (1987). Physical disabilities as risk factors for child maltreatment: A selected review. *American Journal of Orthopsychiatry, 57*, 93–101.

Whitten, C. F., Pettit, M. G., & Fischoff, J. (1969). Evidence that growth failure from maternal deprivation is secondary to undereating. *Journal of the American Medical Association, 209*, 1675–1682.

Wolfe, D. A. (1986, November) A child abuse and neglect early intervention program: Outcome and follow-up. Paper presented at American Association for Behavior Therapy. Chicago.

Wolock, I., & Horowitz, B. (1979). Child maltreatment and material deprivation among AFDC recipient families. *Social Service Review, 53*, 175–194.

Wolock, I., & Horowitz, B. (1984). Child maltreatment as a social problem: The neglect of neglect. *American Journal of Orthopsychiatry, 54*, 530–545.

Woolston, J. L. (1983). Eating disorders in infancy and early childhood. *Journal of the American Academy of Child Psychiatry, 22*, 114–121.

Woolston, J. (1985). Diagnostic classification: The current challenge in failure to thrive syndrome research. In D. Drotar (Ed.), *New directions in failure to thrive: Implications for research and practice* (pp. 225–334). New York: Plenum.

Zeskind, P. S., & Ramey, C. T. (1978). Fetal malnutrition: An experimental study of its consequences on infant development in the caregiving environments. *Child Development, 49*, 1155–1162.

Zigler, E. F. (1983). Understanding child abuse: A dilemma for policy. In E. F. Zigler, C. L. Kagan & E. Klugman (Eds.), *Children, families and government: Perspectives in American social policy* (pp. 331–353). New York: Cambridge.

Zigler, E. G., Kagan, S. L., & Klugman, E. C. (1983). *Children, families and government: Perspectives in American social policy.* New York: Cambridge.

CHAPTER 7

# Sexual Abuse Prevention Education:

## A Review of Evaluation Studies

DAVID FINKELHOR AND NANCY STRAPKO

It has been called the "great social experiment of the 1980s." In an effort to combat child molestation, which researchers in the 1970s found to be affecting as many as a fifth of all children (Peters, Wyatt, & Finkelhor, 1986), educators began to expose millions of American children to what generically have been called child sexual abuse prevention education programs.

These programs, which include films, skits, lectures, coloring books, songs, and puppet shows, usually administered to grade school aged children in a format lasting anywhere from an hour or two to several days, are all intended to convey certain core concepts. First, they teach the concept of sexual abuse, defined by such things as "bad touch" or touching in private places. Second, they teach children to refuse such overtures, no matter from whom they come and to get away from that person. Finally, they encourage children to tell parents and/or adults when such overtures occur.

The programs also may teach a wide variety of other concepts. Usually they try to reassure children that they are not to blame for any such experience. Routinely they try to counter misinformation, for example, that the culprits are primarily strangers. The program sometimes attempt to embrace a larger context of improving children's mental health and social well-being. The Talking About Touching (Beland, 1986) approach, for example, tries to convey to children, along with concern about abuse, the importance of positive and caring touch. The Child Abuse Prevention (Binder & McNiel, 1986) program aims to help children feel generally empowered in their dealings with adults and other children.

The authors wish to thank Kathy Beland, Deborah Daro, Ed Fryer, Raymond Miltenberger, David Nibert, Norman Ostbloom, Carol Plummer, and Andrea Wiseman for help in locating studies; and Donna Wilson for help in preparing the manuscript.

Dr. Finkelhor's effort in this project has been supported by funds from the National Center on Child Abuse and Neglect, National Institute of Mental Health, and the Eden Hall Farm Foundation.

**150**

The programs have won widespread adoption by schools, school boards, and children's organizations such as the Campfire girls. California lawmakers went so far as to mandate that all California children should receive such programs on at least three occasions during their schooling. The ready and widespread adoption of these programs can be ascribed in large part to the extremely high and persistent level of public concern about sexual abuse and the scant number of other easily implemented remedies. Many of the programs have been carefully crafted, and their diligent promotions with their cleverness, humor and appeal have impressed parents and policy makers.

Nonetheless, a variety of questions have been raised about the programs and the great social experiment they have inspired. Most prominently, well-intentioned people have worried about unduly frightening children, perhaps alienating them from family or adults who would fall under a cloud of program-inspired suspicions. The effectiveness of the programs have also been questioned. Were children capable of foiling abusers and protecting themselves in the face of the potentially awesome authority and guile of adults? Promoters of the programs have made concerted efforts to address these questions, with anecdotal but nonetheless reassuring evidence from their extensive experience in teaching programs. These responses have generally allayed the fears of parents and policy makers.

Thus, by and large, these programs have been widely adopted without systematic evaluation. However, concern about research has not been absent. The same California legislation that mandated the programs also provided money to evaluate their impact. The widespread implementation of programs around the country has created a fertile ground for researchers. In the period between 1984 and 1987, a large number of evaluation studies were conducted, and even more are in the offing. In part, because such studies can be done on a small scale without massive research funding, there has been more concerted research effort to study the effect of child sexual abuse prevention education than nearly any other issue within the field of child abuse and neglect. Thus studies have accumulated quickly. The last formal reviews of these studies were done when the literature consisted of just a handful of efforts (Conte, 1984; Daro; Hazzard & Angert, 1986). There are now enough new studies that an updated overall assessment of their findings is in order.

## METHOD

Because so much work is currently in progress, for this review, in addition to searching the literature, we also contacted a network of researchers known to be active in the field. From located studies attention was concentrated on programs where at least one of the functions was to directly train children. Programs that were exclusively focused on parent education were eliminated.

Ultimately, our sample consisted of 25 studies (see Table 7.1), about two-thirds of which had never appeared in a professional journal. The studies

**TABLE 7.1. Studies of Child Sexual Abuse Prevention Programs**

| Study | Source of Sample | Number | Program Presented | Evaluation Method |
|---|---|---|---|---|
| Beland, 1986 | Elementary schools Washington State 2nd & 3rd graders | 314 | Talking About Touching (TAT) | Paper/pencil test |
| Binder & McNiel, 1986 | Elementary school Western city Ages 5–12 | 88 | Child Assault Prevention Program (CAP) | Role play questionnaire |
| Borkin & Frank, 1986 | Preschool children Ages 3–5 | 100 | *Bubbylonian Encounter* (puppet show and coloring book) | Interview |
| Conte, Rosen, Saperstein, & Shermack, 1985 | Day care & elementary school Cook Co., Chicago, IL Ages 4–10 | 40 | Cook Co. Sheriff's office program | Paper/pencil test |
| Daro, Duerr, & LeProhn, 1986 | 7 preschools Southern CA | 505 | CAP, Children's Self-Help, TAT, Touch Safety, Child Abuse Prevention, Intervention & Education, Youth Safety Awareness Project, & SAFE | Story telling, paper/ pencil test |
| Downer, 1986 | Elementary school Seattle, WA Ages 9–10 | 85 | TAT Questionnaire | Puppet show |
| Fryer, Kraizer, & Miyoshi, 1987 | Elementary school Denver, CO K, 1st & 2nd grades | 44 | Children Need to Know Personal safety training program | Role play & questionnaire |
| Garbarino, 1987 | Elementary school Central PA 2nd, 4th & 6th graders | No exact no. reported | *Spiderman* comic book | Questionnaire |
| Kenning, Gallmeier, Jackson, & Plemons, 1987 | Elementary school Midwestern community & Northeastern OK 1st & 2nd graders | 72 44 | CAP TAT | Questionnaire Vignette |

| Reference | Setting | Program | N | Method |
|---|---|---|---|---|
| Kolko, Moser, Litz, & Hughes, 1987 | 3 elementary schools Washington CO, PA 3rd & 4th graders | *Red Flag/Green Flag* (coloring book) *Better Safe Than Sorry II* (Film) | 349 | Paper/pencil test Questionnaire |
| Leake, 1986a | 3 elementary schools San Joaquin Co., CA 1st, 2nd & 3rd graders | CAP | 90 | Role play |
| Leake, 1986b | 3 elementary schools San Joaquin Co., CA 5th graders | CAP & No More Secrets | 45 | Role play |
| Lutter & Weisman, 1985 | Campfire Program Massachusetts | Children's Awareness Training | 323 | Paper/pencil test Role play |
| Miltenberger & Thiesse-Duffy, 1988 | At-Home study Midwestern community Ages 4–7 | *Red Flag/Green Flag* | 24 | One-to-one training by parents Role play |
| Ostbloom, Richardson, & Galey, 1987 | Preschools & elementary schools throughout Iowa Ages 3–7 | *Happy Bear* | approx. 3500 | Skit/questionnaire |
| Plummer, 1984 | Elementary school Southern MI 5th graders | EPSA (Education for the Prevention of Sexual Abuse) | 69 | Role play and film |
| Ray, 1984 | Elementary school Spokane, WA 3rd graders | *My Very Own Book About Me* | 167 | Workbook and movie |
| Sigurdson, Doig, & Strang, 1985 | Elementary school Manitoba, Canada 4tn, 5th & 6th graders | *Feeling Yes Feeling No* | 137 | Videotape and questionnaire |
| Swan, Press, & Briggs, 1985 | Elementary school Ages 8–11 | Bubbylonian Encounters (play) | 68 | Vignettes/questionnaire |
| Wall, 1983 | Elementary school Northern CA 4th & 5th graders | CAP | 147 | Questionnaire |

*continued on next page*

**TABLE 7.1.** *(Continued)*

| Study | Source of Sample | Number | Program Presented | Evaluation Method |
|---|---|---|---|---|
| Wolfe, MacPherson, Blount, & Wolfe, 1986 | 3 Elementary schools Charleston, SC 4th & 5th graders | 290 | You're In Charge | Questionnaire |
| Women Associates Consulting, Inc. n.d. | Elementary school Toronto Grades K–6 | 529 | Missing from Ydob | Interview & questionnaire |
| Woods & Dean, 1985 | Elementary schools Knoxville, TN | approx. 3500 | TAT *Spiderman* comic book | Vignette Questionnaire |
| Wurtele & Miller-Perrin, 1981 | 2 Elementary schools Eastern WA Kindergarten students | 25 | Behavioral Skills Training Program (BST) | Role play |
| Wurtele, Saslawsky, Miller, Marrs, & Britcher, 1986 | Elementary school Eastern Washington State K, 1st, 5th, 6th graders | 71 | Touch Behavioral Skills Training Program | Questionnaire |

covered a wide variety of geographic areas. Most were conducted in the United States, and two reported findings based on research in Canada. All but two of the studies were of elementary and day care students receiving instruction in a standard classroom setting. Miltenberger and Thiesse-Duffy's (1988) study was a home-based study with no in-school instruction, and Lutter & Weisman (1985) was a program adopted and administered by the Campfire organization.

Children in the studies ranged in age from 3 to 12 years, the most common groups being third, fourth and fifth graders, and the range in sample size being 25 (Wurtele & Miller-Perrin, 1981) to over 3,500 (Woods & Dean, 1985). A wide variety of programs were examined, from widely disseminated programs such as Talking About Touching (TAT), Child Assault Prevention program (CAP), the *Spiderman* comic book, and No More Secrets (NMS) to customized or localized programs such as Ostbloom, Richardson, and Galley's (1987) *Happy Bear* and Ray's (1984) *My Very Own Book About Me.*

A wide range of evaluation methods were used in the 21 studies. Eleven studies used paper-and-pencil tests and questionnaires. Binder and McNiel (1986); Fryer, Kraizer, and Miyoshi (1987); Leake (1986a); Plummer (1984); and Wurtele and Miller-Perrin (1981) used role play as a means of evaluating children's knowledge. Ostbloom et al. (1987) and Wolfe, MacPherson, Blount, and Wolfe (1986) used skits in their evaluation. Plummer (1984), Kolko, Moser, Litz, and Hughes (1987), and Ray (1984) had their subjects view short films as part of their evaluation techniques. Downer (1986), Kenning, Gallmeier, Jackson, and Plemons (1987), and Woods and Dean (1985) incorporated vignettes into their study. One study, Fryer et al. (1987) used a unique simulation method, actually staging a situation where each child (K, first or second grader) was approached in the school hall by a strange man who asked if the child would accompany him to his car to help him bring in some cupcakes for his child's birthday party. These scenes were videotaped for evaluation.

## FINDINGS

The studies almost universally found that children acquired the prevention concepts after exposure to the programs. Twenty-four out of 25 studies concurred with this finding. Only Miltenberger and Thiesse-Duffy found that their prevention program, a story book (*Red Flag/Green Flag*) used by parents to teach their 4–7 year-old children, did not produce changes in personal safety knowledge or skills. Leake's (1986) study of fifth grade students also found that while one program (CAP) was effective; another, the No More Secrets (NMS) program, was not effective in teaching fifth grade students to recognize and avoid child abuse and assault. Leake suggests that the difference in performance may have been due to CAP's approach which involved each student by means of role play in contrast to the NMS approach, that is, simply viewing a short film followed by discussion.

Although the studies consistently reported significant learning, they also revealed that certain concepts were learned more easily than others. The facts about what is abuse, at least as conceptualized by the programs, were learned relatively easily. Daro, Duerr, and LeProhn (1986), Garbarino (1987), and Ostbloom et al. (1987) all found that their subjects demonstrated an improved ability to distinguish among various types of touch and to recognize body parts. On the other hand, certain concepts seem to be more difficult to grasp. The most difficult concept seemed to be recognizing that abuse could come from known adults. For example, in Plummer's (1984) study, after the training only 56% of the students believed molesters could "often" be "people I know," and by the eight-month follow up this had slipped to 39%. This backslide at follow up shows the lack of retained knowledge concerning this specific concept. In Ray's (1984) evaluation study, three out of five children incorrectly answered the question: "Do kids ever have touching problems with people they know and like?" Sigurdson, Doig, and Strang (1985) also reported that the most difficult concept to convey to children was the concept that the risk of sexual abuse is not from strangers, but from those who are very close to them, usually relatives.

Some studies also confirm the general principle that concepts are much easier to teach than behaviors. Unfortunately, most studies only looked at knowledge, not at behaviors. But Beland (1986), confirming Plummer (1984), found that the program (*Talking about Touching*) did not have as strong an effect on assertiveness skills (being able to say *no* in an actual role play) as on knowledge and problem solving. This finding was contested, however, by Kenning et al. (1987).

The studies also gave evidence that some children learn the concepts better than others. For example, they confirmed the not unexpected fact that older children learn better than younger children. Conte, Rosen, Saperstein, and Shermack (1985) as well as Sigurdson et al. (1985), Lutter & Weisman (1985) and Wurtele et al. (1986) reported that older children gave a larger number of correct responses to start with and learned more than other children.

More interestingly, Sigurdson et al. (1985) also reported that the females in their study scored higher than the boys. This was in contrast to studies by Ostbloom et al. (1987) and Garbarino (1987) which reported boys scored higher after program implementation. Garbarino's finding is easily explained since he used a special issue of the *Spiderman* comic book, a character with whom the boys were undoubtedly more familiar and with whom they could identify. But for studies in general, the gender differences will have to await further research. The majority of our studies did not examine the comparison between girls and boys.

Programs were compared in but a few of the studies. Woods and Dean (1985), for example, compared the Talking-About-Touching (TAT) with the *Spiderman* comic book approach, finding a greater increase in knowledge with children who had the TAT program. The TAT program probably did better because it involved children to a much greater degree than the passive reading involved in the comic book exposure. Leake (1986a) also compared programs: CAP (*Child Abuse Prevention*) program and NMS (*No More Secrets*). He reported the CAP program was more effective than NMS in teaching fifth grade students to recognize and avoid child abuse and assault. He also found that there was a tendency for NMS to teach children to respond *no* at inappropriate times. Once again, the different approach taken by the CAP presenters may have proven beneficial to the subjects involved. CAP actively involves the participants in role play situations, whereas NMS is a program consisting of a short film followed by discussion.

Wurtele et al. (1986) conducted a study where a program of Behavior Skill Training (BST) was compared with exposure to the prevention movie, "Touch." Consistent with the other studies which found more passive programs less successful, she found that the BST, which included role playing, was more effective than the film. Although Conte et al. (1985) did not do a comparative study, these researchers were disappointed that the children in their evaluation only seemed to have learned half the concepts. They concluded that the short duration of the program was responsible for this shortcoming. So perhaps not surprisingly, it appears that programs with more child involvement and of longer duration seem to be more effective.

Although most programs only tested children immediately after training, some tried through follow ups to see how well children retained their new knowledge. Plummer (1984), Ostbloom et al. (1987), and Lutter & Weisman (1985) measured students at multiple times (2 months and 8 months in the Plummer study and 1 month and 6 months in the Ostbloom et al. study and 6 months and 18 months in the Lutter study). These researchers found that at follow up children knew more than before training, but they also found a discouraging decay in knowledge as time passed. Plummer (1984) reports a significant loss in learning involving a number of concepts. For example, at both 2 and 8 months, 20% of the children had reverted to the conventional idea (contradicted by the program) that promises (to keep a secret) should never be broken, up from 1.4% at posttest. The number of children who were clear on the distinction between sexual and physical abuse dropped from 76.8% correct at posttest to about 45% at two- and eight-month follow up. While three-fourths of the children knew not to blame themselves for getting touched in sexual ways at posttest, this dropped to only half the children by 2 and 8 months follow up. Ostbloom et al. (1987) also found a decline in knowledge after only one month, and at 6 months there was further decline reported. Lutter and Weisman (1985) found decay in knowledge at 6 months, but it was greater among the younger than older children. At 18 months, there was equal and extensive dissipation of knowledge in all age groups. On the positive side, Plummer (1984) reports after 2 and 8 months that three-fourths of the children still knew what to do if touched in an embarrassing way by an acquaintance. At 8 months, 92% still recognized that both boys and girls could be victims of abuse, and over half the subjects continued to know the correct definition of *victim*. Overall, Plummer's (1984) subjects demonstrated that they were less willing to trust in, believe, obey, and rely on any and all adults—and this learning lasted for the full 8 months.

There has been a substantial public and professional concern about whether prevention education may have negative effects on children, an outcome looked for specifically in several studies. Reassuringly, Kolko et al. (1987), Ostbloom et al. (1987), Downer (1986), Binder and McNiel (1986), Conte et al. (1985) were unable to find any negative effects. Binder and McNiel (1986) as well as Lutter & Weisman (1985), asking about possible fearfulness, report that children actually found their programs to be fear reducing and confidence building. In Binder and McNiel (1986) 89% of the children felt safer, while only 3% felt more scared. Studies asking parents and teachers for signs of fear or anxiety, as well as those talking to students directly have failed to find problems. Wurtele and Miller-Perrin (1981) conducted a study entirely devoted to a search for possible negative effects and found none. Instead, parents noticed a significant *decrease* in possible problem behaviors among their children after the training.

On the other hand, by canvassing the research, one can find signs of increased fears or anxieties among some children under some circumstances. One study (Kenning et al., 1987) reports that as a result of children's increased ability to understand the concept of abuse, children may become more fearful in even non-exploitative situations following program presentation. Second graders appeared to have been left somewhat more anxious than first graders. Moreover, in Garbarino's (1987) study, half of the fourth grade boys and girls, and a substantial minority in second and sixth grades as well, said the comic made them feel worried or scared. Girls reported feeling worried or scared more than boys in second and sixth grade (35% vs. 17% in second grade and 30% vs. 17% in sixth grade). Examining the interviews, Garbarino (1987) reveals that most of the children reported feeling "a little" scared or worried, and most said it was because it made them realize "it" might happen to them. Many of the other studies, although they reported no group increase in fear, did not report the actual percentage of children who said it had made them afraid.

On a more encouraging note, the studies generally suggest that the programs prompt children to talk and ask questions about the problem of sexual abuse. Eighty percent of the parents Wurtele et al. (1986) surveyed noted that their children talked to them after the training. And even when they have no specific parent education component, the programs prompt parents to talk to their children. Daro et al. (1986) found that two-thirds of the parents discussed sexual abuse with their children following the program presentation.

The research also confirms educators' observations that the programs prompt children to disclose abuse they may have suffered. Beland (1986) found a doubling in disclosures of abuse during the following year at schools that had implemented programs but no such increase from schools that had not. Curiously, however, 35% of the schools with the programs still did not receive any disclosures, and the average rate for all experimental schools was only two disclosures per school during the year. These low rates may stem from the fact that Beland relied on principals, guidance counselors, and nurses for her information.

By contrast, Kolko et al. (1987), querying children and parents directly, found that 7½% of the children receiving the training reported an abusive experience within 6 months. These children were more likely to have told an adult about the experience (88% did so), and the parents of the group receiving the training, when asked, confirmed that they had indeed received more disclosures about inappropriate touching than had the parents of controls.

## DISCUSSION

It is encouraging to note the sheer quantity of research that is being done concerning sexual abuse prevention education and the pace at which new studies are appearing. Moreover, the findings of this literature have little affect on the enthusiasm of the creators and promoters of the programs. They almost without exception give good marks to the programs, and the cautions they urge are generally those that the educators themselves have already recognized. However, the evaluations to date have been fairly superficial and have not yet addressed several of the harder and deeper questions.

The overwhelming and irrefutable message of the evaluation studies is that children do indeed learn the concepts they are being taught. They learn that some kinds of touching are bad, that this kind of touching can occur with people they know, that they have a right to say *no*, that they should tell adults, and so forth. The better of the studies have also demonstrated that this learning is not simply a rote parroting of ideas but that children can apply the concepts even in imaginary situations and role plays. At least one study using a simulation test suggests that the learning translates into appropriate behavior in the real world, although this and several other studies caution that the acquisition of new behaviors (like assertiveness and the ability to say *no*) is less reliable and less universal than the acquisition of ideas.

The research delineates some other expected characteristics of the learning process. Older children learn the concepts better than younger children, undoubtedly because they are more cognitively developed and have had more practice in the kind of group learning situations that the programs utilize. Some programs seem to work better than others. On this issue, more research is needed, but the present studies do suggest that programs that get children more actively involved; for example, using role plays, do better than those that rely primarily on passive exposure (e.g., film and discussion) or individual study (e.g., workbooks or comic books).

The studies also strongly suggest that the training needs reinforcement at a later time. There is an apparent decay of the learning over time. The more problematic concepts that run most counter to common social assumptions; for example, that offenders can be close family members, tend to evaporate the most rapidly. The decay is apparent even after 1–2 months, suggesting at the least that annual boosters may be required. However, once the learning has been reinforced on several occasions, it is not clear how often it needs to be repeated. Longer term studies will undoubtedly cast light on this question.

On one of the most controversial subjects—whether the programs make children anxious or fearful—the research to date is fairly reassuring. The majority of children do not show signs of fear, according both to their own statements and to the observations by parents and teachers. It would appear that the nature of the program, however, can make a difference in how much fear is experienced. A fairly large minority (quarter to a third) of those exposed to the *Spiderman* comic indicated that it made them feel worried or scared. In the isolated activity of reading a comic book alone, children may feel more anxiety than in a group situation where they experience the direct optimism and strength of the group and the adult leaders. The Spiderman findings, although not manifested in other studies, do indicate that a concern about frightening children is not irrational and that programs need to be careful to design themselves to avoid this effect.

Moreover, the fact that there are some children who may get anxious in response to the programs needs to be the subject of more future research. Unlike the measures of learning, it is not enough for studies simply to show that *as a group* children who receive the programs are not more anxious posttest than pretest or more anxious than the controls. Even if a small number of children get anxious, and this is not true for the group as a whole, this is a worrisome finding and needs to be examined in detail. It is not clear how many children have to get fearful or how symptomatic they have to be before educators should be concerned. But the research needs to address this in greater depth. It is disappointing that only about a quarter of the studies looked at some outcome measure of children's anxiety. Fortunately, at least a couple of those suggest that programs can be implemented that create virtually no anxiety and even decrease it.

Another interesting and encouraging finding from the research is that the programs encourage discussions between children and their parents. Many children go home from the training and talk about what they have learned at home. This happens even in the absence of specific training aimed at the parents. This certainly suggests that one of the best ways to reinforce school-based training is to make sure that parents are familiar with concepts and able to give children boosters.

Curiously, what is perhaps the most important unambiguous finding from the whole experiment with prevention education is something that is only mentioned sporadically in the research literature: Prevention education encourages children to report abuse they have already suffered. Educators who teach these programs all report that they receive many disclosures from children in the aftermath. In fact, most programs have had to develop formal procedures for coping with the raft of disclosures they generally receive.

The research generally confirms the fact that the programs precipitate disclosures, but it gives few specifics about this phenomenon. Researchers have not studied systematically the percentage of children who disclose, the types of disclosures they make, or how these disclosures vary according to type of program, age of children or type of school context. One study (Kolko et al., 1987) reports that about 7½% of the children in the training disclosed abuse in the 6 months following. Another (Beland, 1986) reports a doubling of disclosures at schools where programs are implemented. These encouraging findings support the perceptions of the educators. But many more specifics are needed, both for the educators to help them understand the relative value of their programs and also to assess the general impact of the prevention education process.

## MAJOR UNKNOWNS

### Does It Prevent Abuse?

The most glaring and conspicuous question in the field, however, is whether sexual abuse prevention education really is capable of preventing sexual abuse. The theory behind the programs makes sense, and the evidence that children learn the concepts is a good sign. The central goal of the programs, however, remains essentially untested. There are good reasons to worry, too. Some recent work with molesters, which has tried to better understand their thinking and *modus operandi*, points out the persistence and guile with which they approach children (Conte, Wolf, & Smith, 1987). Given the cleverness, authority, and material resources many adults command, can children ever be expected to win? Moreover, there are good questions about whether prevention concepts will really have application in the heat of a real molester-child interaction. In the emotionally charged interactions between father and daughter, will the concept of bad touch come to mind? Will the admonitions of a school teacher really carry weight in the face of the reassurances of a real life parent? These questions are difficult to answer and the research gives little help.

A major stumbling block is that a research design that would offer the answers has not yet been executed. Any such design would have to have a serious and intensive follow up of children, of the sort that has not yet been done. But more importantly, it would have to resolve a very serious problem: how to get a large sample of young children to talk candidly about abuse and attempted abuse. Obtaining such information from children is certainly not out of the question; investigators looking into allegations of abuse do it routinely. It suggests a design, however, that involves intensive investigation-type interviews with children. Such an interview procedure brings with it a host of attendant ethical questions: 1) whether and how to get parental permission, 2) how to handle the state reporting requirements considering that some disclosures may be of unsuccessful attempts around which the children may not actually be seeking help, and 3) how to keep the interview from being traumatic in and of itself. The researchers who embark on such a study, which would thoroughly screen several hundred normal children for a history of sexual abuse, have their work cut out for them.

Such an intensive study, however, is not the only approach to assessing the ultimate effectiveness of prevention education. There are less challenging designs that could give interim answers. Studies that simply monitor over the years unprompted disclosures from children with and without the education will provide some clues to whether the education is working. There is a problem in that the programs both teach prevention skills *and* encourage reports, so that a high level of disclosures from a trained group does not necessarily mean a failure of the program. The researchers need to look for effectiveness by examining the types of disclosures from the trained versus the untrained group: the trained group should disclose more short-term molestations or attempts at molestation that the children told an adult about right away. In any case, research really needs to start grappling with this part of the problem. It is encouraging to find that children learn the prevention concepts. But until there is evidence that they actually avoid or short-circuit abuse, justified doubts will remain.

### Does It Mitigate Impact of Sexual Abuse?

Even if education programs do not actually prevent sexual abuse, they may well have other important salutary functions. First, they may encourage more immediate reporting. This goal of the programs is widely recognized, and the research suggests that it works. Another potentially salutary function has received less attention: The programs may reduce the trauma of sexual abuse, even when it does occur. One of the most traumatic features of sexual abuse, according to retrospective accounts of victims, is the sense of isolation, of never hearing others discuss problem, of not knowing that such abuse occurs to others. It is possible that when children hear widespread discussions about abuse, it acts to relieve some of the stigma among those who may later become victims.

Of course, it may have the opposite effects as well. Sanford (1980) has cautioned educators against creating additional guilt in victims, who, if they have received prevention education, may feel in addition to everything else, that they were responsible or inadequate because they were not capable of effectively using the resistance tactics that they had been taught. Thus in looking at the impact of prevention education researchers need to look beyond whether it decreases abuse and increases reporting to whether it mitigates or exacerbates the trauma of abuse among victims.

## Effects on Sexuality

The concern that the programs may create anxiety or fear of adults is an issue that researchers appear willing and able to address. Although more such research is needed, the preliminary findings from studies appear encouraging. A more troublesome concern, however, is the effect of these programs on children's sexual development. Most of the programs are not overtly about sexuality and dwell very little on explicit sexual issues, largely because these issues are controversial. It seems plausible, however, that children draw implications about sexuality from the programs. For example, if children have already had peer sexual experiences (playing doctor, etc.), what sense do they make of it after all the discussion about good and bad touching. Are they apt to feel guilty or confused, especially since the programs are unlikely to give such sex play specific endorsement? How many of the children exposed to these programs get the idea that sexual touching is always or almost always bad or dangerous or exploitative? How often are these programs the first thing to come back to mind when children begin to confront sexual issues later on and do they add clarity or confusion to their thinking? These are all important issues that have not been considered very thoroughly by the educators themselves, not to mention the researchers.

Unfortunately, these issues relate to the study of children's sexual development, one of the most unexamined areas in all of social science. The neglect of this subject is due to social taboos, the political controversies that make it very sensitive for adults even as professionals to talk to children about sex, and the ethical ambiguities that surround the problem. Although crucially important, it seems unlikely that sexual abuse prevention researchers will boldly tread where others have retreated. However, such researchers should at least consider the possibility of formulating a few questions to see whether programs have any impact on children's attitudes toward sex. The importance of the subject merits some effort.

## Additional New Directions

The discussion so far has alluded to a number of new methodological directions that research on prevention education needs to pursue. The most obvious, of course, is the truly long-term follow up. The follow-up design as it has been tried to date has focussed primarily on seeing how well children retain their learning, and such studies need to be expanded and developed. The truly long-term follow up should ideally be used to answer the question about whether the training actually prevents abuse. In fact, an ideal design might be to follow children to a point in young adulthood where they could more readily and comfortably answer questions retrospectively about incidents of abuse that may or may not have happened subsequent to their training. In this perspective it might be clear whether or not the programs were effective.

Research studies on the effect of sexual abuse prevention have also mostly had a fairly uniform and predictable format. They are generally either one group pretest-posttest designs, posttest only control group designs, or pretest-post-test control group designs (Campbell & Stanley, 1963). Other important and interesting questions, however, need to be examined outside such normal designs. For example, there is the question of how sex abuse prevention education affects molesters. One piece of evidence indicating the success of the training would be if potential molesters become more wary and less aggressive in their predation. Moreover, if molesters tend to find that more children are refusing their advances or tell stories that suggest the children are using the prevention concepts—this would be welcome evidence, too. Researchers need to be interviewing molesters around these questions with an eye toward examining the effectiveness of prevention education.

Another research direction that falls outside the realm of the classic evaluation design is qualitative studies of children with the training who were victimized nonetheless. As more and more children receive training, an increasingly large amount of reported abuse will involve such children. It may be very enlightening to interview them about why. Had they forgotten their prevention concepts? Did they try them and find that they did not work? Did they fail to see how the prevention concepts applied in the situation they confronted? Any such interview would have to be conducted with great sensitivity so as not to make a child feel guilty for failing to stop abuse. But such a study might provide important insights useful for modifying programs, teaching other skills, or giving children a more realistic assessment of when and how the skills are useful and when they are not.

## CONCLUSION

An impressive quantity of research has been done since 1984 on the impact of sexual abuse prevention education. The most clearly established finding is that children do indeed learn the prevention concepts that the programs teach. However, we do not know yet, and may not know for some time, whether the programs actually help children to avoid abuse. Establishing this is a complex and difficult research task. What we can say, and this is probably the most important finding to date, is that the programs clearly prompt many victimized children to disclose. Since it is in this area, rather than in the prevention area where the programs are most clearly successful, it might make sense to rename the programs "sexual abuse disclosure facilitation programs" or at least "sexual abuse prevention education *and disclosure* programs." The disclosure function of the programs should not be de-emphasized. For even if the programs ultimately were to be shown ineffective in preventing much abuse, the disclosures they prompt are a major accomplishment. They certainly rescue many children, who would not have otherwise been rescued, from extremely troublesome and traumatizing situations, and they short-circuit situations which might otherwise have continued for an extended period of time at much greater ultimate cost to the child's mental health. We certainly think that researchers and educators themselves might place even more focus on the disclosure function and the disclosure successes of these programs.

In addition, it goes almost without saying that research efforts to study sex abuse prevention programs must be broadened and continued. But a larger perspective must also not be lost. Currently in both research and social policy, most efforts at sex abuse prevention *and mitigation* are focussed on teaching these prevention concepts to children. There are a variety of other prevention initiatives that must not be neglected, however. Prevention efforts need to be focussed on parents, adults, and potential abusers, too. For example, we know that children become more vulnerable when they have poor supervision or are emotionally deprived. Parents and other caretakers have the power to address this vulnerability, and programs can support this. We also are beginning to understand some of the roots of molesting behavior, its genesis in childhood, its connection with maltreatment, the ideas and conditions which permit fantasies to be translated into actions. Prevention initiatives need to be directed toward stopping the development of this behavior in potential molesters. It is only by embarking on a variety of initiatives at the same time that we can address all the sources of sexual abuse in our society and have any hope for success in combatting this deeply rooted problem.

## REFERENCES

Beland, K. (1986). *Prevention of child sexual victimization: A school based statewide prevention model*. Seattle: Committee for Children.

Binder, R., & McNiel, D. (1986). *Evaluation of a school-based sexual abuse prevention program: Cognitive and emotional effects*. Paper presented at the 1986 Annual Meeting of the American Psychiatric Association, Washington, DC.

Borkin, J., & Frank, L. (1986). Sexual abuse prevention for preschoolers: A pilot program. *Child Welfare*, 65(1), Jan/Feb.

Campbell, D., & Stanley, J. (1963). *Experimental and Quasi-Experimental Designs for Research*. Chicago: Rand McNally.

Conte, J. (1984). *Research on the prevention of sexual abuse of children*. Paper presented at the Second National Conference for Family Violence Researchers, Durham, NH.

Conte, J., Rosen, C., Saperstein, L., & Shermack, R. (1985). An evaluation of a program to prevent the sexual victimization of young children. *Child Abuse & Neglect*, 9(3):319–328.

Conte, J., Wolf, S., & Smith, T. (1987). *What sexual offenders tell us about prevention: Preliminary findings*. Paper presented at the Third National Family Violence Research Conference, Durham, NH.

Daro, D. (n.d.). *Evaluating child assault prevention classes*. Berkeley: Family Welfare Research Group.

Daro, D., Duerr, J., & LeProhn, N. (1986). *Child assault prevention instruction: What works with preschoolers*. Chicago: National Committee for the Prevention and Child Abuse & Neglect.

Downer, A. (1986). *Evaluation of 'Talking About Touching.'* Seattle: Committee for Children.

Fryer, G., Kraizer, S., & Miyoshi, T. (1987). Measuring actual reduction of risk to child abuse: A new approach. *Child Abuse & Neglect, 11*(2):173–179.

Garbarino, J. (1987). How do children respond to sexual abuse prevention? A preliminary study of the Spiderman comic book. *Child Abuse & Neglect, 11*(1): 143–148.

Hazzard, A., & Angert, L. (1986). *Child sexual abuse prevention: Previous research and future directions*. Paper presented at the American Psychological Association meeting, Washington, DC.

Kenning, M., Gallmeier, T., Jackson, T., & Plemons, S. (1987). *Evaluation of child sexual abuse prevention programs: A summary of two studies*. Paper presented at the National Conference on Family Violence, Durham, NH.

Kolko, D., Moser, J., Litz, J., & Hughes, J. (1987). Promoting awareness and prevention of child sexual victimization using the Red Flag/Green Flag program: An evaluation with follow-up. *Journal of Family Violence, 2*(1):11–35.

Leake, H. (1986a). *A study to compare the effectiveness of two primary prevention programs in teaching children to recognize and avoid child sexual abuse and assault*. Sexual Assault Center of San Joaquin County, CA.

Leake, H. (1986b). *A study to determine the effectiveness of the child assault prevention program in teaching first grade students to recognize and avoid child sexual abuse and assault*. Sexual Assault Center of San Joaquin County, CA.

Lutter, Y., & Weisman, A. (1985). *Sexual Victimization Prevention Project*. Final Report to the National Institute of Mental Health (Grant R18 MH39549).

Miltenberger, R., & Thiesse-Duffy, E. (1988). Evaluation of home-based programs for teaching personal safety skills to children. *Journal of Applied Behavior Analysis, 21*, 81–87.

Ostbloom, N., Richardson, B., & Galey, M. (1987). *Sexual abuse prevention projects*. Des Moines, IA: National Committee for Prevention of Child Abuse, Iowa Chapter.

Peters, S., Wyatt, G., & Finkelhor, D. (1986). Prevalence. In D. Finkelhor (Ed.), *Sourcebook On Child Sexual Abuse*. Newbury Park, CA: Sage Publications.

Plummer, C. (1984). *Preventing sexual abuse: What in-school programs teach children*. Durham, NH: National Conference for Family Violence Researchers.

Ray, J. (1984). *Evaluation of the child sex abuse prevention project*. Spokane, WA: Rape Crisis Network.

Sanford, L. (1980). *The silent children: A parent's guide to the prevention of child sexual abuse*. Garden City, NY: Doubleday.

Sigurdson, E., Doig, T., & Strang, M. (1985). *What do children know about preventing sexual assault? How can their awareness be increased?* Paper presented at the 77th annual conference of the Canadian Public Health Association, Vancouver, BC.

Swan, H., Press, A., & Briggs, S. (1985). Child sexual abuse prevention: Does it work? *Child Welfare, 64*(4), July/August.

Wall, H. (1983). *Child assault/abuse prevention project: Pilot program evaluation.* Concord, CA: Mt. Diablo Unified Schools.

Wolfe, D., MacPherson, T., Blount, R., & Wolfe, V. (1986). Evaluation of a brief intervention for educating school children in awareness of physical and sexual abuse. *Child Abuse & Neglect, 10*:85–92.

Women Associates Consulting, Inc. (n.d.). Toronto: Metropolitan Chairman's Special Committee on Child Abuse Demonstration Project.

Woods, S., & Dean, K. (1985). *Evaluating sexual abuse prevention strategies.* Paper presented at the 7th National Conference on Child Abuse and Neglect, Chicago, IL: November 11–15, 1985.

Wurtele, S., & Miller-Perrin, C. (1981). An evaluation of side effects associated with participation in a child sexual abuse prevention program. *Journal of School Health, 57,* 228–231.

Wurtele, S., Saslawsky, D., Miller, C., Marrs, S., & Britcher, J. (1986). Teaching personal safety skills for potential prevention of sexual abuse: A comparison of treatments. *Journal of Consulting and Clinical Psychology, 54,* 688–692.

# CHAPTER 8

# The Improbability of Prevention of Sexual Abuse

GARY B. MELTON

In the periodic waves of concern about various problems of childhood and family life (see Melton, 1987b), sexual abuse has become the issue of the 1980s. Reporting rates have skyrocketed, criminal prosecution of offenders has become much more common, and the public's eyes and ears have been barraged with the issue in news magazine cover stories, television documentaries, and made-for-TV movies. A cottage industry has arisen for sale of anatomically correct dolls, pictures of missing children, and books and films about sexual abuse (see, e.g., National Committee for Prevention of Child Abuse, 1985/1986).

Legislatures' responses to the discovery of sexual abuse generally have been of two types: a) procedural and evidentiary reforms designed to make prosecution of offenders easier and to diminish stress induced by the legal system on child victim/witnesses, and b) establishment of children's trust funds to support programs intended to prevent child maltreatment. The scope of the latter programs usually extends beyond sexual abuse to other forms of maltreatment, although about one-fourth of the dollars from children's trust funds goes to sexual abuse prevention.

Whether supported by trust funds or other sources, sexual abuse education programs have developed with amazing speed. Although such programs did not exist at all until the late 1970s, over 25 percent of public schools now offer such instruction (Daro, Duerr, & LeProhn, 1987). In the most far-

This chapter is based on a paper presented at the meeting of the American Psychological Association in New York in August 1987.

The ideas for the chapter arose in conversations with Donald Bross. Although our views differ on some key points, Anne Cohn and Deborah Daro also provided stimulating comments on an earlier version of this manuscript. My colleague Mary Kenning assisted with access to unpublished studies.

Financial support for the author's research on sexual abuse has been provided by the National Center on Child Abuse and Neglect (No. 90-CA-1274).

reaching single initiative, the California General Assembly (Maxine Waters Child Abuse Prevention Training Act, 1984) has appropriated $44 million over four years to provide sexual abuse education to every child in the California public schools five times in their school career (once each in preschool, kindergarten, elementary school, junior high, and high school).

I have previously indicated concern that the rash of new legislation altering procedural and evidentiary rules in sexual abuse cases may be unnecessary and ineffective and indeed may have stronger negative side effects than positive direct effects (Lloyd, Rogers, & Melton, 1986; Melton, 1985, 1987a). In that regard, I have argued that legislatures should slow their activity until the legal and psychological bases of such statutory reform are better conceptualized and the effects of the extant legislation are evaluated. Such legislation often has served as a low-cost, quick fix that has satisfied the clamor for legislators to do something about child sexual abuse, but that has diverted attention from more conceptually and empirically based approaches and masked the complexity of the problem.

This chapter has a similar theme. I will argue that psychological theory, the few evaluation studies on sexual abuse prevention programs, and research in analogous contexts all lead to conclusions that the substantial new investment in sexual abuse education programs is unlikely to result in a substantial preventive effect, and that the possibility of unintended negative effects has not been ruled out. Although I can imagine alternative approaches to prevention that follow more logically from what is known about sexual abuse, such conceptually based essentially untried approaches also are fraught with technical difficulty in implementation and may have negative side effects. In short, despite my conviction that population-based preventive approaches are generally the most cost-effective response to problems of children and families (see, e.g., Melton, 1983), I believe that there are inherent obstacles to primary prevention of sexual abuse. Further adoption of such programs should be delayed until the assumptions underlying them have been tested and evaluations have confirmed with reasonable certainty that their effects are substantially more positive than negative.

I am not alone in raising concern about the speed with which state legislatures and local school systems have adopted sexual abuse education programs. In their recent review of child abuse prevention strategies, Wald and Cohen (1986) concluded:

> While parent education programs are benign, the same is not necessarily true of the new wave of sexual abuse education programs. Although there is little in the way of evaluation of such programs, it is quite possible that the materials presented to the children could do more to frighten children than to enable them to protect themselves. . . . We are skeptical that such programs will enable children to resist abuse *within* the family. Moreover, to the extent that legislators believe that they are meeting their obligation to prevent sexual abuse by funding

these programs, such programs may actually end up putting more children at risk, because more meaningful (and expensive) strategies will be ignored.

We want to stress that there is not, as of yet, an adequate basis for concluding that such programs are either good or bad or both. Yet, unlike prevention programs based on causal theories of abusive behavior, these programs have no tested theory: they are based on an unproven assumption that knowledge enables children to protect themselves. This seems dubious to us. We believe that there should be searching evaluations of such programs before they are made a major part of a prevention strategy. (pp. 295–296)

Similarly, in his presidential address to the Division of Community Psychology of the American Psychological Association, Reppucci (1987) also sounded a cautionary note:

I am an advocate of preventive interventions, especially where children are concerned. But I am also an advocate of bringing about change that is based on at least a modicum of information from systematic empirical investigation. In the case of child sexual abuse, we are not ready to move toward primary prevention programs of the sort that are currently sweeping the country. Although some children may be helped by these programs, they may be creating problems for many others and for their families. Nevertheless, many of us are strongly advocating these programs to a fearful public without emphasizing that there may be negative side effects for some children. At the very least, we should be conducting careful longitudinal outcome research, which we are not. (p. 12)

## THE EPIDEMIOLOGY OF SEXUAL ABUSE

To appreciate the difficulty of prevention, knowledge of several facts about the epidemiology of sexual abuse is necessary. First, the problem is one of large scale. Most children are not abused, but sexual abuse is a common event in absolute terms. Although no consensus has emerged about precise prevalence figures for sexual abuse prior to adulthood—in part due to the lack of consensus about the definition of sexual abuse—the median of rates across studies is 20% of females and 7% of males (Peters, Wyatt, & Finkelhor, 1986).

Second, the prevalence of sexual abuse is not strongly linked to demographic factors, thus severely limiting the utility of identification of risk groups as targets for prevention programs. No constellation of social-psychological factors (when aggregated) has accounted for more than about 10% of the variance in prevalence (Finkelhor, 1984). The strongest single factor in prevalence rates is gender, but as shown above, substantial numbers of boys also are subjected to abuse.

Unlike physical abuse and neglect, sexual abuse is unrelated to social class (Peters et al., 1986). High-risk communities may not be possible to identify (unlike physical maltreatment). However, identification of high-risk families may be possible. Elevated risk of sexual abuse, at least for girls, occurs in families that are troubled or in transition—where a parent is absent, a mother is unavailable because of disability or high mother-daughter conflict, parents are themselves in conflict, the mother's educational status is markedly inferior to the father's, and/or a stepfather is present (Finkelhor, 1984; Peters et al., 1986).

Even if it is not possible to identify particularly high-risk families, it may be possible to organize prevention efforts around the family issues that are disproportionately common in families of sexually abused girls. Sexuality itself seems to be a particular source of conflict (Finkelhor, 1984). Sexually abused girls are disproportionately likely to have sexually punitive mothers and unaffectionate fathers and mothers.

Thus there may be some preventive emphases that can be derived from research on risk factors. However, the more remarkable finding is simply how little commonality there is among sexually abused children and their families. With current knowledge, a risk-group approach is unlikely to be very profitable in sexual abuse prevention.

Third, although the modal age of onset of sexual abuse appears to be around 10 or 11 (Peters et al., 1986), many cases occur at younger ages. In Finkelhor's (1984) general-population survey of the Boston metropolitan area, 37% of parents' reports of sexual abuse of their children involved children under age 7. Similarly, in Conte and Berliner's (1981) description of their clinical sample in Seattle, 18.1% of cases involved children age 6 or under, and 40.0% of the victims were under age 10. Therefore, to prevent most cases, prevention efforts would need to be started in the preschool years or, at latest, the primary grades.

Fourth, insufficient knowledge is available about the characteristics of offenders to plan a risk-group approach to them. (The one possible exception is the fact that the overwhelming majority of offenders are male.) Virtually all of the research available is on psychological characteristics of offenders, and most of it consists of clinical descriptions of incarcerated offenders, who are atypical even of apprehended offenders (see Araji & Finkelhor, 1986). Without a population survey, statements about the social characteristics of offenders cannot be confidently made.[1] However, in view of the fact that victim surveys show that the perpetrator in perhaps two-thirds of cases is a relative or acquaintance (Finkelhor, 1984), offenders probably share the socioeconomic diversity of their victims.

To summarize, planners of sexual abuse prevention are faced with trying to prevent a social problem of enormous proportions that seems to be endemic to most identifiable social groups. Little distinguishes victimized children and

---

[1]I recognize the difficulty of conducting such a study. However, it is not impossible. Methods are available to ensure anonymity of response, and they have been used in other contexts for participants to report illegal behavior without fear of detection (see Boruch & Cecil, 1979).

their families from their peers. Little is known about the characteristics of offenders, but it is doubtful that a thorough picture will be much more helpful in delineating a risk profile. It does appear that sexual abuse is typically, although certainly not universally, symptomatic of family problems, even when a family member is not the perpetrator. The epidemiological literature suggests that the tasks involved in primary prevention of sexual abuse are large ones: widespread social change (in view of the pandemic proportions of the problem) and change in the most private aspects of family life.

## SEXUAL ABUSE EDUCATION

### Characteristics

Faced with such a large but hidden social problem, developers of sexual abuse prevention programs have almost always avoided efforts to target families or communities. Instead, they have focused their efforts on changing children's own behavior.

Although the resulting educational programs have differed somewhat in their nuances, the similarities have been much more striking than the differences. Almost all programs have attempted to teach what sexual abuse is, although they frequently do so without direct discussion of sexuality at all. The most specific that programs typically become in discussing the sexual aspects of sexual abuse is to mention protection of private zones or parts of the body covered by a bathing suit.

Instead of directly teaching about sexual abuse, programs typically have described kinds of touch (e.g., *good*, *bad*, *confusing*, *uh-oh*), and some have taught children to rely on their intuition in determining whether a touch is appropriate. Most programs also have emphasized reporting of actual or threatened abuse (e.g., "run and tell"). In that connection, many programs have taught differences between *secrets* and *surprises*, and many have attempted to empower children to exercise control over their bodies by teaching that personal rights are involved or providing assertiveness training.

### Evaluations

Although the literature remains scant, several evaluations of sexual abuse education programs have been conducted in recent years. All of the studies that are available have significant methodological limitations. Nonetheless, when taken together with the theoretical bases for skepticism that we will discuss later, they suggest that sexual abuse education has weak preventive effects at best.

Avoidance of stranger molestation, despite its relative infrequency, has been the most common criterion variable, perhaps reflecting conceptual weaknesses in the programs themselves. Two studies used multiple-baseline designs and very small samples to assess effectiveness of behavioral training to avoid molestation. Using a combination of modeling, rehearsal, and social and material reinforcement, Poche, Brouwer, & Swearingen (1981) trained three preschool children to avoid strangers in the preschool playground by saying that they had to ask their teacher if they could go with an adult and running back to the school playground. The outcome of the training was assessed by having a young man approach the children individually and ask them to leave the school. All three children responded appropriately on follow up.

Peterson (1984) trained two groups of three children how to avoid strangers who seek by phone to determine whether the child is alone or who seek admittance at the door. One group participated in a discussion group about personal safety, and the other used behavioral techniques (e.g., role playing with rewards for successive approximations of desired behavior). Both groups met for about 40 minutes per session in 16 sessions across eight weeks. Success in training was measured by performance on such tasks in a "pretend house." All three children in the behavioral training group scored at full criteria at posttest and five months thereafter. Two of the children in the discussion group scored at full criteria on the door task on the posttest, but this performance was not maintained on follow up. A small improvement was attained by the children in the discussion group on the phone task, but none achieved full criteria.

To determine generalization of training, a confederate of the investigator, posing as a repairman, actually called the child at home or came to the door. Performance was similar to that shown in the pretend house. All three of the children in the behavioral training group refused to admit the stranger at the door, and two of them also called their mothers. They also scored at full criteria on the phone task. However, children in neither group gave safe responses when a stranger was encountered outside the home, a situation on which training had not focussed. Peterson concluded that "there was little evidence that either training method affected competent or skillful behavior either positively or negatively in areas that had not been trained directly" (p. 289).

In the only experimental study of training in stranger avoidance (Fryer, Kraizer, & Miyoshi, 1987a), 44 children in grades K–2 in a Denver school were randomly assigned to such a program or a waiting-list control group. Children in the experimental group participated in eight 20-minute sessions. Children were taught the following rules for interaction with strange adults:

1. Stay an arm's length away.
2. Don't talk or answer questions.
3. Don't take anything.
4. Don't go anywhere. (p. 175)

To assess the effectiveness of training, children were met individually by a confederate on the school grounds who asked them to carry some materials to the school for a play or a party. (A question not addressed by the investigators is how the deception was maintained for multiple trials involving 44 children in the same school.) Children in the experimental group showed improvement after training, although a substantial proportion (21.7%, compared with 47.6% in the control group) complied with the stranger. Self-esteem and knowledge about personal safety was related to compliance rate in the experimental group but not the control group.

Fryer et al.'s (1987b) most impressive finding was that the proportion of children giving unsafe responses actually decreased substantially on a six-month follow-up. However, there are several important qualifiers to this finding. First, the attrition rate was substantial (31.8%). Second, as indicated above, some skepticism is reasonable about the success of the simulation on follow-up. Third, Fryer et al. reported anecdotal data suggesting that such simulations "are sensitive to subtle variations in protocol" (p. 184) and, implicitly, that children may be vulnerable to lures not specifically included in the training.

Studies that assess children's behavior in potentially dangerous situations, even if merely simulated, raise serious ethical issues. Such designs may actually desensitize children to strangers or arouse fear (Conte, 1987). More fundamentally, such observational studies are inherently deceptive and invasive of privacy.

Taking the studies at face value, though, they raise substantial doubt about whether educational programs can succeed in teaching stranger avoidance to young children. Although the studies show that some (but far from all) can be taught to avoid strangers in particular situations that they have rehearsed, the research also suggests that such skills do not generalize to other gambits that perpetrators might use, even when the training is quite intensive. I am not surprised by this finding. The sorts of rules taught in the Denver program provide little guidance to a child involved in a complex social interaction with a strange adult. In view of evidence that perpetrators commonly use sophisticated techniques of persuasion and social reinforcement (Wolf, Berliner, Conte, & Smith, 1987), little reason exists to believe that training in stranger avoidance would significantly diminish children's vulnerability, even if stranger molestation were sufficiently common to merit universal education about the subject.

### Touch Curricula

The most extensive, although still preliminary evaluation that has been reported of typical sexual abuse educational programs was conducted by Daro et al. (1987), who studied children in seven California preschools, each of which used a different curriculum. The length of the training varied from one session of less than a half-hour to 21 sessions of 15–20 minutes each. In a simple pre-post design, participants were asked how a "little bunny" would behave and feel in a variety of touching situations. They also were presented with a situation involving "a big bunny the little bunny didn't know."

On post-test, participants did show significant improvement in ability to distinguish among kinds of touches, offer ways that the little bunny's feelings could be changed by altering the form of touch, and avoid potentially dangerous situations (taking a carrot from a stranger bunny). However, the magnitude of the increases was small, and children still generally scored on the unsafe end of the continuum. Daro et al. concluded that "the instruction still left children unfamiliar with basic safety rules and somewhat confused over the concepts being presented" (p. 10).

In an experimental study of children in a preschool program or an after-school program (10 children in each program) at a Chicago day care center, Conte, Rosen, Saperstein, and Shermack (1985) evaluated the effectiveness of a program implemented by deputy sheriffs. Changes in knowledge and attitudes were assessed with a structured interview covering several major concepts; for example, names for parts of the body, appropriate responses to abuse, permissibility of secret-telling, "OK" and "not-OK" touch. Tapes of the training showed that the deputies emphasized stranger abduction, horror stories about risk, and assertiveness of response more than the curriculum specified.

Prior to training, children in the experimental group knew the correct answers to only 28% of the questions on pre-test. After training, they had improved significantly but still failed almost half of the items. Performance on abstract concepts[2] was especially poor, with preschoolers (4- and 5-year-olds) answering only 3.3 questions correctly (maximum = 22) and school-age children (6- to 10-year-olds) not doing much better ($m$ = 6.1).

Swan, Press, and Briggs (1985) evaluated the effects of *Bubbylonian Encounter*, a videotaped play that is intended to teach the concepts of positive, negative, and "forced sexual" touching. In a quasi-experimental design, children in grades 2 to 5 in a Kansas Catholic school were asked to identify the form of touch involved in five videotaped vignettes. However, the only sexual touching that was shown involved a hand mime by an adult man "to suggest a sexual molestation" of an adult woman. Therefore, "sexual" and "forced sexual" touching were confounded, and it was unclear whether the concepts of appropriate and inappropriate sexual behavior were acquired. Unsurprisingly, most children were able at pretest to identify the forced sexual scenes.

Swan et al. did find a switch in responses to the forced sexual scenes from "Try and stay away" to "Tell someone," although almost no children, even on pretest, indicated that the victim should "Keep it a secret" or "Pretend it didn't happen." A significant increase also occurred in the number of children who acknowledged that a family member "could . . . touch in this

---

[2]Conte et al. did not provide their rule for deciding which items were "abstract" and which were "explicit," and no examples were given. Presumably some of the definitional questions (e.g., the nature of an OK touch) fall into the former category, but this conclusion is conjectural.

way," a change that some unpublished research suggests decays over time (see Finkelhor, 1986b, for review).

In another study of *Bubbylonian Encounter*, Borkin and Frank (1986) used a coloring page and scratch-and-sniff stickers at the conclusion of the puppet show to try to reinforce the concepts in the play that had been shown to preschoolers. Four to six weeks later, coloring pages and stickers were used as memory prompts to recall the play. Almost none of the 3-year-olds and fewer than half of the 4- and 5-year-olds correctly recalled any of the safety rules presented in the play.[3]

Wolfe, McPherson, Blount, and Wolfe (1986) assessed the impact on fourth and fifth graders of brief skits and classroom discussions led by medical students about physical and sexual abuse. Only seven questions, all of them in a true-false format, were included in the evaluation questionnaire. None of the effect sizes were large (maximum of 12.4 percentage points). The questions that obtained a substantial proportion of *wrong* answers (about one-half in the control group and about 40% in the experimental group) all involved debatable propositions (e.g., "If children tell someone they trust that an adult is hurting them, probably no one will believe them").

A few investigators have attempted to create more valid measures. As in most other studies, Kenning (1985) administered a knowledge questionnaire to first- and second-graders in South Dakota who participated in a sexual abuse education program. However, she also presented vignettes with puppets depicting a bully, a stranger, and a familiar adult. In a simple pre-post design, significant changes in knowledge and behavioral responses (i.e., projective responses in the puppet vignettes) were observed. However, the mean differences were of quite small magnitude (1.31 points out of a possible 25 on the knowledge questionnaire; 1.97 out of 46 on the interview). In view of the lack of a control group, such differences simply may have reflected practice effects. Regardless, it is unreasonable to expect such low-magnitude changes to be reflected in behavior in potentially abusive situations.

In an experiment involving elementary-school children in eastern Washington, Saslawsky and Wurtele (1986) used similar procedures. After watching the film *Touch*, produced by Illusion Theatre, children in the experimental group showed low-magnitude gains in knowledge and response to hypothetical vignettes.

In the most sophisticated evaluation thus far, Wurtele, Saslawsky, Miller, Marrs, and Britcher (1986) used the knowledge questionnaire and the "what if" interview to assess the relative impact of *Touch*, a behavioral skills training group, or both interventions. No significant effect of training was shown on responses to the vignettes, but the experimental programs, especially the behavioral skills training, did increase knowledge about sexual abuse. Al-

---

[3]The wisdom of presenting such rewards also is questionable, given that children are invited to report instances of "not OK" touching by adults. Regardless of the actual effects, such temporal contiguity provides some credibility to perceptions that children are being reinforced for reporting abuse.

though the training was not differentially effective across age groups, older children did perform better than younger children.

The literature on the positive effects of typical curricula in sexual abuse education remains largely undeveloped. No large-scale developmental study has been attempted, no study has examined long-term effects or directly assessed effects on rates of abuse or reporting, and only Wurtele et al. (1986) systematically compared curricula or procedures. Nonetheless, one should not ignore the fact that the reported evaluation studies raise questions whether the concept of the touch continuum can be taught to young children and whether, even for older children, substantial gains in knowledge useful for protection against sexual abuse accrue from current prevention programs. The general finding at this point seems to be some increase in knowledge about sexual abuse among older children participating in prevention programs, but such changes are of low magnitude. Even if substantial learning did occur, the question would remain whether increases in children's knowledge result in prevention of abuse. It is noteworthy that the most facially valid measures have shown the weakest effects.

### Negative Side Effects

Research examining negative side effects of sexual abuse education is even less available. All that is known is anecdotal or based on small, unrepresentative samples.

Garbarino (1987) studied children's responses to a special issue of *Spiderman* comic that has been enormously widely disseminated (16 million copies). Seventy-three children in a single elementary school in Pennsylvania were interviewed about their response to the comic. Participants were asked 10 multiple-choice questions about the content of the comic, six of them dealing with sexual abuse. Results showed that most children had comprehended the comic book well. Substantial proportions of children (50% of fourth graders) reported that the comic made them worried or scared, with some evidence that children whose parents read the comic with them experienced greater fear. Garbarino speculated that the latter finding may show that "some parents may not be comfortable discussing these matters with their children and may communicate their own anxiety and fear to the children, thus upsetting the children more than is necessary" (p. 147).

In a simple pre-post study of a sample of 44 first and second graders in a rural Oklahoma school, most of them American Indians, no change was observed after training in scores on the Spielberger State-Trait Anxiety Inventory for Children (STAIC) and in self-reported affective responses to vignettes depicting interaction with an adult in various situations (Kenning, Gallmeier, Jackson, & Plemons, 1987). Although the fact that a generalized increase in anxiety was not observed is obviously positive, Kenning et al.'s results do not prove much, because the sorts of affective responses tapped by the instruments in the study bear little relation to those that commentators have hypothesized. If negative side effects (other than simply waste of resources when training is ineffective) do occur as a result of sexual abuse education, knowledge about them is unlikely to expand beyond mere anecdote[4] until more specific measures are developed (and validated) to assess sexual self-esteem and body image, sexual concepts, beliefs about relationships and affection, and so forth.

In another study using the STAIC as an outcome measure, Kleemeier and Webb (1986) studied elementary-school children in an Atlanta-area school. Knowledge scores and STAIC scores of the treatment group did not change more after sexual abuse education than they changed after no treatment in a comparison group. (The need for proper control groups—a missing element in the majority of the extant evaluation studies—is indicated.) However, the scores correlated with each other moderately negatively. Somewhat contradictorily, weak positive correlations were observed between STAIC scores and prior exposure to information or media presentations about sexual abuse.

Responses on follow-up questionnaires from parents were more troublesome. Although Kleemeier and Webb summarized their findings as showing "few negative reactions," their data indicate that substantial numbers of children showed responses that their parents viewed as aberrant. More than a third of the children were reported to have displayed negative emotional reactions (e.g., irritability, anxiety), and 20% were described as having exhibited negative behavioral responses (i.e., nightmares, 5%; sleep difficulty, 5%; disobedience, 5%; rude to strangers, 10%; reluctance to be touched, 10%). These findings give some credence to concerns both that some children may be frightened by sexual abuse education, and that others may be placed in an untenable position because of family norms about compliance and politeness with adults.

The minimal attention that has been given to discerning possible negative effects of sexual abuse education programs and the dramatic rate of adoption of such programs are remarkable in view of the number of commentators who have raised questions about side effects (e.g., Conte et al., 1985; Finkelhor, 1986b; Garbarino, 1987; Kraizer, 1986; Leventhal, 1987; Reppucci, 1987; Wald & Cohen, 1986). As Finkelhor (1986b) has emphasized, prevention programs may be teaching that sexuality per se is bad, a particularly ironic and tragic possibility in view of the evidence that puritanical family styles and beliefs are risk factors for sexual abuse. Curricula (and outcome measures) rarely have identified positive aspects of sexuality. By implication, as illustrated by Swan et al.'s (1985) evaluation study, sexual touch is "bad," "uh-oh," or "not-OK" touch.

In fact, some sexual abuse education programs may be not only inadvertently teaching that sexuality is bad, but also modeling that talking about it is taboo. A large-scale heterogeneous but unrepresentative survey in northern

---

[4]Of course, more might be learned about untoward (and positive) effects on children or families by systematization of the collection of anecdotes. However, such critical incident reporting requires a level of monitoring and frequency of prompts that may be impractical in a large-scale study.

Virginia showed that about 40% of adults disapproved of teaching correct names for body parts in sexual abuse education (Williams & Stith, 1987). Bowing to political realities, many sexual abuse education programs have avoided using sexual terms at all. If such negligence does have modeling effects, it may actually deter children from reporting abuse or at least make them feel more embarrassed and *dirty* in doing so.

To move to an even hotter issue, about half of the respondents in Williams and Stith's (1987) survey indicated disapproval of teaching "that it is more likely that someone the child knows and loves will sexually abuse him/her." I have already noted the seeming confirmation of myths about stranger abuse in some sexual abuse education and evaluation research programs. I also have noted the apparent instability of knowledge acquired about risk of abuse by a loved adult. As Kraizer (1986) put it, "children are unable to reconcile 'bad' touch occurring with 'good' people, that is, people they love" (p. 259).

Such findings, although not well established, are consistent with cognitive research in adults showing that new knowledge about probability of negative events generally affects perception of risks to the community but not to the individuals themselves (Tyler & Cook, 1984). Apart, though, from the practical problems of attempting changes in personal risk perception, a more fundamental question is whether such changes are desirable. I am not yet prepared to dismiss the collective intuition of much of the public on this point. Although sexual abuse is not a rare phenomenon, it also is clear that most adults are not abusers. Do we really want to communicate that they may be? What are the effects of insisting to children, at least by implication, that they may be at risk from their fathers, stepfathers, grandfathers, uncles, and older male friends? Do we really want children and families to behave as if this proposition were true?

Somewhat less onerously, the hypothesis is reasonable, although unstudied, that children exposed to *touch-continuum* curricula will develop at least transient erroneous beliefs or concerns as a result. As numerous commentators have noted, the experience of sexual abuse is rarely as unequivocally negative or confusing as curricula tend to portray it.[5] Some danger may result from children's mislabeling behavior as abusive (or nonabusive).

In other words, for some children, sexual abuse education may impede

---

[5]Lest I be misunderstood, I certainly am not arguing that sexual abuse is a positive or even neutral experience. Although sexual abuse is not disabling psychologically for most children subjected to it, some measurable negative psychological effects are common, at least in reported cases. Children often report abusive episodes as having been frightening or confusing (Browne & Finkelhor, 1986). However, clinical experience also suggests that children sometimes welcome the affection and attention that often accompanies abuse and find the sexual stimulation to be pleasurable. Although such ambivalence in victims' responses makes the abuse no less *bad* in a moral sense, it does create a problem for those who would label the experience of sexual abuse as *bad touch*. In essence, program designers have assumed that the morality of an interaction is consistently related to how it feels, an assumption that probably is false.

rather than enhance their skill in recognizing inappropriate sexual touching.[6] Anecdotes are common about such negative effects on children's understanding of sexuality and relationships (see, e.g., Kraizer, 1986). For example, after attending a play on sexual abuse prevention, my normally quite verbal and assertive daughter, then in second or third grade, expressed anxiety about telling a male relative that he was hugging her too hard, because she feared that he would think that she was accusing him of sexual abuse.

Typically, such erroneous inferences may be briefly held, and it is unclear how common they are. They also may be sufficiently idiosyncratic that they are difficult to operationalize and study. Nonetheless, the point is that no one yet has tried. Moreover, given that the concepts involved in most of the commonly used curricula are both abstract and usually not fully and openly discussed, it would be surprising if a significant proportion of young children did not draw unintended inferences. Regardless, the studies by Garbarino (1987) and Kleemeier and Webb (1986) do not reduce concern about possible negative side effects.

## Conceptual Problems

### Choice of the Target Group

At root, the major problem in sexual abuse prevention has been a lack of care in conceptualizing both intervention and evaluation. Perhaps the most fundamental conceptual problem in current efforts to prevent sexual abuse is suggested by the following statement of purpose:

> The *ultimate* goal of any program to prevent sexual abuse is to teach behaviors so that when an adult makes a sexual advance toward a child, the child will act in an appropriate manner by saying no and telling a responsible adult what happened. (Leventhal, 1987, p. 169, emphasis added)

Leventhal's comment illustrates the degree of distortion of goals that has occurred in some sexual abuse prevention programs. The ultimate focus on the behavior of potential victims is unjust, besides being of dubious efficacy. Indeed, it is hard to imagine programs to prevent other crimes that could make victim responsibility such a key element and still be politically feasible.

Retorts that such a focus is unfortunate but necessary do not ring true. For example, physical maltreatment of children is usually no less hidden. In fact, given the evidence accumulated in prevalence studies of family violence (e.g., Straus, Gelles, & Steinmetz, 1980), detection of serious physical and psychological maltreatment is no less problematic than detection of sexual abuse. Nonetheless, few programs to prevent physical maltreatment have

---

[6]Even adult professionals are far from unanimous in their attributions of sexual abuse (Atteberry-Bennett & Reppucci, 1986; Boat & Everett, 1987; Haugaard & Reppucci, 1988).

attempted to induce children to keep their parents and teachers from hitting them.

The primary focus on changing behavior of potential victims of sexual abuse is not only unfair but also unrealistic. Telling children that they have control over their bodies makes them no more powerful, a fact to which all children—most American children—who have been corporally punished can attest. For that matter, consider how frequently young children are forced to submit to another form of touch that feels bad—inoculations. Whatever the intent of program leaders, young children are unlikely to perceive themselves as having a right to control over their bodies (Melton, 1980).

More generally, the history of public health shows that prevention programs designed to change individual risky behavior are relatively ineffective. Eliminating or at least reducing opportunities for risky behavior through behavioral engineering usually produces much greater increases in safety than attempts to teach or persuade people to avoid risky behavior when the opportunity is presented (see, Bonnie, 1985; Peterson & Mori, 1985). Research confirms what common sense tells us: childproof caps and lead-free paint prevent poisoning much more effectively than efforts to increase parents' vigilance or diminish children's risk-taking; highway engineering usually has substantially greater effects on pedestrian safety than does safety education; legal regulation of the marketplace affects teenagers' drinking and smoking habits much more than does health education. Similarly, by far the most successful crime prevention programs have been those that create "defensible spaces" (Newman, 1972), thus reducing opportunities for undetected criminal activity.

The general principle that attempted behavior change among vulnerable individuals is not a very successful endeavor may apply with special force to prevention of child sexual abuse. Research on behavior change shows clearly that rehearsal is a critical phase (see, e.g., Bandura, 1977; Meichenbaum, 1977). However, even the best-designed sexual abuse education programs typically go no further in behavioral training than general assertiveness training, which there is little reason to believe generalizes to sexually dangerous situations. Moreover, rehearsal has been found to be especially important in training assertive responses in various situations (McFall & Marston, 1970; McFall & Twentyman, 1973).

Although the ethical problems are obvious in behavioral rehearsal of repelling potential offenders, cognitive rehearsal (which, although less effective than behavioral rehearsal is better than no rehearsal at all), does not present such problems, at least not to the same degree. Nonetheless, because of the politics involved in sex education, most prevention programs are so asexual in content that they do not include even cognitive rehearsal of behavior in high-risk situations.

The public health literature is again instructive. Developmental epidemiological research suggests that experience in managing risk is a strong factor in determining safety. For example, alcohol-related driving problems are disproportionately common in the threshold year for legal drinking, no matter where the minimum drinking age is set (Males, 1986). Similarly, childhood injuries peak at points in development in which children are just beginning to experience opportunities to assume particular risks. For example, toddlers are most vulnerable to poisoning, preschoolers to drowning, and school-aged children to pedestrian accidents (Matheny, 1980). The implication is that, unless the environment is structured to diminish the risk of injury, personal safety instruction is not enough. Children learn how to behave safely by the experience of navigating through various social contexts.

Not only are current sexual abuse prevention programs inconsistent with principles of behavior change, they also generally have failed to consider cognitive-developmental factors that would be expected to affect children's acquisition of concepts taught in sexual abuse education. Just as research on sexual abuse prevention has lacked a developmental approach, programs themselves look remarkably similar across age groups. The language and imagery change a bit, but not the concepts. Little effort has been made to apply an understanding of ways in which the socioemotional and cognitive maturity of children of various ages would affect their understanding of sexual abuse.

Most of the key concepts in current programs are abstract (e.g., the touch continuum) and somewhat removed from the phenomenon that is to be prevented. Not only may young children often fail to comprehend the intended message, a hypothesis that research thus far confirms, but the underlying assumptions about the phenomenology of children's experience also may be wrong. As already noted, the injunction in many programs to children to trust their intuition is based on an assumption that children's social perception is similar to that of adults and that children find sexual arousal to be unambivalently displeasurable (see supra footnote 5). The latter assumption is at least partially disconfirmed by evidence that hypersexualization is a common response to sexual abuse (Friedrich, Urquiza, & Beilke, 1986).

In short, sexual abuse education programs not only do not comport with a just allocation of responsibility. Sexual abuse educators also have shown little awareness of what is known about behavior change and child development.

## OTHER POTENTIAL FORMS OF PREVENTION

### Preconditions for Abuse

The conceptual weakness of current efforts to prevent sexual abuse is also illustrated by the narrowness of focus. In that regard, Finkelhor's (1984) conceptualization of four broad preconditions for sexual abuse is a useful starting point (see Table 8.1), although Finkelhor has acknowledged that the

**TABLE 8.1.    Preconditions for Sexual Abuse**

| | LEVEL OF EXPLANATION | |
| --- | --- | --- |
| | *Individual* | *Social/Cultural* |
| *Precondition I: Factors Related to Motivation to Sexually Abuse* | | |
| Emotional congruence | Arrested emotional development Need to feel powerful and controlling Re-enactment of childhood trauma to undo the hurt Narcissistic identification with self as a young child | Masculine requirement to be dominant and powerful in sexual relationships |
| Sexual arousal | Childhood sexual experience that was traumatic or strongly conditioning Modeling of sexual interest in children by someone else Misattribution of arousal cues Biologic abnormality | Child pornography Erotic portrayal of children in advertising Male tendency to sexualize all emotional needs |
| Blockage | Oedipal conflict Castration anxiety Fear of adult females Traumatic sexual experience with adult Inadequate social skills Marital problems | Repressive norms about masturbation and extramarital sex |
| *Precondition II: Factors Predisposing to Overcoming Internal Inhibitors* | Alcohol Psychosis Impulse disorder Senility Failure of incest inhibition mechanism in family dynamics | Social toleration of sexual interest in children Weak criminal sanctions against offenders Ideology of patriarchal prerogatives for fathers Social toleration for deviance committed while intoxicated Child pornography Male inability to identify with needs of children |
| *Precondition III: Factors Predisposing to Overcoming External Inhibitors* | Mother who is absent or ill Mother who is not close to or protective of child Mother who is dominated or abused by father Social isolation of family Unusual opportunities to be alone with child Lack of supervision of child Unusual sleeping or rooming conditions | Lack of social supports for mother Barriers to women's equality Erosion of social networks Ideology of family sanctity |
| *Precondition IV: Factors Predisposing to Overcoming Child's Resistance* | Child who is emotionally insecure or deprived Child who lacks knowledge about sexual abuse Situation of unusual trust between child and offender Coercion | Unavailability of sex education for children Social powerlessness of children |

Reprinted from *Sexually Victimized Children* by David Finkelhor. Copyright 1979 by David Finkelhor. Published by The Free Press, a Division of Macmillan, Inc. Reprinted by permission.

specific examples listed are often speculative or even in a few instances (e.g., senility) actually disconfirmed by research (Araji & Finkelhor, 1986; Finkelhor, 1986a). The examples are instructive, though, in showing both individual and social factors that might be foci of prevention.

Finkelhor's four preconditions follow a simple logic. (I) Someone must be motivated to abuse a child sexually. Then for the abuse actually to take place, (II) internal and (III) external inhibitors must be overcome, and (IV) the child must be unable or unwilling to resist the offender. Note that current prevention efforts have focused almost exclusively on Precondition IV and then largely in terms of individual factors.

Given the conceptual and empirical limits of current efforts, it is surprising that more attention has not been given to prevention efforts aimed at removing the other three preconditions. However, prevention programs so directed are also apt to reach conceptual or practical roadblocks, at least in the current state of knowledge.

## Prevention of Motivation to Offend

Although it may be possible ultimately to design prevention programs that impede development of motivation to offend, the current state of basic knowledge about offenders is such that few clues are available about preventive strategies. The best documented characteristic of offenders is social ineptitude, especially in regard to women. Therefore, programs to increase heterosexual social skills may be useful, at least on a secondary prevention basis. However, this hypothesis is very speculative and, given the low base rate of offending, may be impractical as a preventive strategy.

Most attention in regard to Precondition I has been given to change of children's behavior. Specifically, the argument is that sexually abused children will become sexual abusers unless they are properly treated. Actually, it is quite clear that the vast majority of abused children do not become abusers, and it is probable that the finding of high proportions of histories of abuse among abusers is an artifact of studying incarcerated offenders (Finkelhor, 1986a). The notion of intergenerational cycles is simple and politically palatable, but, as with physical abuse (Kaufman & Zigler, 1987), childhood history of abuse accounts for little of the variance in prevalence of adults' sexual offenses against children.

Treatment should be available to sexually abused children and their families, but it should be available because children's own experience is important, not because it will prevent abuse a generation later. Moreover, the cycle-of-abuse theory may actually have iatrogenic effects through labeling of abused children as potential abusers and intensification of family stress and guilt.

The intergenerational theory also may have the undesirable effect of diminishing offenders' and potential offenders' subjective responsibility for their behavior. In that regard, the high prevalence of reported histories of abuse among incarcerated offenders not only may reflect the more serious nature of their offenses and their poorer perceived prognosis but also may result from a desire of offenders to present themselves as unfairly punished.

### Strengthening Internal Inhibition

Two general strategies are common as means of inhibiting individuals' motivation to offend. The first, deterrence, is probably unlikely to be very effective in general terms, because of the low risk of detection (cf. Gibbs, 1985). The low rate of recidivism among incest offenders (Finkelhor, 1986a) suggests, though, that specific deterrence strategies of criminal prosecution may be effective in prevention of re-offending among certain types of child molestors.

The second general means of increasing inhibition is through moral suasion (see Bonnie, 1985; Melton & Saks, 1985). However, generalized appeals to conscience have had weak effects in changing habitual behaviors and problems of impulse control. Nonetheless, for potential offenders in situations that pose increased risk of abuse (e.g., conflict-ridden marriages), messages of personal responsibility by men like the potential offenders themselves (as per general principles of modeling) may have some preventive effect (Wolf et al., 1987), although it is still likely to be weak in relative magnitude (i.e., proportion of potential offenses prevented).

### Increasing External Controls

As a general matter, as noted earlier, environmental change is the most effective approach to prevention. However, structuring the environment in order to diminish opportunities for sexual abuse is not an easy task. The most obvious strategy is to increase the vigilance of mothers over their male friends, lovers, husbands, and fathers. However, as suggested earlier in terms of children, changing perceptions about the risk of abuse in the community is one thing; changing perceptions about risk in one's own home is quite another. Again, even if we could do so, it is not clear that it would be desirable to do so, because of the possible negative effects on the quality of relationships and the preservation of family privacy.

### WHERE DO WE GO FROM HERE?

To be clear, I am not suggesting at this point that we scrap all of the sexual abuse education programs that are currently in place. Given the level of investment that has taken place, such a drastic step should not be taken until a more extensive and rigorous body of evaluation research is in place. However, I am arguing that, if research confirms the sorts of negative effects that have been hypothesized and it continues to show at best weakly positive effects, then such programs should indeed be abolished or at least redesigned.

In view of the substantial bases in psychological theory and research to question the direction in which sexual abuse prevention has gone, sexual abuse education programs should not be initiated or expanded until and unless a substantially stronger research base is developed for such programs.

On the other hand, what we do know gives little reason for optimism about prevention in general, even if a more thoughtful approach is taken to program planning. Substantial decrements in the prevalence of sexual abuse may require marked change in societal beliefs about sexuality, the family, and childhood. Such changes are long-term and may be beyond our knowledge about social engineering.

Until then, two strategies deserve greater attention. First, although I am skeptical about the wisdom and the efficacy of attempts to increase vigilance within families, efforts to increase supports for families in transition or under stress are apt over the long term to be the most effective means of prevention, given current knowledge. At the same time, though, it should be recognized that such a strategy is likely to be substantially less effective than analogous programs intended to prevent physical maltreatment. Targeting high-risk families is not as easy as prevention of physical maltreatment, because demographic factors are much less important in sexual abuse. By the same token, variables related to family interaction account for substantially less of the variance in sexual abuse.

Second, emphasis should be moved to basic research. Without more knowledge about the conditions that permit or inhibit abusive behavior, it is unlikely that significant progress will be made in prevention of sexual abuse. Such a research initiative should include attention to normative development of sexual concepts and behavior. As also has been demonstrated in attempts to apply psychology to prevention of teen pregnancy and human immunodeficiency virus (HIV) infection (see Melton, 1986), current knowledge of psychosexual development is grossly inadequate.

Finally, it should be recognized that prevention of sexual abuse is an extraordinarily difficult, indeed improbable exercise. Although it is too early to shut the door to prevention of sexual abuse, ultimately we may reach the unhappy conclusion that our resources are better invested in remediating the effects of abuse than preventing its occurrence.

## REFERENCES

Araji, S., & Finkelhor, D. (1986). Abusers: A review of the research. In D. Finkelhor (Ed.), *A sourcebook on child sexual abuse* (pp. 89–118). Beverly Hills: Sage.

Atteberry-Bennett, J., & Reppucci, N. D. (1986, August). *What does child sexual abuse mean?* Paper presented at the meeting of the American Psychological Association, Washington, DC.

Bandura, A. (1977). *Social learning theory*. Englewood Cliffs, NJ: Prentice-Hall.

Boat, B., & Everett, M. (1987, January). *Interactions of sexually abused and nonabused preschool-age children with anatomical dolls: A comparative and normative study*. Paper presented at the meeting of grantees of the National Center on Child Abuse and Neglect, Washington, DC.

Bonnie, R. J. (1985). The efficacy of law as a paternalistic instrument. In G. B. Melton (Ed.), *Nebraska Symposium on Motivation: Vol. 33. The law as a behavioral instrument* (pp. 131–211). Lincoln: University of Nebraska Press.

Borkin, J., & Frank, L. (1986). Sexual abuse prevention for preschoolers: A pilot program. *Child Welfare, 65,* 75–82.

Boruch, R. R., & Cecil, J. (1979). *Assuring the confidentiality of social research data.* Philadelphia: University of Pennsylvania Press.

Browne, A., & Finkelhor, D. (1986). Initial and long-term effects: A review of the research. In D. Finkelhor (Ed.), *A sourcebook on child sexual abuse* (pp. 143–178). Beverly Hills, CA: Sage.

Conte, J. R. (1987). Ethical issues in evaluation of prevention programs. *Child Abuse and Neglect, 11,* 171–172.

Conte, J. R., & Berliner, L. (1981). Sexual abuse of children: Implications for practice. *Social Casework, 62,* 601–606.

Conte, J. R., Rosen, C., Saperstein, L., & Shermack, R. (1985). An evaluation of a program to prevent the sexual victimization of young children. *Child Abuse and Neglect, 9,* 319–328.

Daro, D., Duerr, J., & LeProhn, N. (1987, July). *Child assault prevention instruction: What works with preschoolers.* Paper presented at the Third National Family Violence Research Conference, Durham, NH.

Finkelhor, D. (1984). *Child sexual abuse: New theory and research.* New York: Free Press.

Finkelhor, D. (1986a). Abusers: Special topics. In D. Finkelhor (Ed.), *A sourcebook on child sexual abuse* (pp. 119–142). Beverly Hills: Sage.

Finkelhor, D. (1986b). Prevention: A review of programs and research. In D. Finkelhor (Ed.), *A sourcebook on child sexual abuse* (pp. 224–254). Beverly Hills: Sage.

Friedrich, W. N., Urquiza, A. J., & Beilke, R. (1986). Behavioral problems in sexually abused young children. *Journal of Pediatric Psychology, 11,* 47–57.

Fryer, G. E., Jr., Kraizer, S. K., & Miyoshi, T. (1987a). Measuring actual reduction of risk to child abuse: A new approach. *Child Abuse and Neglect, 11,* 173–179.

Fryer, G. E., Jr., Kraizer, S. K., & Miyoshi, T. (1987b). Measuring children's retention of skills to resist stranger abduction: Use of the simulation technique. *Child Abuse and Neglect, 11,* 181–185.

Garbarino, J. (1987). Children's response to a sexual abuse prevention program: A study of the *Spiderman* comic. *Child Abuse and Neglect, 11,* 143–148.

Gibbs, J. P. (1985). Deterrence theory and research. In G. B. Melton (Ed.), *Nebraska Symposium on Motivation: Vol. 33. The law as a behavioral instrument* (pp. 87–130). Lincoln: University of Nebraska Press.

Haugaard, J., & Reppucci, N. D. (1988). *Child sexual abuse.* San Francisco: Jossey-Bass.

Kaufman, J., & Zigler, E. (1987). Do abused children become abusive parents? *American Journal of Orthopsychiatry, 57,* 186–192.

Kenning, M. (1985). *Child assault prevention: Program evaluation*. Unpublished doctoral dissertation, University of South Dakota.

Kenning, M., Gallmeier, T., Jackson, T. L., & Plemons, S. (1987, July). *Evaluation of child sexual abuse prevention programs: A summary of two studies*. Paper presented at the Third National Family Violence Research Conference, Durham, NH.

Kleemeier, C., & Webb, C. (1986, August). *Evaluation of a school-based prevention program*. Paper presented at the meeting of the American Psychological Association, Washington, DC.

Kraizer, S. K. (1986). Rethinking prevention. *Child Abuse and Neglect, 10*, 259–261.

Leventhal, J. M. (1987). Programs to prevent sexual abuse: What outcomes should be measured? *Child Abuse and Neglect, 11*, 169–172.

Lloyd, D., Melton, G. B., & Rogers, C. M. (1986). *Sexually abused children and the legal system*. New York: Guilford.

Males, M. A. (1986). The minimum purchase age for alcohol and young-driver fatal crashes: A long-term view. *Journal of Legal Studies, 15*, 181–217.

Matheny, A. P., Jr. (1980). Visual-perceptual exploration and accident liability in children. *Journal of Pediatric Psychology, 5*, 343–351.

Maxine Waters Child Abuse Prevention Training Act, Cal. Welf. & Inst. Code §§18975 to 18979 (West Cum. Supp. 1987).

McFall, R. M., & Marston, A. R. (1970). An experimental investigation of behavior rehearsal in assertive training. *Journal of Abnormal Psychology, 76*, 295–303.

McFall, R. M., & Twentyman, C. (1973). Four experiments on the relative contribution of rehearsal, modeling, and coaching to assertion. *Journal of Abnormal Psychology, 81*, 199–218.

Meichenbaum, D. (1977). *Cognitive-behavior modification: An integrative approach*. New York: Plenum.

Melton, G. B. (1980). Children's concepts of their rights. *Journal of Clinical Child Psychology, 9*, 186–190.

Melton, G. B. (1983). *Child advocacy: Psychological issues and interventions*. New York: Plenum.

Melton, G. B. (1985). Sexually abused children and the legal system: Some policy recommendations. *American Journal of Family Therapy, 13*, 61–67.

Melton, G. B. (1987a). Children's testimony in cases of alleged sexual abuse. In M. Wolraich & D. K. Routh (Eds.), *Advances in developmental and behavioral pediatrics* (Vol. 8, pp. 179–203). Greenwich, CT: JAI Press.

Melton, G. B. (1987b). The clashing of symbols: Prelude to child and family life. *American Psychologist, 42*, 345–354.

Melton, G. B. (1988). Adolescents and prevention of AIDS. *Professional Psychology: Research and Practice, 19*, 403–408.

Melton, G. B., & Saks, M. J. (1985). The law as an instrument of socialization and social structure. In G. B. Melton (Ed.), *Nebraska Symposium on Motivation: Vol. 33. The law as a behavioral instrument* (pp. 235–277). Lincoln: University of Nebraska Press.

National Committee for Prevention of Child Abuse. (1985 and Supp. 1986). *Child sexual abuse prevention resources*. Chicago.

Newman, O. (1972). *Defensible space*. New York: Macmillan.

Peters, S. D., Wyatt, G. E., & Finkelhor, D. (1986). Prevalence. In D. Finkelhor (Ed.), *A sourcebook on child sexual abuse* (pp. 15–59). Beverly Hills: Sage.

Peterson, L. (1984). Teaching home safety and survival skills to latch-key children: A comparison of two manuals and methods. *Journal of Applied Behavior Analysis*, *17*, 279–293.

Peterson, L., & Mori, L. (1985). Prevention of child injury: An overview of targets, methods, and tactics for psychologists. *Journal of Consulting and Clinical Psychology*, *53*, 586–595.

Poche, C., Brouwer, R., & Swearingen, M. (1981). Teaching self-protection to young children. *Journal of Applied Behavior Analysis*, *14*, 169–176.

Reppucci, N. D. (1987). Prevention and ecology: Teenage pregnancy, child sexual abuse, and organized youth sports. *American Journal of Community Psychology*, *15*, 1–22.

Saslawsky, D. A., & Wurtele, S. K. (1986). Educating children about sexual abuse: Implications for pediatric intervention and possible prevention. *Journal of Pediatric Psychology*, *11*, 235–245.

Swan, H. L., Press, A. N., & Briggs, S. L. (1985). Child sexual abuse prevention: Does it work? *Child Welfare*, *64*, 395–405.

Straus, M. A., Gelles, R., & Steinmetz, S. (1980). *Behind closed doors: Violence in the American family*. Garden City, NY: Doubleday.

Tyler, T. R., & Cook, F. L. (1984). The mass media and judgments of risk: Distinguishing impact on personal and societal level judgments. *Journal of Personality and Social Psychology*, *47*, 693–708.

Wald, M. S., & Cohen, S. (1986). Preventing child abuse: What will it take? *Family Law Quarterly*, *20*, 281–302.

Williams, S. B., & Stith, S. M. (1987, July). *Survey results: Needs and interests of students, parents, and professionals for information about sexual abuse*. Paper presented at the Third National Family Violence Research Conference, Durham, NH.

Wolf, S. C., Berliner, L. C., Conte, J., & Smith, T. (1987, July). *The victimization process in child sexual abuse*. Paper presented at the Third National Family Violence Research Conference, Durham, NH.

Wolfe, D., MacPherson, T., Blount, R., & Wolfe, V. (1986). Evaluation of a brief intervention for educating school children in awareness of physical and sexual abuse. *Child Abuse and Neglect*, *10*, 85–92.

Wurtele, S. K., Saslawsky, D. A., Miller, C. L., Marrs, S. R., & Britcher, J. C. (1986). Teaching personal safety skills for potential prevention of sexual abuse: A comparison of treatments. *Journal of Consulting and Clinical Psychology*, *54*, 688–692.

# Child Maltreatment Prevention and Current Treatment Delivery Systems

# CHAPTER 9

# Child Maltreatment Prevention in the Health Care and Social Service System

KEITH L. KAUFMAN, CHARLES F. JOHNSON, DEBRA COHN, AND
JANET McCLEERY

The hospital setting has contributed significantly to the assessment, intervention, and prevention of child abuse from a number of perspectives. Historically, radiological evidence reviewed in this setting provided the first systematic data suggesting that multiple long bone fractures presented as unexplained injuries could instead be the result of intentional acts perpetrated by parents and other caretakers (Caffey, 1957; Woolley & Evans, 1955). This information provided the basis for Kempe's (Kempe, Silverman, Steele, Droegemuller, & Silver, 1962) classic work in defining instances of nonaccidental injury to children as the battered child syndrome. Since this time, the hospital setting has continued to offer empirical information crucial to the development of primary, secondary, and tertiary prevention efforts.

From an ecological perspective, the hospital reflects what Belsky (1980) might refer to as an "exosystem" or a formal social structure that exerts an impact despite the fact that the individual is not actually a part of the structure. The hospital's influence can be viewed at a number of levels. Educational efforts, such as prenatal classes, postnatal instruction and parenting skills workshops, are directed towards the community as a whole. In-service trainings provide medical and psychosocial updates necessary for community physicians and community mental health providers to offer high quality educational, diagnostic, and treatment-oriented services. Finally, prenatal visits, well child visits, annual physicals, and specialty clinics for chronically ill children represent opportunities for hospital personnel to intervene at the individual level.

A third perspective relates to issues of accessibility. The hospital offers a unique opportunity to intervene with individuals across the life cycle (e.g., prenatal visits, labor and delivery, well child visits, school and camp physicals, employment physicals). Health care providers have the opportunity to develop a trusting relationship with both parents and their children, which allows for the discussion of sensitive issues. Such a relationship would seem to enhance parents' help seeking behavior and facilitate parental openness to educational opportunities. The medical setting also represents a conduit to other resources (e.g., mental health services) and social supports (e.g., Big Brothers) which may lead to a reduction in the incidence of child abuse.

The hospital setting has not traditionally been viewed as a center for prevention activities. In fact, many hospitals would be better characterized as tertiary care facilities. As a result, most services are designed to accommodate chronically ill children and their families. Exceptions in the hospital include the emergency room, which deals with acute medical problems and hospital-based poison control centers, which provide a combination of acute care services and preventive programs. Despite the emphasis on tertiary services, hospitals have been involved in primary as well as secondary and tertiary prevention efforts. This contrast exists, perhaps, as a result of a large number of hospitals which have separate child abuse programs or teams that have not been satisfied with simply dealing with abuse in an after-the-fact fashion. Further, the role of the hospital in the medical and psychosocial assessment of alleged cases of abuse has necessitated a balance between research and clinical initiatives which are concerned with the prevention of child abuse and those that enhance diagnostic and treatment services.

While recent reviews of the prevention literature (Rosenberg & Reppucci, 1985; Helfer, 1982; Schmitt, 1980) have discussed a number of hospital-based prevention strategies, it is somewhat surprising that the hospital and health care delivery system has not been used more widely in such efforts. The purpose of this review is to discuss both successful prevention strategies that empirical evidence suggests are well fitted to the hospital environment and those approaches that have demonstrated clinical utility in the hospital and merit further empirical investigation. Primary, secondary, and tertiary prevention efforts will be discussed as well as the role of the professional (i.e., physician, psychologist, nurse, and social worker) in the hospital and social service system. Tertiary prevention efforts (particularly those involving assessment/diagnosis) offer the potential of increasing our knowledge of both victims and perpetrators of abuse. As a result, they may have important implications for the design of primary and secondary prevention programs. For this reason, tertiary approaches have been included in this review, despite the fact that they are typically considered more treatment/assessment oriented. Finally, since the social service system is an integral part of the larger hospital system, it will be discussed primarily in this context.

## PRIMARY PREVENTION

Primary prevention refers to those efforts directed towards ensuring that difficulties do not develop by intervening with a large segment of the population independent of their risk for the particular difficulty. In the area of

TABLE 9.1.    Factors Associated with Families Presenting Minimal Risk of Child Abuse

Child's Characteristics

Likeable attributes
Seen as a separate individual
Healthy
Does not disrupt parents' lifestyle too much
Planned

Parents' Characteristics

Parents share in child-related responsibilities
Stable marriage
Parents exhibit coping abilities to meet baby's needs
Parents had helpful role models growing-up
Parents enjoy personal interests
Parents have their own home and stable living conditions
Future birth control is planned
Mother is intelligent and healthy
Father has a stable job
Father is supportive

child abuse, primary prevention typically takes the form of approaches that strive to enhance parental competencies, coping skills, and resources or those that reduce psychological difficulties that could potentially lead to an at-risk situation. The following section examines the efficacy of such approaches in the hospital setting.

### Parent-Child Bonding

Child development experts have long agreed that a warm and nurturing relationship between the infant and his or her parents is essential for healthy socioemotional and cognitive development (Ainsworth, 1969; Bowlby, 1958). Moreover, findings seem to suggest that a disruption of this process places a child at risk for physical abuse. Bonding is facilitated by physical contact between the parent and the infant. Touching, eye contact, holding, and caressing typically reflect the bonding process and the first few hours of life are thought to be most critical in its establishment (Wilson, 1984). In contrast, "attachment" is considered more of a reciprocal relationship between parent and child that develops gradually during the first year of life (Campbell & Taylor, 1980).

When family circumstances are positive, bonding and attachment are facilitated and the potential for child abuse is minimized. Factors which have been associated with low-risk families are displayed in Table 9.1 and are based upon the work of Gray, Cutler, Dean, and Kempe (1980) as well as Klaus and Kennell (1976, 1982). In contrast, factors which seem to interfere with successful bonding and attachment have also been identified (Gray et al., 1980). Table 9.2 reflects "warning signs" present during prenatal, delivery, and postpartum periods.

TABLE 9.2. Factors Which Seem to Interfere With the Bonding and Attachment Processes Evidenced During the Prenatal, Delivery, and Postpartum Periods

Prenatal Period

Mother's overconcern with baby's sex or performance
Mother's denial of pregnancy
Mother feels depressed, frightened, or alone
Mother states she has "too many" other children
Mother lacks social supports
One parent seriously considered abortion
Family history of abuse or neglect
Parent's living situation is overcrowded or isolated

Delivery Period

Verbal or nonverbal passivity
Hostility
Disappointment over sex of infant
Lack of eye contact
Nonsupportive interaction between parents

Postpartum Period

Mother does not have fun with the baby
Verbalizations directed toward the infant are harsh and negative
Identification of the child with a disliked person
Unrealistic developmental expectations
Mother is very bothered by crying
Mother sees child as very demanding or too messy at feedings
Changing diapers is seen as a very negative task
Mother does not comfort baby
Negativeness of husband or family
Mother lacks social support
Sibling rivalry problems
Husband is very jealous of mother's time with or affection for baby
Mother's complaints about the baby cannot be verified.

Impaired bonding may be due to a lack of responsiveness on the part of either the mother or the infant, or due to separation in the early newborn period as a result of medical complications or hospital policy (Klaus & Kennell, 1976). Early mother-infant contact and more family-centered obstetric care are steps in a process to improve bonding and attachment that should begin with parenting education (Campbell & Taylor, 1980). Primary prevention and early intervention programs must focus on a range of potential problem areas including: (1) prenatal health care and nutrition; (2) educational programs in child development and parenting; and (3) family-centered birth and hospital stay arrangements (Campbell & Taylor, 1980).

Using an outreach approach with high-risk families may bring potentially abusive parents into the helping system. Telephone contacts or home visits, frequent office visits, giving more attention to the mother, emphasizing accident prevention, and using positive reinforcement may be helpful deterrents

(Gray et al., 1980). On the institutional level, hospitals can facilitate bonding by arranging periods of privacy for the new family unit after birth, extending periods of parent-infant contact, and giving complete responsibility to the mother to care for her baby with the nurse or midwife as a consultant (Klaus & Kennell, 1976).

The relatively few studies that have examined these approaches have acquired mixed results. O'Connor, Vietze, Sherrod, Sandler, & Altemeier (1980) found (at a 17-month follow-up) that primiparous mothers assigned to a rooming-in condition were considerably less likely to have been reported for child abuse or neglect than nonrooming-in controls. In contrast, Siegel, Bauman, Schaefer, Saunders, & Ingram (1980) did not find a relationship between early extended contact (i.e., rooming-in) and later child maltreatment. Also problematic is the fact that a later study by O'Connor and his associates (O'Connor, Vietze, Sherrod, Sandler, Gerrity, & Altemeier, 1982) revealed that mothers' risk status interacted with rooming-in (i.e., high-risk mothers were less likely to benefit from rooming-in than low-risk mothers). Fathers have also been the focus of a number of studies (see Parke & Beitel, 1986, for a review); however, none have included child maltreatment as an outcome variable. While a number of other studies also appear in the literature (see Chapter 2 of this volume), it will be difficult to gauge the efficacy of early extended contact on child maltreatment until methodologies are more consistent between investigations, measures are standardized, and fathers are included as participants in these studies.

## Prenatal Information

A number of authors have sought to capitalize upon opportunities for contact between health care providers and parents following delivery. The most popular approach has been to demonstrate newborn capabilities to parents in an effort to facilitate more realistic expectations (Belsky, 1985; Szajnberg, Ward, Krauss, & Kessler, 1987; Widmayer & Field, 1980). Such initiatives have resulted in enhanced parent-child interactions and even positive effects on infant development (Widmayer & Field, 1980).

A slightly different approach undertaken by Gray (1983) involved providing information on a broad range of parenting topics as well as enhanced social support (i.e., volunteer home visits) to a group of middle-class mothers. Results suggested that mothers who received this intervention were more involved with their children and more nurturing than controls at 12- to 15-month follow-up. Differences were not, however, present on dimensions of neonatal perceptions and parenting (see Chapter 2 for more details).

Finally, Parke, Hymel, Power, & Tinsley (1980) utilized a videotape involving fathers feeding, diapering, and playing with their neonates to bolster new fathers' skills. Findings suggested that fathers who viewed the tapes were more knowledgeable, more affectionate, and displayed increased caretaking activities.

Informational approaches show great promise in reducing factors that have been linked to later child maltreatment and neglect. The relatively low cost in providing such services and the ability to tailor information to each parent further enhances their utility. There is a need, however, to examine the relationship between these programs and subsequent rates of abuse and neglect. Establishment of such a link will solidify the usefulness of this approach as a primary prevention tool.

## Well Child Visits—Anticipatory Guidance

For the majority of parents, the primary care physician represents the most consistent source of child care information and guidance available. Much of the general information shared with parents in the hospital, clinic, or private practice setting is within the context of well-care visits. These visits are scheduled visits intended to deal with issues other than acute physical illness. The *Standards of Health Care* from the American Academy of Pediatrics (1977) recommends that children have five scheduled well-care visits during the first year and three during the second year. Despite a decrease in frequency to at least four visits between ages six to 18 years old, a parent complying with this schedule should have ample opportunity to receive adequate child care guidance. Yet, previous findings (Reisinger & Bires, 1980) have suggested that a very small portion of the physician's visit is spent in dealing with anticipatory guidance. Of the 10 to 13 minutes that a physician spent in a typical visit, an average of only 97 seconds was spent on anticipatory guidance with parents of children under five months of age and only seven seconds was spent with adolescents (Reisinger & Bires, 1980). However, recent trends in training pediatric residents (Christophersen, 1986; Kittredge, Espinosa-Charneco, & Olson, 1986) suggests that an increased emphasis will be placed on the role of well-care visits as a preventive tool.

Anticipatory guidance topics covered during well-care visits can vary considerably from practitioner to practitioner. The means of conveying this information may also vary. While many primary care practitioners incorporate anticipatory guidance into their office visits, some have designed separate classes to communicate this information. A number of articles in the medical literature have offered guidelines for anticipatory guidance provided as part of an office visit. Christophersen and his colleagues (Christopherson, Barrish, Barrish, & Christopherson, 1984) have described an anticipatory guidance program that is classroom based and covers information on most of the areas recommended by the Academy of Pediatrics. Classes for parents of infants and parents of toddlers are offered separately. The classes meet two hours per week for four consecutive weeks. Topics for the infant class include: (1) Growth and development; (2) Infant temperament; (3) Parenting; (4) Stressors; (5) Illness; (6) Behavior; (7) Baby sitters and day care. Since inappropriate developmental expectations and punitive and/or ineffective discipline practices constitute major risk factors associated with physical abuse, the well-care visit seems to be a viable primary prevention initiative.

### Reducing Major Life Stressors

Straus' (1980) investigation of family violence in a nationally representative sample of 1,146 families (with children 3- to 17-years old) helped clarify the connection between stress and violence in the home. When major stressors (18 items similar to Holmes & Rahe's Social Readjustment Rating Scale, 1967) were absent, individuals had the lowest rate of violent behaviors indicative of physical abuse. Straus (1980) went on to argue that stress itself does not result in abuse, but rather, it is mediated by other factors. He found that the following factors were associated with high levels of familial violence:

1. Parents who are socially isolated;
2. Parents with low income, education, and occupation;
3. Parents whose marriage is not rewarding or important;
4. Parents who believe that the husband should be the dominant person in the marriage;
5. Parents who believe that physical punishment of children and slapping a spouse are appropriate behavior;
6. Parents whose fathers used physical punishment and who observed their fathers hitting their mothers, thus teaching violence as a response to stress;
7. Parents who engage in physical fights with each other.

With knowledge of these factors in mind, hospital- and clinic-based practitioners could be on the lookout for parents presenting with symptoms of stress, particularly in combination with the mediating factors identified by Straus (1980). When such parents are identified, practitioners could choose to either intervene themselves or make a referral to a psychologist or social worker with greater expertise in the area.

Intervention should focus on reducing the stress itself as well as ameliorating the impact of mediating factors. It is important to recognize, however, that there is likely to be a reciprocal relationship between stress and the mediating factors. As a result, a reduction in one will positively impact the other. Progressive muscle relaxation strategies (Bernstein & Borkovec, 1973) offer a viable approach to stress reduction as do the somewhat more involved cognitive coping techniques (Lazarus & Folkman, 1984). Social networking and involvement in community groups will reduce social isolation, while financial counseling and assistance from state agencies may reduce financial burdens. Parent training classes may be helpful in bolstering parents' repertoire of more positively oriented child-rearing approaches and may reduce their reliance on physically punitive techniques. Finally, marital therapy could be utilized to deal with issues of marital discord and violence.

## The Shaken Baby Syndrome

A variety of informational deficits have been identified as contributing factors in the maltreatment of children (e.g., developmental, discipline). Yet, few, if any, involve the immediate and long-term medical consequences that are frequently associated with the shaken baby syndrome (SBS).

Caffey (1972) was the first to identify this syndrome which was believed to be caused by a whiplash type motion of the head. Differentiated from accidental head injury, this form of child abuse is believed to be the consequence of violently shaking a child. Children below the age of two years old are at the greatest risk for such injuries, due to immaturity of cranial and cerebral structures and the relative weakness of neck muscles supporting these structures (Dykes, 1986). The SBS is typically characterized by the absence of external signs of trauma and the presence of retinal hemorrhages and subarachnoid and/or subdural hemorrhages (Ludwig & Warman, 1984).

The etiology of shaking in SBS is most often *assumed* based upon clinical findings (i.e., retinal hemorrhage, bulging anterior fontanelle, increased head circumference, lethargy, and irritability) and the results of computerized tomography (CT) scans (Duhaime, Gennarelli, Thibault, Bruce, Margulies, & Wiser, 1987). Dykes (1986) suggests that a history consistent with shaking is not always obtained due to a number of factors. First, she believes that many parents are not aware of the relationship between shaking and neurological injury. Second, as a result of not recognizing the connection, many parents do not volunteer the information unless specifically asked. Third, since parents see no danger in this practice, they believe that it is a more socially appropriate discipline practice than hitting the child.

The two largest retrospective studies (Duhaime et al., 1987; Ludwig & Warman, 1984) in the area, to date, reported on 48 and 20 cases of SBS, in patients with mean ages of 7.85 and 5.80 months respectively. In both studies, the most common presenting problems were central nervous system difficulties (e.g., lethargic, floppy/limp, irritable, seizure), respiratory problems, and/or gastrointestinal difficulties (e.g., vomiting, constipation, and feeding problems). Parents or caretakers most frequently reported accidental trauma due to a fall or an accidental blunt trauma. Occasionally they admitted shaking the child (in some cases as part of an effort to perform resuscitation). Findings from the two studies underscored the severe consequences of trauma associated with the syndrome. Duhaime et al. (1987) reported a mortality rate of 27% in their sample, while Ludwig and Warman (1984) reported a 15% mortality rate and a 50% morbidity rate (e.g., motor deficit, blindness, seizures, developmental delay). Many of the children initially free of sequelae later exhibited evidence of morbidity (35%). These results support Caffey's

(1974; 1972) assertion that undetected cases of SBS may be responsible for many cases of mental retardation with unknown etiology.

Despite apparent similarities in the two studies, their conclusions were quite different. Ludwig and Warman (1984) strengthened the position of previous research (Caffey, 1974; 1972) by concluding that the process of shaking a young child/infant was sufficient to cause the mortality and morbidity that they found in their sample. In contrast, Duhaime et al. (1987) indicated that such consequences are "not usually caused by shaking alone" (p. 414). Rather, they suggest that the shaking may be part of a process that leads to a child being thrown down and striking the back of their head. The impact causes focal damage, while the acceleration-deceleration associated with the impact results in shearing forces on the parenchyma and vessels. Further, they state that "fatal cases of the shaken baby syndrome are not likely to occur from the shaking that occurs during play, feeding, or in a swing, or even from the more vigorous shaking given by a caretaker as a means of discipline" (p. 414) unless predisposing factors are present (e.g., collagen-vascular disease).

The difference in findings may be accounted for by three factors. First, Ludwig and Warman's (1984) restricted sample ("Only children injured solely by being shaken were included in the study," p. 104). This excluded children with other evidence of head trauma and the possibility of examining the incidence of both phenomena in the same child. Duhaime et al. (1987) found that 63% of their sample had evidence of both a blunt impact to the head and the SBS. Second, Duhaime et al.'s (1987) report that more than 50% ($N = 7$) of the children who died had evidence of blunt trauma to the head that was only discovered during the autopsy. The study examined a number of biomechanical models (dolls intended to simulate one-month-old infants) which offered acceleration-deceleration data for different types of injuries (i.e., impact and shaking).

The literature on the SBS is relevant to the prevention of child abuse at a number of different levels. From a tertiary prevention perspective, ensuring that emergency room and community physicians are aware of the signs and symptoms of SBS will lead to a proper and timely diagnosis, which is imperative to ensure survival and to minimize morbidity (Ludwig & Warman, 1984). At Columbus Children's Hospital, the Director of the Child Abuse Program (Dr. Charles F. Johnson) has addressed this need in two ways. He has designed a checklist for emergency room and neurosurgery residents which identifies key evaluation areas. These include the use of a CT scan, contacting the neurosurgery-child abuse social worker to assist with history taking, an ophthalmology consultation to assist in identifying retinal hemorrhaging, and a skull series and bone survey (when the child's condition permits) to identify other evidence of abuse. Dr. Johnson has also developed a slide presentation for community pediatricians to familiarize them with the presentation of SBS.

From a secondary prevention perspective, information regarding the consequences of SBS (and associated head traumas) should become a part of all programs directed toward high-risk groups. Further, skills deficits (e.g., anger management, problem solving) and stressors (e.g., inadequate child care) that are likely to lead to situations where this type of incident may occur should be targeted as priorities for intervention.

Finally, Caffey (1974) has suggested two viable primary prevention efforts, neither of which have been pursued. First, that ocular exams become a part of every well-baby visit. This would both improve physicians' skills in differentiating normal and abnormal retinal presentations and increase the probability that chronic and escalating incidents of SBS (and associated head traumas) would be identified prior to a life threatening presentation in the emergency room. Second, that a large-scale educational campaign be undertaken to inform the general public of the consequences of SBS (and associated head trauma).

## SECONDARY PREVENTION EFFORTS

Secondary prevention focusses on the identification of high-risk groups and attempts to ameliorate or reduce the impact of factors which place an individual at-risk. Factors are most often derived from empirical investigations, but could also be gleaned from conceptual and theoretical understandings of etiology. In the area of child abuse, most factors have been identified based upon empirical investigations. Prevention strategies directed toward a number of high-risk groups are presented in this portion of the chapter.

### Screening Approaches to Identify Abusive Parents

Since considerable information is available regarding the characteristics of abusive parents (see Wolfe, 1985, for a review) and the types of interactions they exhibit with their children (Starr, 1988; Dietrich, Starr, & Weisfeld, 1983), it would stand to reason that measures/procedures could be developed to identify parents who, by virtue of these factors, pose a risk for abusing their children. This approach has, in fact, been pursued by a number of authors (Altemeier, O'Connor, Vietze, Sandler, & Sherrod, 1984; Milner, 1986; Schneider, 1982) with varying degrees of success. The Child Abuse Potential Inventory (CAP, Milner, 1986) represents one of the most carefully designed and validated single measures of abuse potential (see Kaufman & Walker, 1986, for a detailed review). Despite impressive reliability and concurrent validity as well as the inclusion of validity, random responding, and lie scales, use of the CAP frequently results in some misclassification of both confirmed abusers and nonabusive controls (4.5% to 14.6% overall).

The literature also contains attempts to predict risk for abuse from multiple measures. For example, in an effort to predict the potential for abuse in a sample of expectant mothers, Altemeier and his associates (Altemeier et al., 1984) administered a structured interview in conjunction with questions regarding life stress, developmental knowledge, and developmental expectations. Even when nonorganic failure to thrive and neglect were included in the definition of abuse, attempts at prediction resulted in a 78% false positive rate.

While these approaches have utility for particular applications (e.g., as a pre-post measure to gauge treatment effectiveness, as part of a more in-depth process), it is important to recognize that their use as part of a general screening initiative is impractical due to the consequences of misclassification (see Parke, 1982, for a detailed discussion). Though the implications of high false negative rates may be obvious (i.e., harm to the child), the consequences of false positives may be somewhat more subtle. Gelles (1975) has suggested that being labeled an abusive parent may lead to characteristics (e.g., depression, anxiety) which are later seen as causal agents in a child's abuse. Further, community rejection due to such a label may contribute to a family's social isolation (Elmer & Gregg, 1967). Also, being labeled "abusive" results in a family's involvement in a network of services that may be more likely to report particular acts as abusive due to the system's sensitivity to such issues. Finally, the fact that misclassification errors may lead to some parents mistakenly being coerced into attending classes, receiving services, etc., engenders legal, ethical, and moral difficulties which cannot be overlooked. Given the nature of child abuse (i.e., a low base rate behavior), it seems unlikely that prediction efforts will ever surmount these concerns. Until they do, screening approaches must continue to assume a limited role in efforts to prevent child abuse.

## Services to Adolescent Parents

Approximately one-million females in the United States under the age of 20 years old become pregnant each year (Elster & McAnarney, 1980). Of these, more than 50% actually carry the child to term (Elster & McAnarney, 1980). Despite a decline in the overall birthrate for American women in the past decade, the number of young teens (10–14 year-olds) having children has continued to increase. Further, the majority of these teenage mothers now choose to keep their babies.

Poor psychosocial and medical outcomes have generally been associated with teenage mothers and their infants. Teenage mothers often have to cope with inadequate social support networks, poor health habits, and a lack of appropriate child-rearing skills (McAnarney & Thiede, 1981). For many teenage mothers, dropping out of school, repeat pregnancy, poverty, and marital instability are common (Whitman, Borkowski, Schellenbach, & Nath, 1987; Presser, 1980). Increased risk for accidents, hospitalizations, school difficulties, developmental delays, and child abuse and/or neglect have been associated with teenage mothers' offspring (Badger, 1985; Garn & Petzold, 1983).

The hospital setting affords a number of opportunities to intervene with pregnant teenagers. Many receive their prenatal care at hospital clinics. Frequently, they have their child delivered by a specialist in obstetrics and finally are referred to a local pediatrician for well child care. Others utilize family medicine practitioners who provide prenatal, obstetric, postpartum, and pediatric care for the mother and child. Teenage parents of low socioeconomic status are typically linked to social service systems and as a result are followed by a caseworker and have access to specialized services (e.g., parenting classes). While the role of teenage fathers has been somewhat neglected in the literature, their inclusion in prevention programs is a necessity to reduce the incidence of child abuse and neglect.

While it is clear that the hospital and social service system are viable and necessary access points for the prevention of child abuse, the topic of services for teenage mothers will not be discussed in detail as part of this chapter. The interested reader is referred to Chapter 3 of this book for a comprehensive review of this area.

## Prenatal/Perinatal Programs

While some examples of prenatal/perinatal programs that would be characterized as primary prevention efforts are reported in the literature (Cooper, Dreznick, & Rowe, 1982; Grindley, 1981), the more methodologically sound studies involved parents already identified as at risk for abuse and neglect (Gray, Cutler, Dean, & Kempe, 1977; Gray, 1983; Olds, Henderson, Chamberlin & Tatelbaum, 1986; Olds, Henderson, Tatelbaum & Chamberlin, 1986; Soumenkoff et al., 1982). The best of these studies were conducted by Olds and his associates (Olds, Henderson, Chamberlin & Tatelbaum, 1986; Olds, Henderson, Tatelbaum & Chamberlin, 1986). They found positive effects for high-risk mothers that received regular nurse home visits in the areas of maternal behaviors, social support, utilization of community professionals, higher birth weights, and longer lengths of gestation. Birth weight and gestation effects were especially pronounced for teenage mothers and mothers who smoked during pregnancy. With regard to postnatal effects, the number of emergency room visits and the rate of child maltreatment were lower for high-risk mothers receiving nurse home visits. Additional details of these investigations are provided in Chapter 2 of this volume.

As stated previously, additional services provided to parents requiring medical prenatal/perinatal care represents a natural linkage. In many cases, a trusting relationship between the parents and the health care professionals is already present. As a result, parents are more willing to become involved with other resources suggested by the health care provider. Visiting nurses, enhancing social networks, and providing parent education would seem to be strategies that have empirical support in decreasing the incidence of child abuse and neglect.

## Medically Ill and Handicapped Children

In ancient times, abuse and murder of handicapped children were commonplace. Such actions were viewed as necessary for the general welfare of the community (Morgan, 1987). Today, values have changed, but the rate of abuse in this population of children continues to be staggering. While only 10% of newborns are considered low birth weight, they comprise approximately 20–30% of the physically abused population (Solomons, 1979; Elmer & Gregg, 1967). Gil's (1970) identification of developmental disabilities in 29% of the 6000 cases of confirmed child abuse he reviewed provides further support for the assertion that a disproportionate number of children who are handicapped are physically abused.

Infants who are born with certain kinds of problems or who are different in some respect (e.g., colic, asthma, eczema, sleep disorders, irritability, premature, excessive crying) seem especially vulnerable to physical abuse (Martin & Beezley, 1974; Ounsted, Oppenheimer, & Lindsay, 1974; Morgan, 1987). Children who are handicapped or who have a chronic medical illness are particularly at risk (Soeffing, 1975; Davidson, 1977; Gray, 1979).

The birth of a child who is medically ill or handicapped creates an unanticipated family crisis as the family mourns the loss of the "idealized child" (Solnit & Stark, 1961). Financial, social, and emotional pressures become a common part of everyday life. Some families are able to adapt and cope with the crisis. For others, however, the care of the child who is medically ill or handicapped becomes overwhelming. Moroney (1981) identified a number of factors related to increased stress in such parents. They included: actual or perceived stigma, extraordinary demands on caregiver's time for child care, decreased personal time for the caregiver, difficulties in managing child behavior, and general feelings of pessimism about the future. Klein and Stern (1971) found that low birth weight infants were from homes with preexisting mental retardation, maternal deprivation, and/or isolation from the mother during the newborn period. Further, Solomons (1979) suggested, "If these stresses are compounded by the initial parental reactions of anger, denial, and guilt, and no long-term relief can be offered to parents, the potential for abuse increases." The severity and social acceptability of the child's handicap or illness and the socioeconomic level of the family also influence parental feelings about the child (Mori, 1983). In addition to stress, unrealistic expectations of the child and parental isolation are also believed to be associated with physical abuse (Mori, 1983; Ramey, Beckman-Bell, & Bowen, 1980; Solomons, 1979; Parks, 1977).

Hammer (1972) identified a number of points in the life cycle when parental stress may be very high, thus increasing the risk of physical abuse. These times include: the child's birth, the point at which a handicap is suspected, at the time of diagnosis, when the child is ready to enter a school program, and when the child reaches puberty. Knowledge of these stress points may increase the professional's ability to prevent abuse.

Professionals in the hospital setting are in a relatively good position to identify stressors related to a chronic illness or a handicap that may lead to physical abuse. In most hospitals, such children are followed regularly in a specialty clinic. A multidisciplinary team is typically an integral part of the clinic's functioning. Physicians and nurses attend to the children's medical needs, psychologists and social workers deal with psychological and psychosocial issues, and physical and occupational therapists provide skills and rehabilitation training. When difficulties are identified, services may either be provided by hospital staff (e.g., parent training, supportive therapy) or through referrals to community agencies (e.g., placement testing in the schools). Additional supportive and educational services are provided to this population in the form of support groups. In some cases, these groups are offered in cooperation with illness/handicap specific community organizations (e.g., Easter Seals).

## Munchausen Syndrome by Proxy

Professionals working in the hospital setting are in a unique position to identify and treat a somewhat unusual form of child abuse known as Munchausen syndrome by proxy (MSBP). Moreover, physicians and mental health professionals are in a unique position to identify adolescents and young adults who will later go on to perpetrate this form of abuse. The term MSBP was first used by Meadow (1977), an English physician, to describe the fabrication of children's medical symptoms by their parents. Named after a famous 18th century storyteller, Baron Von Munchausen of Hanover, the disorder reflects a variety of presentations. Cases have varied along a continuum from parents altering laboratory specimens or falsifying a child's medical history (Verity, Winckworth, Burman, Stevens, & White, 1979; Black, 1981; Meadow, 1984) to parents actually inducing symptoms (e.g., apnea, Berger, 1979; hypernatremia, Rogers, Tripp, Bentovim, Robinson, Berry, & Goulding, 1976; seizures, Greene, Craft, & Ghishan, 1983). In almost all cases, mothers have been identified as the perpetrators (Meadow, 1985) and children below the age of 5-years-old have been at the greatest risk. In most descriptions, fathers are unaware of their wives' activities and are generally considered distant. Evidence also suggests that many of the mothers have their own history of Munchausen syndrome dating back to their adolescence (Meadow, 1985; Chan, Salcedo, Atkins, & Riley, 1986; Jones, Butler, Hamilton, Perdue, Stern, & Woody, 1986; Verity, Winckworth, Burman, Stevens, & White, 1979).

The actual incidence of MSBP is difficult to estimate. While Rosenberg (1987) has discussed 117 cases in a recent review of the literature, other authors have suggested that MSBP is grossly underreported (Meadow, 1985; Libow & Schreier, 1986). Obstacles to accurate identification of cases include perpetrators' vehement denial of allegations, mothers' positive presentation to hospital staff, skepticism on the part of the legal and psychiatric system that children could be victimized by their parents in this fashion, and parents' "doctor shopping" at the first indication of suspicion (Waller, 1983; Chan et al., 1986). When one considers, however, the implications of MSBP, the need to circumvent these barriers becomes clear. As a result of MSBP, many children experience invasive and potentially harmful medical procedures (e.g., surgery), are subjected to frequent hospitalizations, and are emotionally traumatized by their parents' preoccupation with contrived illnesses.

A number of authors have suggested that educating physicians (Waller, 1983) and hospital-based mental health professionals (Chan et al., 1986) would result in an earlier diagnosis in cases of MSBP. A recent study by Kaufman, Coury, Pickrell, and McCleery (1989) indicated that professionals (i.e., physicians, nurses, psychologists, and social workers) associated with medical settings were relatively conversant with MSBP. There was, however, a marked contrast between professionals working in the community and those affiliated with a medical setting. Only 24% of those employed in the community had heard of MSBP, while 86% of those working in medical settings were familiar with the disorder.

A number of prevention initiatives are necessary to impact this form of child abuse. First, educating community mental health professionals would facilitate their ability to identify adult patients whose histories of Munchausen syndrome may put their children at risk for MSBP. Second, educating community physicians would enhance their ability to diagnose such cases and decrease the incidence of unnecessary medical tests and procedures. Finally, the use of formal networks (i.e., communication agreements) developed between community hospitals and private providers would ensure that parents suspected of MSBP were not receiving services for their children at multiple facilities.

## TERTIARY PREVENTION

Tertiary prevention represents after-the-fact attempts to ensure that the difficulty in question will not reoccur. In the case of child abuse, it involves the reporting of abuse, the assessment and diagnosis of the alleged victims, and in some situations their treatment. As stated previously, the section to follow was included in an effort to discuss approaches integral to the hospital setting and often yielding information that may have implications for the development of improved primary and secondary prevention initiatives.

### Physicians' Propensity to Report Child Abuse

One would expect that the reaction of physicians to their legal and moral responsibilities to report child abuse would be favorable. Yet, incidence reports suggest that physicians report a relatively small number of the total cases brought to the attention of state agencies. For example, Franklin County (Ohio) Children Services Board reports that 23,247 phone contacts were made for physical abuse, sexual abuse, neglect, unruly and dependent children, and delinquents in 1985. Of these, 833 were from hospitals and 190 were from "private medical resources." In 1986, the total of 21,999 contacts included 867 from hospitals and 216 from "private medical resources."

In order for tertiary prevention to take place, abuse must first be recognized and reported. Physicians have demonstrated a reluctance to report abuse (Young, 1976). It has been suggested that physicians' propensity to report may be moderated by their specialty area (Chang, 1976). To investigate the possibility that additional experience and education would modify physicians' attitudes about reporting abuse, Morris, Johnson, and Clasen (1985) surveyed 60 pediatricians and 75 family physicians practicing within 50 miles of Columbus, Ohio.

Results of the questionnaire (Figure 9.1) revealed a wide discrepancy between physicians' perceptions of appropriate discipline. Of particular concern was the distinction between what physicians perceived as inappropriate discipline (e.g., hitting with a belt) and what they would report as abuse. One could understand how individuals could have different attitudes about the appropriateness of certain forms of discipline. Their reluctance to report inappropriate discipline, however, despite legal and moral implications, is cause for concern. Results indicated that physicians were still in need of firmer definitions of what constituted abuse. It would seem that this lack of clarity remains a major barrier to appropriate reporting and subsequent tertiary prevention efforts. Fourteen factors were identified as influencing physicians' decisions to report abuse in the simulated cases (Figure 9.2). When queried why *other* physicians do not report abuse, an additional 14, more personal and economic reasons were given (Figure 9.1). Mistrust of social and legal agencies appeared in both lists and precipitated a follow-up study.

A second study examined the etiology of physicians' mistrust of social and legal agencies (Curran, Johnson, & Monk, 1987). Approximately 65% of the respondents had previously reported child abuse, indicating actual experience with the system, knowledge of the abuse diagnosis, and an awareness of reporting requirements. Results suggested that mistrust may be related to their lack of knowledge regarding caseworkers' (Children Services Department [CSD]) responsibilities, skills level, and training. For example, 49% of the physicians did not know the level of education required by CSD and 10% believed that caseworkers could be qualified with a high school diploma or "some college training." Experience with the CSD *improved* attitudes about the agency and knowledge about its functions. Only 13% of the physicians who misunderstood agency functions believed that the agency adequately fulfilled its responsibilities as opposed to 79% of those with an adequate understanding of CSD functions.

Obviously, if physicians in the health care system are to participate in tertiary prevention, their reporting behaviors and attitudes toward service agencies must improve. In addition, other health professionals, including nurses, pedodontists, social workers, and psychologists, must be surveyed to determine their knowledge and attitudes about child abuse and to determine their educational needs.

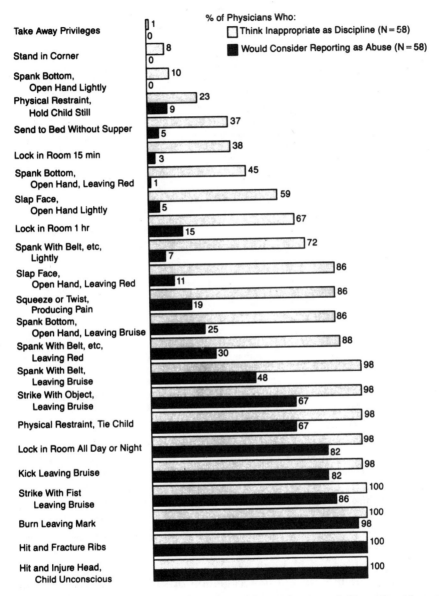

% of Physicians Who:
☐ Think Inappropriate as Discipline (N = 58)
■ Would Consider Reporting as Abuse (N = 58)

| | |
|---|---|
| Take Away Privileges | 1 / 0 |
| Stand in Corner | 8 / 0 |
| Spank Bottom, Open Hand Lightly | 10 / 0 |
| Physical Restraint, Hold Child Still | 23 / 9 |
| Send to Bed Without Supper | 37 / 5 |
| Lock in Room 15 min | 38 / 3 |
| Spank Bottom, Open Hand, Leaving Red | 45 / 1 |
| Slap Face, Open Hand Lightly | 59 / 5 |
| Lock in Room 1 hr | 67 / 15 |
| Spank With Belt, etc, Lightly | 72 / 7 |
| Slap Face, Open Hand, Leaving Red | 86 / 11 |
| Squeeze or Twist, Producing Pain | 86 / 19 |
| Spank Bottom, Open Hand, Leaving Bruise | 86 / 25 |
| Spank With Belt, etc, Leaving Red | 88 / 30 |
| Spank With Belt, Leaving Bruise | 98 / 48 |
| Strike With Object, Leaving Bruise | 98 / 67 |
| Physical Restraint, Tie Child | 98 / 67 |
| Lock in Room All Day or Night | 98 / 82 |
| Kick Leaving Bruise | 98 / 82 |
| Strike With Fist Leaving Bruise | 100 / 86 |
| Burn Leaving Mark | 100 / 98 |
| Hit and Fracture Ribs | 100 |
| Hit and Injure Head, Child Unconscious | 100 |

**Figure 9.1.** Physicians' responses as to why some abuse is not reported. [Reproduced by permission from Morris, Johnson, & Clasen (1985), page 196.]

## Physicians' Ability to Recognize Abuse

Estimates suggest that as many as 25% of all girls and 9% of all boys are sexually abused prior to turning 18 years of age (Finkelhor, 1976). However, as with physical abuse, sexual abuse is considered to be underdiagnosed and

| Factor | % of Physicians* |
|---|---|
| Compatibility of history with physical findings | 85 |
| Seriousness of injury | 58 |
| Familiarity with family | 57 |
| Presence of other injuries | 53 |
| Judgment that injury is "isolated incident" vs. repeated occurrence | 33 |
| Social history: single parent, alcohol, divorce, age | 30 |
| Appropriateness of injury to age of child | 28 |
| Affect or apparent attitude of parent(s) | 24 |
| Physician's own experiences | 20 |
| Affect or response of child | 14 |
| Race | 5 |
| Law requiring reporting of suspicions | 5 |
| Mistrust of social/legal agencies | 5 |
| Wish to give family "second chance" | 5 |

*Physicians who mentioned factor in discussion of at least one sample case photograph.

**Figure 9.2.** Factors that influence physicians' decision to report child abuse. [Reproduced by permission from Morris, Johnson, & Clasen (1985), page 196.]

underreported by the medical community (Pascoe & Duterte, 1981; Jones, 1982). Concerns raised in studies related to physicians' reporting of child abuse (Morris et al., 1985; Curran et al., 1987) would lead one to believe that an inability to recognize signs and symptoms of child sexual abuse may further decrease a physician's willingness to make formal reports. Pascoe and Duterte's (1981) suggestion that uncertainty about diagnostic criteria is related to underreporting in this area further supports this notion.

This supposition led Ladson, Johnson, and Doty (1987) to examine the definitional variables related to recognition of sexual abuse, the technical/medical skills associated with physical diagnosis, and physicians' knowledge regarding venereal disease.

With regard to technical/medical factors, 77% of the physicians indicated that they routinely checked their female patients' genitalia in over 50% of their cases. Only 50% of the physicians, however, examined the size of the vaginal opening in at least 50% of their cases, and only 59% of the physicians correctly identified the hymen on the genitalia photograph. Finally, a horizontal length of vaginal orifice (hymen) of 15mm in a 6-year-old (which is

| Reason | % of Physicians* |
|---|---|
| Abused children seldom appear in private offices | 29 |
| Fear of losing patients | 22 |
| Abuse is a serious accusation: must be sure before reporting | 21 |
| Physician uncomfortable confronting family | 17 |
| Fear of losing rapport with family | 16 |
| Lack of confidence in legal or social agencies | 14 |
| Lack of awareness of problem of child abuse | 12 |
| Fear of court appearance | 10 |
| "I can handle it myself" (office counseling) | 10 |
| Fear of stigmatizing family | 7 |
| Fear of loss of reputation by reporting | 5 |
| Unknown | 5 |
| Too much time involved in reporting | 3 |
| Fear of legal suit for reporting | 3 |

*Some physicians gave more than one reason.

**Figure 9.3.** Physicians' opinions regarding the appropriateness of different forms of discipline. [Reproduced by permission from Morris, Johnson, & Clasen (1985), page 196.]

three times enlarged) was not considered indicative of sexual abuse by 54% of the respondents, despite the fact that the condition of the hymen is considered a major indicator of penetration by the courts.

In response to a question about what organisms should be sought through cultures to evaluate a vaginal discharge, 70% of the respondents answered correctly. As with the study of physical abuse (Morris et al., 1985), there was a major discrepancy between the proportion of physicians who saw the presence of an STD (sexually transmitted disease) in a prepubescent female as raising suspicion of sexual abuse and the proportion who would have reported it as possible sexual abuse.

The study substantiated concerns about the potential for social and cultural taboos, values, personal anxiety, and a lack of medical knowledge about a pathological process to interfere with the recognition or diagnosis of sexual abuse (Brant & Tisza, 1977). In fact, physicians in this study indicated that the poor, urban, white family with five or more children was at greatest risk for sexual abuse. Socioeconomic status, age, sex, and race of the victim should not influence reporting and access to tertiary prevention. In general, the failure of the physician to recognize signs and symptoms of sexual abuse may hinder the court's ability to decide if the child has been abused and may result in the child being placed back into a dangerous environment.

**Interview Strategies Which Reduce System-Based Abuse**

The interdisciplinary team approach to health and social problems represents a model that has been successfully used in the management of child abuse. Teams dealing with child abuse may be composed of varying disciplines and may be organized for different purposes. Hospital-based teams typically diagnose, manage, and make post-discharge plans for children hospitalized due to child abuse (Totah & Wilson-Coker, 1985). Such teams often include a physician, nurse or nurse practitioner, social worker, and psychologist.

In the absence of a functioning team, a suspected child may be interviewed multiple times by police, mental health workers, physicians, lawyers, and parents. A child has a limited tolerance for repeated questioning (MacFarlane & Krebs, 1986). Further, frequent recounting of stressful events by the child may result in additional psychological trauma (American Academy of Child Psychiatry, 1986), withdrawal from further investigation and treatment (Nurcombe, 1986), and termination of court action due to suspected contamination of the child's testimony (MacFarlane & Krebs, 1986; Schetky & Boverman, 1985).

Swift professional intervention using a standardized approach is crucial in protecting an abused child and in offering therapeutic services to the child and family. Recent attempts have been made to standardize the interview process (Boat & Everson, 1986; Friedman & Morgan, 1985; Jones & McQuiston, 1986; White, Strom, Santilli, & Hapin, 1986), but more stringent guidelines and better training of interviewers is needed. Basic aspects of the protocols are controversial and different groups advocate diametrically different approaches. Some emphatically state that extensive background information should be gathered prior to interviewing a child (Boat & Everson, 1986; Conerly, 1986; Friedman & Morgan, 1985; Schlesinger, 1982). Others claim that advance information should be minimized to increase the objectivity of the interviewer (White, 1986a).

There is also a dispute among professionals regarding the optimal number of interviews. Some clinicians believe that one interview is not sufficient to obtain information from a child (Boat & Everson, 1986; White, 1986b). They state that young children require time to establish trust with an interviewer, and that a child's story must be examined for consistency and credibility over time (White & Santilli, 1986). In contrast, others have cited multiple interviews as a problem (Surgeon General, 1986). Some clinical programs, such as Columbus Children's Hospital Child Abuse Team, use only one assessment interview for diagnostic purposes. After rapport is established and the child relaxes during a structured play period, a social worker and a physician jointly interview the child.

In an effort to reduce duplicate interviews, a pilot project was developed which used an interagency team evaluation format. This approach includes a police officer, a mental health worker, and a social worker in a single interview (White & Santilli, 1986). One individual interviews the child while the others observe through a one-way mirror. The drawback of this technique is that it is time consuming, expensive, and often impossible to have representatives of the participating agencies available for each assessment. An alternative approach uses an interview team consisting of a representative of the legal system and a social worker to jointly interview the child (Friedmann & Morgan, 1985). The limitation of this approach is the possibility that two adults may overwhelm the child and receive less information than what they would have individually (Mouzakitis, 1985).

Taping (audio and/or video) interviews is helpful in that multiple agencies can review the tape in lieu of an additional interview as often as they would like without impacting the child (Jones & McQuiston, 1986). Guidelines, however, also need to be developed for the proper use of taping equipment with this population.

In general, practitioners need to remember that it is not only the perpetrator that children need to be protected from. Often, the systems that purport to be protecting the child cause undue trauma and emotional abuse as a result of their approach to acquiring information pertinent to the abusive acts (Tyler & Brassard, 1984). Hospitals and other organizations providing assessment services can help reduce stressful aspects for the child in a number of ways. First, they can standardize their approach to ensure that the child will not have to be reinterviewed as a result of the agency's inability to demonstrate the presence of a standardized approach. Second, they can try to negotiate with the agencies that typically assess an abused child to see if it is possible to arrange for one interview that is acceptable for all parties involved. Finally, they can use audiotapes and videotapes, particularly with young children, to enhance the credibility of the child's testimony.

## THE PROFESSIONAL'S ROLE IN CHILD ABUSE PREVENTION

### The Role of the Physician

The greatest portion of the physician's role in the prevention of child abuse is in the areas of secondary and tertiary prevention efforts. However, physicians do provide some services which fall into the category of primary prevention. For example, many physicians routinely schedule well-child visits for purposes of anticipatory guidance related to infant/child development and discipline. Other physicians work with teenagers at risk of becoming pregnant or teenage parents at risk for abuse. Some physicians have even attempted to assure that child-rearing instruction reach adolescents in the schools (Showers & Johnson, 1984; 1985).

With regard to secondary and tertiary initiatives, physicians assume primary responsibility for assessment in cases involving children who have allegedly been abused. In cases of sexual abuse they conduct a physical examination, collect specimens to determine the presence of STD's, and in some settings they assist in collecting details related to the incident itself. With regard to physical abuse, physicians are frequently asked to examine injuries to determine if they are consistent with parents' explanations. Physicians in the hospital setting are also expected to carefully monitor the interactions of patients who are handicapped and their parents as well as infants and their teenage parents to ensure that patients in these high-risk groups are not being abused. When abuse has already occurred, physicians are asked to determine the need for ongoing medical follow-up and the risks associated with returning a particular child to the care of their parents.

A physician's role in prevention of child abuse is moderated to some degree by their particular specialty. In general, physicians who provide primary care services (e.g., pediatricians, family practitioners) will have the greatest involvement. However, other specialties also afford opportunities. The pedodontist may become concerned with the possibility of neglect due to the condition of a child's teeth, or of abuse as the etiology of an acute dental or oral injury (Sopher, 1977; Malecz, 1979). Physicians in the adolescent medicine area come into contact with sexually active teens as well as teenage parents who may be at risk of abuse. Physicians in the emergency room are asked to evaluate many of the children who are sexually or physically abused. Finally, surgeons may be involved in cases of head injury (i.e., neurosurgeon), fractures (i.e., orthopedic surgeon), or burns (i.e., plastic surgeon).

## The Role of the Psychologist

Psychologists have assumed diverse roles in the prevention of child abuse in the hospital setting. Their expertise in research design, statistical analysis, and skills-based training (e.g., child management skills, stress reduction skills) has facilitated their role as developers of primary prevention initiatives. Psychologists have also contributed in the area of secondary prevention. Parents who are identified as at risk by other hospital professionals are often referred to psychologists for further assessment and treatment. Assessment efforts have focused on the presence of developmental delays, academic difficulties, and behavioral problems in children as well as child management deficits, disruptive levels of stress, a lack of coping/social support resources, and anger/impulse control difficulties in their parents. Treatment approaches have sought to reduce the risk of future abuse that these difficulties present.

With regard to tertiary prevention, the hospital-based psychologist is frequently asked to assess the impact of abuse on the victim and their family.

He or she is asked to make treatment recommendations and sometimes assume the role of the treatment agent. As with secondary prevention, effective treatment (Wolfe, Sandler, & Kaufman, 1981) seems to emphasize remediation of pertinent skills deficits. In some settings the psychologist is also a participant in the initial abuse evaluation. In cases of alleged sexual abuse, this may involve the use of a structured interview, anatomically correct dolls, or drawings, and projective techniques. In all three areas of child abuse prevention, psychologists' research efforts have contributed by ensuring that clinical approaches have an empirical foundation.

## The Role of the Social Worker

The role of the social worker in prevention will vary to some degree depending upon the setting in which they work. The continuum of hospital-linked social services includes the department housed in the hospital itself, the state or county's social service department, and community-based social workers. Hospital- and community-based social workers have been involved in community education (e.g., parenting classes, family planning) intended to prevent (primary) various forms of child abuse. As mentioned previously in this chapter, hospital-based social workers provide a myriad of services to families of handicapped children and teenage parents in an effort to reduce the possibility of abuse. This may include supportive counseling, assisting in the development of social networks, and linking families with services that will improve their housing or financial situation.

Hospitals have consistently relied on social workers to assess alleged victims of abuse and their families. At Columbus Children's Hospital (Ohio), a social worker is on call 24 hours a day for this purpose. That person is expected to perform five essential tasks: 1) Gather specific data regarding the incident from the victim and the victim's family; 2) Help the family understand what has happened to their child and what process will be undertaken by the hospital and social service system as a result; 3) Report the abuse to the proper authorities and serve as liaison to county or state Children Services social workers; 4) Assess the parents' ability to protect the child based upon their social situation, risk factors in the home and parental motivation; and 5) Refer families to other professionals for necessary treatment.

When reports of abuse are made to Children Services social workers (CSSW), a predetermined procedure ensues. CSSWs are mandated to undertake an independent social investigation and assessment within 24 hours of the receipt of a valid report. The CSSW is required to investigate each report, interview all available parties, determine the cause, and notify the local law enforcement agency. A report must be made to the state central registry and any necessary arrangements for protective services must be made. Where abuse is confirmed and the child/children are removed from the home (or custody assumed by the state agency), a "comprehensive reunification plan" is developed by the CSSW. This plan articulates the steps that the family must take before the child/children are (or custody is) returned. The hospital social worker, psychologist and/or physician may all have roles in the completion of this plan. The CSSW is responsible for following the family through these steps until the case is officially closed.

Community Pediatric-Adolescent Services (CPAS) outreach clinics were established as a part of Columbus Children's Hospital's community services to control climbing infant mortality rates (Cohen, V., personal communication, 1987). The social workers in this setting are responsible for educating other clinic staff as well as working with clinic patients. They provide ongoing education and training to clinic patients, make home visits for purposes of in-depth evaluation and skills training, provide supportive counseling, and facilitate patient referrals for adjunctive services (e.g., food stamps). Since they are located in the community, accessibility is much less of a problem for their low socioeconomic status clientele. The neighborhood setting also facilitates the establishment of trust. Since home visits are not uncommon, missed appointments can be more adequately followed up. As a part of the hospital, the community based social worker can also draw upon the resources that the hospital has to offer in meeting their clients' needs.

### The Role of the Nurse

Nurses have played an active role in the prevention of child abuse. Since nurses have traditionally offered preparation classes for childbirth, they have been in an excellent position to provide a broad educational experience to expectant parents regarding child development, child rearing, and common parental expectations. In the outpatient clinic setting, they are responsible for prenatal education as well as ensuring that expectant mothers are following proper health guidelines and are not placing their unborn child at medical risk (e.g., smoking, alcohol/drug consumption). Nurses also provide a large portion of the information presented at "well baby" (or anticipatory guidance) visits. In some practices, such visits are conducted solely by nurse-educators. Nurses have also been involved in teaching classes intended to prepare the general public for the demands of parenthood.

Nurses' inpatient and outpatient positions have also offered opportunities for involvement in secondary prevention. Nurses are the professionals most likely to identify the need for services in at-risk populations (e.g., children who are handicapped and chronically ill). Their primary role in following children who are chronically ill and handicapped through clinic visits and hospital stays affords the opportunity to recognize an increasing risk of abuse and to take appropriate action (e.g., referral for additional services). Teaching teenage parents about proper development and child rearing may also serve a preventive function.

Finally, nurses are also influential in the tertiary prevention area. They perform a key role in the identification of Munchausen syndrome by proxy and other forms of abuse that may actually occur while a child is in the hospital (as an inpatient or outpatient). The "primary nurse" approach means that patients are followed by the same nurse on each stay/visit. This continuity along with careful charting often allows a case to be made when parents are surreptitiously inducing symptoms or falsifying key historical elements and lab samples. Nurses are also responsible for following children who have had injuries or medical difficulties secondary to abuse and to monitor the family to ensure that abuse has not reoccurred.

## FUTURE DIRECTIONS

As stated previously, the hospital setting affords many opportunities for the prevention of child abuse. It is anticipated that the influence of prevention efforts in this setting will continue to increase and that reviews undertaken in the near future will have a richer empirical literature to draw from. A number of training, clinical, and research directions are indicated by the work which has already been completed.

Hospitals should take the initiative in designing and implementing primary prevention programs which: 1) communicate the consequences of shaking an infant/child; 2) integrate developmental and child rearing information into the context of regular prenatal visits; 3) involve all parents in perinatal interventions intended to improve bonding and facilitate realistic expectations; and 4) employ well-child visits as a means of assisting parents in adapting to developmentally related changes in their child. Further, curriculums for medical students and residents should be bolstered to reinforce the importance of anticipatory guidance approaches with new parents.

With regard to secondary prevention, increased efforts in adolescent medicine clinics to discuss family planning and birth control may help reduce the growing numbers of unwanted teenage pregnancies. Additional attention to providing better supportive services (e.g., groups, therapy) to at-risk groups (e.g., handicapped, chronically ill) may also be effective in reducing the incidence of abuse. Community physicians need to be educated to better recognize patients displaying behaviors indicative of Munchausen syndrome. In this way, physicians and mental health professionals may be able to take steps to prevent such persons from going on to perpetrate Munchausen syndrome by proxy. Multiagency case staffings and agreements which allow sharing patient information may also enable hospitals to identify parents who have presented their children to numerous providers seeking questionable services. Finally, educational and supportive services need to be provided in greater numbers to high-risk groups (e.g., teenage parents). A concerted effort should be made to increase the involvement of teenage fathers in the hope that their presence may add to the stability and resources of at-risk families. With regard to tertiary care, hospital-based training programs should ensure that physicians are well versed in identifying presentations of all types of abuse. Medical ethics courses should be modified to deal with issues related to the reporting of child abuse. Agencies (i.e., hospital, law enforcement, Children Services) should be encouraged to conduct joint interviews and investigations which may significantly reduce the trauma experienced by children involved in this process.

Since there is a relative paucity of research literature specifically related to the prevention of child abuse in the hospital setting, there are many areas that need to be pursued. With regard to primary prevention, the following areas are in need of further investigation: the effectiveness and utility of prevention initiatives which are linked to prenatal care; the utility of hospitals offering training for baby sitters in child care skills; what approaches are most useful in reducing SBS; and the effectiveness of programs intended to improve infant-parent bonding. In the area of secondary prevention, there is a need for well controlled studies to determine if "Teen Tot" programs (i.e., skills training and support services for teenage parents) are effective in preventing abuse, and if they are, what components are essential for inclusion. Research should also identify the particular factors that make children who are handicapped and chronically ill particularly at risk for abuse. Once identified, these factors should be used as the basis of research evaluating different intervention strategies. Research directed at identifying effective interventions for adolescents presenting with Munchausen syndrome should be examined as a possible means of reducing the incidence of this form of abuse. Research in tertiary prevention seems to be the most well developed. Still, we know little about the effects of multiple sexual abuse assessments, and which sexual abuse interview approaches (e.g., anatomically correct dolls and drawings) yield the most useful information. Finally, investigations should strive to develop a better understanding of Munchausen syndrome by proxy and effective means of early identification and treatment.

## REFERENCES

Ainsworth, M. (1969). Object relations, dependency, and attachment: A theoretical review of the infant-mother relationship. *Child Development, 40*, 965–1025.

Altemeier, W. A., O'Connor, S., Vietze, P., Sandler, H., & Sherrod, K. (1984). Prediction of child abuse: A prospective study of feasibility. *Child Abuse and Neglect, 8*, 393–400.

American Academy of Child Psychiatry. (1986, February 9). AACP statement on protecting children undergoing abuse investigations and testimony. Adopted by Council.

American Academy of Pediatrics. (1977). Standards of child health care. (Ed. 3). Evanston, IL.

Badger, E. (1985). Teenage mothers and their infants. *Clinics in Perinatal, 12*, 391–406.

Belsky, J. (1980). Child maltreatment: An ecological integration. *American Psychologist, 35*, 320–335.

Belsky, J. (1985). Experimenting with the family in the newborn period. *Child Development*, *56*, 407–414.

Berger, D. (1979). Child abuse simulating "near miss" sudden infant death syndrome. *Journal of Pediatrics*, *95*, 554–6.

Bernstein, D., & Borkovec, T. (1973). *Progressive relaxation training: A manual for the helping professions*. Champaign, IL: Research Press.

Black, D. (1981). The extended Munchausen syndrome: A family case. *British Journal of Psychiatry*, *138*, 466–9.

Boat, B., & Everson, M. (1986). Using anatomical dolls: Guidelines for interviewing young children in sexual abuse investigation. Chapel Hill, NC: University of North Carolina.

Bowlby, J. (1958). The nature of the child's tie to his mother. *International Journal of Psychoanalysis*, *39*, 350–373.

Brant, R., & Tisza, V. (1977). Sexually misused child. *American Journal of Orthopsychiatry*, *47*, 80–90.

Caffey, J. (1957). Some traumatic lesions in growing bones other than fractures and dislocations: Clinical and radiological features. *British Journal of Radiology*, *30*, 225–238.

Caffey, J. (1972). On the theory and practice of shaking infants. Its potential residual effects of permanent brain damage and mental retardation. *American Journal of Diseases of Children*, *124*, 161–9.

Caffey, J. (1974). The whiplash shaken infant syndrome: Manual shaking by the extremities with whiplash-induced intracranial and intraocular bleedings, linked with residual permanent brain damage and mental retardation. *Pediatrics*, *54*, 396–403.

Campbell, S. B. G., & Taylor, P. M. (1980). Bonding and attachment: Theoretical issues. In P. M. Taylor (Ed.), *Parent-infant relationships* (pp. 3–23). New York: Grune and Stratton.

Chan, D., Salcedo, J., Atkins, D., & Riley, E. (1986). Munchausen syndrome by proxy: A review and case study. *Journal of Pediatric Psychology*, *11*, 71–80.

Chang, A. (1976). Child abuse and neglect: Physicians' knowledge, attitudes, and experiences. *American Journal of Public Health*, *66*, 1199–1201.

Christophersen, E. (1986). Anticipatory guidance on discipline. In E. R. Christophersen, J. W. Finney & P. C. Friman (Eds.), *The Pediatric Clinics of North America*, *33*, 789–98.

Christophersen, E., Barrish, H., Barrish, I., & Christophersen, M. (1984). Continuing education for parents of infants and toddlers. In R. F. Dangel & R. A. Polster (Eds.), *Parent Training: Foundations of Research and Practice* (pp. 124–143). New York: Guilford Press.

Conerly, S. (1986). Assessment of suspected child sexual abuse. In K. MacFarlane, J. Waterman, S. Conerly, L. Damon, M. Durfee & S. Long (Eds.), *Sexual abuse of young children: Evaluation and treatment*. New York: Guilford Press.

Cooper, H., Dreznick, J., & Rowe, B. (1982). Perinatal coaching: A new beginning. *Social Casework*, *63*, 35–40.

Curran, C., Johnson, C., & Monk, J. (April, 1987). Mistrust of children's services agencies: One reason why physicians fail to report abuse. Poster session, Landacre

Society Conference. The Ohio State University College of Medicine, Columbus, OH.

Davidson, A. (1977). Child abuse: Causes and prevention. *Journal of the National Medical Association, 69*, 817–820.

Dietrich, K., Starr, R., & Weisfeld, G. (1983). Infant maltreatment: Caretaker-infant interactions and developmental consequences at different levels of parenting failure. *Pediatrics, 72*, 532–540.

Duhaime, A., Gennarelli, T., Thibault, L., Bruce, D., Margulies, S., & Wiser, R. (1987). The shaken baby syndrome: A clinical, pathological and biomechanical study. *Journal of Neurosurgery, 66*, 409–15.

Dykes, L. (1986). The whiplash shaken infant syndrome: What has been learned? *Child Abuse and Neglect, 10*, 211–221.

Elmer, E., & Gregg, G. (1967). Developmental characteristics of abused children. *Pediatrics, 40*, 596–602.

Elster, A., & McAnarney, E. (1980). Medical and psychosocial risks of pregnancy and childbearing during adolescence. *Pediatric Annals, 9*, 89–94.

Finkelhor, D. (1976). *Sexually victimized children.* New York: Free Press.

Friedemann, V. M., & Morgan, M. K. (1985). *Interviewing sexual abuse victims using anatomical dolls: The professional's guidebook.* Eugene, OR: Shamrock Press.

Garn, S., & Petzold, L. (1983). Characteristics of the mother and child in teenage pregnancy. *American Journal of Disorders of the Child, 137*, 365–368.

Gelles, R. (1975). The social construction of child abuse. *American Journal of Orthopsychiatry, 45*, 363–371.

Gil, D. G. (1970). *Violence Against Children: Physical Child Abuse in the United States.* Cambridge, MA: Harvard University Press.

Gray, E. B. (1983). *Final report: Collaborative research of community and minority group action to prevent child abuse and neglect. Vol. I: Perinatal interventions.* Chicago: National Committee for Prevention of Child Abuse.

Gray, J. (1979). Prediction and prevention of child abuse. *Seminars in Perinatology, 3*, 84–90.

Gray, J. D., Cutler, C. A., Dean, J. G., & Kempe, C. H. (1977). Prediction and prevention of child abuse and neglect. *Child Abuse and Neglect, 1*, 45–58.

Gray, J. D., Cutler, C. A., Dean, J. G., & Kempe, C. H. (1980). Prediction and prevention of child abuse. In P. M. Taylor (Ed.), *Parent-infant relationships.* New York: Grune and Stratton.

Greene, J., Craft, L., & Ghishan, F. (1980). Acetaminophen poisoning in infancy. *American Journal of Diseases of Children, 137*, 386–387.

Grindley, J. F. (1981). Child abuse: The nurse and prevention. *Nursing Clinics of North America, 16*, 167–177.

Hammer, E. (1972, November). Families of deaf-blind children: Case studies of stress. Paper presented at the First Regional American Orthopsychiatric Association Conference, Dallas, TX.

Helfer, R. (1982). A review of the literature on the prevention of child abuse and neglect. *Child Abuse and Neglect, 6*, 251–261.

Holmes, T., & Rahe, R. (1967). The social readjustment rating scale. *Journal of Psychosomatic Research, 11*, 213–218.

Jones, D., & McQuiston, M. (1986). *Interviewing the sexually abused child.* (2nd Ed.) Denver, CO: C. Henry Kempe National Center for the Prevention and Treatment of Child Abuse and Neglect.

Jones, J., Butler, H., Hamilton, B., Perdue, J., Stern, H., & Woody, R. (1986). Munchausen syndrome by proxy. *Child Abuse and Neglect, 10,* 33–40.

Kaufman, K., Coury, D., Pickrell, E., & McCleery, J. (1989). Munchausen syndrome: A survey of professionals' knowledge. *Child Abuse and Neglect, 13,* 141–148.

Kaufman, K., & Walker, C. E. (1986). Review of the child abuse potential inventory. In D. J. Keyser & R. C. Sweetland (Eds.), *Test critiques* (Volume V). Kansas City, MO: Test Corporation of America.

Kempe, C. H., Silverman, F. N., Steele, B. F., Druegemuller, W., & Silver, H. K. (1962). The battered child syndrome. *Journal of the American Medical Association, 191,* 17–24.

Kittredge, D., Espinosa-Charneco, M., & Olson, R. (1986). *Residents' Resource Manual for Well Child Care Counseling.* Oklahoma City, OK: The University of Oklahoma Health Sciences Center.

Klaus, H. M., & Kennell, J. H. (1976). Human maternal and paternal behavior. In H. M. Klaus & J. H. Kennell (Eds.), *Maternal-infant bonding.* St. Louis, MO: C. V. Mosby.

Klaus, H. M., & Kennell, J. H. (1982). The family during pregnancy. In H. M. Klaus & J. H. Kennell (Eds.), *Parent-infant bonding* (2nd Ed.). St. Louis, MO: C. V. Mosby.

Klein, M., & Stern, L. (1971). Low birth weight and the battered child syndrome. *American Journal of Diseases of Children, 122,* 15–8.

Ladson, S., Johnson, C. F., & Doty, R. (1987). Do physicians recognize sexual abuse? *American Journal of Diseases Children, 141,* 411–5.

Lazarus, R., & Folkman, S. (1984). *Stress, appraisal and coping.* New York: Springer Publishing.

Libow, J., & Schreier, H. (1986). Three forms of factitious illness in children: When is it munchausen syndrome by proxy. *American Journal of Orthopsychiatry, 56,* 602–11.

Ludwig, S., & Worman, M. (1984). Shaken baby syndrome: A review of 20 cases. *Annals of Emergency Medicine, 13,* 104–7.

MacFarlane, K. (1986). Child sexual abuse allegations in divorce proceedings. In K. MacFarlane, J. Waterman, S. Conerly, L. Damon, M. Durfee, & S. Long (Eds.), *Sexual abuse of young children: Evaluation and treatment.* New York: Guilford Press.

MacFarlane, K., & Krebs, S. (1986). Techniques for interviewing and gathering evidence. In K. MacFarlane, J. Waterman, S. Conerly, L. Damon, M. Durfee, & S. Long (Eds.), *Sexual abuse of young children: Evaluation and treatment.* New York: Guilford Press.

Malecz, R. E. (1979). Child abuse, its relationship to pedodontics: A survey. *Journal of Dentistry for Children, 46,* 25–6.

Martin, H. P., & Beezley, P. (1974). Prevention and consequences of child abuse. *Journal of Operational Psychiatry, 6,* 68–77.

McAnarney, E., & Thiede, H. (1981). Adolescent pregnancy and childbearing: What we have learned in a decade and what remains to be learned. *Semin Perinatal*, 5, 91–103.

Meadow, R. (1977). Munchausen syndrome by proxy: The hinterland of child abuse. *Lancet, 11*, 343–345.

Meadow, R. (1984). Factitious illness: The hinterland of child abuse. In R. Meadows (Ed.), *Recent advances in pediatrics, No. 7*. Edinburgh: Churchill Livingstone.

Meadow, R. (1985). Management of munchausen syndrome by proxy. *Archives of Diseases in Childhood, 60*, 385–93.

Milner, J. (1986). *The child abuse potential inventory manual* (Second Edition). Webster, NC: Psytec, Inc.

Morgan, S. R. (1987). *Abuse and Neglect of Handicapped Children*. Boston: Little, Brown.

Mori, A. A. (1983). *Families of children with special needs: Early intervention techniques for the practitioner*. Rockville, MD: Aspen Systems Corporation.

Moroney, R. (1981). Public social policy: Impact on families with handicapped children. In J. L. Paul (Ed.), *Understanding and working with parents of children with special needs*. New York: Holt, Rinehart, and Winston.

Morris, J. L., Johnson, C. F., & Clasen, M. (1985). To report or not to report: Physicians' attitudes toward discipline and child abuse. *American Journal of Diseases of Children, 139*, 194–197.

Mouzakitis, C. M. (1985). Interviewing in child protection. In C. M. Mouzakitis & R. Varghese (Eds.), *Social Work Treatment with Abused and Neglected Children*. Springfield, IL: Charles C. Thomas.

Nurcombe, B. (1986). The child as witness: Competency and cardibility. *Journal of the American Academy of Child Psychiatry, 25*, 473–80.

O'Conner, S., Vietze, P. M., Sherrod, K. B., Sandler, H. M., & Altemeier, W. A. (1980). Reduced incidence of parenting inadequacy following rooming in. *Pediatrics, 66*, 176–182.

Olds, D. L., Henderson, C. R., Chamberlin, R., & Tatelbaum, R. (1986). Preventing child abuse and neglect: A randomized trial of nurse home visitation. *Pediatrics, 78*, 65–78.

Olds, D. L., Henderson, C. R., Tatelbaum, R., & Chamberlin, R. (1986). Improving the delivery of prenatal care and outcomes of pregnancy: A randomized trial of nurse home visitation. *Pediatrics, 77*, 16–28.

Ounsted, C., Oppenheimer, R., & Lindsay, J. (1974). Aspects of bonding failure: The psychopathology and psychotherapeutic treatment of families of battered children. *Developmental Medical Child Neurology, 16*, 447–456.

Parke, R. D. (1982). Theoretical models of child abuse: Their implications for prediction, prevention, and modification. In R. H. Starr (Ed.), *Child abuse prediction: Policy implications* (pp. 31–66). Cambridge, MA: Ballinger Publishing Co.

Parke, R. D., & Beitel, A. (1986). Hospital-based intervention for fathers. M. E. Lamb (Ed.), *The father's role: Applied perspectives*. New York: Wiley and Sons.

Parke, R. D., Hymel, S., Power, T. G., & Tinsley, B. R. (1980). Fathers and risk: A hospital based model of intervention. In D. B. Sawin, R. C. Hawkings, L. O. Walker, & J. H. Penticuff (Eds.), *Psychosocial risks in infant-environment interactions*. New York: Bruner/Mazel.

Parks, R. M. (1977). Parental reactions to the birth of a handicapped child. *Health and Social Work, 2*, 51–66.

Pascoe, D. J., & Duterte, B. O. (1981). Medical diagnosis of sexual abuse in the premenarcheal child. *Pediatric Annals, 10*, 187–90.

Presser, H. (1980). Social consequences of teenage childbearing. In C. S. Chilman (Ed.), *Adolescent pregnancy and childbearing*. Washington, DC: (DHHS) NIH Publication No. 81-2077.

Ramey, C., Beckman-Bell, P., & Bowen, J. (1980). Infant characteristics and infant-caregiver interactions. In J. J. Gallagher (Ed.), *New directions for exceptional children: Parents and families of handicapped children*.

Reisinger, K., & Bires, J. (1980). Anticipatory guidance in pediatric practice. *Pediatrics, 66*, 889–92.

Rogers, D., Tripp, J., Bentovim, A., Robinson, A., Berry, D., & Goulding, R. (1976). Non-accidental poisoning: An extended syndrome of child abuse. *British Medical Journal, 1*, 793–6.

Rosenberg, D. (1987). Web of deceit: A literature review of munchausen syndrome by proxy. *Child Abuse and Neglect, 11*, 547–64.

Rosenberg, M. S., & Reppucci, N. D. (1985). Primary prevention of child abuse. *Journal of Consulting and Clinical Psychology, 53*, 576–585.

Schetky, D. H., & Boverman, H. (1985, October). *Faulty assessment of child sexual abuse: Legal and emotional ramifications*. Paper presented at Annual Meeting of American Academy of Child Psychiatry and the Law, New Mexico.

Schlesinger, B. (1982). *Sexual abuse of children: A resource guide and annotated bibliography*. Toronto: University of Toronto Press.

Schmitt, B. (1980). The prevention of child abuse and neglect: A review of the literature with recommendations for application. *Child Abuse and Neglect, 4*, 171–177.

Schneider, C. (1982). The Michigan Screening Profile of Parenting. In R. H. Starr (Ed.), *Child Abuse Prediction: Policy Implications* (pp. 105–174).

Showers, J., & Johnson, C. F. (1984). Students' knowledge of child health and development: Effects of approaches to discipline. *Journal of School Health, 54*, 122–4.

Showers, J., & Johnson, C. F. (1985). Child development, child health and child rearing knowledge among urban adolescents: Are they adequately prepared for the challenges of parenthood? *Health Education, 16*, 37–41.

Siegel, E., Bauman, K., Schaefer, E., Saunders, M., & Ingram, D. (1980). Hospital and home support during infancy: Impact on maternal attachment, child abuse and neglect, and health care utilization. *Pediatrics, 66*, 183–190.

Soeffing, M. (1975). Abused children are exceptional children. *Exceptional Children, 142*, 126–33.

Solnit, A., & Stark, M. (1961). Mourning the birth of a defective child. *Psychoanalytic Study of the Child, 16*, 523.

Solomons, G. (1979). Child abuse and developmental disabilities. *Development Medicine and Child Neurology, 21*, 101–6.

Sopher, I. M. (1977). The dentist and the battered child syndrome. *Dental Clinics of North America, 21*, 113–22.

Soumenkoff, G., Marneffe, C., Gerard, M., Limet, R., Beeckmans, M., & Hubinout, P. O. (1982). A coordinated attempt for prevention of child abuse at the antenatal care level. *Child Abuse and Neglect, 6,* 87–94.

Starr, R. (1988). Physical abuse of children. In V. B. Van Hasselt, A. S. Bellack, R. L. Morrison & M. Hersen (Eds.), *Handbook of family violence.* NY: Plenum.

Statt. Sexual Assault Center, Harborview Medical Center, Seattle. (1980). Sexual Assault Center emergency room protocol: Child and adolescent patients. In L. G. Schultz (Ed.), *The Sexual Victimization of Youth* (pp. 83–90). Springfield, IL: Charles C. Thomas.

Straus, M. (1980). Stress and physical abuse. *Child Abuse and Neglect, 4,* 75–88.

*Surgeon General's Workshop on Violence and Public Health Report.* (1986, May). (DHHS Publication No. HRS-D-MC 86-1). Washington, DC: Health Resources and Services Administration, U.S. Public Health Service.

Szajnberg, N., Ward, M. J., Krauss, A., & Kessler, D. B. (1987). Low birthweight prematures: Preventive intervention and maternal attitude. *Child Psychiatry and Human Development, 17,* 152–165.

Totah, N. L., & Wilson-Coker, P. (1985). The use of interdisciplinary teams. In C. M. Mouzakitis & R. Varghese (Eds.), *Social work treatment with abused and neglected children.* Springfield, IL: Charles C. Thomas.

Tyler, A. H., & Brassard, M. R. (1984). Abuse in the investigation and treatment of intrafamilial child sexual abuse. *Child Abuse and Neglect, 8,* 47–53.

Verity, C., Winckworth, C., Burman, D., Stevens, D., & White, R. (1979). Polle syndrome: Children of munchausen. *British Medical Journal, 11,* 422–423.

Waller, D. (1983). Obstacles to the treatment of Munchausen by proxy syndrome. *Journal of the American Academy of Child Psychiatry, 22,* 80–85.

White, S. (1986a, Winter). Uses and abuses of the sexually anatomically correct dolls. Division of Child, Youth, and Family Services. *Newsletter,* American Psychological Association, Division 37.

White, S. (1986b, August). *Mental health evaluator's role in child sexual abuse assessments.* Paper presented at the American Psychological Association Annual Convention, Washington, DC.

White, S., & Santilli, G. (1986). Uses and abuses of sexually anatomically detailed dolls. Unpublished manuscript.

White, S., Stom, G. H., Santilli, G., & Halpin, B. M. (1986). Interviewing young sexual abuse victims with anatomically correct dolls. *Child Abuse and Neglect, 10,* 519–529.

Whitman, T., Borkowski, J., Schellenbach, C., & Nath, P. (1987). Predicting and understanding developmental delay of children of adolescent mothers: A multidimensional approach. *American Journal of Mental Deficiency, 92,* 40–56.

Widmayer, S. M., & Field, T. M. (1980). Effects of Brazelton demonstration on early interactions of preterm infants and their teenage mothers. *Infant Behavior and Development, 3,* 79–89.

Wilson, A. L. (1984). Promoting a positive parent-baby relationship. In C. H. Kempe & R. E. Helfer (Eds.), *The battered child* (4th Ed.). Chicago, IL: University of Chicago Press.

Wolfe, D. A. (1985). Child-abusive parents: An empirical review and analysis. *Psychological Bulletin*, *97*, 462–482.

Wolfe, D., Sandler, J., & Kaufman, K. (1981). A competency-based parent training program for child abusers. *Journal of Consulting and Clinical Psychology*, *49*, 633–640.

Woolley, P. V., & Evans, W. A. (1955). Significance of skeletal lesions in infants resembling those of traumatic origin. *Journal of the American Medical Association*, *158*, 539–543.

Young, M. (1976). A comparison of physician responses to child abuse, Tulsa County, OK; 1969 and 1974. *Journal of Oklahoma State Medical Association*, *69*, 125–7.

# CHAPTER 10

# *Prevention of Physical Abuse of Children Through Parent Training*

THOMAS S. ALTEPETER AND C. EUGENE WALKER

Several authors have recommended that future prevention efforts be multi-faceted, targeting individual, familial, community, and cultural forces believed to contribute to abusive behaviors (Belsky, 1980; Cohn, 1982; Lutzker, 1984; Wolfe, 1985). Although it may be difficult for one prevention program to directly target forces at all levels, an ecological model provides a tentative framework that can be used to more readily identify those factors and their interactions which place individuals at risk for abusive behavior. Presumably, then, reasonable prevention efforts can be directed toward those groups determined to be at high risk.

Perhaps the greatest specific contribution of the ecological paradigm is that it underscores the situational nature of abuse and articulates the hypothesis that parents who are predisposed toward abusive behavior may become abusive as a response to stress-promoting forces both within the family and beyond it. In other words, the greatest risk factors may be situational demands which place subjectively high levels of stress on potentially abusive parents in the absence of adequate support. Wolfe (1985) and others (e.g., Conger, McCarty, Yang, Lahey, & Kropp, 1984; Lahey, Conger, Atkeson, & Treiber, 1984) have noted that the behavior of abusive parents is strongly affected by situational demands and that abusive behavior is strongly associated with high levels of stress and conflict. Specific stressors that might increase risk include factors, both within the family and impinging upon it, that dramatically increase the stress of parenting. These may include aversive child behaviors; single-parent households; large families, particularly if children are closely spaced; low socioeconomic status and unemployment; social isolation, or the lack of an adequate social support system; and so forth. These stressors, when experienced by a parent predisposed toward abuse (e.g., through lack of appropriate parental skills or a history of having had abusive behavior modeled by one's own parents) may precipitate abusive acts towards one's child.

One approach to prevention is to reduce situational stressors which may engender abusive acts in predisposed parents. Several proposed methods to accomplish this goal have been articulated (e.g., Rosenberg & Reppucci, 1985; Wolfe, 1985). This present chapter will focus on programs for teaching/ training high-risk parents alternative behavior management skills and personal coping skills. The aim of this approach is to provide parents with alternative behavior management and coping skills that will enable them to minimize and more adaptively cope with the stressors that they experience. A brief review of the parent training literature will provide a better understanding of this intervention strategy and how it might be put to use in the service of child abuse prevention.

## BEHAVIORAL PARENT TRAINING: ASSESSING ITS IMPACT

Behavioral parent training involves teaching parents to systematically and consistently implement various techniques which are based on both respondent and operant learning principles in managing their children's behavior. This usually involves formal instruction regarding principles of positive and negative reinforcement, extinction, and so forth. In terms of specific techniques, at the rudimentary level parent-therapists may be taught the use of differential reinforcement, often paired with time-out contingencies, to manage various mild to moderate behavior problems, such as noncompliance, temper tantrums, bedtime crying, and similar behaviors (Berkowitz & Graziano, 1972). At more complex levels, parent-therapists may be taught more intricate techniques, such as token reinforcement systems, negative practice, or relaxation training to manage such problems as fire setting (Welsh, 1968), toilet training (Azrin & Foxx, 1976; Walker, 1978; Walker, Bonner, & Milling, 1988), and severe nightmares and sleepwalking (Clement, 1970).

As a strategy for behavior change, parent training can impact the child, the parent, and the broader family system in a variety of ways, all of which serve therapeutic ends. First and foremost, interventions are implemented through the individuals who are most influential in the child's life, in natural settings, and make full use of existing sources of reinforcement. As a result, therapy is potentially available to the child 24 hours per day, 7 days per week, rather than one hour per week. Assuming a minimum degree of cooperation and consistency on the part of parent-therapists, this should yield interventions that are more potent than interventions delivered in more traditional models of therapy. Second, as a consequence of their developing effective behavior management skills through parent training, parents frequently experience an increase in their feelings of competence (Blechman, 1984). Third, parents are typically taught a variety of behavior management skills that are presumably more effective than those they employed prior to training. Parents will hopefully use these skills in future situations to more effectively manage their children's behavior and thereby minimize or prevent further behavioral problems; thus, behavior parent training is a potential preventive measure. Fourth, as a direct result of the increased use of positive reinforcement by the parent, positive transactions will occur more frequently in the parent-child relationship (Eyberg & Robinson, 1982).

In assessing the efficacy of parent training, reviewers have noted that initial studies showed somewhat mixed results and conclusions were difficult to reach due to the limited quality of much of the research. More recently, data from better designed research have become available. Overall, recent studies have demonstrated that parent training is an effective intervention for many childhood problems, and reviewers have been quite positive in their assessment of this method of intervention. Rincover, Koegel, & Russo (1978) reviewed the skills required to be an effective parent-therapist and concluded that most parents could master these skills with appropriate training and professional guidance. Graziano (1977) expressed the opinion that "utilizing parents as cooperative change agents and training them in therapeutic skills may be the single most important development in the child therapy area" (p. 257). Similarly, in assessing the strengths and weaknesses of parent training, Bijou (1984, p. 20) concluded:

> Parent behavioral training currently ranks high among the achievements of behavior modification . . . Everything considered, parent training has as much validity as do other acceptable clinical and remedial practices. It is a feasible and effective way of dealing with children's behavior problems. It is relatively easy to train parents from a wide range of educational and social backgrounds in the essential behavioral techniques.

## BEHAVIORAL PARENT TRAINING: TEACHING EFFECTIVE PARENTING

Recent efforts have been made to extend the parent training paradigm beyond direct treatment for specific behavioral problems into programs that are designed to teach parents effective behavior management skills. One such program, Winning! (Dangel & Polster, 1984b), employs a deductive approach to training. Rather than learning skills to correct or manage a specific behavioral problem, such as noncompliance, temper tantrums, or food refusal, Winning! teaches basic skills that can be applied in a variety of ways, but without focussing the training on the direct application of these skills. The program is structured around 8 basic and 14 advanced lessons, which are further subdivided into short instructional units. Typically, Winning! is implemented in weekly small-group meetings (15 or less per group), although the program provides enough flexibility to be individualized as needed. The meetings have an educational rather than therapeutic focus. Group meetings have been held in a variety of settings, including public libraries, elementary schools, day care centers, and child protective service units. Instructional materials include 14 short booklets and 22 videotape lessons developed specifically for the program. Some of the basic content areas include *praise and affection, rewards and privileges, ignoring,* and *time out.* If a parent has difficulty applying the skills learned through the basic lessons in a particular situation, the advanced lessons are designed to facilitate the generalization of skills to specific problem areas, such as temper tantrums, bedwetting, soiling, school problems, and others.

Dangel & Polster (1984a) reported that over 2,000 families from all socioeconomic levels and several racial minorities have participated in Winning! since 1978:

> Overall, these results indicate that "Winning!" produces substantial desirable changes in parent and child behavior. These improvements occur across a diverse parent and child population: poor, wealthy, minority, nonminority, single-parent, two-parent, referred and voluntary. All parents (in these subsamples) demonstrated mastery of all skills. Observational data show that parents used these skills at various time and activities during the day, that positive changes occurred in untrained behaviors, and that the effects appear to be maintained. (p. 192)

Responsive Parenting (Hall, 1981, 1984) is a large-scale, educational program designed to teach parents to apply principles derived from social learning theory to foster new behaviors in the home setting. The program incorporates large-group didactic presentations, small-group discussions and behavioral rehearsals, and individualized home behavior change projects. A unique feature of Responsive Parenting is the use of selected program *graduates* as subsequent apprentice group leaders. With additional training, they may become independent group leaders; thus some of the positive aspects of self-help groups and paraprofessional helpers are incorporated into this program (Hall, 1984).

Barkley (1987, p. 1) has recently developed a "highly effective, empirically validated program for the clinical training of parents in the management of behavior problem children." The program is organized into 10 sequential steps or integrated instructional units. Each unit is composed of: didactic presentation; opportunities to learn and rehearse specific behavior management skills (e.g., methods to increase compliance, decrease disruptive behavior, the appropriate uses of time-out, etc.); and homework assignments. Barkley (1987) notes that the program is intended primarily for parents of children who display noncompliant behaviors and that the program can be used independently or in conjunction with other therapeutic modalities (e.g., marital and family therapy).

Eyberg (Eyberg, 1986; Eyberg & Matarazzo, 1989; Eyberg & Robinson, 1982) has developed the Parent-Child Interaction Training program, which teaches parents and children a global set of positive interaction skills that can be readily applied to their unique problem situations. The program consists of two phases: the Child-Directed Interaction (CDI) phase, and the Parent-

Directed Interaction (PDI) phase. During the CDI phase, parents are taught several *Do's* and *Don'ts* of interacting with their child through didactic instruction, modeling, and live coaching. These interactions can lead to mutually positive interactions between parents and children (Eyberg & Robinson, 1982). During the subsequent PDI phase, parents are taught behaviors and techniques to increase child compliance in a manner that is fair and noncoercive for the child. For example, parents are taught to give clear, direct commands that are positively stated and that require developmentally appropriate responses from the child. Additionally, parents are taught methods, such as time-out, to manage episodes of noncompliance.

Although these and various other programs (e.g., Systematic Training for Effective Parenting; Dinkmeyer & McKay, 1976) have provided impressive preliminary evidence that parent training programs can be effectively used in a proactive, educative, preventive mode as well as a treatment mode, further research needs to be done. Specifically, the overall impact of proactive, educative programs is not clearly understood, particularly their long-range impact upon parent-child relations. Similarly, it is not known, or at least not reported, if there have been any negative effects or deterioration as a result of involvement in one of these programs. This is a particularly important consideration given the fact that programs such as these will typically be referred families who already experience difficulties in parent-child relations and child behavior management. A related concern is what impact, either positive or negative, these programs have upon individuals who drop out or fail to complete the program. In general, the issues of what motivates premature termination, and whether there are potential negative effects for premature terminators, have not been adequately examined. Finally, comparisons of alternative programs have yet to be carried out to determine the relative effectiveness and cost-effectiveness of competing programs. In summary, then, while systematic parent training programs appear quite promising, they are still in the development and refinement stage, and as such, are in need of additional research.

## BEHAVIORAL PARENT TRAINING IN THE TREATMENT OF CHILD ABUSE

Let us now turn our attention to studies that have investigated the use of behavioral parent training as a mode of treatment for identified perpetrators of child abuse. Although the existing literature relating to child maltreatment is extensive, perhaps the most striking aspect of the literature is the paucity of well designed, empirically based outcome studies. The bulk of the extant literature consists of investigations of the characteristics of perpetrators of abuse, descriptions of consequences of abuse, descriptions of proposals and/or trials of treatment and/or prevention programs without relevant outcome data, as well as essay or opinion articles that are only loosely tied to data. In an exhaustive review of the child maltreatment literature published between 1967 and 1980, Plotkin, Azar, Twentyman, & Perri (1981) found that only about 25% of the 250 articles reviewed were data based, and most of these were case studies. Similar impressions of the literature have been reported by other reviewers as well (e.g., Gambrill, 1983; Isaacs, 1982). Isaacs (1982) observed that methodological weaknesses, such as poor definitions of abuse and abuse populations, inadequate dependent measures, lack of experimental controls, and limited (or no) follow-up data characterize the existing child abuse treatment literature.

More recently, Fantuzzo & Twentyman (1986) established three design criteria for a minimally acceptable outcome study in the area of child maltreatment: 1) adequate matching of subjects on relevant demographic variables, (e.g., history of documented abuse, income, educational level, employment status, etc.); 2) random assignment of subjects to group conditions; and 3) dependent measures that were directly related to incidence rates of abuse. They reported that they could find only two studies (Azar & Twentyman, 1984; Wolfe, Sandler, & Kaufman, 1981) which met all three of the criteria for minimum acceptability, and only two additional studies (Lutzker, Wesch, & Rice, 1984; Reid, Taplin, & Lorber, 1981) which met two of the three criteria. Since Fantuzzo & Twentyman's review, two additional articles have appeared (Brunk, Henggeler, & Whelan, 1987; Wolfe, Edwards, Manion, & Koverola, 1988) that also meet two of the three criteria. In the discussion that follows, these and several additional reports will be reviewed in order to clarify what behavioral parent training has to offer as a mode of intervention for identified perpetrators of child abuse.

## Case Studies

Several early case studies demonstrated that behavioral parent training could be an effective mode of intervention with abusive parents. Jeffery (1976) employed a contingency reinforcement program to increase positive verbal responses from 25% at base line to 70% during home visits, and decrease negative verbal responses from 60% at base line to 70% during home visits, and decrease negative verbal responses from 60% at base line to 20% in the abusive parents of a 6 year old boy. Sandler, VanDercar, & Milhoan (1978) employed contingency contracting, role-playing, and homework assignments as methods of intervention with abusive parents in two referred family units referred with at least one documented incident of child abuse. Increases were noted in positive child-rearing skills, as well as reductions in the rate of aversive parent-child interactions. Reported gains were maintained at a 3-month follow up.

Denicola & Sandler (1980) assessed the contribution of parent training and self-control techniques as methods of intervention with abusive parents in two family units who had at least one documented incident of physical child abuse. Parent training consisted of didactic input concerning behavioral management techniques, modeling, role playing, and parent rehearsal. Self-control techniques included deep muscle relaxation paired with imagery and self-instructional training, after Meichenbaum (1977). During the treatment phase, both parents (perpetrators) and children (victims) decreased the rate of aversive behaviors, and parents increased the rate of child-directed approval behaviors. Gains were maintained, and in some areas, enhanced, at 3-month follow-up. These results suggest that treatment of parents' reactions to stress through anger control training may be an important component to include when working with abusive parents.

Wolfe & Sandler (1981) assessed the contributions of parent training and contingency contracting as methods of intervention with abusive parents in three families with at least one documented incident of child abuse. Parent-training procedures were modeled after those employed by Denicola & Sandler (1980), and contingency contracting was based on the procedures developed by Sandler et al. (1978). During the treatment phase, all three families demonstrated a dramatic reduction in the rate of aversive interactions between parents (perpetrators) and the target child (victim) and an equally dramatic increase in child compliance following parental directives. Each family maintained, and in some cases increased, improvements at 3-, 8-, and 12-month follow ups. The authors noted that homework assignments were not always completed in the absence of contingency contracting and underscored the benefit of positive reinforcement for parents in a training program.

### Experimental Studies

In what Fantuzzo & Twentyman (1986) have described as one of the best studies conducted to date, Wolfe, Sandler, & Kaufman (1981) reported on a competency based parent training program that had both clinic and in-home training components. Sixteen referred family units with at least one documented incident of child abuse participated in the study. Families were randomly assigned to treatment or wait-list control conditions. Controls continued under the normal supervision of the child welfare worker and received typical support services provided by the state. Treatment consisted of weekly 2-hour group sessions conducted in a clinic setting for 8 weeks and concurrent weekly in-home training sessions. The group sessions focused upon instruction in human development and child management, problem solving and modeling of appropriate child management skills, and relaxation and self-control training. The in-home sessions were criterion based and focussed on individualizing the treatment by implementing the new techniques in relevant child-rearing situations. The authors reported that abusive parents interacted in a significantly more positive, constructive manner following training in child management skills. In addition, data from caseworker ratings indicated that families functioned more effectively following behavioral parent training than state supervision alone. Finally, a one-year follow up of agency records revealed no further suspected or reported incidents of child abuse for any families which completed treatment.

Reid, Taplin, & Lorber (1981) reported on a home-based program in which parents were provided training in various behavior management procedures, including the use of reinforcement, time-out, and contingency contracting. Training was provided through didactic instruction, programmed texts (Patterson, 1971), and modeling. Three groups of subjects were included: distressed and abusive family units; distressed but nonabusive family units; and nondistressed, nonabusive family units (i.e., controls). Within the abusive group, there was a significant decrease in the rates of aversive behaviors for mothers and children, but not for fathers.

More recently, Brunk, Henggeler, & Whelan (1987) evaluated the relative efficacy of parent training and multisystemic therapy in the treatment of child abuse and neglect. Abusive and neglectful family units with at least one documented incident of child abuse participated in the study. Families were randomly assigned to two treatment conditions; behavioral parent training or systemic family therapy. In both conditions, treatment consisted of weekly 90-minute sessions for 8 weeks. Parent training was conducted with groups of parents in a clinic setting and was modeled after the treatment protocol employed by Wolfe et al. (1981). Systemic therapy was conducted with each family separately, either in a clinic setting or in the familial homes, and was modeled after Haley (1976) and Minuchin (1974). The authors reported that both parent training and systemic therapy were effective in ameliorating several of the problems commonly experienced by abusive and neglectful families. In both conditions, parents reported significant decreases in psychiatric symptoms, reduced stress, and improvements in their individual and family problems.

### Programmatic Research

We will conclude this discussion by focussing our attention on the programmatic work of Lutzker and his colleagues, who have developed a comprehensive treatment program known as Project 12 Ways (Lutzker, 1984; Lutzker & Rice, 1984; Lutzker, Wesch, & Rice, 1984). Lutzker & Rice (1984) report that Project 12-Ways has been funded by a Title XX Purchase of Service Contract with the Illinois Department of Children and Family Services (DCFS), and all referrals are from DCFS. Two criteria have been established for eligibility in the program: protective service status, and low socioeconomic status (SES). Protective service status means that DCFS has determined, or suspects, that a family is at high risk for child abuse and/or neglect, and low SES has been defined as falling at or below the state's poverty line. Consequently, everyone that is referred to Project 12 Ways is regarded as being at high risk for abuse and/or neglect, and many participants have histories of one or more documented incident(s) of abuse.

Project 12 Ways provides a menu of different intervention modalities, including parent training, stress reduction, assertiveness training, self-control training, basic skills training for children, multiple-setting behavior management training, and several others. The program is considered ecobehavioral because it provides *in vivo* treatment (in homes, schools, etc.) in each of the areas (Lutzker, 1984). Typically, after a referral is made to the program, a behavioral assessment is completed and treatment goals are negotiated. If multiple services are indicated, the needs are generally prioritized and managed in a sequential nature.

The parent training program is modeled after the work of Peed, Roberts, & Forehand (1977). It involves teaching parents to provide: simple, clear, understandable instructions; consistent verbal and social reinforcements for appropriate behavior; and time-out consequences for noncompliance (Lutzker, 1984). In addition, parents may be taught other behavioral procedures, such as token economies, as appropriate. Training is criterion based and parents only progress to more complex concepts and skills once they have demonstrated mastery of the more basic concepts and skills. Lutzker (1984) reports detailed information on the services rendered for fiscal years 1980 and 1981. During each year, the parent training component was the most extensively used modality, having been provided to 42% of the clients in 1980 and 66% in 1981.

A program as comprehensive as Project 12 Ways has the potential to generate an enormous data base which might provide answers to many complex issues surrounding child maltreatment. To date, several case studies have been published which demonstrate the efficacy of the parent training component of the program. For example, Campbell, O'Brien, Bickett, & Lutzker (1983) reported that parent training was successful in teaching a low-income mother to effectively manage her daughter's noncompliant behavior. In addition, preliminary evidence suggests that Project 12 Ways may be reducing the reported rate of abuse in the counties where the program has been implemented (Lutzker, Frame, & Rice, 1982; Lutzker & Rice, 1984).

## Conclusions

The following tentative conclusions are drawn from the foregoing review. First, behavioral parent training appears to be a practical, feasible, effective method of dealing with a wide variety of children's behavior problems. Second, behavioral parent training provides several advantages over alternative models of intervention, as it can be implemented in a relatively brief time frame and the interventions are implemented *in vivo*, or in the natural setting(s) by the individuals most influential in a child's life, thus reducing the artificial aspects of alternative models. Third, behavioral parent training may have considerable preventive potential, depending on the degree of generalization that occurs either spontaneously or as a result of deliberate generalization training components of the overall treatment/training program.

The existing empirical literature focussing on outcome studies of the treatment of child abuse is quite sparse. Thus, conclusions based upon this literature must be regarded as tentative, and in need of additional empirical support. Every aspect of the treatment of both victims and perpetrators of child abuse is in need of well-designed studies to replicate and extend what is currently known. We have a long course to travel before we know which specific treatments produce specific changes in specific individuals under specific conditions, a goal for outcome research in behavior change which was articulated a decade ago (Strupp, 1978). Given the foregoing caveat, behavioral parent training appears at this time to be at least as effective, and perhaps more effective, than alternative methods in the treatment of child abusive parents. It is acknowledged that additional research is needed to amplify the results upon which this impression is formed.

## THE APPLICATION OF BEHAVIORAL PARENT TRAINING TO PREVENTION OF PHYSICAL ABUSE

Prevention programs are generally designed to meet primary, secondary, and/ or tertiary goals. Primary prevention efforts are directed at entire populations or communities with the goal of inhibiting the onset of the particular difficulty or malady in question (e.g., child maltreatment). Alternatively, secondary prevention efforts are directed specifically at subgroups of the population who are determined to be at high risk as a result of their particular life circumstances. Again, the goal is to prevent the onset of the difficulty or malady in question. Finally, tertiary prevention efforts are directed towards individuals who have been identified as exhibiting the difficulty or malady (i.e., known abusers); in this case, the goal is to prevent future incidents of the difficulty. With the dramatic increases in reporting rates of child abuse over the past decade, the need for cost-effective primary and secondary prevention strategies in the area of child maltreatment is self-evident.

Based upon the ecological model of child abuse (Belsky, 1980; Rosenberg, 1987; Rosenberg & Reppucci, 1983, 1985), it has been recommended that prevention efforts target individual, familial, community, and societal forces which are believed to contribute to the final common pathway of abusive behavior (Belsky, 1980; Cohn, 1982; Lutzker, 1984; Rosenberg & Reppucci, 1985; Wolfe, 1985). It has been argued that prevention programs which target one factor, or one level of factors, may be ineffective. Conceptually, the existing parent training literature provides a reasonable base on which to develop a comprehensive, communitywide prevention program to simultaneously target contributory influences at the individual, familial, community, and societal levels as articulated in the ecological model. In addition, based on existing parent training literature, such a prevention program offers the potential to be cost-effective. Let us first turn to an overview of such a proposed program, and subsequently provide a more detailed analysis of how such a program would address forces at the various ecological levels.

A comprehensive prevention program based on a behavioral parent training model could include components at each of the primary, secondary, and tertiary prevention levels. Specific applications of the behavioral training methodology could be adapted to meet primary, secondary, and tertiary goals.

At the primary prevention level, relatively short-term parent training programs, modeled after programs such as Winning! (Dangel & Polster, 1984b), Responsive Parenting (Hall, 1981, 1984), or Parent-Child Interaction Training (Eyberg, 1986; Eyberg & Robinson, 1982) could be made available to parents of all socioeconomic levels. The goals of such a program would be to teach effective parenting and behavior management skills, strengthen parental coping skills, and foster the development of positive parent-child relationships. An assessment of a given parent's behavioral repertoire relative to behavior management skills would not be undertaken. Rather, a broad-based program which focusses on general parent-child interactions and behavior management issues would be utilized. As mentioned earlier, such programs are educationally rather than therapeutically focussed and can be provided in a weekly group format in a wide variety of settings, including schools, libraries, churches, and so forth. Providing parent training groups in such alternative settings would increase the probability of attracting participants who might not attend a program conducted in a mental health center or clinic. Clearly, many parents would benefit from a well developed, broad-based, behavioral parent training program, particularly if it were made available to them at a time when they would be more amenable to input concerning child management, such as a minor crisis. For example, Dangel & Polster (1984b, p. 182) reported that with the cooperation of the local school system, they sent informational fliers home with children's report cards and received 300 calls from parents within 48 hours. Ideally, such a program would be available within a community over an extended period of time, allowing parents to repeat the program as their children mature and present developmentally different behavior management dilemmas. Additionally, such a program could be provided concurrently with one or more communitywide media campaign(s), which would introduce and reinforce the use of alternative, nonviolent behavioral management practices.

At the secondary prevention level, a more focussed, in-depth parent training program could be made available to parents of all socioeconomic levels who were either known to be at high risk as a result of their particular life circumstances, or who perceived themselves to be at risk. The primary goal of such a program would be to inhibit the onset of abuse in these high risk parents; secondary goals would include enhancing parental competencies, increasing the repertoire of parental child management skills, strengthening parental coping skills, and enhancing/fostering the development of positive parent-child relationships. High risk subgroups would be identified on the basis of factors or life circumstances which are generally regarded as increasing the risk of abuse, such as a history of maltreatment in one's own childhood, low socioeconomic status and unemployment, single-parent households, adolescent pregnancy, and so forth. Individuals who fall into one or more of these risk groups could then be actively recruited for involvement in the program. In addition, referrals of high risk parents could be solicited from existing agencies who might have reason to come into contact with such parents.

Again, the program offered at the secondary prevention level could be modeled after one of the several existing, well established programs such as Winning! (Dangel & Polster, 1984b), Responsive Parenting (Hall, 1981, 1984), or Parent-Child Interaction Training (Eyberg, 1986; Eyberg & Robinson, 1982). Such an educationally oriented program is easily implemented in a group format, yet allows enough flexibility to be adapted to the relevant needs of participants. Consequently, at this prevention level, an assessment of a given parent's behavior management skills could be undertaken and areas of deficit could be addressed. In other words, the unique needs and concerns of high risk parents could be specifically addressed in the context of a broad-based, general program. This approach would ensure that the particular circumstances which serve to increase the risk of abuse in the individual family could be addressed, as well as more general issues of behavior management and parent-child relationships.

At the tertiary prevention level, an individualized competency-based parent training program, similar to that employed by Wolfe et al. (1981) could be made available to parents with a known history of abusive behavior. The primary goals of such a program would be to prevent future episodes of abuse; secondary goals would include enhancing parental competencies, increasing the repertoire of parental child management skills, strengthening parental coping skills, and fostering positive parent-child relationships. This program would involve a behavioral assessment for each parent, to identify significant areas of strength and deficit in their behavioral repertoire. Subsequently, various techniques, including didactic instruction in human development and child management, problem solving, modeling and role playing of appropriate child management skills, relaxation and self-control training, etc., would be used to teach more appropriate child management and general parental behaviors.

Similar to the method employed by Wolfe et al., (1981), such a program could utilize both group and individual components so that interventions could be individualized in the most cost-effective manner possible. For example, in Wolfe et al.'s study, the treatment families were provided weekly 2-hour group sessions for 8 weeks and concurrent in-home training sessions. The authors noted that the majority of families attained skills proficiency after 8 in-home sessions, or an average of 8.9 professional hours in the home per family (Wolfe et al., 1981). Assuming an average of five family units per group, this breaks down to an average total cost of 12.1 hours of professional time per family unit.

As an aside, it is instructive to note that the control group employed by Wolfe and his colleagues (1981) consisted of abusive families who were provided "the normal supervision of their child-welfare worker" (p. 635). Outcome data provided by the caseworkers indicated that they viewed the treatment families as functioning more effectively following child-management training than controls who were provided state supervision alone (Wolfe et al., 1981). In other words, the caseworkers themselves regarded abusive parents who were provided 8 weeks of behavioral parent training as functioning more effectively than parents who were provided typical casework supervision. Given these data, it makes sense to routinely provide abusive parents with some form of behavioral parental training as part of the routine casework functions already provided. Caseworkers could be trained to provide these services, or social service agencies could employ behavior therapists trained in behavioral parent training to work with the families. In either case, an immediate improvement in the effectiveness of tertiary prevention efforts would likely be realized.

Recently, Wolfe, Edwards, Manion, & Koverola (1988) reported on an early intervention program for families at risk for child maltreatment that is similar to the secondary prevention program suggested above. Family units were randomly assigned to either an agency-sponsored information group (control), or a behavioral parent training program in addition to the information group (treatment condition). Parent training was conducted in 90-minute sessions and was competency based, similar to the methods employed by Wolfe et al. (1981). Families in the parent training condition completed a median of 9 sessions. Significant improvements in parenting risk and child behavior problems were noted at posttest and 3-month follow up only in the treatment condition. At 12-month follow up, caseworker ratings significantly favored treatment families who received parent training, consistent with the ratings reported by Wolfe et al. (1981).

A comprehensive prevention program based on a behavioral parent training model as proposed above would include components at each of the primary, secondary, and tertiary levels. Let us turn now to a more detailed analysis of how such a program might address various influences at each of the ecological levels, articulated by Belsky (1980) and others, which might contribute to episodes of child maltreatment. First, concerning the level of ontogenetic development, Belsky notes several fundamental experiences as predisposing one toward child abuse, including a history of being exposed to models of aggressive behavior (which may or may not include an actual history of being abused), and an absence of experience in caring for children, or a lack of practice in the parenting role. To some extent, the impact of these influences is directly mitigated through parent training.

First and foremost, through the experience of behavioral parent training, nonaggressive methods of relating with children and managing child behaviors are taught, modeled, rehearsed, and developed. It is likely that a given parent may observe a more effective model in the trainer-therapist than they have previously observed, particularly if their own history includes being abused. Hence, behavior parent training offers the opportunity to learn new, more effective methods for child behavior management and conflict resolution through the direct modeling of the training, thus ameliorating somewhat the negative effects of previous modeling.

Second, parent training provides the parent who may have an absence of experience in caring for children or a lack of practice in the parenting role with an opportunity to gain knowledge and experience under the guidance of a skilled parent trainer. This could be a particularly potent preventive influence for a young parent of a first-born child, who may have little or no experience with young children. Perhaps the most common outcome of such an opportunity would be that a parent would correct grossly mistaken ideas about the sequence and timing of normal child development. Additional outcomes might include the development or refinement of prosocial, nurturant behaviors and an increased repertoire of nonaversive behaviors in interacting with their child.

Next, Belsky (1980) notes that influences at the microsystem level, or within the family itself, may interact with ontogenetic factors to produce child maltreatment. Of particular note at the microsystem level are the following: 1) the interactive process between parent and child, including antecedents and consequences of typical behavioral episodes, whether these include overt abuse or difficult behavior management situations; 2) a particular family's relative ability to tolerate and manage stress; and 3) significant conflict within the marital dyad, with possible displacement of aggression onto one or more children.

Relative to the first area of concern, parent training is specifically designed to examine the behavioral sequences that occur between a parent and a child to aid the parent in altering behavioral sequences toward less aversive and more favorable outcomes. At the primary prevention level, parents would be made more aware of common sequences of interaction that occur between themselves and their children and provided information concerning methods for altering these sequences, such as how to be more attentive to and reinforcing of appropriate child behaviors, how to extinguish misbehaviors, and so forth. At the secondary and tertiary levels, a parent would be made aware of the specific behavioral sequences that occur with his/her child and subsequently be provided with specific training to aid in altering these sequences. For example, a parent may be trained to change environmental or behavioral consequences, or both. Thus, one outcome of behavioral parent training would be a direct change in the interactive process between parent and child, with a decrease in negative interactions and an increase in positive interactions.

Relative to the second area of concern within the microsystem, a family's relative ability to tolerate and manage stress, various forms of parent training have specifically addressed this to a greater or lesser degree. For example, some programs have specifically built stress reduction and stress management procedures into the intervention package (e.g., Denicola & Sandler, 1980; Lutzker, 1984; Wolfe et al., 1981). Assuming the comprehensive program proposed above, stress management and stress reduction components could easily be incorporated at the secondary and tertiary prevention levels, as needed, in response to the individual needs of particular parents.

Relative to the third area of concern within the microsystem (conflict within the marital dyad and possible displacement of aggression onto the child), involvement in behavioral parent training may have a more indirect impact. For example, parent training may serve to limit the degree of displacement of aggression onto a child and help to surface the degree of marital discord, which presumably could then be addressed in an alternative therapeutic form.

Belsky (1980) also notes that influences at the exosystem level, or within the larger social units in which the family is embedded, may interact with ontogenetic and microsystem factors to stimulate child maltreatment. Of particular note at the exosystem level are: 1) unemployment and/or a general lack of monetary resources, and 2) the degree of social isolation of a parent, particularly isolation from larger social support systems which might help prevent or minimize abnormal parenting practices. The impact of behavior parent training on these influences is typically indirect, unless a specific training component is built into the overall program. This has been attempted by Lutzker (1984), who incorporated a training component in job seeking skills. Otherwise, the influences of parent training at the microsystem level, particularly relative to altering behavioral sequences between parents and children and teaching stress management skills, may be sufficiently potent to inhibit the risk of abuse, even in the face of major stressors at the exosystem level.

Finally, Belsky notes that influences at the macrosystem level, or within the larger cultural context in which the social units and the family are embedded, may interact with ontogenetic, microsystem, and exosystem factors to stimulate child maltreatment. Of particular note at the macrosystem level are society's collective attitudes toward children, violence, corporal punishment, and child-rearing practices. The relative impact of a comprehensive, broad-based child abuse prevention program upon collective social attitudes and values would be difficult to predict, much less to assess. However modest influences could be expected and even monitored through specific behavioral indices of social attitudes. For example, if a comprehensive prevention program were implemented within a given community, and it contained effective marketing or public relations components, it may indeed influence specific overt markers of social attitudes, such as an alteration in the policy of corporal punishment in schools, a change in the rates of reporting abuse incidents, or even an increase in the number of monetary donations to agencies which deal with the treatment of child abuse and neglect.

In situations where limited resources would not allow for the development of such a comprehensive prevention program, focussing available resources within the secondary prevention area may prove to be most cost-effective. Many high-risk families are already known to one of several existing medical, social service, and/or mental health agencies. For example, most families who receive AFDC or similar types of support would probably have one or more of the life circumstances which significantly increase the risk of child abuse, such as low socioeconomic status, unemployment, single-parent households, adolescent parentage, and so forth.

Given the existing network of various service agencies, such as social welfare agencies, child guidance clinics, and public schools, providing adequate secondary prevention services to high-risk parents could be a relatively simple and straightforward matter. At a minimum, all that would be required is the development of behavioral parent training programs within the network of existing service agencies and providing these training programs to high-risk families who are known to the agencies. Additionally, insofar as general preventive efforts are part of the mandated mission of federally funded child guidance clinics, the development of such secondary prevention efforts would fall directly under the realm of their existing mission.

## IMPLICATIONS FOR SOCIAL POLICY

The foregoing discussion contains several implications relative to social policy issues that deserve at least brief comment. First, as noted above when discussing the study by Wolfe et al. (1981), outcome data indicated that caseworkers viewed the treatment families, who were provided behavioral parent training, as functioning more effectively than the controls, who were provided standard casework supervision. The results of this study raise the question of whether the provision of behavioral parent training services would be a useful adjunct to standard casework. The point was made that either caseworkers could be trained to provide these services, or social service agencies could employ behavior therapists to provide the services. In either case, an immediate improvement in family functioning might be realized, and the probability of repeat occurrences of abuse would be diminished.

One could easily anticipate (and understand) that many caseworkers would cringe at the prospect of providing yet another service, given the reality that many agencies are not adequately staffed to meet existing service demands, and are operating with limited human and economic resources. Some agencies have been forced into the unfortunate dilemma of either providing less comprehensive services to all who are in need of them, or more comprehensive services to a subset of those in need, and little or no services to the remainder. Clearly, social policy is being forged as choices to resolve these dilemmas are made. The question of whether social service agencies are given sufficient funds to meet the existing service demands must be examined. In many situations, lobbying efforts with state and federal legislators may be required to secure adequate resources to meet the treatment and prevention needs in the area of child abuse.

Second, certain values and attitudes are clearly evident throughout our society that serve to maintain and even foster abuse. The ecological model reviewed above suggests that incidents of abuse occur within a context of cultural attitudes which legitimize physical forms of behavioral control or discipline such as corporal punishment, and which view physical force and violence as acceptable means of resolving conflict. Consequently, many have appropriately advocated changes in social policy, such as passing statutes to prohibit the use of physically forceful methods of discipline, whether in the home or school. While these advocacy efforts are indeed necessary and appropriate, it is our view that insufficient attention has been focused on providing adults with opportunities to learn alternative, nonviolent behavior management skills. As pointed out above, a history of being exposed to models of aggressive behavior (which may or may not include an actual history of being abused) as a method of conflict resolution is a factor which increases the risk that one will respond to conflictual or stressful situations in a violent or aggressive, perhaps abusive, manner. We would suggest that efforts to change social attitudes and values might be more successful if such efforts are tied to programs that offer and promote reasonable nonviolent alternatives, such as behavioral parent training programs.

Third, an enormous amount of our nation's resources, in terms of both money and human effort, are currently being spent through various state and federal programs to assist the poor and the underprivileged (a high risk group for child maltreatment, considering their life circumstances such as low socioeconomic status, unemployment, and so forth). Aid to Families with Dependent Children (AFDC), and similar so-called entitlement programs, are just a few examples of our nation's extensive investment in providing for the underprivileged. At the same time, we lack a consistent, coherent policy regarding the provision of such aid, as Gil (1976) and others have observed. What does an unemployed, poor, single mother of several young children need in order to provide a minimally adequate existence for herself and her children and to reduce the risk of child maltreatment? Perhaps she needs more than minimal financial resources to adequately parent her children.

Clearly, many such parents need social resources as well, such as the availability of adequate child care and preschool services, the availability of social supports upon which to call in times of stress or need, the opportunity to learn about normal child development and how to appropriately stimulate and reinforce one's children, the opportunity to learn various parenting and child management skills, and so forth. Although some such parents may have access to these resources through a variety of channels (e.g., extended family, church groups, etc.), there is no integrated social policy which recognizes these needs and attempts to meet them. If we as a society aspire to provide aid to families with dependent children, then policies developed to provide such aid should be realistic about the types of aid needed and then provide the financial support for programs that would be designed to meet these needs.

Fourth, as noted above, there is in existence an extensive network of various service agencies that could provide adequate secondary prevention services to high-risk parents in a relatively simple and straightforward manner. The simplest model would involve developing behavioral parent training programs, within the network of existing service agencies, and providing these training programs to high-risk families known to these agencies. Insofar as prevention efforts are part of the mandated session of child guidance clinics, the development of such secondary prevention efforts would seem to fall into the realm of their existing mission. Many child guidance clinics currently offer limited parent training programs or services that are consistent with this proposal and could easily adapt or expand their existing program(s) to meet the secondary abuse prevention goals, given adequate funding.

Finally, perhaps existing and/or expanded services available in child guidance clinics as discussed above could be combined with the notion of providing more comprehensive aid to families with dependent children, so that both goals could be met in a cost-effective manner. Conceptually, there is no reason why a comprehensive program of aid to such families could not be provided in a coherent package, with one component to the program used as a reinforcer for participation in other parts of the program. For example, what if the AFDC program were altered such that participation in various parent training components (provided through child guidance clinics) were required, and the existing financial assistance were provided contingent upon participation in the parent training program? In this scenario, parent training programs could be targeted at the secondary prevention level, as discussed above, with the primary goal of inhibiting the onset of abuse in these high-risk parents, and secondary goals including enhancing parental competencies, increasing the repertoire of parental child management skills, among others. In addition, parents could complete a basic training program and then be required to participate in periodic follow up or maintenance programs, allowing for ongoing support and the opportunity to address new developmental and behavioral management issues as they arise.

All components of such an expanded AFDC program could fall under one or another existing agencies (e.g., social service agencies and child guidance clinics) and be consistent with the mandates of these agencies, thus avoiding the necessity of creating a new level of bureaucracy. The additional costs which would accrue would result primarily from the additional clinical and support personnel required to provide such expanded services. And, although there would be additional costs, the program would be a relatively cost-effective method for providing child abuse prevention services, services which generally are not being provided at the present time. Needless to say, such a program should be implemented gradually with careful research at each stage to document effectiveness and improve procedures.

Implementing such a program would obviously require that various social policies and legislative statutes related to the provision of welfare and mental health services be modified. At a minimum, funds would need to be allocated to support such a program. In addition, as it has been proposed, legislative changes would be required in the AFDC program to allow for such mandated parent training programs. Consequently, legislative lobbying would be required before this type of program could be initiated.

## SUMMARY AND RECOMMENDATIONS FOR FUTURE RESEARCH

In this chapter, we have examined the literature on behavioral parent training, with a particular focus on studies that attempted to treat physically abusive parents. Behavioral parent training has been found to be a practical, feasible, and effective method of intervening with a wide variety of children's behavior problems. Although the empirical literature specifically focussing on outcome studies of the treatment of abusive parents is sparse, the impression formed from this literature has been that behavioral parent training is at least as effective, and perhaps more effective, than alternative methods of intervention.

In the present chapter, we extrapolated what was gleaned from this literature to address issues of child abuse prevention. We reasoned that the existing parent training literature provides a reasonable base upon which it would be possible to develop a comprehensive prevention program to simultaneously target influences at the individual, family, community, and society levels as articulated in the ecological model by Belsky and others. In addition, it was observed that such a comprehensive program could be adapted, as needed, to meet primary, secondary, and tertiary prevention goals. A model program was then proposed, and an effort was made to articulate how such a program would address various influences at each of the levels in the ecological model. Finally, several social policy issues which were implied in the foregoing were briefly discussed.

There are many needs for additional research in all areas of child abuse, including theoretical issues, treatment, and prevention. Specific recommendations for future research relative to prevention based upon a parent training model are briefly highlighted below.

First, as Rosenberg & Reppucci (1985) have argued, additional ecologically oriented research is needed to identify the necessary and sufficient conditions of child abuse. Until such conditions are more adequately understood, all efforts at prevention must be based upon unproven hypotheses and assumptions. For example, in the present chapter, prevention strategies based upon the behavioral parent training literature are proposed. At the same time, we have extrapolated a strategy that goes beyond the empirical evidence, which may prove to be more or less useful. The same could be said for any proposed prevention program at this point in time, given our limited understanding of the necessary and sufficient conditions of child abuse.

The ideas and proposals articulated in this chapter contain many areas for additional research. At the simplest level, the effectiveness of behavioral parent training as a prevention strategy needs additional empirical support. To date, only one preliminary study has examined the efficacy of such an approach (Wolfe et al., 1988). Exploratory efforts to demonstrate effectiveness should be undertaken and should include outcome measures relating to both short-term or proximal objectives, such as changes in parent-child interactions, parental child management behaviors, and so forth, as well as more distal goals, such as the impact upon incidence rates of child abuse. At the same time, it is our opinion that the extant literature supporting behavioral parent training as an effective treatment model provides a sufficient foundation to argue for the implementation of communitywide prevention programs based upon the behavioral training model. Such programs would provide both the opportunity to assess the overall effectiveness of the parent training model as a prevention strategy, as well as allow for the examination of more specific issues, such as the relative effectiveness at primary, secondary, and tertiary prevention levels.

One specific proposal noted above is the incorporation of behavioral parent training into the usual and customary social casework services provided to families reported for suspected abuse. This proposal offers the possibility of a cost-effective method of increasing prevention effectiveness. There seems to be no reason why this could not be assessed and implemented immediately.

In order to adequately assess the impact of behavioral parent training as a prevention strategy, ongoing and long-term follow-up data must be obtained relevant to both immediate and distal prevention goals. In addition, effective prevention may require that parents have the opportunity for periodic follow up or maintenance programs, allowing for ongoing support and the opportunity to address new developmental and behavior management issues as they arise. Consequently, relatively long-term programmatic research is necessary, and funding sources will need to consider allocating monies to support well designed long-term projects.

## REFERENCES

Azar, S. T., & Twentyman, C. T. (1984). *An evaluation of the effectiveness of behaviorally vs. insighted oriented group treatment with maltreating mothers.* Paper presented at the annual meeting of the Association for the Advancement of Behavior Therapy, Philadelphia, PA.

Azrin, N., & Fox, R. (1976). *Toilet training in less than a day.* New York: Pocket Press.

Barkley, R. A. (1987). *Defiant children: A clinician's manual for parent training.* New York: Guilford Press.

Belsky, J. (1980). Child maltreatment: An ecological approach. *American Psychologist, 35,* 320–335.

Berkowitz, B. P., & Graziano, A. M. (1972). Training parents as behavior therapists: A review. *Behavioral Research and Therapy, 10,* 297–317.

Bijou, S. W. (1984). Parent training: Actualizing the critical conditions of early childhood development. In R. F. Dangel & R. A. Polster (Eds.), *Parent training: Foundations of research and practice.* New York: Guilford Press.

Blechman, E. A. (1984). Competent parents, competent children: Behavioral goals of parent training. In R. F. Dangel & R. A. Polster (Eds.), *Parent training: Foundations of research and practice.* New York: Guilford Press.

Brunk, M., Henggeler, S. W., & Whelan, J. P. (1987). Comparison of multisystemic therapy and parent training in brief treatment of child abuse and neglect. *Journal of Consulting and Clinical Psychology, 55*, 171–178.

Campbell, R., O'Brien, S., Bickett, A., & Lutzker, J. (1983). In-home parent training, treatment of migraine headaches, and marital counseling as an ecobehavioral approach to prevent child abuse. *Journal of Behavior Therapy and Experimental Psychiatry, 14*, 147–154.

Clement, P. W. (1970). Elimination of sleepwalking in a seven-year-old boy. *Journal of Consulting and Clinical Psychology, 34*, 22–26.

Cohn, A. H. (1982). Stopping abuse before it occurs: Different solutions for different population groups. *Child Abuse & Neglect, 6*, 473–483.

Conger, R. D., McCarty, J. A., Yang, R. K., Lahey, B. B., & Kropp, J. T. (1984). Perception of child, child rearing values, and emotional distress as mediating links between environmental stressors and observed maternal behavior. *Child Development, 55*, 2234–2247.

Dangel, R. F., & Polster, R. A. (Eds.). (1984a). *Parent training: Foundations of research and practice.* New York: Guilford Press.

Dangel, R. F., & Polster, R. A. (1984b). WINNING!: A systematic, empirical approach to parent training. In R. F. Dangel & R. A. Polster (Eds.), *Parent training: Foundations of research and practice.* New York: Guilford Press.

Denicola, J., & Sandler, J. (1980). Training abusive parents in child management and self-control skills. *Behavior Therapy, 11*, 263–270.

Dinkmeyer, D., & McKay, G. D. (1976). *Systematic training for effective parenting (STEP).* Circle Pinces, MN: American Guidance Service.

Eyberg, S. M. (1986). *Parent-Child Interaction Therapy: Integration of traditional and behavioral concerns.* Paper presented at the Annual meeting of the American Psychological Association, Washington, DC.

Eyberg, S. M., & Matarazzo, R. G. (1989). Training parents as therapists: A comparison between individual parent-child interaction training and parent group didactic training. *Journal of Clinical Psychology, 36*, 492–499.

Eyberg, S. M., & Robinson, E. A. (1982). Parent-child interaction training: Effects on family functioning. *Journal of Clinical Child Psychology, 11*, 130–137.

Fantuzzo, J. W., & Twentyman, C. T. (1986). Child abuse psychotherapy research: Merging social concerns and empirical investigation. *Professional Psychology: Research and Practice, 17*, 375–380.

Gambrill, E. D. (1983). Behavioral interventions with child abuse and neglect. *Progress in Behavior Modification, 15*, 1–56.

Gil, D. G. (1976). Primary prevention of child abuse: A philosophical and political issue. *Journal of Pediatric Psychology, 1*, 54–57.

Graziano, A. M. (1977). Parents as behavior therapists. In M. Hersen, R. M. Eisler, & P. M. Miller (Eds.), *Progress in behavior modification* (Vol. 4). New York: Academic Press.

Haley, J. (1976). *Problem solving therapy.* San Francisco: Jossey-Bass.

Hall, M. C. (1981). *Responsive parenting manual* (rev. ed.). Shawnee Mission, KS: Responsive Management.

Hall, M. C. (1984). Responsive parenting: A large-scale training program for school districts, hospitals, and mental health centers. In R. F. Dangel & R. A. Polster

(Eds.), *Parent training: Foundations of research and practice*. New York: Guilford Press.

Isaacs, C. D. (1982). Treatment of child abuse: A review of the behavioral interventions. *Journal of Applied Behavioral Analysis, 15*, 273–294.

Jeffery, M. (1976). Practical ways to change parent-child interaction in families of children at risk. In R. E. Helfer & C. H. Kempe, (Eds.), *Child abuse and neglect: The family and the community*. Cambridge, MA: Ballinger Publishing Co.

Lahey, B. B., Conger, R. D., Atkeson, B. M., & Treiber, F. A. (1984). Parenting behavior and emotional status of physically abusive mothers. *Journal of Consulting and Clinical Psychology, 52*, 1062–1071.

Lutzker, J. R. (1984). Project 12-Ways: Treating child abuse and neglect from an ecobehavioral perspective. In R. F. Dangel & R. A. Polster (Eds.), *Parent training: Foundations of research and practice*. New York: Guilford Press.

Lutzker, J. R., Frame, R., & Rice, J. (1982). Project "12-Ways": An ecobehavioral approach to the treatment and prevention of child abuse and neglect. *Education and Treatment of Children, 5*, 141–155.

Lutzker, J. R., & Rice, J. M. (1984). Project 12-Ways: Measuring outcome of a large in-home service for treatment of child abuse and neglect. *Child Abuse and Neglect, 8*, 141–155.

Lutzker, J. R., Wesch, D., & Rice, J. M. (1984). A review of project "12-Ways": An ecobehavioral approach to the treatment and prevention of child abuse. *Advances in Behavioral Research and Therapy, 6*, 63–74.

Meichenbaum, D. (1977). *Cognitive behavior modification: An integrative approach*. New York: Plenum Press.

Minuchin, S. (1974). *Families and family therapy*. Cambridge: Harvard University Press.

Patterson, G. R. (1971). *Families: Applications of social learning to family life*. Champaign, IL: Research Press.

Peed, S., Roberts, M., & Forehand, R. (1977). Evaluation of the effectiveness of a standardized parent training program in altering the interaction of mothers and their noncompliant children. *Behavior Modification, 1*, 323–350.

Plotkin, R. C., Azar, S., Twentyman, C. T., & Perri, M. G. (1981). A critical evaluation of the research methodology employed in the investigation of causative factors of child abuse and neglect. *Child Abuse and Neglect, 5*, 449–455.

Reid, J. B., Taplin, P. S., & Lorber, R. (1981). A social interaction approach to the treatment of abusive families. In R. Stuart (Ed.), *Violent behavior: Social learning approaches to prediction, management and treatment*. New York: Brunner/Mazel.

Rincover, A., Koegel, R. L., & Russo, D. C. (1978). Some recent behavioral research on the education of autistic children. *Education and Treatment of Children, 1*, 31–45.

Rosenberg, M. S. (1987). New directions for research on the psychological maltreatment of children. *American Psychologist, 42*, 166–171.

Rosenberg, M. S., & Reppucci, N. D. (1983). Child abuse: A review with special focus on an ecological approach in rural communities. In A. W. Childs & G. B. Melton (Eds.), *Rural psychology*. New York: Plenum Press.

Rosenberg, M. S., & Reppucci, N. D. (1985). Primary prevention of child abuse. *Journal of Consulting and Clinical Psychology, 53,* 576–585.

Sandler, J., VanDercar, C., & Milhoan, M. (1978). Training child abusers in the use of positive reinforcement practices. *Behavior Research and Therapy, 16,* 169–175.

Strupp, H. H. (1978). Psychotherapy research and practice: An overview. In S. L. Garfield & A. E. Bergin (Eds.), *Handbook of psychotherapy and behavior change: An empirical analysis* (2nd ed.). New York: Wiley.

Walker, C. E. (1978). Toilet training, enuresis, encopresis. In P. Magrab (Ed.), *Psychological management of pediatric problems: Vol. 1. Early life conditions.* Baltimore: University Park Press.

Walker, C. E., Bonner, B., & Milling, L. (1988). Incontinence disorders: Enuresis and encopresis. In D. K. Routh (Ed.), *Handbook of Pediatric Psychology* (pp. 363–398). New York: Guilford Press.

Welsh, R. (1968). Stimulus satiation as a technique for the elimination of juvenile fire setting behavior. Eastern Psychological Association, Washington, DC.

Wolfe, D. A. (1985). Child-abusive parents: An empirical review and analysis. *Psychological Bulletin, 97,* 462–482.

Wolfe, D. A., Edwards, B., Manion, I., & Koverola, C. (1988). Early intervention for parents at risk of child abuse and neglect: A preliminary investigation. *Journal of Consulting and Clinical Psychology, 56,* 40–47.

Wolfe, D. A., & Sandler, J. (1981). Training abusive parents in effective child management. *Behavior Modification, 5,* 320–335.

Wolfe, D. A., Sandler, J., & Kaufman, K. (1981). A competency-based parent training program for child abusers. *Journal of Consulting and Clinical Psychology, 49,* 633–640.

CHAPTER 11

# Child Maltreatment Prevention and The Legal System

N. DICKON REPPUCCI AND MARK S. ABER

Laws seek to prevent harm by regulating conduct in several ways (Levine, Ewing, & Levine, 1987). First, laws are enacted that specify what acts will be punishable as crimes on the theory that forewarning and punishing offenders will reduce the frequency of those prohibited and undesirable acts in the future (Hall, 1960). Second, laws regulate conditions affecting health and safety by providing civil, and sometimes, criminal sanctions for those who cause accidents that injure others on the theory that penalties for negligent acts will motivate prospective culprits to be more cautious. Third, laws confer benefits on certain classes of individuals in order to prevent harm. Finally, laws prevent harm by protecting individual rights against unwarranted interference by government or private citizens. For example, courts are frequently called upon to protect individuals from alleged abuse of official authority that violate fundamental principles of our democracy, such as freedom of speech or freedom of religion.

Once a law, a regulation, or a judicial declaration of rights is in place, it provides the basis for a demand for legal protection to prevent future harm (Levine et al., 1987). In some cases, the court orders defendants to stop engaging in certain activities (e.g., to stop segregating a school system) or to act to promote change (e.g., bus to desegregate schools). Class action suits allow individuals to request that the courts use their powers to achieve change in large institutions. These suits are favored if the goal is institutional reform because if won by the plaintiffs, systemwide relief often seems appropriate to the courts. *Brown v. the Board of Education* (1954), for example, had the impact of desegregating schools nationwide and thus served as a broad reaching preventive intervention.

Appreciation is expressed to Jeffrey Haugaard and Elizabeth Scott for many stimulating discussions about this topic over the past several years. We also appreciate Debra Mundie's help in the manuscript's preparation.

Since the official discovery of child abuse by Kempe and his colleagues in 1962, the legal system has played a prominent role. In the interest of protecting children from harm, child abuse reporting laws swept the nation in the late 1960s. Their explicit goal was not only to identify ongoing child abuse in order to stop it and to prevent future harm to the individual children involved, but also to act as a deterrent to other potential abusers. However, these laws have also had the effect of intruding on the constitutionally protected right of family autonomy (see *Prince v. Massachusetts*, 1944), and many parents have suffered as a result of being wrongfully charged with being abusive (Schultz, 1988). Other more direct forms of primary prevention have been suggested by reformers, e.g., to require mandatory child development classes for all prospective parents (Feshbach & Feshbach, 1978), which also invade family privacy. More recently, a number of reforms in the trial arena have been enacted in order to increase the likelihood that child sex abuse offenders can be prosecuted more effectively, thereby sending a clear message to other potential abusers. Again, several of these reforms may be at the expense of constitutionally guaranteed defendants' rights (Haugaard & Reppucci, 1988). A delicate balancing act between the competing interests of the state, parents, and children has developed (Reppucci, Weithorn, Mulvey, & Monahan, 1984). The purpose of this chapter is to examine the impact of these concrete attempts to use the legal system to combat the problem of child maltreatment and to highlight the ethical dilemmas that these changes have caused.

## CHILD ABUSE REPORTING LAWS

In order to understand the potential preventive impact of child abuse reporting laws, several historical trends in the evolution of these laws need to be considered. Between 1962 and 1967, all 50 states, Washington, DC, and the Virgin Islands enacted reporting laws. The scope of these early laws was relatively narrow. Their primary function was identification of ongoing abuse. While it was hoped that bringing abuse to public attention would serve to deter or prevent new cases of abuse, strictly speaking prevention was not a primary goal. In 1974, however, with the passage of the federal Child Abuse Prevention and Treatment Act, an explicit legislative effort was made to prevent child abuse. Similarly, child abuse reporting laws should be distinguished from statutes that outlaw and impose criminal sanctions for child abuse, and thereby seek to deter or prevent abuse. Thus, separate laws have been enacted to serve three related but distinguishable functions: identification, prevention and criminal prosecution (deterrence). Since the mid-1970's, perhaps in response to the failure of the Congress to fund prevention efforts adequately, the identification and prevention functions of the reporting laws have become blurred.

During the past 25 years, most states have modified their reporting laws many times (e.g., California has amended its statutes 15 times since 1963).

Changes have occurred in each of the seven primary elements of reporting laws: 1) definition of reportable conditions; 2) persons mandated to report; 3) degree of certainty required for a report; 4) sanctions imposed for failure to report; 5) immunity for good faith reporters; 6) abrogation of certain communication privileges; and, 7) reporting procedures (Education Commission of the States, 1978). In each of these areas, considerable debate has arisen concerning the proper scope of the law. One consideration that underlies this debate has been the extent to which such laws should serve a preventive function. While the reporting laws were designed for the purpose of identification of children in trouble, and as such are neither preventive nor investigative tools, many proposed and adopted reforms have sought to increase the preventive function of reporting statutes. The discussion which follows will highlight some of the legal implications and social costs of broadening reporting laws to encompass a preventive function.

## Definition of Reportable Conditions

Perhaps the most direct consideration of a preventive function for reporting laws has occurred in the context of debate about the definition of reportable conditions. One aspect of this debate has focussed on the breadth of the definition, because there is remarkably little agreement as to when a court should find a child abused or neglected (Rosenberg & Hunt, 1984; Wald, 1975). Most relevant to the present discussion of prevention is whether definitions of reportable conditions should include "threatened abuse or neglect." The impetus for inclusion of threatened harm is to identify the child in peril as quickly as possible, and to prevent through direct intervention by Child Protective Services (CPS) the occurrence of dangerous behaviors. A number of state statutes have adopted such a provision. The standards for these provisions differ from state to state, but generally, the definition of threatened harm is left to the discretion of the reporter (Meriwether, 1986). In this vein, child advocates have recently drawn attention to the threat of harm imposed on fetuses by pregnant women who abuse alcohol or drugs. Assuming that maternal substance abuse during pregnancy is threatening to the child, several courts have jailed women to limit their access to drugs and alcohol and thereby prevent damage to the fetus. Civil libertarians have raised concerns about this practice, arguing that it opens the door to state intervention in a wide variety of cases involving less severe behavior by pregnant women. Where will the line be drawn?

Related to the issue of threatened harm is the debate about whether definitions of child maltreatment should focus on the perpetrator's (usually a parent's) behavior or demonstrable harm to the child. If the concept of threatened harm is to have any force in the law, the definition of child maltreatment must focus on the perpetrator's behavior. Some have argued that efforts to predict future danger to a child based on psychological profiles of parents or caretakers are simply too inaccurate to support investigation by child protective services (Goldstein, Freud & Solnit, 1979; Wald, 1975). Given this, most statutes focus on recent past parental behavior defined as "capable of harming the child." These statutes are based on the assumption that, absent significant change in the family's circumstances, such behaviors indicate a reasonable likelihood that the child will be threatened again and will eventually suffer maltreatment.

## Mandated Reporters

Parallelling the trend to broaden the definition of reportable conditions has been the trend to broaden the scope of individuals mandated to report suspected maltreatment. This trend has been motivated by a desire to identify the child in peril before the damage becomes severe. While most early laws mandated only physicians to report, over time a much broader spectrum of professionals who are likely to have close contact with children have been explicitly included in many state statutes. Today, the list of mandated reporters often includes coroners, medical examiners, mental health and social service workers, law enforcement and school officials, attorneys, day care staff, foster care providers, and clergy (Mitchell, 1987). In the extreme, a number of states require "any person" who suspects abuse to file a report.

## Degree of Certainty

The degree of certainty that a potential reporter must have in order to be required by law to make a report of suspected maltreatment has also been the subject of some controversy. The standard for certainty employed in reporting laws varies from state to state. Three typical examples of statutory language are "cause to believe," "reasonable cause to know or suspect," and "reasonable suspicion." Whether these differences actually serve as useful guides for the behavior of the average reporter is questionable. In theory, however, the statutory language used to define the degree of certainty has important legal implications as it is used in determining liability for failure to report. Language which includes the word *reasonable* denotes an objective standard: what a reasonable person in similar circumstances would believe to be the case, whether or not the reporter actually formed the belief (Sussman, 1974). Conversely, the words *believe* or *suspect*, standing alone, denote a subjective standard under which only the reporter is required to hold the requisite opinion or belief. Use of an objective standard thus simplifies enforcement of penalty provisions (Meriwether, 1986). Thus, to the extent to which such liability serves as an impetus for reporting, the statutory language used to define degree of certainty will determine the degree to which the reporting laws prevent further child maltreatment.

## Sanctions for Failure to Report

Currently, the majority of state statutes defines failure to report suspected maltreatment as a crime, usually a misdemeanor punishable by fine and/or jail sentence. Nevertheless, data from the 1979–1980 National Incidence Study suggest that professionals report only about 33% of suspected cases (Burgdorf, 1981). Additionally, in some states general tort liability has been imposed on nonreporters for damages to the child (Brown & Truitt, 1978; Meriwether, 1986). Despite these sanctions, prosecution of professionals for failure to report has been extremely rare (Aaron, 1981). With the recent prosecution of several psychologists, however, there is some indication that such prosecutions may become more common (Denton, 1987).

## Immunity for Good Faith Reporters

In cases of erroneous reports, all states provide immunity from prosecution for reporters who make reports in good faith. Immunity clauses are intended to encourage reporting. Only cases in which it can be proven that a reporter knowingly made a false report is that person liable for damages suffered by those subject to investigation following a report. In practice, of course, demonstrating that a report was knowingly false is extremely difficult and immunity is preserved for nearly all reports.

## Abrogation of Communication Privileges

Another effort made in most state statutes to facilitate reporting is the abrogation of certain communication privileges. Privileged communications, those protected from presentation into evidence at a judicial proceeding, between patient and physician, husband and wife, and psychotherapist and client are nullified for the purpose of reporting in nearly all states.

## Reporting Procedures

Most reporting laws specify the procedures that must be followed to report a case of suspected child maltreatment. Some of these procedures have preventive implications. First, most statutes require that an oral report be made immediately or as soon as practically possible, followed within a brief time by a written report. The obvious goal here is to minimize the opportunity for further incidences of maltreatment. Second, in most states, among the various types of information that must be included in a report is the reporter's name. Some states, however, allow reporters to remain anonymous. In many states, grants of anonymity are made only to permissive reporters while mandated reporters are required to divulge their identities (Meriwether, 1986). Finally, most states require that the records of unfounded cases be expunged from the state central registry. The criteria used to determine what constitutes a founded case varies from state to state and in some states is left undefined.

## IMPLICATIONS OF PREVENTIVE TRENDS IN REPORTING LAWS

The preventive benefits that have resulted from historical evolution of the reporting laws must be considered against the cost of increased state intrusion into the constitutionally protected right of family autonomy. Inclusion of a threatened harm provision, broadening the scope of mandated reporters, relaxing the degree of certainty required for a report, providing immunity for good faith reporters, all increase the preventive function of the reporting laws but also theoretically carry with them increased risk of overreporting and increased numbers of unsubstantiated reports, with potentially serious consequences for the families involved. Given the paucity of available data it is difficult to evaluate the real costs of these trends.

We do know that there has been a steady increase in the number of child maltreatment reports every year since national statistics have been available (American Association for Protecting Children, 1986). Moreover, while rates of reports have steadily increased, the percentage of those reports that are substantiated (variously referred to as "unfounded" or "not indicated") has steadily decreased. At the national level, the number of maltreatment reports has risen over 12 times since 1963, from approximately 150,000 to over 1.9 million in 1985 (American Association for Protecting Children, 1987). Between 1975 and 1985, however, the national percentage of substantiated reports fell from 65% to about 40%. Each year over half a million families are investigated for reports that are unsubstantiated. In states with large urban populations, where child protective services are more heavily taxed, substantiation rates are even poorer. For example, in New York State between 1974 and 1984 the number of maltreatment cases increased from below 30,000 to over 80,000, while the percentage of substantiated cases fell from 50% to 35% (Eckenrode, Powers, Doris, Munsch, & Bolger, 1988). Still there is much we do not know about the meaning of these figures.

Some of the increase in reporting may be attributed to real changes over the years in the actual incidence of child maltreatment, but these changes are likely small compared to increases due to a better educated and more aware public. It remains unclear to what extent increases in reports are attributable to the trends toward *preventive* reporting laws described above, although it seems safe to assume that such factors have contributed to the increase. All else being equal, broader definitions of maltreatment, increasing numbers of individuals mandated to report, relaxed criteria for certainty of reports, etc., should result in greater numbers of reports.

Data addressing the extent to which these preventive trends have contributed to the declining percentage of substantiated reports is sorely needed. From a utilitarian policy perspective, it would be useful to have this information. Presumably, some relatively small increase in the rate of unsubstantiated cases might be tolerable if accompanied by a relatively large increase in the rate of substantiated cases. Unfortunately, such an evaluation is very difficult, if not impossible, to make. Comparisons between states with and without a threatened harm provision, for example, would have to control for, at minimum, potential differences across states in definitions of abuse and neglect and in child protective service investigatory resources and procedures. Within state comparisons of pre- and post-enactment of a threatened harm provision might be more viable but still would need to control for base rate increases in reporting due to factors such as increased child protective service resources to handle reports and increasing public awareness of child abuse and neglect. To the authors' knowledge, no such analysis has been attempted.

In the absence of such data, less direct evidence may be considered. Some unsubstantiated cases involve reports of poor child treatment and care that may warrant legitimate concern but simply do not meet the legal criteria of child abuse or neglect. While hard evidence is lacking, there is a general consensus that cases of this type are increasingly being reported to child protective service agencies in the absence of other, more appropriate family-oriented social-services, by concerned citizens and professionals who hope that by making the report necessary support services will be provided to the family before child abuse or neglect occurs full blown (Besharov, 1988). Reporting laws that have broadened the definition of child maltreatment and reduced the standard for certainty required for a report may be contributing to this phenomenon.

There is some evidence that reports made by professionals are more likely to be substantiated than are reports made by nonprofessionals (Eckenrode et al., 1988; Groeneveld & Giovannoni, 1977). It is not yet clear why this is the case, but taken together with considerable evidence that 1) many professionals show a high degree of noncompliance with reporting statutes (Bailey, 1982; Brown & Truitt, 1978; Burgdorf, 1981; Collier, 1983; Miller & Miller, 1983; Swoboda, Elwork, Sales & Levine, 1978; Weisberg & Wald, 1984), and 2) professional reports are more often associated with cases being brought to court (Eckenrode et al., 1988), it is likely that professionals reserve reporting for the most severe cases of maltreatment. Perhaps professionals, due to increased contact with and better understanding of child protective services, simply report those cases that they are relatively confident can be substantiated.

There is also evidence that anonymous reports are less likely to be substantiated than other reports. Adams, Barone, & Tooman (1982) reported that of 1,037 anonymous reports made in Bronx County during a 2-year period, over 87% were unfounded; and of those 129 that were founded, over half had been previously reported or were still active. Similarly, national statistics suggest that substantiation rates are lower for anonymous reports, e.g., only 25% in 1978 (Department of Health and Human Services, 1980).

It is widely recognized that resources for child protective service agencies around the country have been inadequate to respond to this rising tide of reports. Consequently, child protective personnel are left in the unenviable position of investigating increasing numbers of unsubstantiated reports while having fewer and fewer resources left to provide treatment for substantiated cases. This situation is all the more distressing because it is not known what proportion of unsubstantiated cases result from well-intentioned but mistaken reports of suspected abuse and what proportion represents real cases of child abuse or neglect that, due to the difficulty of producing convincing evidence upon investigation (especially when investigative agencies are overtaxed for both time and resources), cannot be proven.

In any event, unsubstantiated reports of the former type exact several costs. First, the cost to the families involved can be substantial. Investigation for suspected abuse is unlikely to be benign. Depending on how thoroughly CPS investigates the report, school officials, employers, neighbors and extended family, among others, can be contacted regarding the suspected abuse (Hardin, 1988). Clearly the potential for social stigma can be high, both for the parents and for older children. Furthermore, investigation often produces at least temporary disruption of family functioning, including disruption of parent-child relations, especially when either the parent or child is removed from the home, and loss of either parent's time at work to participate in investigations and hearings. Second, and not insignificantly, given the necessity of focussing limited child protective services on those cases of severe child abuse and neglect, there is the cost to the child protective service system of paper work and staff time for investigation.

## PROCEDURAL REFORMS IN THE COURTROOM

A second area in which major changes have occurred since the popular discovery of child abuse, especially child sexual abuse, has been in the area of courtroom procedure (McLain, 1987). The view of many clinicians is that child victims of abuse are further traumatized by their involvement in the prosecution of their abuser. Therefore, a major goal has been to revamp the procedure in order to prevent children from experiencing the stress and trauma of testifying. Most of these changes have been specific to victims of sexual abuse. This specificity has been questioned because other children, such as those who witness the killing of a parent, may be equally or more traumatized by the event and by having to testify about it (Goodman & Rosenberg, 1987).

Three changes in trial procedures have been enacted in several states to reduce the trauma to child witnesses and to increase the possibility of successful prosecution of offenders: 1) broadening of the types of out-of-court statements that can be admitted; 2) increased use of videotaping of the child's testimony outside of the court; and 3) shielding the child from the defendant during the child's courtroom testimony. It should be noted that there is no empirical evidence to demonstrate that these innovations actually do reduce the trauma to the children; however, there is much acceptance of this reasoning based on clinical experience reported by many professionals. It is also extremely important to note that all three innovations involve restrictions on the rights afforded the accused in a criminal trial, especially the Sixth Amendment right "to be confronted with witnesses against him." This confrontation clause eliminates the danger to the defendant of being convicted on the basis of hearsay evidence and provides the defendant with the opportunity for cross-examination.

Before proceeding to discuss each of these innovations, it is worth mentioning that much empirical research (for a brief review, see Haugaard and Reppucci, 1988) has been focussed on the issue of children's competence to testify in the first place. Although until recently, in most states young children were presumed incompetent to testify, a presumption that could be challenged (*Wheeler v. United States*, 1895), Federal Rule of Evidence 601 states that no one can be declared incompetent on the basis of age and eliminates the challenges to children's competence per se. Although this new rule does not allow every child to testify since each child must meet the requirements of every other person who wishes to testify, it does change the burden of proof to a different party because the child must be found incompetent rather than competent (Mahady-Smith, 1985).

## Use of Out-of-Court Statements

Hearsay is defined as "a statement, other than one made by the declarant while testifying at the trial or hearing, offered into evidence to prove the truth of the matter asserted" (Federal Rule of Evidence 801). For example, if a child told her mother that the neighbor had sexually molested the child, and the mother is allowed to testify during the neighbor's trial that the child told her of the abuse and the child does not testify, this is hearsay. The potential for misuse is great because of infringement on the defendant's constitutional rights to cross-examine the accuser. Strictly speaking, any use of hearsay would seem to be prohibited by the Sixth Amendment. However, the Supreme Court has not found this to be the case and has allowed for certain exceptions (*Mattox v. United States*, 1895). In *Ohio v. Roberts* (1980), the court held that hearsay statements do not deny the accused the right to confrontation if two requirements are met: the witness is unavailable and the statement has "sufficient indicia of reliability" (*Mitchell Law Review*, 1985, p. 812). A child could be found to be unavailable because of being 1) too young to testify and therefore incompetent, 2) mentally infirm at the time, e.g., was very emotionally upset, or 3) meaningfully emotionally harmed as a result of having to testify.

If the child is found to be unavailable, then the child's out-of-court statement must have indicia of reliability. The Supreme Court has enunciated four criteria for assessing reliability (*Dutton v. Evans*, 1970): a) The statement contains no express assertion of facts previous to the incident described, b) Cross-examination would not indicate that the witness had a lack of knowledge of the incident, c) There is only a remote possibility that the witness recollection is faulty, and d) The statement is such that there is no reason to suppose that the witness purposely misrepresented the defendant's involvement. Although subsequent lower court decisions have held that not all four criteria must be met for reliability to be declared (Bulkley, 1985), it is clearly left up to the trial judge to interpret the criteria in each individual case.

The hearsay exceptions that are most likely to occur in a child sexual abuse trial are those involving an "excited utterance" defined as a "spontaneous declaration made by a person immediately after an event and before the mind has an opportunity to conjure a falsehood" (*Black's Law Dictionary*, 1979, p. 1173), and statements made to a physician during the diagnosis and treatment of an injury. Most hearsay in child sexual abuse cases has been admitted under the excited utterance exemption. For example, in *United States v. Nick* (1979), a three-year-old boy's statement to his mother about a sexual attack he had experienced an hour or two before was deemed admissible because the child was found to be too young to testify. Statements made to a physician in the course of a physical examination for an injury are admissible to the extent that the information obtained by the doctor was needed for the proper diagnosis and treatment of the injury (*United States v. Iron Shell*, 1980).

Several states have enacted special hearsay statutes for child sexual abuse trials. The language of the Washington statute has served as a model for the laws of several other states and has been held constitutional by the Washington supreme court, although it has not been reviewed by a federal court (*Harvard Law Review*, 1985).

> A statement made by a child when under the age of ten describing any act of sexual conduct performed with or on the child by another, not otherwise admissible by statute or court rule, is admissible in evidence in criminal proceedings . . . if: (1) the court finds, in a hearing conducted outside the presence of the jury that the time, content, and circumstances of the statement provide sufficient indicia of reliability; and (2) the child either: (a) testifies at the proceedings; or (b) is unavailable as a witness, provided that, when the child is unavailable as a witness, such statement may be admitted only if there is corroborative evidence of the act. (Graham, p. 164)

There are several advantages to the adoption of a statute in this form. It aids in the prosecution of sex offenses against children because courts are no longer required to stretch the requirements of the excited utterance exemption. It provides clear guidelines for the admission of hearsay evidence, thereby increasing the certainty as to which types of out-of-court statements will be admissible. It helps to avoid the wrongful conviction of alleged perpetrators by requiring either direct testimony by the child or other corroborative testimony; in other words, the statement of one adult who was not a witness to the abuse cannot be used alone to convict the defendant. Finally, it discourages constitutional challenges enunciated by the Supreme Court (*Harvard Law Review*, 1985; *Mitchell Law Review*, 1985).

## Use of Videotaped Testimony

Videotaped testimony taken outside the courtroom is designed to replace the testimony of the child in open court. Statutes allowing for such videotaping are based on the assumption that the act of testifying in a strange situation in front of a large number of strangers is, in itself, traumatic for the child and consequently reduces the value of the child's testimony (*Harvard Law Review*, 1985; *Mitchell Law Review*, 1985). Videotaped depositions tend to be taken before the judge in chambers in the presence of the district attorney, the defendant, and his attorneys. Examination and cross-examination of the alleged victim are allowed. The intent is to keep the essential aspects of the trial situation while eliminating the public aspect of the trial. Nevertheless, videotaped testimony is technically hearsay testimony because it is made outside the presence of the jury.

State statutes vary in their requirements for admissible videotaped testimony. For example, the Arizona, Kentucky, and Texas statutes do not allow face-to-face confrontation between the defendant and the child during the videotaping, although the defendant can hear the testimony from an adjacent room and the defendant's attorney is present with the child. In several states, it is required that the trial judge make a ruling of unavailability of the child to testify before allowing the videotaping to occur. Although the various statutes providing for videotaping have not been challenged in the federal courts, several have been challenged in state courts and been upheld (e.g., *State v. Melendez*, 1982; *Commonwealth v. Stasko*, 1977). Although some legal commentators (Clark-Weintraub, 1985; *Harvard Law Review*, 1985) suggest that components of some state statutes may make them unconstitutional, especially provisions for removing the defendant and those not requiring a previous finding of witness unavailability, the general view is that the statutes that require unavailability and videotaping in the presence of the defendant will probably be found constitutional.

Whitcomb (1985) has pointed out that videotaping, although praised by its proponents, is seldom used in the states where it is authorized. She reasons that many prosecutors consider the deposition environment to be more traumatic than the courtroom. The judge may not be present to monitor the behavior of the defendant or the counsel; small rooms which entail closer proximity of the child and the defendant are the norm for depositions; and victim advocates may not be permitted to attend. Moreover, if a finding of unavailability is required, the child often has to undergo a battery of psychiatric and medical tests or both by examiners for the defense and the prosecution. As a result, some prosecutors believe that any child who can successfully cope with the investigation process leading up to the deposition can succeed at the trial as well.

## Shielding the Child Witness from the Defendant

Several states have enacted statutes allowing the defendant to be screened from the child witness during the child's testimony. Some of the statutes require that the defendant be able to see the witness, e.g., through a one-way mirror; others merely mandate that the defendant be able to hear the witness. In some states, the child can testify via closed-circuit television, allowing the judge, jury, and defendant to see the child, while the child is unable to see into the courtroom (*Harvard Law Review*, 1985).

The major concern regarding the procedural safeguard of shielding is whether the defendant has a right to face-to-face confrontation of the witness. In 1981, the California supreme court reversed the conviction of a man for sexual abuse on the grounds that during the trial he was seated so that he could hear but not see the child witness and thus was not afforded his right to confrontation (*Herbert v. Superior Court*, 1981). In order to protect the defendant's right to confront an accuser, California law now requires that in instances where the child testifies from another room via closed-circuit television, the defendant's face must appear on a television monitor in the room where the child is located.

The only Supreme Court decision to deal with this issue (*Coy v. Iowa*, 1988), an Iowa law approved the placement of a large screen between the defendant and the child witnesses during the children's testimony. After certain lighting adjustments in the courtroom, the defendant was able to perceive the witnesses dimly, and the witnesses could not see the defendant at all. This arrangement was found unconstitutional because the defendant's "constitutional right to face-to-face confrontation was violated (p. 4934)." Although this decision clearly raises the constitutionality of all of the various state statutes regarding shielding, Justice O'Connor, joined by Justice White, in a concurring statement to form the majority opinion carefully pointed out that Iowa was the only state that authorized the particular type of screen used in this case. She emphatically stated that, "While I agree with the Court that the Confrontation Clause was violated in this case, I wish to make clear that nothing in today's decision necessarily dooms such efforts by state legislatures to protect child witnesses (p. 4934)." Furthermore, "the Court has time and again stated that the Clause 'reflects a *preference* for face-to-face confrontation at trial,' and expressedly recognizes that this preference may be overcome in a particular case if close examination of 'competing interests' so warrants (p. 4934)." Justice O'Connor concluded that, "In short, our precedents recognize a right to face-to-face confrontation at trial, but have never viewed that right as absolute." . . . and . . . "our cases suggest that the strictures of the Confrontation Clause may give way to the compelling state interest of protecting child witnesses (p. 4934)." Thus, the door was left open to courts and legislatures to develop constitutionally sound modifications of the Confrontation Clause as a means of shielding child witnesses.

Two years later, the United States Supreme Court dealt with the question that it avoided in *Coy v. Iowa*; that is, whether the right to face-to-face confrontation of a child victim-witness can be abridged when the state offers a particularized finding of necessity. In *Maryland v. Craig* (1990), a day care operator appealed her conviction of several offenses related to sexual abuse because the trial judge had allowed the use of one-way closed-circuit television. Justice O'Connor, writing for a five-member majority, upheld the conviction and cited psychological research in the Court's holding "that, if the State makes an adequate showing of necessity, the state interest in protecting child witnesses from the trauma of testifying in a child abuse case is sufficiently important to justify the use of a special procedure that permits a child witness to testify at trial against a defendant in the absence of face-to-face confrontation (p. 3169)." Justice O'Connor emphatically concluded that "Indeed, where face-to-face confrontation causes significant emotional distress in a child witness, there is evidence that such confrontation would in fact disserve the Confrontation Clause's truth seeking goals (p. 3169)." Goodman, Levine, Melton, & Ogden (1991) point out that although the Court did not determine the level of emotional distress sufficient to justify the absence of face-to-face confrontation, the majority did state that as long as the finding of trauma is specific to confrontation and not to the courtroom generally and is more than a witness's mere anxiety about testimony, then its absence may be permissible. However, the vociferous dissent of the four justices in the minority, authored by Justice Scalia, insures that controversy about the wisdom of special procedures to protect child witnesses, even in carefully selected cases, will continue, and that further litigation to test *Craig's* limits is likely (Goodman, et al., 1991).

## CONCLUSIONS

Both the child abuse reporting laws and the innovative courtroom procedures we have discussed have been designed to protect children from individual or system abuse. Certainly in many instances these laws have been successful at accomplishing this goal. However, in other instances they have been less successful and have intruded on the constitutional rights of others. Competing interests require that the goals of the reporting laws be balanced against the privacy rights of families and that new courtroom procedures be balanced against the right to face-to-face confrontation between child witnesses and accused perpetrators.

Helping professionals have been in the forefront in the call for laws to protect victims of child abuse from further abuse as well as to prevent it from ever occurring. For example, Feshbach and Feshbach (1978) have proposed "to invade family privacy (p. 168)" by requiring that childrearing practices be assigned public status. At the same time helping professionals have tended to be unclear in their definitions of child abuse (Giovannoni and Becerra, 1979), especially child sexual abuse (Attebury-Bennett, 1987), and, for the sake of child saving, have been quite willing to trammel constitutional safeguards for both families and alleged adult perpetrators. Other more legally oriented commentators (e.g., Melton, 1985) have been less willing to give up the safeguards. For example, Justice Scalia, in regard to the Confrontation

Clause, stated, "That face-to-face presence may, unfortunately, upset the truthful rape victim or abused child; but by the same token it may confound and undo the false accuser, or reveal the child coached by a malevolent adult. It is a truism that constitutional protections have costs (*Coy v. Iowa*, 1988, p. 4933)."

Notably missing from our discussion of either the reporting laws or procedural reforms was empirical evidence, psychological or legal, to buttress the positions taken by either advocates or opponents. The major finding regarding reporting laws is that since their implementation, the number of people reported for possible child abuse has increased significantly. However, of the cases reported, as few as 35% have been founded or substantiated. Of course, we do not know how many of the unsubstantiated cases really were abuse cases because there have been no follow-up studies of reported families. Child protective service workers, who are placed in the precarious position of having to decide at what point the child should be removed from the home, do not want to separate children from parents needlessly; however, they are confronted with the knowledge that a wrong decision could result in a serious or even fatal injury to the child. Stories by workers who realized too late that they incorrectly judged the home situation and should have intervened sooner are all too prevalent. Yet little is said of the many cases in which falsely accused parents have suffered the loss of their children and/or total disruption of their family life. We need data, carefully collected and analyzed, to determine the outcomes for families and children impacted by the reporting laws.

Moreover, we have no evidence for the hypothesized deterrent effect of the laws. An assumption that has powered these laws has been that not only can the state intervene to protect children currently being abused but that the laws themselves will deter potential abusers from engaging in abusive behaviors. Unfortunately, the problem of determining impact seems unsolvable until we are able to arrive at baselines for abuse in our society. Until we can show a percentage decrease in this baseline figure, we have no evidence for prevention.

Similar concerns plague the courtroom procedural reforms. No available empirical evidence indicates the percentage of children traumatized by testifying, which children are at the greatest risk for trauma, the types of abuse that cause the most trauma to a child testifying about them, or the value of these new procedures for reducing this trauma.

Haugaard & Reppucci (1988) have strongly urged the undertaking of research to measure the effects of these procedural changes. For example in an effort to determine the effect of testimony via closed-circuit television or videotape, they suggest that:

> In an experimental situation, it would be possible to present a child's testimony live to one group of adults (representing a jury) and at the same time videotape it to show to another group of adults. Differences in the adults' reactions to the

testimony, if any, would provide preliminary information about the effects of videotaped testimony. In a similar type of situation, the reactions to testimony given by a child who is shielded from a "defendant" could be compared with the reactions to the same testimony given while the child is able to see the "defendant." (p. 368)

Although neither the legislative nor the judicial branches of government are well-known for their intensive use of empirical data, the constitutional rights that are at stake require that social scientists provide as much systematic data as possible so that such information can be taken into account when developing legal safeguards. We want to be able to protect children, and this protection should be based on empirically validated assumptions not mythology. There is often a tendency to assume that parents are abusive because they have been investigated by protective services, or that a defendant is guilty simply because enough evidence exists to allow for a trial. This is despite the fact that we all know that presumption of innocence is a cornerstone of our judicial system. There is too much at stake for families and alleged perpetrators to have their constitutional rights abridged in any way without compelling evidence to do so. At least in regard to the preventive goals of the reporting laws and the courtroom procedural changes, this evidence does not yet exist.

## REFERENCES

Aaron, J. (1981). Civil liability for teacher's negligent failure to report suspected child abuse. *Wayne State Law Review, 28*, 183–213.

Adams, Barone, & Tooman (1986). The dilemma of anonymous reporting in child protective services. *Child Welfare, 61*, 4–5.

American Association for Protecting Children (1986). *Highlights of official child neglect and abuse reporting 1984, 8.* Denver, CO: American Humane Association.

American Association for Protecting Children (1987). *Highlights of official child neglect and abuse reporting 1985, 9.* Denver, CO: American Humane Association.

Atteberry-Bennett, J. (1987). *Child sexual abuse: Definitions and interventions of parents and professionals.* Unpublished doctoral dissertation, Institute of Clinical Psychology, University of Virginia, Charlottesville.

Bailey, M. (1982). The failure of physicians to report child abuse. *University of Toronto Law Review, 49*, 49–66.

Besharov, D. J. (1988). Child abuse and neglect reporting and investigation: Policy guidelines for decision making. *Family Law Quarterly 22*(1), 1–15.

*Black's Law Dictionary.* (1979). (5th ed.). New York: Western.

Brown, R. H., & Truitt, R. B. (1978). Civil liability in child abuse cases. *Chi-Kent Law Review, 54*, 687–752.

*Brown v. Board of Education of Topeka*, 347 U.S. 483 (1954).

Bulkley, J. (Ed.). (1985). *Child sexual abuse and the law* (5th ed.). Washington, DC: American Bar Association.

Burgdorf, K. (1981). *Results of the National Incidence Study*. Washington, DC: National Center on Child Abuse and Neglect.

Clark-Weintraub, D. (1985). The use of videotaped testimony of victims in cases involving child sexual abuse: A constitutional dilemma. *Hofstra Law Review*, *14*, 261–296.

Collier, S. A. (1983). Reporting child abuse: When moral obligations fail. *Pacific Law Journal*, *15*, 189–215.

*Commonwealth v. Stasko*, 370 A.2d 350 (1977).

*Coy v. Iowa*, No. 86-6757. In *United States Law Week*, *56*, (6-28-88), 4931–4938.

Denton, L. (1987). Child abuse reporting laws: Are they a barrier to helping troubled families? *APA Monitor*, *18*, 22–23.

Department of Health and Human Services (1980). *National analysis of official child neglect and reporting*. DHHS Publication Number (OHDS) 80-30271.

Department of Health and Human Services (1981). *Study findings: National study of the incidence and severity of child abuse and neglect*. DHHS Publication Number (OHDS) 81-30325.

*Dutton v. Evans*, 400 U.S. 74 (1970).

Eckenrode, J., Powers, J., Doris, J., Munsch, J., & Bolger, N. (1988). Substantiation of child abuse and neglect reports. *Journal of Consulting and Clinical Psychology*, *56*, 9–16.

Education Commission of the States (1978). Report No. 106. *Trends in child protection laws—1977*, 18–21.

Feshbach, S., & Feshbach, N. D. (1978). Child advocacy and family privacy. *Journal of Social Issues*, *34*, 168–176.

Giovannoni, J. M., & Becerra, R. M. (1979). *Defining child abuse*. New York: Free Press.

Goldstein, J., Freud, A., & Solnit, A. (1979). *Before the best interests of the child*. New York: The Free Press.

Goodman, G. S., & Rosenberg, M. S. (1987). The child witness to family violence. In D. J. Sonkin (Ed.), *Domestic violence on trial: Psychological and legal dimensions of family violence*. New York: Springer.

Goodman, G. S., Levine, M., Melton, G. B., & Ogden, D. W. (1991). Child witnesses and the Confrontation Clauses: The American Psychological Association Brief in *Maryland v.Craig*. *Law and Human Behavior*, *15*, 13–30.

Graham, M. H. (1985). Child sex abuse prosecutions: Hearsay and confrontation clause issues. In J. Bulkley (Ed.), *Papers from a National Conference on Legal Reforms in Child Sexual Abuse Cases*. Washington, DC: American Bar Association.

Groeneveld, L. P., & Giovannoni, J. M. (1977). Disposition of child abuse and neglect cases. *Social Work Research and Abstracts*, *13*, 24–30.

Hall, J. (1960). *General principles of criminal law* (2nd ed.). Indianapolis, IN: Bobbs-Merrill.

Hardin, M. (1988). Legal barriers in child abuse investigations: State powers and individual rights. *Washington Law Review*, *63*, 493–604.

*Harvard Law Review*. (1985). The testimony of child victims in sex abuse prosecutions: Two legislative proposals. *Harvard Law Review*, *98*, 806–836.

Haugaard, J. J., & Reppucci, N. D. (1988). *The sexual abuse of children: A comprehensive guide to current knowledge and intervention strategies*. San Francisco, CA: Jossey-Bass.

*Herbert v. Superior Court*, 117 Cal. App. 3d 661 (1981).

Kempe, C. H., Silverman, F. N., Steele, B. F., Droegemueller, W., & Silver, H. K. (1962). The battered child syndrome. *Journal of the American Medical Association, 181*, 17–24.

Levine, M., Ewing, C. P., & Levine, D. I. (1987). The use of law for prevention in the public interest. In L. Jason, R. Selner, R. Hess, & J. Moritsugu (Eds.), *Communities: Contributions from allied disciplines. Series in Prevention in Human Services, 5*, 239–276.

Mahady-Smith, C. M. (1985). The young victims as witness for the prosecution: Another form of abuse? *Whittier Law Review, 7*, 639–661.

*Maryland v. Craig*, 110 S. Ct. 3157 (1990).

*Mattox v. United States*, 156 U.S. 237 (1895).

McLain, L. (1987). Maryland's statutory hearsay exception for reliable statements by alleged child abuse victims: A hesitant step forward. *University of Baltimore Law Review, 17*, 1–39.

Melton, G. B. (1985). Sexually abused children and the legal system: Some policy recommendations. *American Journal of Family Therapy, 13*, 61–67.

Meriwether, M. H. (1986). Child abuse reporting laws: Time for a change. *Family Law Quarterly, 20*(2), 141–171.

Miller, J., & Miller, M. (1983). Protecting the rights of abused and neglected children. *Trial, 19*, 68–72.

Mitchell, M. H. (1987). Must clergy tell? Child abuse reporting requirements versus the clergy privilege and free exercise of religion. *Minnesota Law Review, 71*, 723–778.

*Mitchell Law Review*. (1985). Minnesota's hearsay exception for child victims of sexual abuse. *William Mitchell Law Review, 11*, 799–823.

*Ohio v. Roberts*, 448 U.S. 56 (1980).

*Prince v. Massachusetts*. 321 U.S. 158 (1944).

Reppucci, N. D., Weithorn, L. A., Mulvey, E. P., & Monahan, J. (Eds.). (1984). *Children, mental health, and the law*. Beverly Hills, CA: Sage.

Rosenberg, M. S., & Hunt, R. D. (1984). Child maltreatment: Legal and mental health issues. In N. D. Reppucci, L. A. Weithorn, E. P. Mulvey, & J. Monahan (Eds.), *Children, mental health, and the law*. Beverly Hills, CA: Sage.

Schultz, L. G. (1988). *One hundred cases of wrongfully charged child sexual abuse: A survey and recommendations*. Unpublished manuscript, West Virginia University, School of Social Work, Morgantown.

*State v. Melendez*, 661 P.2d 654 (1982).

Sussman, R. (1974). Reporting child abuse: A review of the literature. *Family Law Quarterly, 8*, 245–277.

Swoboda, J. S., Elwork, A., Sales, B. D., & Levine, D. (1978). Knowledge of and compliance with privileged communications and the child abuse reporting laws. *Professional Psychology, 9*, 448–457.

*United States v. Iron Shell*, 633 F.2d 77 (1980).

*United States v. Nick*, 604 F.2d 1199 (1979).

Wald, M. (1975). State intervention on behalf of 'neglected' children: A search for realistic standards. *Stanford Law Review*, *27*, 985–989.

Weisberg, R., & Wald, M. (1984). Confidentiality laws and state efforts to protect abused or neglected children: The need for statutory reform. *Family Law Quarterly*, *18*, 143–212.

*Wheeler v. United States*, 159 U.S. 523 (1895).

Whitcomb, D. (1985). Prosecution of child sexual abuse: Innovations in practice. In *Research in Brief*. Washington, DC: National Institute of Justice.

# Future Directions of Child Maltreatment Prevention

CHAPTER 12

# The Prevention of Child Maltreatment: Programming, Research, and Policy

JOAN KAUFMAN AND EDWARD ZIGLER

Despite programming and legislative efforts, child maltreatment continues to be a pervasive social problem. Epidemiological studies show that over one million children are maltreated each year (National Center on Child Abuse and Neglect, 1981). Although a recent study suggests that the percentage of all children subjected to the most severe forms of violence has decreased from 3.6% to 2% over the past decade (Gelles & Straus, 1985), overall rates of child maltreatment have increased. Last year, approximately 2,000 children died due to maltreatment—half as a result of physical abuse and half as a result of neglect (Daro & Mitchell, 1987).

The design and implementation of effective prevention efforts requires a thorough understanding of the causes of child maltreatment. Belsky (1980), in extending the work of Garbarino (1987), proposed the most comprehensive model of abuse to date. He integrated Bronfenbrenner's (1979; 1977) conceptualization of the contexts in which development occurs with Tinbergen's (1951) analysis of ontogenetic development, and organized the factors associated with the etiology of abuse into a framework comprised of four ecological levels: the ontogenetic, microsystem, exosystem, and macrosystem. On the ontogenetic level, Belsky gave characteristics of parents who mistreat their children, such as a history of abuse or experiences of stress. On the microsystem level, he discussed aspects of the family environment that increase the likelihood of abuse, such as having a poor marital relationship or a premature or unhealthy child. On the macrosystem level, he included work and social factors, such as unemployment and isolation; and on the exosystem level, he depicted cultural determinants of abuse, such as society's acceptance of corporal punishment as a legitimate form of discipline.

Consistent with the views of Cicchetti and Rizley (1981), we believe that a complete conceptualization of the factors associated with the etiology of abuse should include both risk and protective factors. Risk factors (e.g., history of abuse, poverty) increase the likelihood of abuse occurring and

TABLE 12.1.   The Causes of Child Maltreatment

| Ontogenetic Factors | Microsystem Factors | Exosystem Factors | Macrosystem Factors |
|---|---|---|---|
| | | Risk Factors | |
| History of abuse | Marital discord | Inadequate health | Economic recession |
| Alcohol abuse | Single parenthood | care facilities | Cultural acceptance |
| Stressful experiences | Premature or | Social isolation | of corporal |
| Low IQ | unhealthy child | Unsafe | punishment |
| Psychiatric and | | neighborhood | View of children as |
| physical illnesses | | | possessions |
| | | Protective Factors | |
| History of a positive | Supportive spouse | Good community | Economic |
| relationship with | Economic security | social and | prosperity |
| at least one | Grandmother or other | health services | Culture opposed to |
| caregiver | adult in home to | Affordable quality | violence |
| Good interpersonal | assist with child | day care | Culture opposed to |
| skills | care | Strong informal | the use of |
| High IQ | | social supports | corporal |
| | | Respite care | punishment |
| | | facilities | |

protective factors (e.g., being involved in a relationship with a supportive spouse) decrease the likelihood of abuse. Although protective factors are implied in Belsky's model, their explicit delineation is useful to both service providers and policy implementers. Table 12.1 includes examples of risk and protective factors which have been organized using Belsky's ecological framework.

Some protective factors that are apt to decrease the likelihood of maltreatment occurring on the ontogenetic level are having a high IQ and good interpersonal skills. On the microsystem level, being involved in a relationship with a supportive spouse and having economic security are protective factors. Good social supports and living in a community with ample social and health services are protective on the exosystem level. Living in a culture that is opposed to violence and does not believe corporal punishment is an acceptable form of discipline are protective factors on the macrosystem level.

These factors interact in complex ways (see Kaufman & Zigler, in press, for further discussion). An appreciation of the risk and the protective factors that affect the potential for maltreatment within any one family system is important when designing prevention strategies, identifying target populations for intervention efforts, and studying the effectiveness of prevention programs.

In this chapter, the importance of these risk and protective factors are highlighted in relation to programming and evaluation efforts. Theoretical and applied implications of child maltreatment research are also discussed, and then policy issues pertinent to the prevention of child maltreatment are considered.

## PROGRAMMING EFFORTS

In this section, the province of child maltreatment prevention programming efforts is defined, and issues related to identifying high-risk individuals for intervention purposes are discussed. Current strategies for the prevention of child maltreatment are then reviewed, and differences in the approaches used to prevent the various forms of maltreatment are highlighted.

### Defining the Province of Child Maltreatment Prevention Programming Efforts

The term *child maltreatment* must be defined before the province of its prevention can be delineated. Over the past decade, there has been considerable debate over what constitutes maltreatment (see Aber & Zigler, 1981; and Zigler, 1980, for discussion). Definitions range in scope from an emphasis on serious physical abuse (Kempe, Silverman, Steele, Droegemueller, & Silver, 1962) to a broad focus on the failure of the environment to meet the child's developmental needs (Alvy, 1975). At this writing, there is considerable debate concerning the appropriateness of including "emotional abuse" under the rubric of maltreatment (see *American Psychologist*, February, 1987, Special Issue on Emotional Maltreatment; and Garbarino, Guttman, & Seeley, 1986, for further discussion). For the purposes of this chapter, however, the definition of child maltreatment will be limited to incidents of physical abuse, sexual abuse, and neglect that are associated with imminent risk of serious bodily injury (Solnit, 1980).

Prevention efforts are typically categorized as primary, secondary, or tertiary (Lorion, 1983). In the area of child maltreatment, primary intervention efforts aim to completely avoid the onset of parenting dysfunction; secondary intervention efforts attempt early detection of parenting problems so remediation procedures can be applied; and tertiary interventions are treatment-oriented services designed to rehabilitate maltreating parents. Although tertiary intervention efforts are usually not considered prevention per se—estimates of recidivism rates for maltreating parents range from 20%–85% (Williams, 1983), and over 60% of child abuse mortalities occur to children who have already been identified as at risk (Gelles, 1984)—the creation of successful tertiary/treatment interventions to prevent the reoccurrence of maltreatment must be considered an integral component of prevention planning.

### Targeting Individuals For Prevention Efforts

Although secondary and tertiary intervention efforts are by definition targeted towards individual parents, much debate has centered on whether primary prevention efforts should be targeted towards high-risk individuals or high-risk communities. In order to identify parents at risk of abusing their children for primary prevention purposes, written questionnaires (e.g., Milner, 1986; Schneider, Helfer, & Pollock, 1972); standardized interviews (e.g., Altemeier, O'Connor, Vietze, Sandler, & Sherrod, 1984); and direct parent-child observation techniques (e.g., Gray, Cutler, Dean, & Kempe, 1976) have been devised. The utility of all these procedures is questionable, however (see Starr, 1982 for a review of the literature). For example, it has been shown that maltreating parents have not responded consistently to risk inventories (Schneider, Hoffmeister, & Helfer, 1976); and when a controlled experimental investigation was conducted, professionals skilled in working with abusive families were unable to differentiate the abusive parents from demographically matched nonabusive parents using direct parent-child observation techniques (Starr, 1987). Even supposing that the reliability and predictive power of these procedures could be improved, given the low base-rate (incidence) of abuse, many nonabusive parents would inevitably be falsely labeled at risk (see Kaufman & Zigler, in press, for further discussion). In fact, even if these screening processes could correctly label abusers and nonabusers 95% of the time, misclassifications would still occur in 50% of all identified cases.

To illustrate, consider a sample of 1,000 parents. A 5% abuse rate implies that 50 of these parents are abusers, and 950 are not. If 95% of the abusers were correctly identified, only three parents would have escaped detection. With comparable predictive power for detecting nonabusers, 902 parents would be correctly classified and 48 parents would be falsely labeled potential abusers. Forty-seven abusive parents would have been correctly identified, and 48 nonabusive parents would have been falsely accused, resulting in half of all the identified parents being misclassified. It is simply not statistically feasible to accurately predict a low base-rate phenomenon like child abuse.

The issue of misclassification is not merely an abstract, statistical question (Daniel, Newberger, Reed, & Kotelchuck, 1978). Child abuser is an extremely value-laden and derogatory term, so the cost of mislabeling parents potential abusers must be weighed seriously (see Solnit, 1980, for further discussion). We agree with Garbarino (1980) and others who suggest that, given the limited effectiveness of screening instruments, and the problems associated with predicting a low base-rate phenomenon, primary prevention strategies should be aimed at high-risk communities and not high-risk individuals. In contrast to a prediction approach to prevention, we advocate the implementation of voluntary services to ameliorate the conditions that promote abuse—services like those that are outlined in the following section.

## Intervention Strategies to Prevent Child Maltreatment

Numerous strategies are employed to prevent and treat child maltreatment. Since these have been described in the preceding chapters, we will only briefly outline the types of programs that have been devised. Then we will examine them in relation to the risk and protective factors previously delineated, and discuss them with regard to principles developed from experience in the field of early childhood intervention.

Programs designed to prevent and treat child maltreatment are as diverse as the etiological factors associated with its occurrence. In fact, just as risk and protective factors that influence the likelihood of maltreatment can be organized in an ecological framework, so, too, can existing prevention and treatment programs. For example, primary and secondary preventions at each of the ecological levels include, on the ontogenetic level, stress management skills training (Egan, 1983) and job search assistance (Lutzker, Welsch, & Rice, 1984) programs. On the microsystem level there have been efforts to enhance the quantity and quality of interactions between mothers and their newborns (O'Connor, Vietze, Sherrod, Sandler, & Altemeier, 1980; Kempe, 1978), and home health visitors have been used to provide social and medical support to parents from high-risk groups (Olds & Henderson, in press; Siegel, Bauman, Schafer, Saunders, & Ingram, 1980). On the exosystem level programs to facilitate informal community supports (Pancoast, 1980), and develop social and health services in communities (Cohn, 1982) have been implemented; and on the macrosystem level, national campaigns have been conducted to affect public awareness about the problem of child abuse and influence attitudes about corporal punishment.

In addition to these prevention strategies, tertiary/treatment interventions at each ecological level include the use of various individual-oriented therapeutic interventions (i.e., Connor, 1987; Galdston, 1975), home safety skills training programs (Lutzker et al., 1984), efforts to locate foster and adoptive homes for abused children (Rosenstein, 1978), and the establishment of a federal agency to coordinate child maltreatment services (Child Abuse Prevention Act, 1974). Table 12.2 contains a comprehensive list of prevention and treatment strategies organized using the ecological framework. Many of these intervention ideas reflect the suggestions of a National Conference that was held in Philadelphia in 1978 (Gerbner, Ross, & Zigler, 1980).

Since the causes of child maltreatment are not independent, an intervention that focusses on one cause is apt to influence other causes as well (Cohn, Gray, & Wald, 1984). Nonetheless, we agree with others (i.e., Helfer, 1982; Morse, Hyde, Newberger, & Reed, 1977; Olds, & Henderson, in press; Rosenberg & Reppucci, 1985), that the best prevention and intervention strategies are multifaceted.

For example, the home-visitation program developed by Olds and his colleagues (1986; 1987) for single, low-income, expectant mothers has three components: parent education concerning fetal and infant development; enhancement of the informal supports available by encouraging friends and relatives to be involved in the home visits; and the linkage of family members with other formal health and human services including day care, health care, and job training opportunities.

TABLE 12.2  Prevention and Intervention Strategies

| Ontogenetic Level | Microsystem Level | Exosystem Level | Macrosystem Level |
|---|---|---|---|
| Psychotherapeutic interventions for abusive parents (Galdston, 1975) | Marital counseling (Lutzker, et al., 1984) | Develop community social and health services (Cohn, 1982) | Campaigns to increase public awareness (Cohn, 1982) |
| Treatment programs for abused children (Connor, 1987) | Home safety training (Lutzker et al., 1984) | Crisis hotlines (Johnston, 1976) | Formation of NCCAN grants for research |
| Alcohol and drug rehabilitation (Lutzker, Wesch, Rice, 1984) | Health visitors (Olds & Henderson, in press) | Training Professionals to Identify Abuse (Loadman & Vaughn, 1986) | Establishment of a National Commission on Child Abuse and Neglect |
| Stress management skills training (Egan, 1983) | Enhancement of parent-infant contact and interactions (O'Connor et al., 1980) | Location of foster and adoptive homes (Rosenstein, 1978) | Require states to adopt procedures for the prevention, treatment, and identification of maltreatment (Child Abuse Prevention and Treatment Act of 1974) |
| Job search assistance (Lutzker et al., 1984) | Parents aids programs (Adnopoz et al., 1987) | Facilitate informal community supports (Pancoast, 1980) | |
| | Education for parenthood programs (Zigler, 1980) | Establish family planning centers (Cohn, 1982) | Legislative efforts to combat poverty (Albee, 1980) |
| | Parenting skills training (Wolfe & Harlon, 1984) | Establish coordinating agency for child maltreatment services (Shay, 1980) | Establish laws against corporal punishment in the schools (Zigler, 1980) |
| | | Parents anonymous groups (Lieber, 1983) | Research incidence maltreatment and effectiveness of prevention & treatments (Zigler, 1980) |
| | | Respite child care facilities (Cohn, 1981) | |

Recent evaluations (Olds, 1987; Olds et al., 1986) suggest that the program succeeded in improving the birth weight and gestation age of the children born to smokers and young adolescent mothers; enhancing participants' informal social supports; and promoting increased use of community services. Twenty-four months postpartum, nurse-visited homes were equipped with more appropriate play materials, program participants were observed to punish their children less frequently; and among the subsample of women most at risk for parenting problems (i.e., women with multiple risks—unwed, young, and poor), fewer incidents of verified child abuse and/or neglect were reported. Forty-six months postpartum, nurse-visited women had fewer subsequent pregnancies and were more likely to have worked during the follow-up time period than comparison mothers.

The effectiveness of the home-visitation program was enhanced by: the use of multiple, ecologically sensitive prevention strategies; the coordination of program services with existing community services; and the provision of continuous, long-term assistance. These three ingredients are essential for successful intervention with high-risk families—especially the last of these three aspects.

There was a time in the field of early childhood intervention when people believed that short-term improvements in a chronically depriving situation could have long-term benefits. As Zigler and Berman stated (1983):

> Development is a continuous process; experiences at any given age are affected by and built on experiences that have come before. . . . Intervention at later stages of life can no more wipe out a history of disadvantage than can a brief early intervention inoculate a child against continuing disadvantage. . . . The most successful intervention should comprise a series of dovetailed programs, independently available as the need requires, with each appropriate for a particular stage of development—prenatal, infancy and toddlerhood, preschool and early elementary school years, middle childhood, and adolescence.

The majority of prevention efforts targeting neglect and physical abuse incorporate at least one of the three ingredients which we feel are essential for successful intervention. Attempts at sexual abuse prevention, however, have taken a divergent course. Almost all sexual abuse prevention interventions focus on teaching children how to say *No!* (see Conte, Rosen, & Saperstein, 1984, for a review). In fact, there are over 100 such prevention programs marketed nationally (Krugman, 1985). In the next section, the goals of these programs are considered in relation to what is known about the prevalence and nature of child sexual abuse (p. 898).

### Child Sexual Abuse Prevention

Prevalence rates of sexual abuse vary greatly. Finkelhor (1984) estimates that 12% of all adults were sexually abused before the age of 16. This rate was computed defining sexual abuse as forced intercourse, attempted intercourse, oral-genital contact, fondling of the sex organs, fondling of body parts through clothing, exhibitionism, and unwanted sexual requests. When the latter three categories, which have different social policy implications than the first four, are removed from the analysis, the rate of sexual exploitation drops to 5%. Although the true rate of sexual abuse is difficult to obtain for methodological reasons, including the identification of abuse victims and production of a representative sample of respondents, it is likely that the actual rate of sexual abuse is not nearly as high as some researchers (i.e., Dubowitz, 1986) and the popular press suggest.

Many parents are convinced of the importance of prevention programs by being told that more than 80% of all sexually abused children are exploited by someone they know. While there is research to support this claim (Gomes-Schwartz, 1984), information concerning the pervasiveness of sexually abusive experiences is equivocal, and findings on the effectiveness of child-focussed prevention efforts are highly questionable.

Child sexual abuse prevention programs that teach children to say *No!* have been shown to promote disclosure among children who have been abused (Garbarino, 1987), but beyond this, few positive gains have been noted. Content analyses of program materials suggest that younger children have difficulty understanding the prevention self-defense concepts (Conte, Rosen, Sapersten, & Shermack, 1983), and follow-up studies show that there is significant reduction in retention of prevention material two months after program completion (Plummer, 1984). In one evaluation study, 94% of the children could define assertiveness after prevention training, and only 47% could give an example of an assertive reply to a puppet role-played abusive situation (Downer, 1984). Moreover, in another study, when children were asked about experiences of inappropriate touches that occurred in the 6 months after program completion, both experimental and control groups reported such experiences (Kolko, Moser, Litz, & Hughes, in press). Although no systematic investigations have been conducted to evaluate possible negative consequences, particularly fear and anxiety, "Anecdotal evidence suggests that some children in some programs may have at least temporary (if not permanent) negative reactions as a result of prevention" (Conte, 1984, p. 5).

### Prevention Strategy Assumptions and Cautions

There are at least three implicit assumptions in a strategy designed to teach children to resist inappropriate advances. 1) There is widespread belief that all children are at equal and serious risk of sexual exploitation. Some groups of children and families have been shown to have increased prevalence rates of sexual abuse (i.e., single-parent families, step-families, children of teen mothers). An alternative to universal prevention programming would be to offer intervention services to these groups. 2) The most effective approach to prevention efforts is to educate children about the dangers of sexual assault. Since many children are sexually exploited by strangers and neighbors while their parents are at work, and 2 million children between the ages of 7 and 12 return home from school to an empty house (Congressional Record, January, 1979), an alternative way to protect children in this situation is to establish and extend after-school programs. Such programs would not only decrease the risk of sexual abuse, but also help prevent accidents that often occur when children are unsupervised. 3) Children should be responsible for preventing their own sexual exploitation. Most programs based on this assumption attempt to teach children strategies to discourage offenders. Since adults have the ability to outwit or physically overpower children, and 84% or more of all advances by adults involve some form of manipulation, threat, and/or use of aggression (Gomes-Schwartz, 1984), assertiveness training for children seems a futile endeavor. Adults must accept responsibility for protecting children and keeping other adults' behavior within appropriate bounds. They have a much greater capacity to achieve this aim than children.

Although a few novel approaches to the prevention of sexual abuse have recently been suggested (i.e., Gilgun & Gordon, 1985; Jenny, Sutherland, & Sandahl, 1986; Ounce of Prevention Fund, 1987), the child assertiveness training bandwagon continues to receive widespread support. Ways to revise and expand these programs are currently being considered. For example, Conte, Rosen, and Saperstein (1984) suggest that:

> As professionals' experience increases with sexually abused children, new prevention content (for programs) is identified. For example, the limited amount of information available about the Manhattan Beach California Day Care abuse case suggests new concepts which should be taught children to debunk the lies, manipulations, and coercions adults use to engage and maintain children in sexual abuse. It appears that one of the things we need to teach children is how to overcome the fear created by watching small living animals crushed to death before their eyes and being told that the same thing would happen to their parents if they told about the sexual abuse (p. 15).

Given the available anecdotal evidence about childrens' reactions to these prevention programs as they exist, intensifying their content as suggested above seems inadvisable. It is dangerous to assume that prevention strategies will have only positive or, at worse, neutral consequences. The long-term follow-up of the Cambridge-Somerville Project, a classic early example of preventive work, attests to the need to heed this caution (McCord, 1978). This program provided prevention-oriented counseling to a group of randomly selected adolescents judged to be at risk for serious delinquency. At long-term follow-up, program participants were more likely than individuals excluded from the intervention to have continued criminal activity and show evidence of alcoholism and mental illness. While we all want to *Do something!* to prevent child sexual abuse, prevention strategies must be designed judiciously, or those intended to be aided by the prevention may end up adversely affected.

**Summary**

In this section, the prevention of child maltreatment was defined to include primary, secondary, and tertiary intervention efforts. Many different prevention strategies were outlined, and the need to design preventions judiciously was highlighted by a discussion of current sexual abuse prevention strategies. Child maltreatment is a complex phenomenon. Its prevention requires coordinated, ecologically sensitive, multifaceted, and continuous programming efforts. In order for the relative effectiveness of competing intervention strategies to be determined, however, systematic evaluations must be conducted.

In the next section, evaluation and other child maltreatment research issues are discussed.

## CHILD MALTREATMENT RESEARCH

Program development must be guided by studies on the etiology and sequelae of child maltreatment, and the effectiveness of different prevention and intervention strategies. Research on the causes and effects of maltreatment suggest target populations and problems for intervention efforts, and the results of evaluation studies determine the most effective intervention programs. In this section, issues pertinent to program evaluation will be discussed, together with some of the basic and applied uses of the findings of child maltreatment sequelae research.

### Evaluation Studies

Most of the research on the effectiveness of different prevention (Garbarino, 1986) and intervention (Wald, Carlsmith, Leiderman, de Sales French, & Smith, 1986) efforts have produced equivocal findings. Since the risk and protective factors associated with the etiology of maltreatment also influence the likelihood of a given intervention strategy being successful, it is not surprising that mixed results have emerged. Future investigators need to address questions not only about what works, but for whom, how, and why (Zigler & Weiss, 1985). Studies looking for simple main effects—Does the program work or not?—are bound to produce conflicting results. In this section, a number of methodological considerations associated with the design of evaluation studies are discussed. For an in-depth treatment of evaluation research issues, readers are referred to Guttentag & Struening (1975) and Struening & Guttentag (1975).

### Program Documentation

Before beginning an evaluation study, the goals and the means developed to achieve the objectives of the intervention program should be clearly delineated (Twain, 1975). The congruence between intended and actual program operations can then be examined. Since many intervention strategies are tailored to meet the needs of individual participating families, differential treatment histories of experimental and comparison subjects must be carefully monitored (Lorion, 1983). In addition, staff-client ratios, staff training and supervisory procedures, and the nature of interagency contacts—factors which may impact on the quality of services received and influence the success of replication attempts—should also be documented.

## Experimental Design

Random assignment of experimental and comparison subjects is one of the strongest research procedures for determining treatment effects. The necessity of withholding services to parents in need, however, is an obstacle to using this type of experimental design in prevention and intervention programming efforts (Seitz, 1987). Although experimental and comparison subjects have been randomly chosen in some investigations (i.e., Olds, Henderson, Chamberlain, & Tatelbaum, 1986), once there is sufficient reason to believe that a given intervention is sufficiently effective that withholding it may have adverse consequences, the use of this type of research procedure becomes increasingly questionable. As an alternative, a number of quasi-experimental designs can be implemented, such as treatment partitioning, which involves random assignment of subjects to alternative treatment programs; time-lag procedures, which involve identifying control subjects before a program is implemented, while it is in operation ("waiting list" controls), or after it is discontinued; or drawing subjects for comparison groups from neighboring communities that do not have comparable service facilities (See Cook & Campbell, 1979; and Seitz, 1987 for further discussion).

## Sampling Considerations

In evaluation studies, large samples are needed in order to reach meaningful empirical conclusions, since the magnitude of program effects may be obscured by variability within the experimental and comparison groups. This variability within groups increases the error term used in statistical analyses and makes it more difficult to detect program effects. When longitudinal, follow-up data is desired, loss of subjects due to attrition should be anticipated. For example, one 18-month follow-up study of confirmed sexual abuse cases lost nearly 20% of their subjects due to attrition. Some families refused to continue contacts with researchers, and others simply could not be found despite extensive staff efforts to track changes of address and telephone numbers (Gomes-Schwartz, 1984). This rate of subject loss is comparable to, and somewhat lower than those reported by other investigators (Powell, 1987). Research samples should be large enough to accommodate these expected losses.

In addition to sample size, numerous subject characteristics must also be considered in evaluation studies. Since not all maltreating families are the same, it is likely that interventions will be more or less effective with families that exhibit different forms of maltreatment and possess different strengths (protective factors) and weaknesses (risk factors). Demographic characteristics of program participants should be well documented, and maltreatment related variables such as type, duration, and severity must also be obtained. In addition, potential mediating variables, such as parental alcohol or drug abuse, psychiatric illness, or mental retardation should also be assessed. Although experimental and comparison subjects can only be matched on a few of these variables, assessing these potential sources of variation will increase the interpretability of research findings, and help to account for successful and non-successful intervention outcomes.

The one variable that experimental and comparison subjects are most often matched on is socioeconomic status (SES). While this helps to remove a number of sources of nonexperimental variation within and between groups, it also obscures the impact of environmental factors on the lives of program participants. Consequently, it sometimes is advisable to employ a three-group research design, including a target/maltreatment group which will be predominantly low SES, a demographically matched low SES comparison group, and a middle SES comparison group (i.e., Aber & Allen, 1987). Use of the two comparison groups permits an analysis of the independent effects of programming efforts and environmental factors on outcome measures. For example, a given intervention may reduce the incidence of nutritional and medical neglect within a high-risk sample, but this reduced rate may still exceed the rate of these types of neglect within more advantaged populations, highlighting the need for more aggressive interventions.

## Outcome Criteria

Evaluation studies of preventive interventions should assess both anticipated direct and indirect effects (Zigler & Berman, 1983). The anticipated direct effect of most prevention efforts is a reduction of child maltreatment. This can be assessed in terms of a reduction in incidence or a reduction in severity (Garbarino, 1986). Accurate measurements of incidence, however, are difficult if not impossible to obtain, since reported incidents of child maltreatment (Gelles & Straus, 1985) and maltreatment related deaths (Jason, Carpenter, & Tyler, 1983) are known to be inaccurate. Furthermore, the true and reported incidence of maltreatment may be positively related under some conditions, negatively related under others, and unrelated under still others (Garbarino, 1986). For example, significant increases in child abuse reporting are associated with increases in public awareness and coordination of treatment programs within a community (Barth & Schlesler, 1985). Does this mean prevention and treatment efforts lead to increases in the incidence of abuse? In all probability, it does not.

There are no guaranteed methods to obtain an accurate assessment of incidence trends, but multiple sources including hospital records, state registries, and private agencies files should be assessed. Direct interviews with parents can be conducted as well, and indicators of both decreased incidence and reduced severity should be examined.

The direct effects anticipated by different prevention programs will vary according to the particular goals of the intervention effort. Whether the goal of the intervention is health care or home safety, multiple indices of project outcome should be obtained to correct for reporter bias (Cowen, 1978). Both program participants and service providers, albeit for different reasons, are subject to producing biased response sets. Obtaining data from multiple sources permits analyses of discrepancies and increases the interpretability of empirical findings. In addition to specific target outcomes, a number of the indirect effects may result from intervention, as well. Changes in life stress (i.e., Egeland, 1986), social supports (i.e., Barrera, 1980), or parenting attitudes (i.e., Newberger & Cook, 1983) can be assessed as possible indirect effects of interventions. Inclusion of these types of variables in outcome studies may suggest mechanisms by which programming effects are achieved and maintained. While no study can assess all possible outcome criteria, some direct and indirect effects should be examined, with the choice of constructs to be assessed dictated by the focus of the intervention and the characteristics of program participants.

### Data Analysis

Since simple main effects of program benefits are not likely to be observed consistently, the impact of multiple risk and protective factors on treatment effectiveness should be tested statistically according to specific hypotheses. For example, it might be hypothesized that families experiencing greater numbers of stressful life events will benefit less from intervention efforts than families whose lives are less chaotic. In addition, the quality of the families' social supports may be expected to mediate the impact of the life stresses and improve program effectiveness. Path analytic techniques can be used to test these and other competing hypotheses. In addition, tests for unidirectional and bidirectional effects, direct and indirect effects, and spurious effects due to correlations among the independent variables can also be conducted (Pedhazur, 1982).

### Summary

There is no such thing as a *quick and dirty* study in the area of child maltreatment research. Evaluation studies are difficult and time consuming to conduct. To avoid obtaining uninterpretable results, however, researchers should anticipate equivocal findings and assess potential mediating factors so variation in intervention effectiveness can be explained.

### MALTREATMENT SEQUELAE RESEARCH

In the recent past, child maltreatment was criticized for its isolation from other more developed research areas (Zigler, 1976). The use of traditional research paradigms has improved the quality of child maltreatment research and increased the interpretability of empirical findings.

Research in the area of child maltreatment has important theoretical and practical implications. While studies are needed to identify targets of intervention efforts, research in this area can also help enhance our understanding of normal and atypical developmental processes—especially those associated with the etiology of psychiatric disorders (Cicchetti & Rizley, 1981). In this section, findings of studies on the sequelae of maltreatment are briefly reviewed, and then the theoretical and practical implications of research in this area are discussed.

It is only within the past 10 years that systematic investigations have been conducted to determine the effects of maltreatment on children's socio-emotional development (Aber & Cicchetti, 1984). Many of these studies were guided by an organismic perspective (Sroufe, 1979), which views development as a series of qualitative reorganizations among and within behavioral and biological systems. Within this perspective, healthy development is defined in terms of inter-related social, emotional, and cognitive competencies. Specific issues, similar to those outlined by Erikson (1950), are believed to be related to each developmental period, and competent functioning at one stage is believed to increase the likelihood of successful adaptation in the future (see Cicchetti & Schneider-Rosen, 1986, for further discussion).

In accordance with this view, a number of studies have evaluated maltreated children's functioning using age-appropriate, stage-salient assessment procedures. Studies have investigated the quality of maltreated children's attachment relationship to their primary caregiver in infancy (Egeland & Sroufe, 1981; Schneider-Rosen, Braunwald, Carlson, & Cicchetti, 1985), development of self and autonomous functioning in toddlerhood, (Egeland & Sroufe, 1981; Schneider-Rosen & Cicchetti, 1984), and peer relations (Kaufman & Cicchetti, in press) and effectance motivation during the early school-aged years (Aber & Allen, 1987). In all these studies, maltreated children were found to be significantly impaired.

Although most of these studies were cross-sectional in design, when children were studied over time the adverse sequelae cited above were also evidenced at each developmental stage (Egeland, Sroufe, & Erickson, 1984). In addition, a continuity of adaptation was observed, such that those children who were maladjusted at one point in time were most likely to be maladjusted in the future. The quality of a child's attachment relationship to their primary caregiver in infancy was one of the best predictors of child functioning during the preschool years (Farber & Egeland, 1987).

It has been suggested that internal working models of attachment relationships experienced in infancy play a significant role in personality development (Bowlby, 1973; Bretherton, 1985). Variations in attachment relations and their corresponding internal schemata have been evoked to explain the process by which maltreating experiences lead to adverse developmental sequelae. Organismic theorists, however, recognize genetic, biochemical, and neurological, as well as psychological and environmental influences on development. Whether genetic, biochemical, or neurological factors can also explain the observed adverse developmental outcomes of maltreated children cannot be determined, however, because these factors were not assessed in any of the studies cited above. It is likely that all these factors interact in complex ways to produce the observed deviant outcomes.

For example, studies with nonhuman primates (Hofer, 1987; Reite, 1987) and infants (Tennes, 1982) have shown that disturbances in attachment relations produce significant physiological as well as behavioral consequences. These studies have found that early mother-infant interactions are important for the regulation of numerous infant biological systems, including the regulation of neurochemical and neuroendocrine secretions.

Abnormalities in these secretions have been implicated in the etiology of many psychosocial and psychiatric disorders, and abnormalities in these secretions have also been linked to genetic factors and inherent or environmentally induced (i.e., through physical assault) neurological impairments (Ciaranello, 1983). Whether or not genetic, biochemical, and neurological deficits are implicated in the etiology of the pathology shown by maltreated children can only be determined if their influences are simultaneously investigated together with standard psychosocial measures. It is likely, as stated previously, that these factors interact in complex ways with psychological variables, such as an individual's internal working models of relationships, to produce adverse developmental sequelae. For example, a history of abuse (Garbarino & Plantz, 1984; Lewis, Shanok, Pincus, & Glaser, 1979), lower socioeconomic status (Robins, 1966), genetic (Hutchings & Mednick, 1975), and neurological (Lewis et al., 1979) factors have all been implicated in the etiology of juvenile delinquency. In order to better understand the independent and interactive effects of these factors, however, it is necessary to conduct prospective longitudinal investigations which assess multiple influences on development.

Despite shortcomings in elucidating the processes by which adverse developmental outcomes are obtained, the results of child maltreatment sequelae research have suggested a number of targets for prevention and intervention strategies including efforts to improve mother-child attachment relations (i.e., Siegel et al., 1980) and use of peer-oriented therapeutic interventions for maltreated children (Connor, 1987). Examination of the affects of multiple risks and protective factors on child outcomes will also help to identify and/or confirm other targets for intervention efforts. For example, assessments of perinatal risk may help explain variation in the outcome of maltreated children, such that those children who were brought into the world the most constitutionally vulnerable may be found to be the subgroup of maltreated children who later in childhood appear most adversely affected by experiences of abuse and neglect. This finding would further substantiate the value of prenatal and perinatal care and home health visitor programs.

## Summary

Studies on the sequelae of child maltreatment can enhance understandings of developmental psychopathology and inform intervention policy planning.

In order to maximally accomplish these aims, however, prospective longitudinal multidisciplinary studies, which incorporate assessments of risk and protective factors at numerous levels of analysis, must be conducted.

## CHILD MALTREATMENT: A MACROSYSTEM PERSPECTIVE

The majority of prevention and intervention strategies discussed focus on the ontogenetic, microsystem, and exosystem levels. Child maltreatment, however, occurs within a greater social context, highlighting the need for macrosystem level interventions as well. Worsening economic conditions (Elder, Liker, & Cross, 1984) and increases in poverty (Pelton, 1978) are two macrosystem factors that have been repeatedly implicated in the etiology of maltreatment. Although most poor people do not maltreat their children, and poverty, per se, does not *cause* abuse and neglect, the correlates of poverty, including stress, drug abuse, and inadequate resources for food and medical care, increase the likelihood of maltreatment. In this section, we consider current poverty trends, additional social problems affected by poverty increases, and relevant macrosystem level interventions.

### Poverty Trends

In the current economic market, a job is no longer a guarantee against poverty. Recent estimates suggest that two million parents working full time live in poverty (Heintz, 1987), and the number of employed men between the ages of 20 and 24 earning enough money to keep a family of three above the poverty line has dropped to 42%, from 60% in 1963. Since 1974, the proportion of young workers employed in manufacturing jobs has declined 25%, while the percentage of young adults working lower paying service jobs increased 20%. It is estimated that the earnings of young men have dropped nearly 30% between 1973 and 1984; and while all groups have been affected by these changes, Black youths have suffered the most severely, with earning losses approaching 50% (Children's Defense Fund, May, 1987).

Economic trends leading to the reduction of male earning power, together with numerous other social and economic factors have resulted in drastic increases in poverty rates. The most recent Census Bureau reports suggest that 13.6% of all persons in the United States, and 22% of all children under the age of six, are below the poverty line (Bureau of Census, 1987). Of households headed by a mother younger than 25, three out of four are poor (Children's Defense Fund, January, 1987).

### Social Problems Associated with Increases in Poverty

Worsening economic conditions and increases in poverty rates are not only associated with increases in child maltreatment. Basic skills and educational deficits (Children's Defense Fund, May, 1987), teen pregnancy (Children's Defense Fund, January, 1987), and infant prematurity and low birth weight (Miller, 1987)—also associated with increases in poverty—are additional problems currently receiving a lot of political attention. Links among these problems, and between these problems and child maltreatment have also been documented.

Figure 12.1 illustrates the relationship among various social problems. As can be seen in the diagram, in some cases the relationships between the problems is unidirectional; in other cases it is bidirectional. References accompanying the diagram highlight the association among the depicted social problems, and report magnitude when reliable estimates could be obtained.

The purpose of depicting these relationships is not to get lost in a quagmire of statistical associations, but to highlight that the problem of child maltreatment prevention must be considered in a context with other pertinent social issues. Solutions to these problems are rarely conceived in conjunction with one another; however, programs aimed at lowering poverty rates can help to reduce the incidence of child maltreatment, and have impact on other social problems at the same time.

## Macrosystem Interventions Aimed at Poverty

The Welfare Reform acts of the House and the Senate are the most relevant legislative acts aimed at poverty under consideration at this writing. In this section we will discuss the intent of these bills, an outcome study on the effectiveness of the New York State Welfare Reform program, a program similar to the programs outlined in the House and Senate bills, and some problems in achieving the aims of these proposals.

The House of Representatives and the Senate Welfare Reform bills are similar. The acts do not claim to be the solution to all the problems of the current welfare system, but rather a "foundation for systematic change by making an investment in America's poor families." The legislators recognize that the "investment will cost money now . . . (but it is) . . . expected to save money in the long run as it creates a future of hope and economic independence for many of America's poor children" (Family Welfare Reform Act of 1987, H.R. 1720).

Both the House and Senate bills contain a mandatory welfare-to-jobs component, provisions for training and remedial education of welfare recipients, subsidies for child care expenses, work incentives which allow families to exclude a portion of their earned income from their net income in calculating eligibility for partial government assistance, transitional health care benefits to families leaving the welfare program, plans to extend eligibility of aid to two-parent families, and measures to determine paternity and enforce child support to reduce the cost of federally funded child assistance. Although a similar voluntary welfare-to-jobs program in Massachusetts, the Employment and Training Choices (E-T) Program, has placed 30,000 recipients in full-

1. One-third of all teens that give birth rely on the welfare system for support (Children's Defense Fund, January, 1987).

2. Prior to the birth of their first child, approximately half of all teen mothers are in the lowest quartile on measures of socioeconomic standing (Broman, 1981).

3. Child maltreatment rates are approximately 50% higher in working class families (Straus, 1979) and 300% higher in families with incomes below the poverty line than they are in middle income families (Pelton, 1978).

4. Women in the lowest social classes have a 50% greater risk of a preterm birth, and a 95% greater chance of a low birthweight delivery (British, 1978).

5. One-half of all poor youth have basic reading and writing skills in the bottom fifth among their age group (Children's Defense Fund, May, 1987).

6. Youths 20–24 years old with skills in the bottom fifth for their age group are five times more likely to be out of work than youths with average skills (Children's Defense Fund, May 1987).

7. Teen mothers are approximately two times more likely to maltreat their children than older, more economically advantaged mothers (Broman, 1981).

8. A disproportiate number of adolescent mothers report experiences of sexual victimization as children (Ounce of Prevention, 1987).

9. Infant prematurity has been identified as a risk factor for child maltreatment (Hunter, Kilstrom, Kraybill, & Loda, 1978).

10. Although 17% of all births are to teenagers, infants of teens comprise 24% of all low weight births (National Center for Health Statistics, 1980).

11. Of all teens that have babies, 61% will never finish high school (Children's Defense Fund, January, 1987).

12. Teens with poor basic skills are five times more likely to become mothers before 16 than those with average skills (Children's Defense Fund, January, 1987).

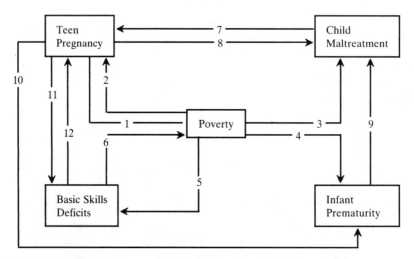

**Figure 12.1.** Interrelationships among social problems associated with poverty.

time jobs and reduced its caseload 4% in three years, much can go wrong in programs of this kind without proper planning, as a study of New York City's welfare-to-jobs initiatives demonstrates (Sebestal & Sklar, 1987).

New York City's Employment Opportunities (EO) Program for Welfare recipients required all employable, able-bodied adults whose children were 6 years of age or older to participate in job training or employment activities. No additional funds were provided, however, to assure proper implementation and administration of programming efforts. The results were disastrous. Caseworkers were insufficiently trained on the details of the program, and staffing shortages left caseworkers responsible for processing 27 clients a day. Clients, consequently, received minimal orientation to the program and inadequate screening to determine the most appropriate training or work assignment. Most recipients were given workfare assignments which provided minimal training experience. Although 80% of participants received evaluations of *good* or *excellent* from workfare supervisors, only 3% of workfare assignments lead to unsubsidized jobs. In addition, sanctions leading to termination and grant reductions were applied indiscriminately and often unlawfully, as is evident by the fact that 98% of all Fair Hearings involving work-related sanctions produced decisions favorable to the recipient. (Fair Hearings typically favor recipients in 50% of all cases.) Shortages in appropriate training slots and adequate daycare provisions were also noted. There were 10,000 slots for individuals to receive intensive remediation and 38,000 recipients in need of such training; and an estimated 25,000 daycare and after-school care positions available for the 50,000 children in need of such supervision (Sebestal & Sklar, 1987).

Considerable planning and resources are required if the federal welfare-to-jobs program is to avoid the pitfalls of the New York program. Without such efforts, those intended to be aided by the program may end up most adversely affected. Shattered parental hopes, inadequate child care facilities, and sanctions leading to grant terminations of family aid bode poorly for the children of the mothers mandated to participate in the welfare-to-jobs program. Rather than increase the "hope and economic independence" of America's poor children and help prevent child maltreatment by reducing poverty, the proposed Welfare Reform bills may inadvertently victimize the children it proposes to help.

Each new program must incorporate what has been learned from the failures of its predecessors. Although an appreciation of the types of problems that can arise when attempting to promote social change can lead to inaction, poverty, child maltreatment, and the other social problems previously discussed cannot be prevented through inaction. Social change requires systematic, comprehensive, and relentless efforts.

## CONCLUSION

In order for the goal of child maltreatment prevention to be achieved, ecologically sensitive, multifaceted, and continuous intervention programs must be utilized. Each well-intentioned intervention will not be successful, but through well-designed evaluations, the effectiveness of future efforts can be increased, and the hiatus that separates the intention and realization of prevention aims can be diminished.

## REFERENCES

Aber, L. & Allen, J. (1987). Effects of maltreatment of young children's socioemotional development: An attachment theory perspective. *Developmental Psychology, 23*, 406–414.

Aber, L. & Zigler, E. (1981). Developmental considerations in the definition of child maltreatment. In R. Rizely & D. Cicchetti (Eds.), Developmental Perspectives on Child Maltreatment. New Directions for Child Development (Vol. 11). San Francisco: Jossey-Bass Inc., Publishers.

Adnopoz, J., Nagler, S. & Sinanaglu, P. (1987). The family support Service: Servicing families in crisis. Paper submitted for publication. *American Journal of Orthopsychiatry.*

Albee, G. (1980). Primary prevention and social problems. In G. Gerbner, C. Ross, E. Zigler (Eds.), Child Abuse: An Agenda for Action. New York: Oxford University Press.

Alvy, K. T. (1975). Preventing Child Abuse. *American Psychologist, 30*, 921–928.

Altemeier, W., O'Connor, S., Vietze, P., Sandler, H., & Sherrod, K. (1984). Prediction of Child Abuse: A Prospective Study of Feasibility. *Child Abuse and Neglect, 8*, 393–400.

*American Psychologist.* Special issue on emotional maltreatment. Volume 42, 1987.

Barrera, M. (1980). A method for the assessment of social support networks in community survey research. *Connections, 3*, 8–13.

Barth, R. & Schlesler, D. (1985). Comprehensive sexual abuse treatment programs and reports of sexual abuse. *Children and Youth Services Review, 7*, 285–298.

Belsky, J. (1980). Child maltreatment: An ecological integration. *American Psychologist, 35*, 320–335.

Bowlby, J. (1973). Attachment and Loss: Vol. 2 Separation. New York: Basic.

Bretherton, I. (1987). Attachment Theory: Retrospect and Prospect. In I. Bretherton & E. Waters (Eds.) Growing Points in Attachment: Theory and Research. Monographs of the Society for Research in Child Development. Series #209. Volume 50.

Bronfenbrenner, U. (1977). Toward an experimental ecology of human development. *American Psychologist, 32*, 513–531.

Bronfenbrenner, U. (1979). *The ecology of human development.* Cambridge, MA: Harvard University Press.

Bureau of the Census. March, 1987. *Money income and poverty status of families and persons in the United States.* U.S. Department of Commerce.

*A children's defense budget: An analysis of our nation's investment in children.* Children's Defense Fund, 1987.

Children's Defense Fund. (January, 1987). *Adolescent pregnancy: An anatomy of a social problem in search of comprehensive solutions.*

Children's Defense Fund. (May, 1987). *Declining earnings of young men: Their relation to poverty, teen pregnancy, and family formation.*

Ciaranello, R. (1983). Neurochemical aspects of stress. In N. Garmezy & M. Rutter (Eds.), *Stress, coping, and development in children.* New York: McGraw Hill.

Cicchetti, D., & Rizley, R. (1981). Developmental perspectives on the etiology, intergenerational transmission, and sequelae of child maltreatment. *New Directions for Child Maltreatment, 11,* 31–55.

Cicchetti, D., & Schneider-Rosen, K. (1986). An organizational approach to childhood depression. In M. Rutter, C. Izard & P. Read (Eds.), *Depression in children: Developmental perspectives.* New York: Guilford Press.

Cohen, S., Gray, E., & Wald, M. (1984). *Preventing child maltreatment: A review of what we know.* Chicago, National Committee for Prevention of Child Abuse.

Cohn, A. (1981). *An approach to preventing child abuse.* Chicago, National Committee for Prevention of Child Abuse.

Cohn, A. (1982). Stopping abuse before it occurs: Different solutions for different population groups. *Child Abuse and Neglect, 6,* 473–483.

Cook, T., & Campbell, D. (1979). *Quasi-experimental design and analysis issues for field settings.* Chicago: Rand McNally.

*Congressional Record,* January 15, 1979. S76–S77.

Connor, M. (1987). *Treatment programs for abused children.* NCPCA Working Paper No. 37. Chicago: National Committee for Prevention of Child Abuse.

Conte, J. (1984). Research on the prevention of sexual abuse of children. Paper presented at Second National Conference of Family Violence Researchers. Durham, NH, August 7–10, 1984.

Conte, J., Rosen, C., & Saperstein, L. (1984, September). *An analysis of programs to prevent the sexual victimization of children.* Paper presented at the Fifth International Congress on Child Abuse and Neglect, Montreal, Canada.

Conte, J., Rosen, C., Saperstein, L., & Shermack, R. (1983, November). *An evaluation of a program to prevent the sexual victimization of young children.* Paper presented at the National Association of Social Workers Professional Symposium. Washington, DC.

Cowen, E. (1978). Some problems in community program evaluation research. *Journal of Consulting and Clinical Psychology, 46,* 792–805.

Daniel, J., Newberger, E., Reed, R., & Kotelchuck, M. (1978). Child abuse screening: Implications of the limited predictive power of abuse discriminants from a controlled family study of pediatric social illness. *Child Abuse and Neglect, 2,* 247–259.

Daro, D. & Mitchell, L. (1987). *Deaths due to maltreatment soar: The result of the 1986 annual fifty-state survey.* NCPCA Working Paper No. 8. National Committee for Prevention of Child Abuse, Chicago.

Downer, A. (1984). *Evaluation of talking about touching.* Seattle, WA: Committee for Children.

Dubowitz, H. (1986). *Child maltreatment in the United States: Etiology, impact, and prevention.* Background paper prepared for the Congress of the United States, Office of Technology Assessment.

Egan, K. (1983). Stress management and child management with abusive parents. *Journal of Clinical Child Psychology, 12,* 292–299.

Egeland, B. (1986). *Life stress scale and scoring manual.* University of Minnesota. Unpublished manuscript.

Egeland, B., & Sroufe, L. A. (1981). Developmental sequelae of maltreatment in infancy. In R. Rizely & D. Cicchetti (Eds.), *Developmental perspectives on child maltreatment. New directions for child development* (Vol. 11). San Francisco: Jossey-Bass.

Egeland, B., Sroufe, L. A., & Erickson, M. (1984). The developmental consequences of different patterns of maltreatment. *Child Abuse and Neglect, 7,* 459–469.

Elder, G., Liker, J., & Cross, C. (1984). Parent-child behavior in the Great Depression: Life course and intergenerational influences. In P.B. Baltes and O.G. Brim (Eds.), *Life-span development and behavior* (Vol. 6). New York: Academic Press.

Erikson, E. (1950). Childhood and Society. New York: Norton Press.

Farber, E., & Egeland, B. (1987). Invulnerability among abused and neglected children. In E. J. Anthony & B. Cohler (Eds.), *The invulnerable child.* New York: Guilford Press.

Finkelhor, D. (1984). *Child sexual abuse. New theory and research.* New York: The Free Press.

Fontana, V. (1970). *The maltreated child: The maltreatment syndrome in children.* Springfield, IL: Charles C. Thomas.

Galdston, R. (1975). Preventing the abuse of little children: The parents' center project for the study and prevention of child abuse. *American Journal of Orthopsychiatry, 45,* 372–381.

Garbarino, J. (1980). Preventing child maltreatment. In R. Price (Ed.), *Prevention in mental health.* (Vol. 1). Beverly Hills: Sage.

Garbarino, J. (1986). Can we measure success in preventing child abuse? Issues in policy, programming, and research. *Child Abuse and Neglect, 10,* 143–156.

Garbarino, J. & Plantz, M. (1986). Child abuse and juvenile delinquency: What are the links? In J. Garbarino, C. Schellenbach, J. Sebes, and Associates (Eds.), *Troubled youth, troubled families.* New York: Aldine.

Garbarino, J. (1987). Children's response to a sexual abuse prevention program: A study of the *Spiderman* comic. *Child Abuse and Neglect, 11,* 143–148.

Garbarino, J., Guttman, E., & Seeley, J. (1986). The psychologically battered child: Strategies for identification, assessment, and intervention. San Francisco: Jossey-Bass.

Gelles, R. (1984, August). *Applying our knowledge of family violence to prevention and treatment: What difference might it make?* Paper presented to the second National Conference for Family Violence Researchers. Durham, NH.

Gelles, R., & Straus, M. (1985, November). Is violence towards children increasing? Paper presented at the seventh National Conference on Child Abuse and Neglect. Chicago.

Gerbner, G., Ross, C., & Zigler, E. (1980). *Child abuse: An agenda for action.* New York: Oxford University Press.

Gilgun, J., & Gordon, S. (1986). Sex education and the prevention of child sexual abuse. *Journal of Sex Education and Therapy*, *11*, 46–52.

Gomes-Schwartz, B. (1984). Nature of sexual abuse. In B. Gomes-Schwartz (Ed.), *Sexually exploited children: Service and research project*. Draft Final Report. Office of Juvenile Justice and Delinquency Prevention, U.S. Department of Justice, March, 1984.

Gray, J., Cutler, R., Dean, J., & Kempe, C. H. (1976). Perinatal assessment of mother-baby interaction. In R. Helfer & C. H. Kempe (Eds.), *Child abuse and neglect: The family and the community*. Cambridge: Ballinger.

Guttentag, M., & Struening, E. (1975). *Handbook of evaluation research*. (Vol. 1). Beverly Hills: Sage.

Heintz, S. (1987). *Investing in poor families and their children: A matter of commitment*. Final report, Part I: One child in four. A policy development project of the American Public Welfare Association and the National Council of State Human Service Administrators.

Helfer, R. (1982). A review of literature on the prevention of child abuse and neglect. *Child Abuse and Neglect*, *6*, 251–261.

Hofer, M. (1987). Early social relationships: A psychobiologists view. *Child Development*, *58*, 633–647.

Hughes, D., Johnson, K., Rosenbaum, K., Simmons, J. & Burtler, X. (1987). The health of America's children. *Maternal and child health data book*. Washington: Children's Defense Fund.

Hunter, R., Kilstrom, N., Kraybil, E. & Luda, F. (1978). Antecedents of child abuse and neglect in premature infants: A prospective study in a newborn intensive care unit. *Pediatrics*, *161*, 629–635.

Hutchings, B. & Mednick, S. (1975). Registered criminology in the adoptive and biological parents of registered male criminal adoptees. In R. R. Fleve, D. Rosenthal, & H. Brill (Eds.), *Genetic research in psychiatry*. Baltimore: Johns Hopkins University Press.

Jason, J., Carpenter, M., & Tyler, C. (1983). Underrecording of infant homicide in the United States. *American Journal of Public Health*, *73*, 195–197.

Jenny, C., Sutherland, S., & Sandahl, B. (1986). Developmental approach to preventing the sexual abuse of young children. *Pediatrics*, *78*, 1034–1038.

Jenny, C., Sutherland, S., & Sandahl, B. (1986). Developmental approach to preventing the sexual abuse of children. *Pediatrics, 78*, 1034–1038.

Johnston, C. (1976). *The art of the crisis line: A training manual for volunteers in child abuse prevention*. Oakland, CA: Parent-Stress Service, Inc.

Kaufman, J., & Cicchetti, D. (in press). The effects of maltreatment on children's socio-emotional development: Assessments in a day camp setting. *Developmental Psychology*.

Kaufman, J., & Zigler, E. (in press). The intergenerational transmission of child abuse. In D. Cicchetti and V. Carlson (Eds.), *The Handbook of Child Maltreatment*. Cambridge: Cambridge University Press.

Kempe, C. (1978). Child abuse: The pediatricians role. *American Journal of Diseases of Children*, *32*, 1255–1260.

Kempe, C., Silverman, F., Steele, B., Droegemueller, W., & Silver, H. (1962). The battered child syndrome. *Journal of the American Medical Association, 181*, 17–24.

Kolko, D., Moser, J., Litz, J., & Hughes, J. (in press). Promoting awareness and prevention of child sexual victimization using the Red Flag/Green Flag Program: An evaluation with follow-up. *Journal of Family Violence.*

Krugman, R. (1985). Preventing sexual abuse of children in day care: Whose problem is it anyway? *Pediatrics, 69*, 1150–1151.

Lewis, D., Shanok, S., Pincus, J., & Glaser, G. (1979). Violent juvenile delinquents: Psychiatric, neurological, psychological, and abuse factors. *Journal of the American Academy of Child and Adolescent Psychiatry, 18*, 307–319.

Lieber, L. (1983). The self help approach: Parents Anonymous. *Journal of Clinical Child Psychology, 12*, 288–291.

Loadman, W., & Vaughn, M. (1986). Child abuse prevention: implementation and evaluation considerations for the special education professional. *Maladjustment and Therapeutic Education, 4*, 20–28.

Lorion, R. (1983). Evaluating preventive interventions: Guidelines for the serious social change agent. In F. Felner, L. Jason, J. Montsuger, & S. Farber (Eds.), *Preventive Psychology: Theory, Research, and Practice.* New York: Pergamon Press.

Lutzker, J., Welsch, D., & Rice, J. (1984). A review of project 12-Ways: An eco-behavioral approach to the treatment and prevention of child abuse and neglect. *Advances in Behavior Research and Therapy, 6*, 63–73.

Martin, H., & Beezely, P. (1974). Behavioral observations of abused children. *Developmental Medicine and Child Neurology, 19*, 25–73.

McCord, J. (1978). A thirty-year follow-up of treatment effects. *American Psychologist, 33*, 284–289.

Miller, C. (1987, April). *Infancy to adolescence: Opportunities of success.* Hearing Summary, Washington, DC.

Milner, J. S. (1986). *The child abuse potential inventory: Manual* (2nd ed.). Webster, NC: Psytec.

Morse, A., Hyde, J., Newberger, E., & Reed, R. (1977). Environmental correlates of pediatric social illness: Preventive implications of an advocacy approach. *American Journal of Public Health, 67*, 612–615.

Newberger, C., & Cook, S. (1983). Parental awareness and child abuse: A cognitive developmental analysis of urban and rural samples. *American Journal of Orthopsychiatry, 53*, 512–524.

O'Connor, S., Vietze, P., Sherrod, K., Sandler, H., & Altemeier, W. (1980). Reduced incidence of parenting inadequacy following rooming in. *Pediatrics, 66*, 176–182.

Olds, D. (1987, April). *Long-term impact of nurse home-visitation: Time and risk factors as conditioners of program effect.* Paper presented at the biennial meeting of the Society for Research in Child Development, Baltimore, MD.

Olds, D., & Henderson, C. (in press). The prevention of maltreatment. In D. Cicchetti and V. Carlson (Eds.), *The handbook of child maltreatment.* Cambridge: Cambridge University Press.

Olds, D., Henderson, C., Chamberlin, L., & Tatelbaum, R. (1986). Preventing child abuse and neglect: A randomized trial of nurse home visitors. *Pediatrics, 78,* 65–78.

Ounce of Prevention. (1987). *Child sexual abuse: A hidden factor in adolescent sexual behavior.* Chicago: Ounce of Prevention Fund.

Pancoast, A. (1980). Finding and enlisting neighbors to support families. In J. Garbarino & S. Stocking (Eds.), *Protecting children from abuse and neglect.* San Francisco: Jossey-Bass.

Pedhazur, E. (1982). *Multiple regression in behavioral research: Explanation and prediction.* New York: Holt, Rinehart & Winston.

Pelton, L. (1978). Child abuse and neglect: The myth of classlessness. *American Journal of Orthopsychiatry, 48,* 608–617.

Plummer, C. (1984, April). Research prevention: What school programs teach children. Paper presented at the Third National Conference on Sexual Victimization of Children, Washington, DC.

Powell, D. (1987). Methodological and conceptual issues in research. In S. L. Kagan, D. Powell, B. Weissbound, & E. Zigler (Eds.), *America's family support programs: Perspectives and prospects.* New Haven: Yale University Press.

Quinton, D., & Rutter, M. (1984). Long-term follow-up of women institutionalized in childhood: Factors promoting good function in adult life. *British Journal of Developmental Psychology, 2,* 191–204.

Reite, M. (1987). Some additional influences shaping the development of behavior. *Child Development, 58,* 596–600.

Richmond, J., & Janis, J. (1980). Child health, policy, and child abuse. In G. Gerbner, C. Ross, E. Zigler (Eds.), *Child Abuse: An agenda for action.* New York: Oxford University Press.

Rolf, J. (1985). Evolving adaptive theories and methods for prevention research with children. *Journal of Consulting and Clinical Psychology, 53,* 631–646.

Rosenberg, M., & Repucci, N. D. (1985). Primary prevention of child abuse. *Journal of Consulting and Clinical Psychology, 53,* 576–585.

Rosenstein, P. (1978). Family outreach: A program for the prevention of child abuse and neglect. *Child Welfare, 57,* 51–525.

Sacher, E. (1985). Disorders of feeling: Affective diseases. In E. R. Kandel & J. H. Schwartz (Eds.), *Principles of Neural Science.* New York: Elsevier.

Schneider, C., Helfer, R., & Pollock, C. (1972). The predictive questionnaire: A preliminary report. In C. H. Kempe & R. Helfer (Eds.), *Helping the battered child and his family.* Philadelphia: Lippincott.

Schneider, C., Hoffmeister, J., & Helfer, R. (1976). A predictive screening questionnaire for potential problems in mother-infant interaction. In R. Helfer & C. H. Kempe (Eds.), *Child abuse and neglect: The family and the community.* Cambridge: Ballinger.

Schneider-Rosen, K., Braunwald, K., Carlson, V., & Cicchetti, D. (1985). Current perspectives in attachment theory: Illustrations from the study of maltreated children. In I. Bretherton & E. Waters (Eds.), *Growing points in attachment theory and research.* Monographs for the Society for Research in Child Development, Vol. 50.

Schneider-Rosen, K., & Cicchetti, D. (1984). The relationship between affect and cognition in maltreated infants: Quality of attachment and the development of visual self recognition. *Child Development, 55*, 648–658.

Sebestal, F., & Sklar, M. (1987). *Hope or hassle: A study of New York City's Welfare to Work initiative for AFDC recipients.* Rochester, NY: Statewide Youth Advocacy, Inc.

Seitz, V. (1987). Outcome evaluation of family support programs: Research design alternatives to true experiments. In S. L. Kagan, D. Powell, B. Weissbound & E. Zigler (Eds.), *America's family support programs: Perspectives and prospects.* New Haven: Yale University Press.

Select Committee on Children, Youth, and Families. *Abused children in America: Victims of official abuse: A report of the Select Committee on Children, Youth, and Families.* House of Representatives, March 3, 1987.

Shay, S. (1980). Community council for child abuse prevention. In R. Helfer & C. H. Kempe (Eds.), *The battered child.*

Siegel, E., Bauman, K., Scharer, E., Saunders, M., & Ingram, D. (1980). Hospital and home support during infancy: Impact on maternal attachment, child abuse and neglect, and health care utilization. *Pediatrics, 66*, 1183–1190.

Solnit, A. (1980). Too much reporting and too little services: Roots and prevention of child abuse. In G. Gerbner, C. Ross & E. Zigler (Eds.), *Child Abuse: An Agenda for Action.* New York: Oxford.

Sroufe, L. A. (1979). The coherence of individual development. *American Psychologist, 34*, 834–841.

Starr, R. (1987). Clinical judgment of abuse proneness based on parent-child interaction. *Child Abuse and Neglect, 11*, 87–92.

Starr, R. (1982). *Child abuse prediction: Policy implications.* Cambridge: Ballinger.

Straus, M. (1979). Family patterns and child abuse in a nationally representative American sample. *Child Abuse and Neglect, 3*, 213–225.

Struening, E., & Guttentag, M. (1975). *Handbook of Evaluation Research* (Vol. 2). Beverly Hills: Sage.

Tennes, K. (1982). The role of hormones in mother-infant transactions. In R. Emde & R. Harmon (Eds.), *The development of attachment and affiliative systems* (pp. 75–80). New York: Plenum.

Tinbergen, N. (1951). *The study of instinct.* London: Oxford University Press.

Twain, D. (1975). Developing and implementing a research strategy. In M. Guttentag & E. Struening (Eds.), *Handbook of evaluation research* (Vol. 1). Beverly Hills: Sage.

U.S. Bureau of the Census, Current population reports, Series P-60, No. 157. *Money income and poverty status of families and persons in the United States: 1986.* Washington: U.S. Government Printing Office.

Wald, M., Carlsmith, J., Leiderman, P., DeSales French, R., & Smith, C. (1986). *Protecting abused/neglected children: A comparison of home and foster placement.* Unpublished manuscript.

Williams, G. (1983). Child abuse reconsidered: The urgency of authentic prevention. *Journal of Clinical Child Psychology, 12*, 312–319.

Wolfe, D., & Manion, I. (1984). Impediments to child abuse prevention: Issues and directions. *Advances in Behavior Research and Therapy, 6*, 47–67.

Zigler, E. (1976). Controlling child abuse in America: An effort doomed to failure. In *Proceedings of the First National Conference on Child Abuse and Neglect.* D. Adamovics, (Ed.), Washington, DC: Department of Health, Education, and Welfare.

Zigler, E. (1980). Controlling child abuse: Do we have the knowledge and/or the will? In G. Gerbner, C. Ross & E. Zigler (Eds.), *Child Abuse: An agenda for action.* New York: Oxford.

Zigler, E., & Berman, W. (1983). Discerning the future of early childhood intervention. *American Psychologist, 38,* 894–906.

Zigler, E., & Weiss, H. (1985). Family support programs: An ecological approach to child development. In N. Rapoport (Ed.), *Children, youth, and families: The action-research relationship.* (pp. 166–205). New York: Cambridge.

# Author Index

# Subject Index